Intimate Ironies

Intimate Ironies

MODERNITY AND THE MAKING OF
MIDDLE-CLASS LIVES IN BRAZIL

Brian P. Owensby

Stanford University Press
Stanford, California
1999

Stanford University Press
Stanford, California
© 1999 by the Board of Trustees of the
Leland Stanford Junior University
Printed in the United States of America
CIP data appear at the end of the book

To my parents,
who first took me to discover Latin America

Acknowledgments

As was so often true of the people who are the focus of this book, I have lived beyond myself by accumulating debts. None of my creditors would ever collect. In any event I am fairly certain I could never fully repay them.

I have been fortunate over the years to have financial support for my work. This project would never have gotten off the ground without help from the Program in Latin American Studies at Princeton University, which subsidized two preliminary research trips to Brazil. An eighteen-month trip in 1990–92 was generously funded by two Fulbright grants, one from the Institute for International Education and one through the Fulbright-Hays program. The Fundação Getúlio Vargas sponsored me while in Brazil. A Mellon Post-Enrollment Fellowship and the Princeton Society of Fellows of the Woodrow Wilson Foundation supported a year's worth of writing. The University of Virginia invested two summer research grants toward completion of the book. Finally the Princeton University History Department gave me the final push with an award that enabled me to take a semester off from teaching in order to revise the manuscript.

It all began years ago when Prof. Stanley Stein and Prof. Michael Jiménez allowed me to write a historiographical paper for which there was little historiography. Between that paper and this book there is a great distance, but I covered it because they let me go off on my own. Their support as friends and as mentors was invaluable. I also recall with gratitude an important conversation with Professor Frank McCann in Rio de Janeiro at a time of doubt. He reminded me that I needed to be true to the lives of my subjects, wherever that might lead. Professor Jeremy Adelman made helpful suggestions at several points along the way. Professor Thomas Skidmore read various versions of my work and encouraged me from afar over a number of years.

I am grateful as well to the many scholars and archivists at the Fundação Getúlio Vargas's Centro de Pesquisa e Documentação, the Biblioteca Nacional, and the Arquivo Nacional, also in Rio de Janeiro, the Edgard Leuenroth Archive at Unicamp, the Biblioteca Municipal, and the Serviço Social da Indústria in São Paulo. I also owe an immense debt to the many archivists and functionaries who helped me in *sindicatos* and associations. My special thanks go to those who were willing to talk to me about their lives: Augusto de Angelo, Prof. Júlio Maia de Albuquerque Arantes, Profa. Rita Bauser, Dr. José Feliciano Castellano, Col. Asdrubal Esteves, Hélvio Pinheiro Lima, Paulo Mota Lima, Durval Coutinho Lobo, Mario Martins, Armando Peixoto, Dr. Júlio Arantes de Sanderson Queiroz, Dra. Maria de Lourdes Brescia Ribeiro, Herculano M. de Siqueira, and Nelson Werneck Sodré.

I have been happy in friendship over the years. In Princeton I was part of a circle of friends and peers who supported and challenged me early in the project. Mere mention of their names will have to do, though I owe them far more: Barbara Corbett, Marcus Daniel, Dina Hurvitz, Nimrod Hurvitz, Linda Lierheimer, Eve Niedergang, David Nirenberg, Jane Dailey Nirenberg, Dror Wahrman, Noa Wahrman, and Andy Weiss. Peter Johnson never failed me with apt bibliographical tips. While in Brazil I worked with and relied on Mark Adamson, Peter Beattie, Sueann Caulfield, Professor Sydney Chaloub, Jean and Francine Daudelin, Scott and Ann Hildula, Roger Kittleson, Professor Nancy Naro, Quélia Quaresma, Danyel and Cynthia Sak, Ken Serbin, and Gail Trainor. My special thanks go to the law firm of Pinheiro Neto in São Paulo and in particular to my good friends Caio Leonardo and Sylvia. In Rio, Sra. Nice Mucemuci generously put me up. Here in Charlottesville I have had the support of a number of energetic colleagues and students in the University of Virginia history department who have read and commented on all or part of the book: Cindy Aron, Ed Ayers, Alon Confino, Rebecca Deschweinitz, Purnima Dhavan, Lara Diefenderfer, Lori Gates, Bob Geraci, Tamara Giles-Vernick, Steve Innes, Nelson Lichtenstein, Peter Onuf, Brad Reed, Sophie Rosenfeld, Ajay Skaria, and Olivier Zunz. I also am grateful to Luís Soares for his bibliography, conceptually challenging conversations, and encouragement. At Stanford University Press, Muriel Bell, and John Feneron saw me through and understood that behind books there are people. Two anonymous readers made comments that encouraged me to sharpen important aspects of the argument, for which I thank them. I am especially grateful to Professor Herbert "Tico" Braun, an uncommon colleague, reader, critic, mentor, friend, and cycling partner.

The language of gratitude quails in the face of those relationships that go beyond debt. My in-laws, Bev and Patsy Blackwood, have cheered me on these many years. My siblings, Marc, Craig, and Lauren, have always taken the time to find out what was up with the project and to let me know I could depend on them. My parents, Walter and Susan Owensby, made this book happen. They taught me about the large and the small in life. Dad showed the way. Mom never doubted. My wife, Bronwyn Black-wood, has been a loving companion in everyday life. My daughter, Amanda, has lightened my spirit by reminding me again and again of the comedy of life.

                                                                    B.P.O.

Contents

Tables

A Note on Orthography

I have done my best to reproduce all names and titles as they appeared in the original sources despite the fact that the Portuguese orthography was so variable in the sources I relied on.

Intimate Ironies

1

Directions

A NOVEL THAT appeared in Rio de Janeiro and São Paulo in 1945 tells the story of several people who struggle with an identity and a way of life still relatively new in Brazil at the time. One of the central characters of the prosaically titled *Middle Class* is a young man who until recently had lived on his father's estate in the rural Northeast. Like so many others in twentieth-century Brazil, he had heard about the vibrant metropoles of the South. Life in the countryside seemed vapid by comparison. And so, taking the money his father offered him, Torquato had decamped for São Paulo. Thrust into a competitive world, he had known what to do. Thanks to a friend he had landed his current job as a traveling salesman for a shoe manufacturer. Now he criss-crosses the state of São Paulo by rail, going from town to little town, persuading local shopkeepers and haberdashers to order the shoes produced by factory workers back in the state capital. He is good at what he does, a man on the move.

Yet Torquato's life is not free of doubt. His sharpest misgivings come during bouts of introspection while riding the trains. "Why this life-and-death struggle"? he wonders on one of his trips. He works hard, travels constantly, has no rest, while the company's owner lives off his efforts; it does not seem fair, especially since he has forgone the easy life on his father's *fazenda* (estate). Were not he and the factory workers who made the shoes "the real authors of progress," due a share of the profits? Momentarily seized by the question, he quickly comes to himself. He and the workers could never join together to oppose the boss. "Equality," Torquato whispers under his breath, would lead to "inversion, only inversion! And that is not possible. The middle class will always have to exist, just as will the rich and the poor classes. They are all necessary and can never disappear. It would be utopian to affirm otherwise. What each must do is help the others lead dignified lives within their proper social spheres."[1]

In 1949 Brazilians read the sequel to a work of fiction that one reviewer had referred to as "the perfect middle-class novel."[2] Like its best-selling predecessor, this book is the story of Dona Lola, housewife and aging widow of a hard-working commercial employee. In one scene Dona Lola is returning to São Paulo from holiday at her wealthy son's house. Lulled by the sway of the train, she mulls over her recent visit. Julinho had done well in life, no doubt, but what had he meant by saying that he belonged to one class, the rich, and she to another, the middle class? And what was this class struggle that people kept talking about? Julinho had once been like the rest of the family. Now he was rich. But his sister Isabel was not rich. Why so great a difference? Dona Lola thought for a while. Isabel's children might not be wealthy, but they had ambition: Silvia wanted to be a pianist; Carlos, a doctor; Eduardo, an engineer. They would make their way more through "intelligence and knowledge" than through money. Julinho's children, on the other hand, were like "pretty oranges with no juice." Wanting a tang for life and paralyzed by the privileges of money, they cared little for study. Was this "class struggle?" After all, if "the middle class to which I belong far outnumbers the rich," Dona Lola muses, might it not be that we of "the poor class will swallow the rich," whose only consolation will be their money?[3]

Torquato's and Dona Lola's thoughts and confusions condense much of what had become an unavoidable feature of Brazilian social life by 1950—the aspirations and anxieties of urban middle-class people puzzling over where they fit into a rapidly changing society that was coming to think of itself in class terms. Their lives were taken up by a concern for status, the pursuit of success through merit, dependence on patronage, an irreducible affinity for respectable employment, a tortured desire for conspicuous consumption, a preoccupation with class, a desperate desire for moral superiority. All this is the stuff of lives that have remained largely in the shadows of the histories told of nineteenth- and twentieth-century Latin America.

We begin with these interior moments because they blur the distinction between intimate, everyday lives and the abstractions of class, ideology, and politics: Torquato's flash of solidarity with workers flares from a private resentment over lost status and extinguishes itself in an equally private anxiety over a new-found, ill-defined social station; Dona Lola's ruminations occur at the juncture of family relationships, perceived social difference, and a language of class still strange to her. In the spirit of confronting these uncertainties on their own terms, this book explores how middle-class lives were made through the imperfect meshing of the very small with the very large in the complex gearing of everyday life. This approach is rooted in the idea that social identities and political sensibilities take shape historically through the interplay of the global and the mundane in myriad individual lives of making do.[4] A middle class materialized, in other words, as people like Torquato and Dona Lola struggled to impose order on their own lives and, through their own lives, on society in general. The tension between their yen for coherence and the instability of the social and political categories available to them is the focus of this book.

In 1883 abolitionist Joaquim Nabuco complained of his native Brazil that "the middle classes, the driving force of nations, are nowhere to be found." The country's troubles, he implied, were rooted in this absence.[5] Seventy years later French sociologist Jacques Lambert examined Brazil's social structure and proclaimed that "it is above all in the ascension of the middle classes that the new Brazil differs so profoundly from the old one." Breaking with "archaic complexes," liberal professionals, public functionaries, commercial employees, military officers, private-sector bureaucrats, and others in Brazil's fledgling "urban middle class," said Lambert, were adopting "new modes of living, new ideas, and new ideologies without offering any resistance." They were leaving hierarchy behind and ushering in a "modern" and more fluid "individualist society that neither agreed with nor accepted patronage." Perhaps most important, they were positioning themselves to "make their will triumph in national politics."[6]

What joined these comments across seven decades was a sense that the middle class represented the key to Brazil's historical evolution. This was no mere coincidence. Although separated by seventy years Nabuco and Lambert both drew on a reified notion of the middle class, what may be thought of as the myth of an individualistic, meritocratic, and progressive middle class. This congratulatory tale has a long history.[7] The narrative begins with a titanic struggle in which England's emerging business class of the eighteenth and early nineteenth centuries vanquishes a moribund aristocracy and marches through the nineteenth century to economic, political, and cultural preeminence. This prosperous and confident middle class quickly became a symbol of social stability amidst the tumult of Dickensian England. As early as 1855 William Makepeace Thackeray, with a sidelong glance to the "idle, profligate, and criminal . . . men of rank and fashion," insisted that "it is to the middle class that we must look for the safety of England."[8] So tightly was the idea of the middle class en-

twined with Britain's progress over the latter half of the nineteenth century and so great other countries' desire to reproduce British success that
by century's end the middle class as abstract idea was severed from historical specificity.

By the turn of the twentieth century, as Nabuco's 1883 comment suggests, the words *middle class* could easily be used to judge a nation's prospects.[9] In 1907, for instance, English historian A. F. Pollard heralded "the
advent of the middle classes" and the rise of the national state as the two
indispensable "factors" in the triumph of modernity over the Middle
Ages.[10] Deracinated from historical context, the middle class easily came
to stand for the ideal of private prosperity and public virtue thought crucial to the smooth functioning of modern societies. This is what allowed
Lambert to make the claims he did for the Brazilian middle class of 1953.*
Ignoring Brazil's own history, he held the Brazilian middle class to an idealized standard more mythical than real. According to this view, the middle class was the social embodiment of progressive modernity, avatar of a
supposedly reproducible, universal, and teleological process. Few social
and political ideas of the twentieth century have proven more durable and
seductive.

Lambert was among the earliest proponents of what came to be known
as modernization theory. Its basic idea was that successful development
depended essentially on replacing certain cultural values of "traditional"
societies—hierarchy, patronage, status—with "modern" ones—individualism, merit, egalitarianism.† Amidst cold war tensions development

---

*Lambert's middle class of white-collar employees and professionals was a very
different social group from the business middle class Nabuco seemed to have been referring to. Lambert was drawing on what may be thought of as the more commonly
used definition of the middle class in the twentieth century—a social group compris-
ing educated salary earners and professionals—as opposed to the business and manufacturing middle class usually connected with nineteenth-century England. (Some,
however, have argued that the nineteenth-century English middle class was a far more
diverse group, embracing those in commerce, professional life, rentiers, and others of
"independent income." See Morris.) The history of how the term *middle class* was
transformed has yet to be told. In European historiographies it is still common to refer to the educated, white-collar salary earners as the lower middle class or petite
bourgeoisie. See Mayer; Kocka, "The Middle Classes"; Blackbourn.

†Examples of this school of thought are legion, stretching back to the 1950s. See,
e.g., Harrison. The basic problem with this approach as applied to Latin America is
not that it was "ahistorical, but rather that its account of the actual historical development of the West was a misleading and mistaken one. . . . The historical record
simply does not match the picture of Western development one gleans from the works
of the modernization theorists. That view of Western history stressed the lack of con-

studies and modernization theory sought to spell out the conditions that would allow what were referred to as traditional and underdeveloped nations to become modern, prosperous, and democratic capitalist societies. Nor was this merely a goal to be striven for. Rather, the achievements of the "mature" industrial societies in North America and Northern Europe were taken to represent the culmination of a world historical process which, extended to lesser developed countries, would check the course of communism.[11]

Without ever pinning down what they meant by the term, modernization theorists often put the middle class at the crux of this process. By rejecting patronage and hierarchy, by embracing individualism and merit, it would deliver Latin American nations from "backwardness."[12] Through the 1950s optimists expected—hoped—that Latin America's middle classes would dampen, perhaps ultimately eliminate, social unrest from modernizing nations.* By the mid-1960s this vision proved chimerical. Political tensions, especially between organized workers and employers,

---

flict and the continuities of the process; it tended to collapse a complex series of long-term changes into a single 'transition.'" Roxborough, 757.

*This was a central if implicit premise of the Alliance for Progress, a foreign policy initiative of the Kennedy and Johnson administrations that took shape in reaction to the Cuban revolution. Broadly, the Alliance promised $20 billion to help Latin American countries lay the foundation for self-sustaining economic growth. See Morley, 131–35. Although the project advanced on numerous fronts and did not explicitly comment on the middle class, the middle class came to be seen as a counterweight to what John Foster Dulles called "the lower classes," who could not be trusted to pursue "democracy as we know it." Hunt, 166. It was assumed that the middle class would spearhead reform and by their "passionate devotion to constitutional government" avoid extremism. See Humphrey, 25; Nehemkis, 238–39. Howard Wiarda has noted that this idea of "salvation through the middle class" was rooted in the notion that "if only we could create in Latin America more middle-class societies, then more stable, more just, more democratic, and more anti-communist attitudes would surely prevail." Wiarda, 105. This indulged a series of facile assumptions, as a critic from the early 1960s noted: "The fundamental error in the U.S. approach . . . has to do with its definition of the middle class. U.S. scholars, politicians, and journalists have gleefully discovered a Latin American middle class and, without pausing to find out what kind of middle class it really is, they have proceeded to credit it with all sorts of qualities it does not possess. In fact, the only claim which the Latin American urban middle groups have to the description 'middle class' is based on the fact that they are in the middle, between the traditional aristocracy and the peasants and the workers." Claudio Véliz in *The World Today* (Jan. 1963), 22–23, quoted in Nehemkis, 238 n. 2; Wiarda, 105. Put another way, U.S. policy makers ingenuously invoked the idea of the middle class in hopes of promoting modernization. While Véliz has a point, it is important to note that his argument also relies on the idea of the middle class, for he asserts the nonexistence of Latin American middle classes by concluding that they do not measure up to an ideal he leaves unstated.

exploded into open conflict in some of Latin America's most modernized nations, among them Brazil, Argentina, and Chile, just as the economic growth that was supposed to vault these nations to self-sustaining prosperity slowed.

When military regimes, often with broad middle-class support or acquiescence, suspended democratic governments, starting with Brazil in 1964, many scholars lost faith in the prospects for Latin America's modernization and concluded that middle classes could not advance the region's development. Some simply turned away from the middle class as a suitable subject of scholarly inquiry. Others concluded that Latin America's cultural distinctiveness precluded a middle class.[13] Either way, the absence of a middle class became a crucial measure of Latin America's social and political instability, a confirmation of what had long been thought to be Latin America's "pathology."[14] Further embarrassment to the generalizations undergirding modernization theory could be avoided only by making the Latin American middle classes into an exceptional case. The middle class was shrugged off the scholarly agenda.*

Opponents of modernization theory had no greater use for the middle class. Concerned above all with seeking an explanation for Latin America's "underdevelopment," dependency thinkers rejected the assumption that cultural values could explain Latin America's "backwardness." Instead, they stressed Latin America's economic subordination to the United States and Europe and the relationship between elites and subjugated masses. Middle classes appeared in these narratives as extras, and then only when they seemed to play a role in the unfolding of economic dependence.[15] Subsequent historical analysis has reflected the logic of the excluded middle.[16] Great strides have been taken to recover the lives and experiences of rural and urban elites, peasants, workers, and the poor. But social and political relations have come to be represented in terms of polar opposites: employers and workers, elites and masses, rich and poor, capital and labor, oppressors and oppressed. In the process the middle class has been thought to have "no political horizons of its own."[17]

---

*John Johnson proposed an ambitious research agenda for Latin America's middle classes in 1958 with his seminal book *Political Change in Latin America*. Operating from a critical perspective within the liberal framework of modernization theory, Johnson set out the elements of a non-Marxist class analysis by which to understand the middle class and by extension class society more generally in Latin America. His proposal fell before the ideological battles between modernization theorists and those employing a dependency framework. *Political Change* remains an indispensable starting point for understanding the middle class in Latin America.

Stepping into the breach left by these antagonists, this book seeks to enrich the social and political history of Latin America in light of the middle class.* The point is not merely to "put the middle class back in." Rather, I am broadly interested in how the ambiguities of everyday middle-class lives have put the meaning of modernity at issue in Latin America and elsewhere. I focus, therefore, on the experience of men and women who after roughly 1920 found themselves swept up in the turmoil produced by the eruption of market relations, the state, and politics at the very center of daily life. I do not reject the idea of modernization, only the notion that it can be understood as the teleological unfolding of modernity. Indeed, modernization is central to my account, but modernization as a "maelstrom"— of technological change, new forms of power, demographic upheavals, movements of populations, urban growth, challenges to stable identities, mass communications, bureaucratic expansion, social movements, and deepening market relations—that has kept social lives in the twentieth century "in a state of perpetual becoming."[18] This becoming, in turn, has been anything but linear, for the changes generally thought to be characteristic of modernity have been deeply intertwined with what are usually called traditions. In Brazil, thus, the market mentalities, meritocracy and egalitarianism, professionalization, consumer culture, and social identities typically connected with the notion of the middle class are inseparable from a disdain for manual labor, an insistence on social hierarchy, and the presumed naturalness of patronage, time-tested values and practices constantly renewed and folded into modern social life.†

*The need for scrutiny of the middle class is obvious. On the one hand, it is difficult to find an important synthesis of twentieth-century political and social history in Latin America that does not rely explicitly on the middle class as a social group and sometime political actor. On the other hand, there has been very little systematic inquiry into the politics, social experience, culture, and values of middle-class people. In other words, historians who have wanted to make generalizations about Latin American society and politics have found themselves forced to use the concept of middle class operationally, even though they have known very little about it empirically and analytically. A Brazilian historian framed the problem some years ago: "In relation to the function of the 'middle class,' the common feature of Brazilian 20th-century historiography is a recognition of their role and agreement on the importance of that role. As for anything else, everything is in dispute" (N. Sodré, 51–54). See endnote 20, this chapter.

†This approach draws on the insights of scholars who have argued that modernity is experienced not as the passing of tradition in the face of modern developments, but as the unpredictable mixing of the traditional and the modern. See Hess and Matta, 270–91; Canclini; Rowe and Schelling. This is no different from what happened earlier in Europe and the United States, except that European and American continuities

A defining aspect of the tensions inherent in this process is that the experience of being modern was mediated by the image of an idealized modernity located outside Brazil. Through newspapers, books, magazines, advertisements, radio shows, photographs, and movies, growing numbers of Brazilians from the nineteenth to the twentieth century came into contact with the idea of what it was to be modern. It was an idea that took life from the visions of modernity issuing from New York, Paris, London, and Los Angeles, where it was supposed the modern had already been achieved.* And since by the 1920s the celebratory middle-class storyline had become normative for modern societies, middle-class Brazilians could not help but conduct their lives in tangled relation to the middle-class ideal. Amidst the commotion and swirl of rapid change, they, perhaps more keenly than other Brazilians, experienced modernity through the incongruity and dissonance of trying to live by an ideal they could never quite live up to.[19]

The middle-class lives explored in this book embrace the experience of families headed by literate, white-collar employees and professionals, and to a lesser extent the self-employed, who did not engage in manual labor and who were overwhelmingly white or light skinned.[20] They were the accountants, bank clerks, bookkeepers, commercial employees, doctors, engineers, government functionaries, journalists, lawyers, managers, military officers, office professionals, salesmen, shopkeepers, and supervisors who got their livings in the expanding urban service sectors of Rio de Janeiro and São Paulo up to 1950. But a bloodless list of occupations tells less than half the story. For the middle class was also a state of mind oriented to

----

appear invisible because their historical experiences were folded into the narratives that were taken as the basis for an abstract theory of modernization.

*The issue of how the idea and ideal of modernity came to be diffused remains largely unexplored. Mass consumption and technological changes in communications are at the center of the process. See, e.g., Nolan, 108–27; Rosenberg, 87–107. What is at stake is a sense of the broader frame within which Western modernity can be understood. As Berman points out, the reality of modernization has been full of dissonance and conflict, in the West and elsewhere. Berman, 245. Over the twentieth century, many in the West, and this would include Latin America, managed to forget the messy realities of modernization and instead came to imagine that modernity could be seen as the outcome of a relatively smooth process of transition from traditional to modern societies. This was the fundamental move of post–World War II modernization theory, of which Lambert was an early proponent. Over the postwar period the notion of a seamless modernization came to embody the dominant view of how modernity had been attained in the North Atlantic. A history of the spread of this idea would require a cultural, social, political, intellectual, and economic history of the media through which the vision of modernity was projected onto the world at large and how that vision was received.

a dynamic social and economic arena. In Rio de Janeiro and São Paulo, though not only there, the middle class consisted of men and women who worried about small incomes and demanded respectable status, who worked hard to earn educational credentials so they might succeed on their own merits and still assiduously sought patrons, who aspired to prestigious professional positions and often settled for much less, who at times imagined themselves friends and colleagues to their bosses and still demanded deference from those below, who insisted on keeping a maid and scrimped so that they could afford to, who consumed manufactured goods and went into debt doing so, who allowed professional organizations to speak for them and yet resisted becoming members, who struggled to believe in electoral politics and yet crowded the margins of public life, who feared the lower classes and distrusted elites and still hoped that morality could anchor the social order.

These people lived as much by their yearnings and fantasies as by objective reality. They faced lives of possibility defined by markets, shifting hierarchies, the potential for mobility, and certain imagined political relationships that allowed a wide array of people to take up middle-class roles in explicit and implicit comparison with others.[21] These possibilities, in turn, were mediated by the language of class.[22] This premise is central to my focus on the period from roughly 1920 to 1950, since before 1920 there is no evidence of widespread use of specific terms denoting social middleness.[23] No particular unity is implied here. Sometimes shared experiences were the basis for common cause. Other times they were not. Consequently, the middle class was anything but compact. Incomes, status, mobility, and access to patronage varied dramatically. Even the language of self-description remained unstable throughout the period, as Dona Lola's equation of "middle class" and "poor class" suggests.

The making of a single class may be understood as the history of how the notion of class came to be articulated from a particular point of view—in this case, from the middle outward. Of course, no single perspective is comprehensive or seamless. Tensions, half-articulations, and meaningful silences abounded, so that the lived reality of class was characterized by the fluidity and contingency of its identification with a particular language of class.

In Brazil this contingency derived partly from the fact that Brazilians so often took the language of class to be an objective description of social divisions in a modernizing society. The middle class in particular was understood in terms of a standard to be met. Use of the term implied invidious comparison, so that the existence of a Brazilian middle class was always unsettled in relation to what were assumed to be proper European and American middle classes.* For example, a 1940 article entitled "On the Meaning and Value of the Middle Classes" noted that doubts had often been expressed as to the existence of the middle classes in Brazil because they did not look like the Belgian middle classes.[24] In the process of trying to affirm the "meaning and value" of the Brazilian middle class, the author could not avoid calling its existence into question. This was not just a trap of language. It reflected as well the ambivalence of those who imagined social identities partly in relation to a foreign model that seemed always to jangle with actual experience.[25]

Social lives are cobbled together from the bits and pieces of day-to-day existence. Politics flows from no one fountainhead. The connections between lived experience and the wider meanings ordinarily attributed to politics are revealed by an eclectic array of sources. Particular themes are animated through overlay and contrast. Insights into a competitive social order derive from memoirs, letters to potential patrons, and manuals written for white-collar employees as well as from the publications of white-collar occupational groups. In direct but also off-handed ways, these documents speak to issues of status and social hierarchy, market relations, and the taxonomy of class. In a powerful manner they illumine the interaction between the new and the old in a modernizing Brazil. Mass-circulation magazines, housekeeping manuals, novels set in middle-class homes and work places, and surveys conducted by Brazil's first market-research organization afford a glimpse into issues of domesticity, consumption, and gender roles in the experience and representation of work and home. In a country of 75 percent illiteracy they evince an emerging urban culture no longer limited to elites. Clues to middle-class politics run through all of the sources and may also be found in the records of social work schools, the programmatic literature of political movements and parties, and in the commentary of those who tried to write the middle class

---

*Observers in Britain, France, and the United States have long talked about their middle classes in explicit or implicit comparison to the middle classes of other countries. See, e.g., Blumin, 240–49; Wahrman, 273–97. The differences among the cases may be that in Europe (especially in nineteenth-century England) and in the United States the idea of the middle class was still being imagined into existence and could not yet be thought of as a fully developed model. In contrast, by the 1930s and 1940s the idea of the middle class had been so long a part of the language of social description in the West that Brazilians could easily see themselves as trying to live up to a static model, just as twentieth-century Americans could see themselves as trying to live up to a fully realized notion of a middle class rooted in a mythologized past.

into the political script. Because sources illuminating those concerns are concentrated in Rio de Janeiro and São Paulo, I have focused on those two cities without limiting myself to them.

The architecture of the interpretation offered here relates the small to the large, the everyday to a broader narrative of social and political change. Chapter 2 traces the transition from a slave society to a competitive social order and tracks the gradual opening of a social middle from the mid-nineteenth century up to roughly 1930. Chapters 3, 4, and 5 treat diverse aspects of an emergent middle class in the face of deepening market relations, an expanding state, and the thickening of class relations during the 1920s, 1930s, and 1940s. By exploring the manifold ways middle-class men and women confronted a changing social order through hierarchy, competition, patronage, mobility, consumption, and domesticity, these chapters reveal how the actions, words, and imaginations of middle-class people, and of the people around them, constituted a middle-class worldview at the core of which was an anxiety produced by the counterpoint of experience and ideal. Chapters 6 and 7 analyze efforts within the middle class to create space for active political expression amidst the crisis of mass politics. Chapter 8 characterizes the middle class's precarious political situation in electoral populism up to 1950. Chapter 9 considers middle-class ambivalence toward politics as such and the tenuous alternatives that grew out of it.

Political history has generally concerned itself almost solely with the activities of well-organized groups, whether of elites or oppositional vanguards or, more recently, with the pervasive micropolitics of human relations.[26] Neither of these models is adequate to the task of retrieving a meaningful sense of mid-century politics in Brazil. One assumes that the unorganized are largely irrelevant to political analysis. The other fails to connect micropolitics to the politics of parties, ideologies, and platforms. One way to bridge the gap is to recognize that the instinct to confront society individually is in constant tension with the impulse to respond collectively. Close attention to the "nature, texture, and structure" of everyday life reveals something of how and why people, as individuals and as groups, opt for or against collective politics to express their interests and what attitudes toward the means and ends of political activity they bring to their choice.[27]

The middle class has in many ways been the central symbol of twentieth-century social life in the West, a reflection of Western anxieties and hopes. And though it has been more prominently discussed at certain times than others, debate over its place and role in modern societies has been continuous. This is hardly surprising, for the stakes are considerable. The middle-class narrative constitutes a principal thread in the broader story of modernization and liberal-democratic capitalism. Through it the triumphal epic of development culminating in prosperity and stability came to be projected onto the historical experience of Latin America. Countries such as Brazil were found hopeful or wanting, depending in part on whether they could boast a middle class. The ideal of the middle class thus became one of the ways the United States and certain European countries, through invidious comparison with countries labeled less developed, made the Panglossian assumption that their social problems were a thing of the past and that these other countries would soon follow—so that the West as a whole could "settle down and be comfortable in a world where tranquillity is secure."[28] Middle-class Brazilians shared a lust for the tranquillity promised by an idealized modernity. Their experience was otherwise. To understand the middle class in Brazil—and elsewhere—is to embrace this ambiguity. In doing so, it is possible to recover the insight that middle classes have been "vitally important" in Latin American history in a way that respects the particularities of that history and still speaks to the broader account of Western modernization.[29]

"YOU'D BETTER HURRY. It's disappearing. Besides, it never really existed anyway." This was so common a response among Brazilians to whom in the early 1990s I described my still-vague project on the middle class that I began to fear I had chosen the wrong topic. Over time I came to understand that such statements—asserting its existence in part by denying it—defined the middle-class situation. For the Brazilian middle class had long been as much a matter of dreams as of concrete reality. During the 1990s the dreams either were becoming nightmares or were being shown up for illusions. Inflation, confiscatory government policies, unemployment, despair of ever becoming "First World"—all seemed to challenge the notion that there could be anything like a durable Brazilian middle class. Doubts were most commonly expressed at the level of casual conversation among those who thought of themselves as middle class. But these anxieties were not only private. Newspapers articles and magazine features, even television reports, contributed to the curious sense that the middle class was becoming ever more tangible just as it was said to be vanishing. This was possible because in countless unconscious and conscious ways middle-class Brazilians judged their own lives according to the idea of the middle class, a "myth of the modern world" so compelling that they rarely had occasion to reflect upon its role in their lives.[30] This book is the story of how such lives came to pass,* lives that unsettle the notion of the normative modernity that the middle class has been taken to represent.† And not only for Brazil.

*The origins of the idea of the middle class have led me to an implicitly comparative perspective. Such an approach is something of an antidote to the subtle ways the assumptions of modernization have been implicated in European (especially English) and American historiographies: students of Latin America have long asked themselves why Latin America *failed* to live up to the *successful* modernization of the so-called First World. This has made it difficult to understand Latin American history on its own terms. My focus remains on everyday lives, but these lives are part of a broader story about the tensions between Brazil's cultural and historical particularities and the supposed universalities of modernity. At a number of points in the text I have addressed myself to these tensions in discursive notes located at the bottom of the page. Their purpose is to suggest through comparisons with the United States and Europe that individualism, egalitarianism, consumption, associational spirit, political involvement, and meritocracy not be taken for granted in understanding the middle class in Brazil—or anywhere else.

†There is a kind of countermyth of the modernizing middle class in Germany's *mittelstand*, which has tended to be depicted as inherently reactionary and authoritarian. Some have begun to challenge this simplistic view, arguing that the German middle class was far more complex. See Blackbourn. My work on the Brazilian middle class, which reacts against the simplifications of modernization theory and dependency, is of a piece with other efforts to recover the middle class for historical analysis from easy assumptions of whatever species.

2

Into the Middle of a
Competitive Social Order

To the middle of the nineteenth century the institutions and mind-set of hierarchy and personal dependencies so pervaded Brazil's social, political, and economic life that there was little room for alternative imaginings of society. On the *fazenda* (estate) and in the cities day-to-day life and political relationships were played out according to the brutal familiarities of slavery and the "anxious connections" of patronage in the context of a society deeply imbued with a consciousness of rank.[1] The crucial transformation after 1850 was the unfolding of a "competitive social order" defined by a generalized struggle among individuals at all social levels for jobs, status, and material goods.[2] Of course, markets were hardly new in Brazil, but only after mid-century, and particularly after the abolition of slavery in 1888, did they become central to everyday lived experience.

A society of "castes and estates" did not simply give way to a "competitive social order."[3] Rather, the mentality and practice of markets combined unstably with the ethos of slavery and patronage. An expanded sense of possibility unsettled the culture of rank and hierarchy, allowing ever greater numbers of people to imagine that social place was perhaps not so firmly fixed after all. Yet a disdain for manual labor and the vagaries of patronage continued to ground status. Structural continuities too shaped Brazil's social order in the twentieth century. State-supported agricultural exports continued to dominate the economy throughout the period up to 1930, even as industry began to develop. Against this backdrop the instabilities and uncertainties of a developing competitive social order were the stuff from which middle-class lives materialized.

The Culture of Slave Society at
Mid-Nineteenth Century

Slave society reached its zenith shortly after Brazil's independence from Portugal in 1822. In the countryside and cities black and mulatto slaves made up the bulk of the work force and a third or more of all Brazilians. Economic output beyond export commodities—principally sugar, cotton, and coffee—and basic foodstuffs for internal consumption remained economically and socially insignificant. There was little industrial production. Sugar factories in the Northeast employed a minute work force of variable composition: some used only slaves; others relied on slaves who operated relatively autonomously, approximating low-wage free labor; many mixed slave and free labor. Only a very few employed free labor exclusively.[4] Wage labor, then, remained the exception to the rule in an essentially rural economy.

Land- and slave-owning elites stood at the pinnacle of an entrenched patriarchal culture. While many *fazendeiros* owned homes in northeastern coastal cities or interior towns, the plantation defined social life for the great landowners. Inclined to familial, personal, and hierarchical relationships, they reinforced their dominance over clients through *compadrio*, becoming godparents to the children of their lessers, acting as protectors and benefactors in exchange for loyalty and deference. These lords of the land cultivated aristocratic mores, indulged ostentatious displays of wealth, and sought titles of nobility as badges of position and privilege. Local, state, and national politics worked more through dense networks of personal relationships than through ideology or political party.

Elite women led ambiguous lives at the center of these families. Cloistered in the *casa grande* (big house), largely excluded from the affairs of men, they nevertheless wielded considerable personal authority over house slaves. They also participated in the web of dependence, coercion, and personal relationships that held the fazenda together, directing commemorative activities and reinforcing kinship networks. When their husbands died, they often assumed control of fazendas, at times involving themselves in local politics.

On the land and in small towns hard by, such families brandished enormous powers. Slaves and free rural workers were utterly subordinate to large landowners. As a contemporary observed, planters had no time for "the free man who desires . . . an increase in salary and constantly aspires to rise out of his position of lowly day laborer to obtain a higher one more independent and convenient."[5] Scattered tenant farmers, technically free, were, in fact dependent on landlords. As a result, no substantial population of independent small farmers or rural wage workers offset the power of the fazendeiros. Indeed, the three decades after independence marked a period of sharp conflict between squatters who lacked clear legal title to their plots and plantation owners who wanted more land on which to produce sugar and coffee for export or foodstuffs for local consumption.[6]

Above all, fazendeiros prided themselves, as they had for centuries, on their leisure and the fact that they did not soil their hands with manual labor. This disdain for hand work reached far deeper than the thin crust of the elite. An English traveler to Brazil in the 1850s remarked that Brazilians would "starve rather than become mechanics."[7] Artisans often hired other people's slaves to carry their tools in public. Surgeons might not be able to marry into elite families, as surgery was thought to be too much like the hand work barbers did. And a traveling salesmen could think that he was complimenting a rich woman's dessert pastry, only to find that he had insulted her, since baking was manual work left to slaves.[8]

A further consequence of the plantation economy was that up to 1850 cities lacked the complexity and density to make them magnets for the ambitious. Respectable, that is, nonmanual, work was hard to come by. Those with pretensions to respectability disdained the trades, long the province of slaves and freedmen.[9] Even in Brazil's largest cities export elites did not constitute enough of a market to sustain a large nonproducing population. There were few teachers because there were few schools, few bank clerks because there were few banks. Few pursued military careers, as local militias held pride of place over the federal army. Commercial employees might avoid the most degraded manual labor but only rarely secured remunerative positions. *Doutores*—sons of fazendeiros, poor relatives of traditional families, and *rara-avis* "poor-boys-made-good" who were emerging from the law and medical *faculdades* (faculties) created after independence—generally faced bleak prospects in private practice.

For them patronage remained everywhere common coin, both in hiring and promotions. Aspirants to law practice were best advised to find sponsors, particularly well-connected, wealthy relatives. In this way youths of moderate fortune, even a few mulattos, gained an education and, more important, made advantageous friendships for the future. Those who found no patron after graduation became, according a mid-century observer, a "plague of doctors without clinics, *bacharéis* [law faculdade graduates] without jobs."[10] The growing numbers who hankered for respectable work began to look to the expanding state and federal bureaucracies. Yet entry into the bureaucracy offered no escape from the dependence of patronage. Those lacking political connections and family backing or disinclined to servility had little chance of rising in the civil service.

For none was this more pressing an issue than the throng with pretensions to respectability. Few could realistically aspire to a bacharéis's ring and diploma. Most contented themselves with nonmanual employment, if they could find it, and struggled to keep up appearances on a small income. British travelers remarked on the not uncommon phenomenon of a "dandified-looking gentleman" investing meager earnings in Parisian fashions so as not to be found "wanting in ability or in acquirements."[11] Among such people sartorial competition was rife. On Sundays, when faculdade students preferred light clothes to the heavy frock coats, top hats, canes, and black shoes they sported during the week, lowly commercial clerks bathed, dressed to kill, doused themselves with perfume, and swaggered with fancy canes in imitation of their betters.[12] They would step out to cafés and bars, mingling with students, professionals, military officers and other *pessoas decentes* (respectable people) who gathered there.

Even the respectable poor might nurture dreams of moving beyond their station through work or connections. They too turned to state bureaucracies, often as a first resort. As early as 1846 a Rio newspaper noted that "instead of learning the trade of sailor, stonemason, or carpenter, the sons of poorer families continue to seek public employment."[13] More commonly, those who moved up did so on their own initiative. For example, before the railroads, muleteers might rise from what elites saw as vagabondage. During the 1850s and 1860s Domingos Custódio Guimarães was able to parly a string of mules into several plantations and two titles of nobility.[14] Most did not scale these heights, but the very fact that it was possible meant that elites' close attention to rank did not signify social stasis. It was, rather, the sign of a social order in which the possibility of mobility was widely recognized as real. Precisely the likes of Guimarães the muleteer made rank matter so deeply; each individual had "constantly to define and redefine his or her own position vis-à-vis others."[15]

The least of the respectable poor lived at the margin of penury. Dr. Antônio Corrêa de Sousa Costa studied the dietary and living conditions of the Carioca (residents of the city of Rio de Janeiro) "poor class" in 1865. In addition to blacks, mulattos, and poor whites who worked as journeymen and day laborers, the doctor found public functionaries, commercial employees, many of them recent immigrants, and "whites of a better class who had fallen into poverty."[16] These people cleaved tenaciously to their sense of re-spectability, knowing that genuine poverty was real and looming.

Corrêa's description suggests that the dominant, socially perceived division after master-slave was rich-poor, with little sense of an intermediate station. Tradesmen and artisans, often freedmen and mulattos, were considered manual workers pure and simple, notwithstanding their skills and whether or not they owned property. Above them, by one contemporary account, about 8 percent of the population lived just "tolerably."[17] Lacking the "possessions and social role" of the razor-thin layer of the truly "influential people," they had only lightness of skin, literacy, and some minimal capacity for "intellectual work" between them and the "workers giving off a vile miasma of *cachaça* [cane liquor] and cigarette smoke."[18] As compared with the "class of well-off citizens," these vaguely middling sorts could easily see themselves as poor, shifting as best they could, fearing all the while that destitution would strip them of their minimal dignity and status. From above wealthy Brazilians sniffed at all below. One foreigner remarked at mid-century that nowhere did elites "pay great[er] regard to distinction and rank and perhaps in no other language are those so precisely determined."[19]

Market Relations to 1900

Economic expansion after 1850 catalyzed gradual change in this society of distinction and rank. The Northeast was in decline. Sugar was being successfully cultivated and refined elsewhere, and lands worked hard for three centuries were exhausted. By contrast, between 1820 and 1880 coffee exports from the South increased by over 1,000 percent and grew from 19 to 63 percent of total exports as earnings quadrupled.[20] By 1880 coffee earnings had soared to five times that of 1841–50. The coffee boom intensified pressure on land and labor after mid-century, squeezing smaller fazendeiros.

Through the colonial period small holders had lived comfortably without being wealthy, enjoying the respectability and independence of being land and slave owners, passing their land on from generation to generation through elder sons. At the end of the colonial period new laws sought to break up large fazendas by requiring division among all surviving sons. The law had the opposite of its intended effect. Property holders found themselves dividing and subdividing their land. Over the generations holdings shrank, and many sons could not avoid selling their plots to larger fazendeiros. This trend was especially marked in the state of Rio de

Janeiro during the 1850s and the state of São Paulo during the 1870s, when many small farms were swept up by large fazendeiros with the gleam of coffee profits in their eyes.[21] Nor could small holders compete with large plantations for labor.[22] As a result, many of these farms went bankrupt or were absorbed by larger neighbors.

The dwindling of small holdings alongside the expansion of large fazendas spelled decline for many young men, who often left for the cities in search of opportunity. At the same time coffee planters began to push mass European immigration after abolition of the transatlantic slave trade in 1851. From 1850 to 1872 a quarter of a million immigrants arrived in the coffee fields of the Center-South. While some returned to Europe, many subsequently found their way to urban areas, plying artisanal trades and keeping shop, making over the complexion of cities. In 1870 foreigners made up a third of Rio's 235,000 inhabitants.[23]

These developments transformed Rio de Janeiro and São Paulo into cynosures of culture, cosmopolitanism, and what was coming to be thought of as progress. Elites spoke French. Electric lights lit downtown areas by the 1880s. Faculdade graduates, bored by the pace of rural life, increasingly chose to remain in the city after completing their studies, seeking to establish private practices, gain political influence, or secure bureaucratic posts. In Rio brokers of all nationalities hustled after consignments and commissions. Clerks, merchants, and civil servants met in the streets, the cafés, and on the trams to the suburbs, where many lived in houses with separate bathrooms, bedrooms, gardens, and, said one traveler, "wheezy and asthmatic pianos." Ladies had even begun to appear in public, quite a "modern sight," commented this same observer. They made the rounds of the linendrapers, tailors, stationers, jewelers, hatters, grocers, and butchers, ladening their slaves or servants with bundles and packages.[24]

A growing population of people neither rich nor poor took advantage of new entertainments: circuses, bullfights, horse races, and beer gardens, where clerks, merchants, and public employees relaxed under the trees. Roller skating, the "fashionable" English and Parisian pastime, was all the rage in São Paulo by the 1870s. Meanwhile untold numbers of journeymen, carters, and domestic servants, and tens of thousands of factory workers, labored all day at backbreaking jobs and then returned to the growing wretchedness of tenements known as *cortiços*, or beehives. According to a member of Congress, these people, especially with the influx of freedmen from the countryside, represented a "growing social danger."[25]

Initially the transformation of Rio de Janeiro and São Paulo was intimately linked to the expansion of slavery in their immediate hinterlands.

After the transatlantic slave trade ceased, coffee planters simply could not recruit enough immigrants to meet labor needs. They began to look to the slave-rich plantations of the Northeast. The internal slave trade brought hundreds of thousands of slaves from declining sugar plantations to the states of Rio and São Paulo. Between 1823 and 1872, the number of slaves in the states of Minas Gerais, Rio de Janeiro, and São Paulo doubled to nearly 800,000. By 1887, a year before the abolition of slavery, two-thirds of Brazil's slaves lived in these three states.[26]

Yet by the 1870s many believed that slavery was doomed. The slave population was not being replenished from outside and after the Free Womb law of 1871 could not reproduce itself from within. So, despite the internal trade, slaves as a proportion of total population in the coffee regions declined from about 25–30 percent to roughly 10–20 percent between the 1850s and the 1870s. Free labor took on an expanded role in São Paulo's coffee fields, especially with the spurt of European immigration after 1875. City dwellers felt the gradual shift away from slavery early on. The number of slaves in the city of Rio de Janeiro dropped after 1850, as plantations demanded more hands. Between 1864 and 1887 slaves as a proportion of Rio's urban population plummeted from over 100,000 (nearly half of Rio's total population) to under 10,000 (as Rio grew to half a million).[27] In 1872, 37 percent of servant women in Rio de Janeiro were slaves, down from 43 percent just two years earlier. Even among city dwellers who continued to own slaves the line between slave and employee was beginning to blur, for by the late 1870s it was common to rent house slaves out to those who could no longer afford slaves of their own.[28] Quite simply, slavery was becoming a less notable feature of everyday life for growing numbers of Cariocas.

With the tailing off of slavery, the rise of immigration, and the boom in coffee exports, urban areas began to show signs of a more generalized market orientation. From 1870 to 1889 tens of thousands of free wage laborers went to work in hundreds of new industrial establishments in and around the cities of Rio and São Paulo.[29] Prospects for those who worked at nonmanual jobs improved considerably. A growing demand for accountants, clerks, bookkeepers, supervisors, and white-collar employees within the coffee sector opened new paths of opportunity to young strivers of modest origins. Sons of immigrants made up roughly one-third of those employed in commerce in Rio by 1872.[30] The fortunate might start sweeping the floor at an import-export house, move up to traveling representative, and ultimately become a partner in the firm.[31]

Some took this new sense of possibility very seriously. Despite working long hours for low pay, and often under conditions indistinguishable from workers in small manufactories, commercial employees in retail stores and import-export houses did not identify with manual workers. They saw themselves as "future honorable merchants."[32] So there could be no mistake about their status, 43 of these men established an organization in 1880 to represent Rio's 15,000 to 20,000 clerks.[33] The founders of the Rio de Janeiro Association of Commercial Employees were primarily retail salesmen or clerks (then known as *caixeiros*): Antônio Mathias Pinto Jr. earned a salary as a clothing salesman; Armando de Figueiredo was a Portuguese immigrant who started working as a salaried employee in the coffee trade at age twelve; Joaquim Telles worked on salary and commission as a traveling salesman; Vitorino José de Carvalho, a Portuguese tailor who in 1866 had come to Brazil from Portugal, where he had belonged to Lisbon's association of commercial employees, ran a small retail business with his own employees.[34]

The association reflected a growing pride of calling among commercial clerks, who sought for themselves what they saw as the relative prestige and status of commercial employees in Europe. They were among the first to articulate a basis for social standing not directly linked to the ownership of land or slaves. The distinction between employer and employee was left hazy. Bosses encouraged their clerks to think in these terms, insisting that "merchant and commercial employee differ only in degree, like first and second cashier or like the bookkeeper from his assistant."[35] For the most part, caixeiros were only too happy to indulge the conceit.

Opportunity for some was risk for others. The respected urban professions could not accommodate all of the young graduates emerging from the faculdades. In 1883 abolitionist Joaquim Nabuco highlighted the dilemma of a fluid social order even for those from good families, noting that "the nation is made up of the very poor, since the dependents of slave holders rapidly fall into the same condition [of poverty] themselves."[36] If most doutores did not fall so far, it was by grabbing onto the lifeline of public employment. Many of these reluctant bureaucrats—a tiny fraction of the population—imagined themselves poets, novelists, or politicians. Oftentimes they showed up at the office only to pick up a paycheck, leaving Nabuco to fume that the civil service had become "a refuge for the heirs of ancient, wealthy and noble families that had thrown away their fortunes." Pointedly he insisted that *empregomania* (employment mania) and the "epidemic of bureaucratism" were "direct result[s] of slavery." A "lack of credit and commerce and the primitive structure of our economy," he wrote, had left only "narrow alleyways" of advancement or "closed doors" for those in the "so-called independent professions" of law, medicine, and engineering. Consequently, too many "lived with [their] eyes turned toward the munificence of the state."[37]

Prospects for faculdade graduates simply were not what they had once been. Growing competition between those of modest origin and the doutores of good families for a limited number of respectable jobs dulled the luster of the faculdade ring. Even a few mulattos were finding opportunities in the army, the schools, and the civil service. Young social climbers of all backgrounds increasingly chafed against a system that emphasized patronage over merit and privileged the sons of traditional families. Yet, as the director of a private secondary school in Vassouras, Rio de Janeiro, noted, "Under the conditions molding our society, a man who does not proudly possess a gallery of illustrious ancestors, a man who has only ability and respects his backbone so highly that he refuses to curve it, that man is almost always mad."[38]

By the 1870s such "mad" ones were clamoring for expanded educational opportunities and a curb on patronage. *Concursos* (competitive examinations) were instituted for a variety of government positions previously doled out exclusively according to sponsorship. Legislation in 1878 loosened regulations on institutions of higher education. Further reforms in 1891–92 extinguished the states' monopoly on the creation of faculdades and allowed any private person or association to found one, subject to government inspection.[39] Faculdades proliferated "wildly" thereafter, according to a commentator in 1917, and young men quickly filled classroom benches.[40] Legal and institutional developments, then, contributed crucially to an evolving sense of market competition as a basis for success in nonmanual occupations. For though it was still nigh impossible to secure a government job without a patron, the idea was gaining purchase that a show of merit could bolster connections in hiring and promotions. In other words, a new form of social competition was taking shape in which individuals vied in a market for qualifications, even as they sought to protect and advance themselves through nonmarket patronage and relationships whenever possible.

Eighteen eighty-eight marked a symbolic and structural watershed for a Brazilian social order on the cusp of the twentieth century. By the mid-1880s slavery was economically moribund and philosophically bankrupt. Abolition represented the triumph of the liberal notion of market competition as the basis of social life. Free-market labor relations spread rapidly, if unevenly. Cities and coffee plantations led the way. Immigration exploded; nearly three-quarters of a million immigrants entered the state of São Paulo in the decade after abolition.[41] People flooded into the cities of Rio and São Paulo from the hinterlands and from the Northeast. Industry, railroads, credit institutions, and commerce all burgeoned. The nonmanual job base began to broaden, though economic expansion did not translate into a sharp break with the mid-century economy of more limited opportunities. Despite its growth, the nonmanual sector remained in thrall to import-export commerce and to government bureaucracy.[42]

Nor was there a rupture between slave society and the emergence of a competitive social order. Slavery's racial legacy weighed heavily on the society that was taking shape in Rio and São Paulo after 1888. A few mulattos did manage to escape the destiny of "manual or mechanical professions" into the commercial sector or into what the 1872 census generously defined as the "liberal professions": lawyers, doctors, public servants, teachers, midwives, pharmacists, and artisans.[43] Most did not.[44] And because social position depended on respectability and patronage, whites and even nonwhites from humble backgrounds who found niches in the nonmanual occupations tended to embrace or acquiesce in the mores of newfound status and privilege, including those regarding race. In doing so, they became agents of cultural continuity amidst the dramatic changes that were defining their place in a modernizing society.

Increasingly dense market relations impelled this process. By 1900 wages and salaries were the rule rather than the exception in urban industry and commerce and in certain areas of agricultural production, such as coffee. In these sectors labor was a commodity bought and sold. Most city dwellers depended exclusively on their capacities, manual or intellectual, to survive. Despite stiff competition cities had become the new promised land. A character in a 1902 novel entitled *Chanaan* (Canaan) characterized rural life as "sad and tedious." "You'll get bored, I assure you," he said to a friend. "Perhaps it would be better to go to Rio or São Paulo. For these are the great commercial centers where you'd easily find a job."[45]

In these cities the ideology of market individualism advanced. Brazilian intellectuals, such as Joaquim Nabuco and later Rui Barbosa, as well as Protestant missionaries from Britain spoke passionately in favor of individual responsibility, individual rights, individual advancement, individual salvation.[46] In the face of cultural continuities Brazilian thinkers began to reconceptualize the social order. Darwin's theory of evolution, extended to the social realm by Herbert Spencer, offered a powerful explanation for the relentlessly competitive cast of economic and social relations in the modern world. As though with the sweat of the chase in their eyes and the scent of the kill in their nares, from behind their desks Brazilian positivists wrote about the concept of survival and the importance of natural selection. The inferior would be separated from the superior, ensuring progress for nations as well as individuals.[47] Journalist Euclides da Cunha made a morality play of these ideas in his widely read account of the federal government's military campaign against the millenarian community at Canudos. *Os sertões* told of an epic struggle between the modern and the traditional, civilization and barbarism. Brazilians, wrote Da Cunha, had to compete or perish.[48] Those who would not, principally the Brazilian *mestiço* (person of mixed race), were obstacles to evolution and progress.

For a modernizing elite, among them many students at the faculdades in Rio and São Paulo, the comfortable notions of old simply were out of time. The ideals of patriarchy and the reality of patronage had not fallen, but neither were they any longer the unrocked pillars of society. A commercial culture had matured enough by 1900 that an influential few could see competition and struggle as defining metaphors of social life in Brazil's largest cities. Even so, the fact remained that individuals in Brazil could never forget that they lived in a plural and relational society defined principally by a web of families, *compadrio*, and patronage.

New social divisions inconceivable in a stable agrarian patriarchy seemed to reflect recent changes. In 1880 businessmen favoring industrialization founded the Industrial Association to push their interests against landowners and import-export merchants. Over the next twenty years they advocated for manufacturing.[49] Similarly, printers, carters, shoemakers, textile workers, railroad and customs workers in Rio began to move beyond mutual assistance to militancy in the early 1880s. The reformist Partido Operário (Workers' party), founded in 1890, framed a new set of issues—wages, housing, social security, education—and stumped for collective bargaining. Several labor newspapers began to circulate in port and industrial cities, stressing radical themes. The first socialist conference was held in Rio in 1892. Tentative and disjointed though it was, this new militancy, by seeking collective redress for the inequities produced by a market for labor, obliquely indicated the advent of a competitive social order.

Through the nineteenth century politics had been little more than a struggle for power among factions led by prominent families, a matter of patronage, clientage, and bureaucratic intrigue. So, while roughly half of all free males (10 percent of the total population of 10 million) were registered to vote through the 1870s, elections were more theater than open contests.[50] Liberals and Conservatives alternated in power, guided as much by patronage and spoils as by policy and ideology. In the 1880s new interests began to make claims against a system that had been in place since roughly the 1840s. By 1889 the old arrangement could not withstand the pressures mounting against it, especially the escalating demands of São Paulo's vigorous coffee export sector.

Declaration of the Republic in 1889 thus marked a watershed in the history of Brazilian politics and political culture. Though flawed, the Empire's political system had enjoyed remarkable stability for nearly fifty years. By overthrowing it, São Paulo's powerful coffee planters, with the help of military officers in Rio and ranchers in Minas Gerais, sought free rein to push regional agendas oriented to the export economy. The expansion of railroads and shipping through the 1870s and 1880s and the surging demand for coffee led Paulista (from the state of São Paulo) planters to believe their interests were not best served by a strong, centralized political power. With the constitution of 1891 they opted instead for a federalism that all but precluded national government from intervening in affairs of the various states.[51]

Despite the Republic's break with the past and its apparent adherence to liberal political doctrine, politics remained a game for elites. Indeed, a smaller proportion of the population appeared on the voting rolls throughout the Republic than had been the case during the Empire in 1872. From the 1890s onward governors delivered votes in Congress for the national president, who in turn helped ensure that the dominant Republican party in each state won its elections without opposition. The system was founded on patronage controlled by the *coronéis* (local political bosses in the countryside), who were usually fazendeiros or their allies. In theory only the literate could vote; in practice rural workers who could barely sign their names voted as directed by their coronéis in exchange for favors, jobs, loans, land use, and the security of having a patron and protector in the often violent Brazilian backlands. Tax collectors, teachers, justices of the peace, and judges were under the power of local bosses, and even priests and government employees often found it necessary to play their part in local elections.[52] The center of political gravity remained in the countryside.

Urban politics followed the rural pattern. Working through political bosses and electoral corporals, *figurões* (grand figures) rather than coronéis controlled vast networks of government patronage. The lieutenants in this system were usually lawyers and doctors, or at times teachers and journalists, who attended public ceremonies in the name of the *figurão* and provided professional services and personal favors to clients. They stood over the *cabos* (corporals), often mid-level public servants owing their jobs to patronage, who wore down their soles trucking in the currency of small favors to voters. Within this vertical structure there was little opportunity or incentive for political opposition along party lines.[53]

So effective was the political class at tamping down dissent that protests erupted only episodically. The first occurred during the political uncertainty attending the birth of the Republic. A passel of disaffected professionals and salaried employees in Rio—shopkeepers, teachers, bookkeepers, some doctors, lawyers, engineers, pharmacists, and especially commercial clerks and public functionaries—founded the Jacobino movement (a rhetorical rather than ideological reference). These young men, who felt they faced limited professional opportunities, sought to carve out political space for those excluded from the patronage networks of the agrarian, export elite. Jacobino clubs opposed the "know it all bacharéis," "the degree-holding directors of the nation's affairs," who sought only to safeguard and augment their own privileges. Hoping for greater opportunity, these Young Turks believed the Republic could assure "social and material progress." They frothed nationalistic against the Portuguese, who they said monopolized commerce, and the British, who sought to maintain Brazil's subservience to English industry.[54]

The political legacy of Jacobinismo was mixed. No ongoing movement formed, no lasting ideology took shape. In part, this was because so many Jacobinos appear to have been public employees. As such, their livelihoods depended crucially on the bacharéis against whom they railed. During the confusing early years of the Republic, when the control of patronage was up for grabs, some had been emboldened. After 1894, however, new political forces turned patronage against the Jacobinos, squelching dissent. Nor did the movement lay the foundation for any kind of cross-class alliance. Despite rhetorical appeals to Rio's still inchoate working class, manual workers appear to have had relatively little to do with the Jacobinos. Still, the movement represented the first time white-collar employees who saw themselves as outside the elite had expressed themselves explicitly on their own behalf, and they had done so by linking fears over mobility and job status to a vague disgruntlement with the political status quo.

Emergence of a Social Middle, 1900–1920

By the final quarter of the nineteenth century the roots of a society and culture defined by fazenda and slavery were withering. The most dynamic forces in this continuing process were coffee exports, growth of industry, and expansion of the state. All converged, at times collided, in Brazil's largest and most enterprising cities.

In São Paulo coffee exports roughly doubled between 1889 and 1913. Over the same period the number of industrial establishments in the state jumped from 200 to over 4,000, many, perhaps most, owned by immigrants.[55] To meet an urgent demand for labor, the government actively promoted European and later Japanese immigration. Between 1900 and 1920 nearly 1.5 million foreigners entered Brazil, over half of them to work in the coffee fields or factories of São Paulo state, Brazil's new economic dynamo.[56] By 1920, over 100,000 people labored in São Paulo's industrial park.[57]

Rio experienced the end-of-the-century boom differently. During the 1890s the Paraíba Valley in the valley of Rio de Janeiro declined as a center of coffee production, marking the end of a cycle that had begun decades earlier. Many who tilled now exhausted fields, planters and laborers alike, decamped for the city of Rio and its environs, providing the hands for a significant expansion of industry. Between 1889 and 1920 the number of industrial establishments grew tenfold to over 1,500, employing 150,000 men and women.[58] Rio's real businesses after the turn of the century, however, were imports and government. No longer a major coffee exporter, Rio became after 1900 Brazil's principal importer of foreign manufactured goods. In 1906, for example, the port at Rio accounted for only one-seventh of exports, but nearly half of Brazil's imports, though Rio continued to be involved with the export trade, now as regulator and financier.[59] The increasingly complex task of managing foreign trade—the coffee valorization program that supported prices for Paulista coffee planters as of 1906, the imposition of tariffs, the collection of revenues, the manipulation of exchange rates, the managing of money flows—fell to swelling ranks of government and private-sector bureaucrats. Aspirants to these positions were never in short supply. The federal budget for civil administration reflected this fact, more than doubling between 1872 and 1920, as the number of federal civil servants quadrupled to 40,000, 40 percent of whom lived and worked in Rio.[60] Rio's new economic role was that of distributor of imported goods, Brazil's largest consumer market, and hub of government.

The pace of urbanization picked up considerably in both cities after 1900. São Paulo was transformed from a town of 65,000 in 1890 to a metropolis of nearly 600,000 in 1920, 24,000 of whom labored in factories of 500 or more workers.[61] So vigorous was São Paulo's growth that one foreigner noted in 1910 that the city was the "briskest and most progressive place in all Brazil . . . giv[ing] the impression of energy and progress." The city positively tingled with the excitement of great purpose. A Brazilian bureaucrat echoed the confidence: "São Paulo is equipping itself to be a great industrial center, something like Chicago and Manchester combined."[62] This optimism was made material in the modern conveniences and diversions now available to those with some money. In 1913, for instance, the city was served by 30 gramophone shops, 46 cinemas, a roller-skating palace, new cafés, and a Parisian-style cabaret, not to mention the numerous boutiques catering to those with the taste and pocketbook for imported goods. New social differences were being etched on the city's physiognomy. The showy downtown, with its large retail concerns, elegant hotels, and well-appointed shops, stood in ever starker contrast to the dingy streets of working-class districts, with little more than dry-goods stores, small cafés, and ubiquitous *botequims* (stand-up, sidewalk bars).[63]

In Rio the successes of the import-export economy galvanized elites to make over a tired colonial façade. Population growth throughout the nineteenth century and the presence of the port had made Rio a cramped and unhealthy place. Fearing that the city might become a tropical backwater compared with Buenos Aires (often referred to as the "Paris of South America), Rio undertook the "Haussman-ization" of its downtown in 1904. Narrow streets were ripped up, old buildings razed, and unsightly *cortiços* erased to make way for broad avenues lined with cafés, haberdashers, and fashionable stores. In 1905 Avenida Central cut a swath through the old city, displacing thousands of poor people, connecting the city center to the waterfront, a "sublime example," according to one newspaper, "of the material progress which Rio de Janeiro is determined to achieve."[64] By the 1920s the city once again rivaled Buenos Aires. Greater Rio's population shot up to 1.2 million.[65] Skyscrapers, clubs, cars, and art nouveau architecture dotted the urban terrain. Sidewalk cafés and movie theaters proliferated. At the same time the poor continued to live in degrading and unhealthy *favelas*, which were creeping up many of Rio's slopes from the valleys.

Central to Rio's and São Paulo's emerging urban culture was the spread of literacy among city dwellers. In both cities literacy rose from under 50 percent in 1887 to 75 percent in 1920, even as the national rate remained at about 25 percent.[66] This dramatic leap reflected developments in the non-manual urban labor market in the early decades of the twentieth century. Between 1900 and 1920 the number of people in the liberal professions, public and private administration, the officers' corps, and commerce dou-

TABLE I

Occupational Breakdown of Work Force, Rio de Janeiro, 1906, 1920

(Number in each occupational group per 1,000 men,
1,000 women, and 1,000 people regardless of sex)

	1906			1920		
	Men	Women	Both	Men	Women	Both
Agriculture, extraction	86	23	66	80	13	64
Domestic servants	88	757	303	35	492	149
Rentiers	8	11	9	10	19	12
Industry	224	146	197	182	289	208
Transportation	86	1	59	119	9	91
Commerce	231	8	59	227	25	77
Public administration	47	1	32	67	9	53
Private administration	0	0	0	26	5	20
Liberal professions	35	22	32	48	89	56
Bank clerks	3	0	2	8	1	6

SOURCE: Census 1920, vol. 2, part 1, cxxi.

bled to over 800,000 in all Brazil. In Rio white-collar employees and professionals made up 20 to 30 percent of the half-million strong work force in 1920. São Paulo's white-collar sector was smaller but also probably neared 20 percent of the work force.[67]

Table 1 shows that in Rio de Janeiro during this period greater opportunities opened up in every segment of the nonmanual sector—public and private administration, liberal professions, commerce, and bank employment—leading to use of the label *gente de colarinho e gravata* (collar-and-tie people). Most of these, according to a 1911 sociological study, were not poor, but neither were they "happy practitioners of mammonism."[68] The presence of women in such jobs marked a significant shift. The 1920 census noted that an "appreciable number of women" now worked outside the home at nonmanual jobs, especially in teaching, commerce, and public administration. An explanatory note hastened to add that unlike Europe women, who were "competing notably" with men, Brazilian women "still enjoyed ... the privilege of living, for the most part, under the care of a head of family whose job it is to maintain the family home."[69]

Expansion of nonmanual sectors occurred just as the manual work force appears to have been industrializing. Between 1906 and 1920 the number of people employed in factories far surpassed those in construction or in independent artisanal production. Many artisans were forced into wage labor during these years. This had the effect of putting greater social distance between a broadened group of respectable employees and swelling ranks of deskilled laborers.[70] Another significant trend in the manual sector was the rising proportion of women working at industrial jobs, predominantly textiles. This was paralleled by a drop in the proportion of lower-class women earning wages in domestic service, as Table 1 shows. For many, factory jobs were an opportunity for economic advancement and greater independence.[71]

The demand for professional qualifications and higher education grew in direct proportion to expansion of the nonmanual sector. In 1911 educational reforms further eased regulations governing institutions of higher learning. By 1932 there were nearly 40 faculdades in Brazil just in the traditional areas of law, medicine, and engineering. Fourteen faculdades were founded in Rio alone between 1906 and 1920.[72] As a result, the liberal professions grew sevenfold over the period.[73]

New opportunities propelled people of diverse backgrounds toward an urban economic arena increasingly defined by market relations. The sons of oligarchical families and their "poor cousins" from downwardly mobile elite families continued to curry favor within the circuits of patronage.[74] Success there led to positions of prominence and influence in government, politics, business, and intellectual circles. Those who enjoyed less success in "the struggle for life" joined what Tobias Monteiro called in 1917 a veritable army of "educated men" who were turning the state into a job service for the needy.[75] These young strivers simply expected more than their faculdade degrees could be counted on to deliver.

With intensified competition, patronage seeped into nontraditional areas alongside more meritocratic practices. It was not uncommon in the 1920s for aspirants to bank positions to be *"afilhados"*—to have a "godfather" or sponsor who helped them be hired, promoted, or transferred. *Padrinhos* might be traditional patrons, or they might be patrons of a new sort, clients of a bank linked to more dynamic sectors of the economy, people more likely to be comfortable with market relations.[76] At the same time banks increasingly emphasized merit as a way of choosing among the growing numbers of applicants with sponsors.[77] Markets and patronage, then, were becoming complementary strategies for making one's way in the economic world. Monteiro noted, for instance, that cheating on exams in the faculdades was rampant, suggesting that students understood just how important credentials had become as badges of merit and social qualification.[78]

The relative few from privileged backgrounds also contended in ever closer quarters with the sons of immigrants and Brazilians of modest origins for positions and social standing. Banished early on from the loam of patronage on which *bacharelismo* (the system of status and privilege rooted in possession of a degree) flourished, ambitious immigrants often turned to business. By the 1920s immigrants of Italian origin had become the main fragment of São Paulo's industrialists.[79] Far more commonly immigrants constituted an important segment of the urban artisanate. Upwardly mobile sons considered their father's professions beneath them and set out for the *faculdades*. Already in 1910–11 Italian surnames were not unusual within the liberal professions in São Paulo.[80] According to the census, foreigners made up 12 percent of Rio's lawyers, doctors, and teachers and nearly a third of its intellectuals and men of letters in 1920.[81] By the late 1920s and early 1930s sons of moderately successful Brazilians and foreigners were entering the new professional areas of teaching, engineering, economics, and other occupations that had appeared with an industrializing economy and an expanding state.

Not all who sought it attained economic security or independence. Many sons of tradesmen, artisans, small manufacturers, and shopkeepers ended up among the mass of Brazilians clinging to respectability at the lower end of the white-collar labor market. Typically they came to the cities from the interior in search of nonmanual work. Paulo Mota Lima, for instance, left his native Alagoas for Rio in the early 1920s, prompted by his father to flee limited opportunities in the "intellectual professions."[82] Others like Lima made do with the minimal dignity of avoiding manual labor and attempted to establish relationships with potential patrons, often preferring low-level collar-and-tie jobs in government, even when paid less than many in the trades or commerce.[83] Yet others attended military schools, since the officers' corps came to be considered a more respectable career choice as of the 1890s.

Immigrants more often than Brazilians opted for petty commerce. In 1920, for instance, more than 40,000 foreigners were employed in commerce in the city of Rio de Janeiro, compared with 26,000 native-born Brazilians.[84] Long shut out of government jobs and the liberal professions, recent immigrants turned to commerce as a principal means of advancement during the first two decades of the twentieth century. This process was helped along by Brazilian shopkeepers' long-standing practice of passing their shops on to employees rather than to more status-conscious sons who felt commerce beneath them, a custom that dovetailed with many foreigners' hopes for betterment through self-employment. Immigrants often sacrificed the continued education of a child in order to gain independence.[85] Edmundo Cardoso was such a one. Son of an Italian photographer living in São Paulo, he stopped going to school at fifteen to manage a shoe store for the owner. When years later the owner retired, Cardoso took the shop over and made it prosper.[86] Cardoso's trajectory was typical of immigrants, who frequently numbered among the small and medium businessmen who owned property but were by no means rich. Meanwhile, the sons of Portuguese merchants went off to study and frequently "ended up doutores, poor and obscure, at the back of some government office, having spent every last penny of the inheritance."[87]

Immigrants' success in commerce sparked an increased sense of competition among commercial employees. While much clerking still required little beyond literacy, basic figuring, good manners, and light skin, the pressure for educational credentials was beginning to grow. In 1920, for instance, Professor Créten of the American School of Commerce in Rio (a slick combination of French intellectual prestige and American know-how) exhorted Brazilians not to leave "modern and intelligent commerce" to Portuguese, Syrian, and Lebanese immigrants. Ambitious young men, insisted Créten, should forsake the bacharéis's life of dull routine in a government ministry and instead pursue commercial education at the American School.[88]

Whether they attended a faculdade, a military school, or a commercial school, many if not most of these young men had little purchase in the *alto mundo* of high society. A contemporary sociological observer described graduates as a "very curious and disarticulated class" that was obliged to "keep up appearances."[89] As a consequence, whether fallen from higher status or risen from modest beginnings, these salaried employees and professionals fixed their attention on the bacharéis, who still called the tune in public life. European fashions, polished manners, and an air of cultivated propriety borne lightly by elites were the hard-earned privileges and burdens of their epigones below. For apart from a desire to imitate their social betters, clients understood that patrons paid close attention to the minutiae of fashion, etiquette, and culture in deciding whom to take on.

The galloping commercialization of life in Rio de Janeiro and São Paulo led to a dramatic shift in the nature and composition of voluntary associations between 1900 and 1920. As the economy grew and diversified after 1890, voluntary associations moved away from religion and neighborhood and toward occupational and economic concerns as bases for organization.[90] From 1880 to 1920 white-collar employees and professionals founded dozens of associations, declaring themselves ready to collaborate with government. Some of these new organizations began to act more and more as interest groups. Expressing themselves on questions of salary and cost of living, pressing government for concessions, they made Rio in 1920 a vibrant "arena of conflicting bankers and tellers, industrialists and laborers, shoemakers and shopowners, bureaucrats and clerks."[91] Local newspapers devoted considerable attention to associational life, prominently reporting meetings and demands against government. But none of these groups came close to having the influence of the economically powerful—planters, industrialists, and import-export merchants—who, in the words of one pundit, could always "obtain what they want from Congress."[92] Lacking clout of their own, most white-collar associations avoided confrontation and instead sought to rub shoulders with political movers and shakers. For if economic and occupational identities were taking firm root by 1920, it was alongside the stout older growth of bacharelismo and patronage.

Expansion of white-collar associational life during the first two decades of the twentieth century was paralleled by the emergence of militant labor organizations demanding higher wages, better working conditions, and greater political participation. A social democratic journal began to publish in 1900, mixing socialist and reformist ideas. In 1902 the Second Socialist Congress met in São Paulo. Organized workers founded the Brazilian Socialist party, adopting a program that divided the social world into "two distinct classes: capitalists and workers." They called for an end to private property.[93] The notion of classes in conflict was relatively new in Brazil. Through most of the nineteenth century Brazilians had imagined and experienced their country as one of rich and poor, whose relations were mediated principally by hierarchical obligations between patrons and clients.

The wave of strikes that swept São Paulo, Rio de Janeiro, and to a lesser extent other cities between 1917 and 1921 was, for this reason, an important point of inflection in the history of Brazilian social life and politics. In 1917 public protests against rising food prices culminated in a general strike in São Paulo. Forty-five thousand workers walked off their jobs. Led by immigrant anarchists, workers struck 124 times in Rio and São Paulo alone between 1917 and 1920.[94] While this upheaval finally calmed in 1921, when the federal government began to deport foreign "agitators" and imprison others who sought to "subvert the present social order," elites, whatever their disagreements with each other, understood that all was not as it had been.[95] As a Paulistano (a person from São Paulo) industrialist put it in 1918, "Workers' discontent is a new force that really exists."[96]

In 1919 reformist intellectual, orator, and lawyer Rui Barbosa saw in labor's stridency a chance to crack open the closed political system that had been in place since declaration of the Republic in 1889. Where in an earlier election he had waxed democratic against fraud and *politicagem* (political chicanery), in 1919 he began to speak of "the people," in which he very prominently included "workers," even though his principal audience remained urban, white-collar employees and professionals. Against a backdrop of strikes and growing public concern over "the social question," Barbosa claimed that much-needed social reforms were hostage to political forces impervious to challenge.[97] Barbosa lost the election but garnered 30 percent of the vote. Since, except for 1910, winning margins in every election between 1889 and 1918 had exceeded 90 percent, the outcome in 1919 and Barbosa's appeal to the working class and "the people" was a sign that politics had begun to spill over the dikes of oligarchic containment.[98]

The perceived successes of working-class militants up to 1920 bred resentment among white-collar employees and professionals, especially during the inflationary years following World War I. In February 1921, after more than three years of strikes and uprisings by factory workers, the *Correio da Manhã*, Rio's main newspaper, ran an editorial denouncing a planned strike by elements of the working class.[99] The editorialist declared that he did not oppose a workers' strike in principle. He was concerned, rather, that the "working class" had "advanced the furthest and grabbed the most for itself," securing an "advantageous position" vis-à-vis "intellectual workers": lawyers, doctors, pharmacists, and servants of the state. The working class had already won significant concessions that made it better off than "other classes in society," seethed the writer. "Except for the monied and the monopolists, it can be said that the workers now occupy the most comfortable and best remunerated position in the social hierarchy." Why, there were even some workers who earned *more* than some liberal professionals. Thus, if anyone had "the right to lob dynamite at public buildings as a sign of their disdain for ruling institutions," it was these beset intellectual workers.

There are two noteworthy elements in this piece. First, the author counterpoised to factory workers a broad social group, neither rich nor poor, made up of people who depended almost entirely on salaries for their livelihoods. Although their work involved what the writer called "mental" rather than "muscular" effort, these lawyers, doctors, pharmacists, and public functionaries had no special advantages and felt themselves to be none too secure in their positions. Second, while incensed with the constituted authorities, the author was also extremely wary of organized factory workers. He referred explicitly to the "working class" as a separate and identifiable social group with a distinct and potentially dangerous political agenda. His language hummed with resentment toward uppity manual workers who had already obtained concessions but who, by depicting themselves as the "eternal victim of society," always pushed for more. Faced with collective action among his social inferiors, the author neither proposed that the "much-scorned liberal class" organize on its own behalf, nor did he demand anything from government. He confined himself to complaining about the supposed advances of working people, as though it were somehow unfair that they should have banded together to advance their interests.

The Predicament of Promise Amidst Crisis

A letter to the editor of the *Correio da Manhã* in April 1921 testifies to a creeping sense of irreconcilable class difference between manual workers and white-collar employees. Initially the public functionary who wrote the letter adopted an inclusive rhetoric, asking "whether or not the unfortunate middle classes and the working class can continue to live in this country" in the face of the rising cost of living. Yet in the next breath he revealed a narrower agenda, asserting that "the middle classes, which are made up of public employees and those employed in commerce, suffer more than the working class because, as you well know, they are obliged to maintain a certain standard of living to which the working class is not subject."[100] He continued with an "optimistic" account of earnings and expenses for his family, "which consists of myself and my wife, our four children under six, and two servants." After all basic expenses, he had a small balance for clothing, calico dresses, books, and medical bills. This balance itself and the servants distinguished him from most industrial workers, who barely made it from one day to the next, with no thought of books or calico dresses, much less someone to wait on them. Odds are that his laundress was the wife of just such an industrial worker, a common arrangement among working-class families. "I could spend less," the writer concluded, "but this would subject my family to an atmosphere of promiscuity and bad examples."

This man's anxiety was emblematic of a wider fact of Brazil's rapidly changing social order in the early 1920s: relative standards of living for many white-collar employees and professionals appear to have been converging with those of the lower class at just the time a sense of class difference was beginning to take root in the Brazilian social and political landscape. In 1911, sociologist Arthur Guimarães had concluded that whereas the average Carioca working-class family of four could get by on 250 mil réis a month, the family of four headed by a nonmanual employee needed at least 1,500 a month.[101] But, according to one study, this difference eroded after World War I. Between 1914 and 1928, when the cost of living nearly tripled, public functionaries' real wages fell by about 25 percent, compared with about 10 percent for unskilled manual workers.[102] The surge of inflation after 1918 reflected a deepening crisis in the agro-export economy. A 60 percent drop in international coffee prices after the war led to government price supports, effectively the printing of money, even as industrialists were winning relaxed exchange policies and higher tariffs on imports. In short, inflation represented the way white-collar employees and professionals and manual workers experienced the growing tensions between entrenched coffee interests and rising industrialists.[103] Finally the government's inability or unwillingness to expand bureaucracy apace with the demand for respectable employment exacerbated the crisis of the collar-and-tie sector during the 1920s. Between 1920 and 1927 real spending at all levels of government stagnated. This hit federal bureaucrats hardest, especially in Rio, where a huge proportion of the national budget went to pay functionaries' salaries.[104]

Not everyone in the white-collar sector experienced the 1920s as an economic downturn. Despite the growing coffee crisis and the lull in textile manufacturing after 1925, the Brazilian economy struck off in new directions during the 1920s. Modernization and diversification were the order of the day in industry. Pig iron, cement, electrical hardware, textile machinery, sugar-processing equipment, automobile parts, tools, agricultural implements, gas appliances, watches and weighing devices, rayon textiles, new chemical products, and toys all began to be produced in growing quantities after World War I.[105] In turn industrial diversification and urban growth generated a greater demand for supervisors, managers, accountants, typists, and clerks to work in industrial offices, and more salesmen, professionals, brokers and office employees to staff the growing service sector of the urban economy. In effect, collar-and-tie employees and professionals faced new opportunities, on the one hand, and stagnation in the public sector and the pinch of rising prices, on the other—they were living the predicament of promise amidst crisis.

Frustration among white-collar families sharpened during these years as pent-up consumer demand ran headlong into the rising cost of living. The consumption crisis before 1920 had been severe. Declining imports during World War I had not begun to recover until 1919. Just as consumption opportunities were returning to normal, however, inflation took off, as Table 2 shows.

TABLE 2

Cost of Living, Rio de Janeiro, 1920, 1924, 1928

(base 1912 = 100)

Year	Food	Fuel	Clothing	Rent	Servants	Household	Total
1920	170	208	200	150	137	150	167
1924	244	222	240	250	200	267	242
1928	245	195	320	305	300	310	269

SOURCE: Ministério da Fazenda, Serviço de Estatística Econômica e Financeira. *Índice do custo da vida*, 1942.

Rising prices appear to have strained family budgets. *Vida Doméstica*, a widely read monthly magazine of the period, offers a window onto tensions of the everyday economic life of white-collar employees and professionals in Rio and São Paulo during the 1920s. On the one hand, the signs of competition, of people on the make, of a dynamic economy and its rewards were rife. Regular advertisements for "commercial schools" encouraged young men to learn bookkeeping, accounting, and other business skills so that they might move into nonmanual occupations and propel themselves upward.[106] Rio's Association of Commercial Employees shared the enthusiasm and openly exhorted its members to upward mobility.[107] Correspondence courses did a brisk business, with degrees for everything from commerce to accounting, to foreign languages, to art, to engineering. For those who had not broken through yet, the Magnetism Institute published a book guaranteed to help people succeed in work and commerce, to improve vision and memory, and to bring in money.[108]

With the right job and some money, it became possible to dream of buying a home. One advertisement put it this way: "It is no longer a privilege of the rich to own and live in a comfortable house. . . . There is luxury and there is comfort. For those favored by fortune, both can be had. For the others, comfort is sufficient and that is what can be had with a modest house in good artistic taste."[109] Nor was this just an empty dream. Middle-income dwellings constituted about 70 percent of all housing stock built in Rio between 1925 and 1929.[110] Accompanying the advertisements for houses were others for furniture, refrigerators, radios, watches, record players, typewriters, cameras—the stirrings of a consumer culture, rooted in the "improved general conditions among the middle class," that would come of age only in the 1930s and 1940s.[111]

At the same time signs of belt-tightening and even hardship were common. A 1924 *Vida Doméstica* article entitled "The Difficulties of the Rio

Home—Chronicle of a Head of Family" stated the matter plainly: "Really, the budgetary disequilibrium of housewives has reached the limit. It is now impossible to make ends meet *within* the budget." No talk of home ownership and refrigerators here. Vegetable gardens made a comeback as a way of combating the rising cost of living. Many people moved from homes to apartments or from larger to smaller apartments. Others gave up their servants. Young people put off marriage because they could not hope to save enough money to live on their own. Mothers had to tighten the budget elsewhere in order for their daughters to have a *fantasia* (costume) for Carnival.[112] According to a woman's magazine, *donas de casa* (housewives) were having to learn to "spend like [their husbands] know how to earn" in the face of renewed consumer possibilities and diminished spending capacity.[113]

Hardship varied by family and circumstance. Families of public functionaries, commerce and banking employees, and small shopkeepers tended to live closer to the boundary with the lower class, while a greater proportion of middling professionals and managers were less immediately threatened. Common to all was the reality and dawning awareness of a social condition, precarious and uncertain, of being neither rich nor poor, of being "obliged to maintain a certain standard of living," as the letter writer had put it, and of competition in a collar-and-tie employment market as the stuff of which destinies were being fashioned.

Employers and government helped reinforce the sharpening perception of a socially—and ultimately politically—meaningful difference between nonmanual employees and industrial manual workers. In 1925 a São Paulo bank employees' magazine reprinted a letter from a bankers' journal warmly congratulating that city's bank employees' association for refusing to organize, a natural outcome "given that they occupy a higher social level than factory workers, because of their manners, their education, and the environment in which they were raised."[114]

A report prepared on behalf of employers for the National Labor Council made more or less the same point in the mid-1920s. "Intellectual workers" were entitled to holidays because time off would not affect their daily lives, "at least on the moral side."[115] Holidays would allow the intellectual worker needed rest to recover from his "intense mental effort," which, as a later report noted, was something not experienced by "a manual worker, whose brain does not expend energy."[116] And "since the home of the brain worker is welcoming and pleasant, he will return to his office with his psyche intact, as he does not stray from his customary habits; he uses his leisure for diversions, but is careful to avoid subaltern activities that would alter his moral fabric." Not so the industrial worker, whose physical life was "purely animal" and whose home was little more than a "campsite." He would "kill his long free hours in the *rua* [the street, referring to unstructured social space outside the home]," prey to "latent vices" and "subaltern instincts." Vacation time for workers could have no effect other than to "unsettle the moral equilibrium of a whole social class within this nation."

This document should not be taken for more than it was. Meant to justify employer opposition to vacation laws, it argued that workers could not be trusted with idle time. Still, it is significant that the means to this end involved drawing a line between manual workers and nonmanual employees. The life of the "intellectual worker," the moral benchmark by which factory workers were judged dangerous, was obviously idealized. Not all white-collar employees, or even liberal professionals, lived in "welcoming and pleasant" homes. Yet the ideal is telling. While brain work had long been distinguished from manual labor, increasingly articulate industrialists were using this old notion as a social buffer between themselves and potentially contumacious factory workers. In doing so, they helped to crystallize and give new meaning to the difference between manual workers and nonmanual employees. By defining these groups in terms of each other, one with negative and the other with positive connotations, employers simultaneously imbued office employees with a certain status and rationalized the closer supervision of factory workers, often by white-collar employees themselves.

Not surprisingly, questions of class difference began to hold a genuine fascination for collar-and-tie Brazilians during these years. Though eager to remain a cut above manual workers, some probably were troubled by the growing distance. Paschoal Lemme, son of a Rio dentist and himself a teacher in the 1920s, hinted at this sentiment. Lemme wrote in his memoirs that he had the "most vivid recollections" of an "extraordinary" book he had read as a child, a novel entitled *O coração* (The heart) by Edmundo Amici, translated from Italian into Portuguese in a cheap edition.

The narrative chronicles the life of Henrique, a young schoolboy. Much of the novel focuses on letters exchanged between the lad and his middle-class parents. One of the missives from father to son addresses the issue of relations with working-class people. Henrique had written to his father worried that as he advanced in school he would lose the working-class friends with whom he had grown up. His sage father reminds him that it need not be so, because even once he is in the university, he can seek them out in their stores and shops, and so learn a great deal about their way of life. It would be a great mistake to lose these friends, father counsels son, for once Henrique has grown up, it would be much harder for him to make friends "outside your own class." There is a clear distinction between classes, admits the father, but perhaps workers are the more meritorious, since they derive so little benefit from their own work. He advises his son, and the young Paschoal as well, to "honor and respect" these "noble" people, paying little attention to "differences of fortune or class" so prized by "vile men." If 40 years later you should run into an old companion wearing a mechanic's smock, says the father in closing, I should hope you would embrace him as the friend he has always been.[117]

Lemme's experience with this book is illuminating, for among other things it suggests the power of reading among even modest collar-and-tie people trying to make sense of a changing social order. The importance of Lemme's strong reaction to O *coração* is that at its center was a vision of society in which class differences were offset by genuine fraternity between unequals. This view of the social world amounted to the hope that the mutual obligations and respect of a properly functioning patriarchal hierarchy could salve the injuries of class. If by the late 1920s this was at best idealistic, it represented nevertheless a potent desire that personal relationships anchored in hierarchy could secure social peace.

The desire may have been less realistic in Brazil than in Italy, given the association of class with race. As far back as the 1870s Brazilian intellectuals had sought some explanation for the backwardness of their country. Drawing on the writings of French positivist Auguste Comte and English empiricist Herbert Spencer, positivist Sílvio Romero struggled to articulate a defensible position that would make clear the inferiority of Afro-Brazilians without relegating Brazil to an inherently secondary status vis-à-vis the supposedly more developed Europeans. Romero's solution involved the progressive whitening of Brazil's population, through immigration and miscegenation, until blacks and Indians were completely absorbed. This idea carried over to the twentieth century. In 1911 a student of the matter predicted that by 2011, Brazil would be 97 percent white, and only 3 percent mulatto. By the 1920s the "whitening ideal" was widely accepted as the basis for Brazil's future greatness. After World War I Brazilian eugenicists continued to explore the idea, seeking to clarify the problem of race and offer concrete solutions to it.[118]

While most people probably did not spend a great deal of time thinking about it, the culture and ideology of race bolstered the position of those whose social status was rooted in the white-collar sector. Since darker-skinned people tended disproportionately to work at manual jobs and since this fact was so ingrained, the white or near-white men who constituted the vast majority of those in the emerging collar-and-tie employment sector, and their families, benefited from racial cleavages and assumptions in hiring, promotion, housing, patronage, social contacts, and education. They held the upper hand in the innumerable daily interactions of life in a competitive social order where skin color and status converged to give some leverage over others.

Despite advantages relative to inferiors, those in the emerging social middle walked a tight line between confidence and diffidence as they faced the future. Inflation, a strident working class, and heedless elites seemed to threaten hard-won status gains. Discontent moved some to join organizations in an uncoordinated bid for political voice. On February 13, 1920, a crowd of elegant elites and a sizable clutch of petty bureaucrats, commercial employees, bank clerks, and teachers gathered at the Historical and Geographical Institute in downtown Rio to hear Dr. Alvaro Bomilcar deliver a rousing philippic founding the Nationalist Social Action (ASN). Invoking the spirit of patriots long dead and echoing the Jacobinos of the 1890s, Dr. Bomilcar reminded his "fellow citizens" that the "interests of foreign capitalism," prominent among them the British, had established a "monopoly" over commerce and industry, excluding native Brazilians from the benefits of their own economy.[119]

For tens of thousands of collar-and-tie employees and professionals, whose horizons were expanding within a competitive social order but whose prospects were still conditioned by the world of petty patronage and the import-export economy, nationalism verging on nativism appears to have been a plausible and easily digested explanation for Brazil's social ills. Through the ASN they could protest their plight without having to confront harder questions about their place in a changing society. The organization thus pursued reforms—curbs on inflation, government fiscal responsibility, electoral honesty, regulation of foreign trusts, social benefits for all workers, rent control, expanded educational opportunities— even as it condemned materialism and egoism and insisted on the need for moral order through Catholic discipline, corporate hierarchy, and organic unity.[120]

Yet just as the ASN gained notoriety and influence, its leaders began to soft-pedal reform. In the tight web of political patronage the bacharéis and other faculdade graduates who headed the organization saw an advantage in cozying up to the elites they had been criticizing. Bomilcar himself, for example, began to claim that Brazil's elites were not the problem; foreign monopolists in league with a "traitorous press" were.[121] It is hard to say whether the ASN's rank and file shared this embrace of oligarchic rule. Moral concerns probably resonated with many, as did fear of working-class upheaval. Others surely followed Rio's feisty press, which was highly critical of elite politics. For them it must have been hard to credit Bomilcar's defense of Brazil's elite.

The ASN's decline by the mid-1920s suggests that Bomilcar and other leaders misread the depth of discontent against the oligarchy. By 1925 collar-and-tie people on the whole appear to have been less reluctant to oppose the government than they had been in the early 1920s. The labor actions of 1917–21 had faded somewhat from memory, and the government had continued to repress working-class activists after the strikes had ended. Labor newspapers were closed, *sindicatos* (unions) raided, rallies stopped, and leaders arrested throughout the 1920s. Factory owners promised that workers identified as militants would "disappear for some time, until the atmosphere of agitation has passed."[122] Between 1925 and 1927 workers struck only seven times in Rio and São Paulo.[123] Quite simply, organized labor did not appear to present the same threat to society it had earlier in the decade. Free of the incubus of imminent working-class uprising, salaried collar-and-tie men could be more receptive to antioligarchic sentiment and more open to calls for greater political participation.

These calls came from within the one institution widely seen as not wholly subservient to the Republican political oligarchy, the military. In 1922 a group of junior officers, the *Tenentes* (lieutenants), launched a barracks revolt in Rio demanding higher pay, readier promotion, and greater recognition of the army's role in Brazilian society. The Copacabana Revolt was followed two years later by another in which the Tenentes took control of the city of São Paulo for two weeks. Calling for the overthrow of President Artur Bernardes, they no longer spoke solely for an aggrieved army but now claimed to represent "national interests" and "fellow citizens." Through manifestoes, press releases, and irregular journals they called on "the people" to assert their "interests and rights" against the oligarchy in order to "republicanize the Republic."[124] By insisting on the "moralization" of politics—the secret ballot, measures against electoral fraud and administrative corruption, greater educational opportunities, broader powers for the judiciary, centralization of the state, accountability of the public fisc, reduced taxes, and limits on federalism[125]—the Tenentes achieved a measure of autonomy in relation to dissident elites.

The Tenentes' rhetoric must be understood in context. References to "the people"—roughly synonymous with the politically relevant citizenry—were hardly new to Brazilian political language in the 1920s. The Old Republic, against which the Tenentes were reacting, had been forged in the 1890s largely by excluding the vast majority of the citizenry from active political participation in the affairs of the nation. A contemporary noted in 1891 that the people had had nothing whatever to do with the birth of the Republic, at least in Rio. Another concluded that "the people" had been reduced to the level of "dull beasts" at the birth of the Republic, not knowing what it meant.[126] Voting rates and electoral margins indicate close control of the political system. Between 1898 and 1919 those voting in presidential elections only once surpassed 3 percent of Brazil's total population.[127]

A decade and a half into the Republic many elites came to see the poor as irrational and those who would speak on their behalf as dangerous. In Rio in 1904 manual workers and the unemployed, goaded by educated professionals, rose up and rioted against an obligatory small-pox vaccination imposed by political elites. The Revolt Against the Vaccine took on a significance that transcended the narrow issues that had sparked it; for though civil rights and outrages against morality had triggered it, the uprising represented an early, if unfocused, challenge to the oligarchy's political hegemony.[128] Here for the first time in the Republic poor people, violent and chaotic from the perspective of elites, appeared on the stage of politics not as dependents who took direction from patrons but as a group loosely referred to as the people. Perhaps not surprisingly, later reformers were cautious in referring to the people, seeing them as requiring "an example to follow" because they "lack any knowledge about questions of state."[129]

Thus, when in the mid-1920s the Tenentes called on the people to oppose the oligarchy, they tapped into a deep vein of political meaning that ran along the fault lines of political exclusion set by the Republic and later elitist reformers. The 1920s differed importantly from earlier attempts at reform in two ways. First, patron-client politics in the cities simply lacked the efficacy it retained in rural areas. Second, literacy rates in Rio and São Paulo had risen over preceding decades—three out of four Cariocas and Paulistanos could read by 1920—allowing a substantial majority of these urban populations to follow newspaper reports about and manifestoes issued by the Tenentes. In short, more people than ever before could imagine making up their own minds about political questions.

The Tenentes appear to have enjoyed support within a highly literate, still vaguely defined social middle. The officers themselves hailed from middling backgrounds. They were secondary-school or military-school graduates, sons of military officers, teachers, small property owners, public functionaries, shopkeepers, and bookkeepers. They spoke the language of liberal reform—secret ballot, judicial independence, what they called "administrative moralization," education—scanting attention to workers' concerns, such as length of workday, wages, working conditions, and the right to organize and strike. Indeed, their focus prompted the Communist party to characterize *Tenentismo* as a "reactionary movement of the petite bourgeoisie."[130]

There is no warrant to conclude that workers were uninterested in reform, however. The Communists did not speak for most workers, and the rhetoric of Tenentismo was not intended to make explicit class distinctions. Quite the opposite: the Tenentes had cause to broaden their appeal, since urban workers constituted a growing segment of the electorate. Workers participated in elections throughout the 1920s and had every reason to be frustrated with the limitations and corruption of Republican government. Nor was there a contradiction between electoral process and working-class concerns, even among revolutionary firebrands. The Bloco Operário Camponês (Worker and Peasant Bloc [BOC]), for example, ran its own candidate in the 1930 presidential election under the slogan, "A vote for the BOC is a vote for revolution." This implied no wide community of interest between collar-and-tie people and manual workers beyond a vague opposition to the oligarchy. The point is that in Tenentismo's rhetoric both groups were emerging from political exclusion as part of a socially heterogeneous people, rather than as distinct interest groups or politically constituted classes.

By the late 1920s popular sentiment had given the Tenentes some leverage in elite politics. In 1926 the recently founded São Paulo Democratic party (PD) began to voice themes Tenentismo had been raising for two years, the moralization of politics and the welfare of the working classes. Where the Republican party of São Paulo held to time-tested methods of repression and exclusion, the PD offered narrow concessions to ease tensions and seemed willing to tolerate expanded political participation.

This strategy garnered support among urban groups generally, notwithstanding the party's obvious connection to elites.[131] Fully 40 percent of the PD's rank-and-file membership was drawn from the urban collar-and-tie sector. Just over 30 percent came from the ranks of manual workers, especially factory workers, artisans, and skilled laborers.[132] The PD's organizational success in São Paulo inspired civil servants, students, engineers, and commercial clerks to join a Rio PD after 1926.[133]

The final chapter in the process of broad-based political disaffection with the status quo came with the appearance of the Liberal Alliance (AL), a loose amalgam of opposition political groups that emerged as the active force for reform and ultimately revolution in 1930. Founded by dissident elites who wanted to run their own candidate against the Republican party's official candidate in the elections of 1930, the AL pitched its rhetoric to "the Brazilian people ... conscious of its rights" and incorporated a by-now familiar litany of reformist measures: the secret ballot, provisions against electoral fraud, judicial reform, and protection of workers' interests, including the eight-hour workday, vacations, and minimum wages.[134] These were not gratuitous concessions. They were an effort to garner as much urban support as possible, since without urban votes, the AL had no chance of confronting the electoral power of the coronéis in the countryside.

Relative success in securing broad urban backing did not mean an absence of class tensions within the elite-dominated AL. Manual workers and collar-and-tie people all suffered 60 percent inflation between 1920 and 1929. Yet the latter may have felt particularly beset as they seemed to lose ground to workers. A pamphleteer plucked hard on the taut strings of status anxiety when he wrote in 1929 that "the distinction between workers and nonworkers is disappearing completely. In the law, teaching, letters, arts, industry, and even commerce there are poor people who work hard but are miserably paid and who would be envious of the lives led by many so-called 'workers.' "[135] By 1930 collar-and-tie Cariocas and Paulistanos in large numbers appear to have opposed what was now widely spoken of as the oligarchy and to have been eager for greater political participation and social inclusion under the tutelage of dissident oligarchs in the PD and AL. At the same time they lived in fear of workers as a constant threat to their precarious perch in a hierarchical society.

BY 1930 A SOCIAL MIDDLE of urban, white- or light-skinned, white-collar salarymen and their families was emergent in the cities of Rio de Janeiro and São Paulo. For several decades the day-to-day decisions and actions of myriad individuals—the déclassé descendants of traditional families, and the upwardly mobile sons of immigrants and lower-class Brazilians, all struggling to adjust to the challenges and uncertainties of an increasingly competitive and diversified social order—had eroded the social hierarchy of mid-nineteenth-century slave society. Economic competition and self-reliance were more deeply implicated in the work lives of collar-and-tie men than at any time past. Still those who could bring connections to bear were far more likely to succeed than those who could not. Most others had only their professional qualifications to go on. Educational opportunities offered greatly improved chances for social betterment and contributed to a more profound and generalized sense of the irreducible dignity and status of nonmanual employment (and the indignity of manual labor). While hardly new, this sensibility was newly important, for it grounded social differentiation between the nonmanual employees and industrial workers who were concentrated in Brazil's largest cities.

This was no monolithic urban middle class. As a social group it was still incipient during the 1920s. The sons and occasionally daughters of declining elites, recent immigrants, and native-born Brazilians were beginning to rub shoulders in commerce, journalism, insurance companies, brokerage houses, public employment, banks, factories, and schools. New opportunities did not make such people confident and secure as a group. Their "social and economic base was not in small property, but in activities such as the state and services subsidiary to the social structure of large property."[136] Compared with elites—fazendeiros who had moved to cities, import-export merchants, and a small but growing class of industrialists—their dependence on patronage and their vulnerability to inflation bespoke economic and social weakness. Yet they did not stop to think about whether they were living up to some abstract notion of modern, prosperous individualism; they simply strove as best they could, recognizing the virtual impossibility of making it in a competitive social order wholly on their own.

3

Shifting Hierarchies

IN LATE JANUARY 1928 a young man wanders into a bookshop in downtown Rio de Janeiro. Clerk in the office of a nearby business, he stops in during his lunch hour to peruse recently arrived books. While leafing thoughtfully through one of the volumes, he is accosted by another patron. The two strike up a conversation. After a short while they take their discussion to a café up the street, where they continue to chat about history, law, sociology, and politics. After an hour or so they cut short their lively exchange; both need to return to work. The young man spends the rest of the afternoon at his desk typing, calculating, handling money, checking inventory, and keeping accounts. On his way out he exchanges pleasantries with his boss, who compliments him on the day's work. Proud of his accomplishments, he rides the trolley home, ruminating on his witty and civilized talk earlier in the day, with no thought of joining workers gathering at the *botequims* along the way.

This was the image of commercial clerks Col. Leite Ribeiro sought to project in a 1927 radio address on the proper relationship between bosses and employees.[1] At the time his words did not reach many such employees; only the affluent owned radio sets in the late 1920s. But Rio's Association of Commercial Employees was so impressed that it reprinted the colonel's commentary in its own bulletin in January 1928. There clerks read that they were nothing like their "ancestors in times past." Now they were a "mixture of manual laborer with polyglot, of mechanic with man of letters." Newly developed office techniques, "modern accounting methods," nighttime foreign-language classes, books, magazines, and movies, "All this," said Ribeiro, "made the clerk [*caixeiro*]—or as we call him more politely today, commercial employee—a civilized social being," no longer part of a "brutish, unthinking, silent mass." He is "sufficiently educated, intellectually and morally, to devote himself to the success of the business to which he is linked."

What might commercial employees have made of Ribeiro's words in 1928? On the one hand, he was complimenting them, including them in the embrace of the respectable, which set them apart from those who lacked culture and earned their livings at degraded labor. It was a paean achingly resonant. Yet perhaps it was all rank flattery. He seemed to take for granted that commercial clerks, as "civilized beings," would utterly subordinate their interests to employers'. So how far could his encomium be trusted?

The issue of how middle-class people imagined their social position must be addressed through the tensions inherent in Ribeiro's remarks. Stretched between a building impetus toward social leveling and the insistent momentum of social hierarchy, those who were coming to recognize themselves in a still congealing social middle had to decide what relation they bore to the better off, for whom they often worked, and to workers, who, while dangerous and uncouth, often stood up for themselves before employers. In their personal lives such men—and increasingly women— doubtless resolved the dilemma in many different ways. At the level of the public representation of social experience, however, something more like a consensus took hold after 1930: there was to be a boundary between collar-and-tie employees and professionals, on the one hand, and mere manual workers, on the other. The voices of individuals and of white-collar associations founded during the 1930s and 1940s strove mightily to establish this border. In the process they located collar-and-tie employees and professionals within a new taxonomy of class. This is why even commercial clerks, those most in danger of being confused with their social inferiors, could assert in 1948 that they were part of the Brazilian "middle class," if "poorly disguised" because of the ravages of inflation and small salaries.[2]

New relations of work and class crystallizing within a modernizing economy underlay this process. Despite global depression Brazilian industrial output surged throughout the two decades between 1930 and 1950.[3] Cities grew apace. Rio's population doubled between 1920 and 1950, to nearly 2.5 million. São Paulo exploded from around half a million to over 3 million during the same period. Politics were transformed. In response to growing working-class militancy—referred to by elites and politicians as the "social question"—the national state took control of labor-management relations during the 1930s, creating a regime under which workers belonged to unions approved and monitored by a federal labor ministry. As part of its effort to keep social peace, the state also took a more active role in promoting industrialization. The net effect of these initiatives was that the state required larger budgets, more agencies, and more bureaucrats to staff them than ever before.

Collar-and-tie employment expanded with industrialization, urbanization, and growth of the state. Between 1920 and 1950 the service sector of the economy, principal source of collar-and-tie job opportunities, grew from 15 to 22 percent of the Brazilian work force, outstripping the manufacturing sector.[4] In 1940 collar-and-tie employees and their families probably made up anywhere from a sixth to a third of Rio de Janeiro's 1.5 million people.[5] Some white-collar sectors swelled dramatically. In Rio the number of private-sector management positions tripled to well over 21,000 in 1950. Burgeoning financial services catering to the cities' fast-growing economies meant ever more employees in banking, real estate, and credit firms. In Rio 3,000 people were employed in these areas in 1920; by 1950 over 25,000 were.[6] General office jobs also grew, as indicated in 1950 by the appearance of a census category "occupations related to the functioning of offices." Far more women than in earlier times entered the nonmanual work force, especially as public servants, teachers, sales clerks, social workers, and typists.[7] Responding to the state's broadened responsibilities, employment in health, education, welfare, and civil service all increased substantially between 1920 and 1950. Public-service payrolls often outran budgets.[8]

Certain nonmanual sectors declined in significance with the expansion of salaried employment. In both Rio and São Paulo those who kept small stores or operated small manufactories made up a diminishing share of the nonmanual work force from 1920 to 1950.[9] Off-the-rack clothing, mass-produced shoes, household goods, and food all squeezed small producers and retailers as never before. Unable to compete against large factories and imported goods, some passed into the ranks of nonmanual salary earners. Others took up manual labor in factories. Independent professions underwent a similar transformation. The total number of lawyers and doctors in Brazil continued to grow but represented a dwindling proportion of the nonmanual work force. Unable to establish practices of their own, many graduates sought posts in government or social services, took up salaried middle-management positions in public and private administration, or settled for jobs in commerce and banking.[10] By 1950 *faculdade* graduates were more likely than at any time in the past to be workaday salary earners rather than autonomous professionals.

Thus, while the independent middle sectors were not altogether eclipsed during this period, they were increasingly overshadowed by the emergence of a middle-income salariat. As one contemporary noted, the dominant characteristic of the Brazilian middle class, as against its Belgian counterpart, was not "autonomous work," that is, shopkeepers and professionals in private practice, but salaried employment.[11] In sum, the urban middle class was born of a thoroughgoing process of urbanization and "salarization" that had its start in the nineteenth century. By the 1920s and 1930s collar-and-tie employees and professionals shared the broad experience of salaried, nonmanual work in an economic regime mediated by patronage as well as by market forces.

What privileges the decades after 1920 in this account is the linking of hierarchy to social class, a process neither automatic nor self-generating. For those in an emerging middle class, work amounted to more than a job description; it was above all a way of coming to grips with a rapidly changing social world and their place in it. During the 1930s and 1940s white-collar organizations through their editorial voices, and white-collar individuals through everyday choices about how to conduct themselves, pushed a hierarchical division between manual and nonmanual work and between those with culture and those without as ordering principles of a class-divided society. In doing so, they recast deep-rooted aspects of social hierarchy in a new context. In subtle ways they also subverted it. Through their insistence on a measure of professional dignity vis-à-vis elites, hierarchy became less a holdover from Brazil's past than an instrument for negotiating a competitive social order.

Handling "Natural Differences"

In 1956 British sociologist Bertram Hutchinson undertook a study of occupational prestige in Brazil. He asked 700 university students in São Paulo to rank 30 professions, among them doctor, public servant, and garbage collector, in order of social worth. Their answers revealed a clearer separation between manual and nonmanual occupations in Brazil than in England. Whereas in England office clerks were lumped together with manual workers, in Brazil they were "included in a higher group, of entirely nonmanual occupations, such as shipping clerks, traveling salesmen, and small shopkeepers."[12]

Hutchinson's conclusions were not merely the musings of a foreign interloper. Brazilian intellectuals frequently commented on their culture's special disdain for manual labor. One astute observer remarked in 1949 on the "revulsion for manual labor . . . *any* manual work" in Brazilian society.[13] Even Catholic writers who sought to rescue manual labor from degradation under capitalism referred to the distinction between manual and nonmanual labor as an "irreducible reality." Intellectual work, they said, was not, in itself, superior to manual work, but it would constitute an "immoral inversion of function" to go against the "natural human tendency . . . from manual to intellectual work."[14]

This sentiment reached well beyond intellectual and academic circles. Between 1920 and 1950 numerous collar-and-tie associations promoted a public discussion of the social meaning of work and hierarchy. At a time when notions of class were taking root in everyday life and politics, these organizations demanded distinction between those who worked with their heads and those who worked with their hands.

Perhaps the most careful parsers of the subtle grammar of work, because they had the most at stake, were those nearest the line dividing manual from nonmanual workers—commercial employees. Commercial work had long ranged widely across the manual-nonmanual spectrum. In the nineteenth century, caixeiros had lived at the stores where they were employed, suffered terrible working conditions, and endured great indignities for low pay. Through a life of privation and loyalty to their employers they might inherit the shop, especially if the shopkeeper's son went to a faculdade or sought a place in the bureaucracy. Meanwhile their social position remained unsettled. Much of their work involved lifting and wrapping, though because they might also deal with customers and do some figuring and since most were minimally literate, they could make some claim to respectability.

As collar-and-tie opportunities grew over the first three decades of the twentieth century, commercial clerks struggled to secure their "little place in the sun."[15] Their spokesmen knew they could not claim the status of liberal professionals. Not only did too many clerks perform manual tasks, but as a practical profession oriented to money, clerking was widely seen as incompatible with a life of cultivated refinement. Even so, many were determined not to be leveled down into what they saw as the undifferentiated ranks of manual workers. For instance, one author redefined commercial clerks as "commercial assistants," which he felt would distinguish them from "workers," who performed exclusively manual labor, and "servants," who performed personal services for others.[16]

Many clerks saw their chance in office work. Wants ads of the 1930s and 1940s reveal a growing demand for office employees with skills beyond minimal literacy and figuring. More exact accounting and bookkeeping practices, larger and more complicated filing systems, greater contact with clients and customers, larger pools of office employees to be managed, stenography and foreign languages, typewriters and adding machines—all pointed to an increasing specialization of nonmanual work. Night and correspondence courses proliferated in Rio and São Paulo, galvanizing many clerks to seek new opportunities. By attending school and acquiring skills, commercial employees could more easily believe they were "civilized" in ways workers were not. Even clerks more closely identified with the labor movement characterized themselves first as "intelligent people" and only second as workers. "The time is past," insisted one publication, "when commercial auxiliaries were relegated to an inferior situation, specifically in matters of culture. From the modest little clerk to the present-day commercial assistant there is an enormous distance." Now they were prized guests at the best boarding houses, and pretty girls wanted them as husbands, or so it was said.[17]

This hopeful hymn, as much aspirational ideal as faithful description, probably represented a minority of those employed in commerce at any given time. Perhaps half of all clerks were young and poorly paid *balconistas*, counter and store clerks who often performed physical labor, had at best some secondary-school education, and enjoyed little social standing. They were generally looked down upon by those who worked at purely clerical or administrative tasks, a kind of aristocracy among commercial employees. One accountant, for instance, argued that it was "perfectly natural and just" that "office employees," who probably made up somewhere between a quarter and a half of those laboring in commerce, should work fewer hours than "retail clerks," "since mental work burns more matches."[18] The fact that many, and by 1950 perhaps half, of these low-level clerks were women reinforced the distinction between "intellectual" and manual work.[19]

A static picture of commercial employment occludes as much as it reveals. Even among those who performed little if any manual labor, many were poorly paid, discharged routine tasks, and did not attend foreign-language and accounting classes at night. Commercial work was a last redoubt within the nonmanual sector for those unable to find jobs calling for higher skills and offering better salaries. It was a place where many got stuck, with little hope of moving up to better positions.[20] But commerce was also a staging area to move up in life. According to one study, nearly half of all commercial employees in Rio were under 20, and 63 percent were single in 1949.[21] Like Fausto de Pinho Tavares, a law student who worked at a commercial firm in Belo Horizonte in 1940, many clerks worked part-time in order to pay for school.[22] If Tavares did not succeed in establishing a legal practice of his own, as most did not, then perhaps with the right credentials, hard work, and often connections, he could someday become a higher-echelon employee, an accountant, or a middle manager in a sizable concern.[23] At worst he could console himself (though it might be cold comfort) that he was a "polyglot," a "man of letters," "civilized"—social identities to which most manual workers, commonly illiterate and always poor, could never aspire.

It is important to note the glissade from a simple manual-nonmanual dichotomy, which the nature of commercial work could not wholly sustain, into notions of cultural elevation and competence. The slippage is critical because it establishes the links among culture, work, and class, suggesting how those so inclined could anchor their place in the social hierarchy. It also hints at why commercial employees might have been willing to accept Ribeiro's words; he was describing them as so many of them wanted to be seen. As novelist Oswald de Andrade put it in his 1944 novel *Chão*, commercial employees beheld themselves with a kind of "aristocratic romanticism in the face of the proletariat, to which they did not want to belong." Even women clerks refused to "mix with the factory girls."[24]

Bank employees also hankered for "social projection."[25] Bank work seems to have been a respectable fallback for those with educational or social credentials who failed to find work in what one author referred to as the "more seductive" liberal professions.[26] It also appears to have been a respectable career path for those of more modest origin and lesser education who might otherwise have taken jobs in commerce.[27] Indeed, the insistence that all bank clerks were "intellectual workers" entitled to "a certain social standing" was the social glue for a group of people drawn from varied backgrounds.[28] According to one publication in 1942, the teller had to be "diligent, active, discreet, prudent and capable; he must know how to deal with the public (and everyone knows what an arduous task that is); he must lead a normal private life and an irreproachable public life; he must have polished manners, be polite, have general knowledge, in short, possess the qualities that will allow him to perform his work well and with dignity."[29]

While some doubtless chafed at maintaining respectability on pitiable salaries, the rewards of such employment were great enough that the competition for bank positions was intense. In 1935 an officer of a conservative bank employees' association blamed low salaries in the profession on "the very strong prejudice against work that depends on physical effort," a holdover from slavery, he said. As a result, young men preferred low-paying jobs with a title—office clerk, accountant, section chief—to better-paying jobs utterly lacking "hierarchy." So deep ran the prejudice, wrote this author, that "a brother, who is a public servant, full of conceit because he is chief of a section but also full of debt in consequence of his small salary, is ashamed to introduce his brother who is a small farmer, though he is not embarrassed constantly to be asking him for loans to cover his permanent deficits."[30]

Mid-level public functionaries faced a somewhat different problem than bank or commercial employees in their bid for social recognition. Civil servants had long been condemned as "parasites" and bad workers.[31] According to the prevalent mythology, functionaries were nothing more than the "poor cousins" and clients of traditional families, who abused the public fisc by showing up once a month to retrieve their paychecks.[32] As the legend went, these people could not be troubled to work and used public office to subsidize their poetic and political aspirations.

Thus, when civil servants in the 1930s and 1940s lay claim to respectability, they did so on two fronts. They cast intellectual work in a new role by demeaning the lax life of the *faux* literati and playing up technical expertise for productive ends. Functionaries, unlike *bon vivant bacharéis* and manual workers, insisted one civil servant, necessarily possessed the "intelligence of scholars" and were given to "serious thinking and study."[33] Most were not nearly so well endowed. Nevertheless, the image gave all functionaries a means of one-upping indolent elites and setting themselves off from social inferiors.

The vehemence with which civil servants claimed their status must be understood in the context of what was happening in the liberal professions. It is commonly assumed that lawyers, doctors, and engineers belonged to an elite class by dint of their education. But while a few circulated in the highest levels of society, most had no choice but to scrabble for a living. Unable to make a go of it as private practitioners, young graduates stampeded public and private bureaucracies, industrial laboratories, newspapers, and unions in search of stable, salaried employment.[34] They accepted the status of "employee," gladly or reluctantly depending on individual circumstance and predisposition. According to one doctor in 1945, medicine had been "industrialized," so that most physicians now lived on salary, working for employee associations or the state.[35] Much the same was said of the professions in general,[36] for most could not avoid "renting out their intellectual or technical capacities" and subordinating their work to the hierarchy of a business or government office.[37]

Part of the quandary for these new employees was whether and at what price they might benefit from labor legislation mandating social security and retirement, and regulating salary, length of workday, and vacation. As the new laws applied only to "workers," some collar-and-tie associations began to concede that "between the manual and the intellectual proletariat there is no difference in the effects of social legislation."[38] Many did so with great trepidation. In some cases they were hoist by their own petard. In 1942 a judge denied a journalist protection under the labor laws because of the "natural differences of economic inferiority that separate the manual worker from the technical and intellectual worker." While the decision was reversed on appeal, the initial ruling indicates the ambivalent position collar-and-tie people occupied in Brazil's unsettled social order.[39]

The willingness of collar-and-tie employees to bear the label "worker," then, did not imply social leveling. Doyens of the liberal professions, usually connected to traditional families, jealous of their independence, and financially flush enough to maintain private practices, doubtless thought as much. But beyond limited concessions, the new breed of employees stubbornly insisted on remaining "intellectuals." The implications of this quandary were troubling for many. A university graduate hunched over a government or company desk might claim to be a worker as defined in the new labor laws and still arrogate to himself the social privileges of his bacharéis's ring and diploma, but he knew that the truly independent professionals continued to look down on their bureaucratic colleagues for drawing a paycheck.

Salaried liberal professionals countered this withering gaze by trying to redefine what it meant to be a professional. When in 1942 sociologist Gilberto Freyre accused Brazil's engineers, architects, and chemists of being just a bunch of "bacharéis with fingers full of rings, who never descend from their dignity to smear themselves with grease or paint in working on a house or a bridge or in a laboratory," the São Paulo engineers' association responded hotly. No one denied that most Brazilians thought "physical or manual labor not suitable to the superior man." Still, the editorial finger wagged, "it must be recognized that we have made progress." Where once gentlemen had slaves to carry their packages and umbrellas, "today we can see on buses and trolleys collar-and-tie gentlemen on their way home, not hesitating to dangle from their fingers packages bound with twine." Moreover, most were not afraid of "heavy work." And few "lived in the comfort of a mansion."[40] Whether or not rhetoric met with reality, these engineers positioned themselves against the traditional elite by manipulating the manual-nonmanual distinction to their advantage.

Among the lower ranks of educated professionals, those with only secondary-school degrees, the prestige of the *doutor* continued to be the
point of social reference. For instance, accountants, most of whom could
boast only secondary-school or technical educations, were extremely
pleased to be included among the liberal professions by a 1933 law defining occupational status.[41] They might not command the prestige and deference enjoyed by doutores, but they could garner the considerable respect
or at least derive the market advantage due their relative scarcity. Here
too the disdain for manual labor ran deep. An influential national opinion
magazine reported in 1941 that experts were frustrated with Brazilian
secondary-school students who persistently eschewed "manual training"
courses—what in the United States was called shop—and preferred the
culture-laden classes in literature, languages, philosophy, and the more
ethereal professions related to them. The explanation, according to one
expert, was that students confused "manual training" with "professional
training," which was taught at special industrial schools intended for and
attended exclusively by factory workers. Only by substituting for *manual
training* the term *steriometry*—"a limpid word, which encompasses functions and goals, sounds pleasing, does not offend the ear, and even has
something noble about it"—could the prejudice against the courses be
overcome.[42] It is doubtful many minds would have been changed.

If those in more established occupations were having difficulties during
the 1930s and 1940s, not a few white-collar types were riding high on a
"veritable avalanche of new professions" being thrown up by industrial
expansion and economic development.[43] Economists, engineers, statisticians, chemists, architects, advertising experts, well-trained accountants,
insurance-, real estate-, and stock brokers, and others with business and
managerial skills were in great demand.[44] Virtually all, as the association
of advertising professionals put it, sought to "elevate their art to the dignity of a respectable profession."[45]

Managers may have had the best of this boom. With the specialization
of industrial and government work tens of thousands of young men took
up administrative and supervisory positions in the public and private sectors. Managerial work varied in nature and compensation. Educated supervisors in private companies "were very well remunerated," according
to one study, and tended to be promoted by merit. Because of their "moral
qualities" and their "broad general culture" these administrators were
seen as belonging to a higher social class than manual workers.[46] An enu-
meration of the personal qualities required of managers—tact, honesty,
optimism, self-control, enthusiasm, sympathy, dignity, firmness, patience,

balance, decisiveness, imagination, valor—bespeaks an effort to mold a personality type to fit the new supervisory role.[47] Public administrators too were thought to have the "greatest future," and examinations for admission to the ranks of "administrative technicians," and even to less prestigious government positions, were heavily contested.[48]

The government's deepening intervention in the relationship between capital and labor also created collar-and-tie opportunities. Social work and government labor law, for instance, were new career paths keyed to what was widely seen as growing class conflict in Brazilian society. Social work was conceived as a means of addressing the worst and most dangerous ills of an industrial economy. The social worker's job, as described by the Ministry of Education and Health in 1941, was to "enlighten and readjust" disruptive and disorderly manual workers.[49] Though the profession drew on a wide variety of disciplines, including the male bastions of medicine, law, and pharmacy, women predominated among social workers trained and put to work in the late 1930s and 1940s. It was commonly argued that women were the ideal social workers because of their softer touch in relationships with other people.[50] Government labor lawyers, almost always men, were thought to be more confrontational. Graduates of the better law schools, they were supposed to adjudicate disputes between employers and employees without favoring one party over the other. Their broad charge was to ensure social peace. In the process, they, along with social workers, helped institutionalize the manual-nonmanual divide and put some in the position to police the border between the two in a way that allowed private interests and the public good to converge.

Those in older occupations doubtless worried that they were being pushed down toward a line they dare not cross. Shopkeeping still represented a route to modest comfort and security, especially among the descendants of Rio's and São Paulo's immigrants. But even as Miguel Chaloub, son of Syrian parents who immigrated to Brazil in 1892 and moved to Rio in 1907, was making a go of his decidedly "modern" clothing and accessories store in an "elite" Rio neighborhood,[51] shopkeepers' publications were decrying the plight of these "heroic pioneers of progress,"[52] who faced ever higher taxes, fines, and regulations that made it difficult for them to keep abreast of inflation.[53] The life of the small merchant was becoming more tenuous.

Their social position was being eroded from two sides. New labor laws strained relations with employees, because workers could now denounce violators to the authorities. Merchants were profoundly discomfited by this turn, arguing that "if we disregard hierarchy, which is the base of all social organization ... we walk toward the abyss."[54] Yet the generalized bid for social recognition among collar-and-tie employees was altering the meaning of social hierarchy. While shopkeeping had never enjoyed great prestige, it was losing ground as schooling and the acquirements of culture spread among other professions. Merchants' sons had always gravitated to the faculdades. Now there were many more paths to higher-status positions than ever before. It was no longer enough to be "a simple seller," said a popular monthly magazine.[55] Recent changes demanded more. The sentiment is perhaps best captured in Erico Veríssimo's novel *Crossroads*, where a son's decision to join his father in the dry-goods business is met by a mother's tirade: "Is that why a man studies ten years? Is that why he strives for a diploma? So that he can be a storekeeper like his father who never learned anything except multiplication, addition, subtraction, and division?"[56]

The Importance of Being Culto

At bottom this mother's exasperation was a complex fugue among educational credentials, social competition, and the status deriving from cultural attainment. In a competitive market, education was becoming a *sine qua non* of collar-and-tie employment. The rising stock of diplomas was the most obvious sign of this development. But much more was going on. According to one writer, employers in the 1940s hired managers and office employees on the basis of their "diplomas," less as proof of their abilities than as an indication of their "social qualifications," their "total social status."[57] The idea was that a more intangible notion of status should be relevant in hiring. One magazine noted that "general culture and a capacity for technical development," which workers "unhappily lacked," distinguished engineers from the skilled artisans with whom they so often competed for construction projects.[58] Others who concerned themselves with managerial issues insisted that "preparatory studies" in addition to "intellectual and moral qualities, general culture and specialized knowledge" should be the prime determinants in hiring public functionaries and bank employees.[59] Civil servant José Moacir de Andrade Sobrinho's 1940 essay held as unassailable that the public functionary's "cultural patrimony" should determine his income, lest he be lumped together with illiterates.[60]

The appeal to culture spread rapidly from the 1930s forward. White-collar publications pushed the idea that their members were *culto* (cultured or cultivated). The vehemence of the claim varied with the group in question. Lawyers and doctors appear to have felt little need to speak publicly about their cultural attainments. Possession of a university ring and membership in a traditional profession were prima facie evidence of being culto. Others were more aggressive. For example, a candidate for the presidency of a São Paulo public servants' association knew an opportunity when he saw one and promised that his administration would create humanities courses for its members, because "culture is a good that we know how to appreciate."[61] He won. This desire to "cultivate intelligence" was the impetus that drove most large collar-and-tie associations to build libraries, classroom complexes, and theaters during the 1930s and 1940s. Rio's Association of Commercial Employees, in an ad featuring a fellow in suit and tie thoughtfully absorbed in a book, exhorted its members to use the library, to bring out the "latent forces of your spirit," because "knowledge is the capital that produces the most and the only wealth that will accompany a man until his last day."[62] What better response to the likes of a São Paulo accountant who demanded that his association establish humanities courses like the ones doctors and lawyers already enjoyed? "And what of the accountant?" he asked. "Is he an inferior kind of professional, of the mechanical arts, whose work is independent of reasoning?"[63]

As this man's exasperation suggests, a primary goal in claiming to be culto was to project a certain ascendancy over social inferiors: workers and poor people. In advancing this cause, white-collar associations often found ready allies among employers. Many businessmen had little stake in the traditional sense of culto as the province of a small elite. Since the nineteenth century those with faculdade degrees had looked down on business as a lesser activity. Immigrants who successfully clambered up the social ladder through commerce had little concern to preserve a status from which powerful Brazilian families had barred them for so long. Moreover, many employers hoped that white-collar employees who felt themselves a cut above manual workers would forgo collective action. As early as 1925 a banker's journal stated hopefully that surely its employees would not form a union, given that their manners and education put them at a "higher social level" than factory workers.[64] Bank employee associations, those more closely identified with the labor movement as well as conservatives, eagerly agreed with the second part of the statement, insisting that as *"homens cultos"* (cultivated men) a certain deference was due their "culture and erudition."[65]

What these publications meant when they used the word *culture* or referred to their members as culto was never quite clear. But, then, vagueness may have been the point. Ideally someone who was culto bore the imprint of refinement, knowledge, and polish characteristic of those cut from superior social cloth: the small circle of bacharéis and other elites of the late nineteenth and early twentieth centuries whose status was an inherent attribute of their birth, education, manners, and ease of life. When in the 1920s white-collar associations and individuals began to insist publicly that their members also were culto, they were altering the sense of the term. As set forth in the pages of association publications, culto was less the mark of an individual than a label claimed on behalf of an occupational group, a collective will to status.

The mere fact of an institutional claim to culto status meant little if individual members did not at least make a good show of striving toward the ideal. Collar-and-tie publications constantly reminded members to use the library, avail themselves of the record collection, attend the theater, and take classes. Many surely did. One São Paulo bank employee wrote an article on the perils of directionless autodidacticism. Too many of his colleagues, he complained, read frivolously, wasting time and squandering opportunities to better themselves. Far preferable, he counseled his fellows, to study only great literature: Homer, Aristotle, Plato, Dante, Shakespeare, Goethe, Hugo.[66]

The frequency of such exhortations suggests that for most collar-and-tie professionals and employees the desire to be culto was in good measure instrumental. Willing to have their associations push for culto status collectively, individuals appear to have pursued the ideal halfheartedly at best. One group tried to spark greater interest among its members by linking the acquisition of culture to career advancement: "COLLEAGUE! If you aspire to a higher position, think first about the cultural level of your spirit. Sign up today for the self-improvement class sponsored by the Bank Functionaries Union ... Results are sure to follow."[67] There can be no more eloquent testimony to the dissonances of the changed and uncertain meaning of culto.

Amidst the swirl of meanings, pursuit of the status of culto had its own dangers and dilemmas. Perhaps the most vivid and intimate rendering of them is a fictional account, Jacy Pacheco's *Bank Clerk ... (Miseries of a Profession).*[68] If Pacheco is to be believed, few were more obsessed with the question of culture than bank employees. Pacheco's protagonist, Fernando, is a teller at a well-regarded bank. Miserable at his job, bored with the routinized work, he supports his union and lives in constant fear of being fired, for he cannot "resign himself" to his situation and wait for a chance to move up.

Refusing to lash himself to a career, he is easily led astray by the siren of culture. Dire circumstance moves him to introspection and existential lament. He begins to frequent cafés, where he falls in with a crowd of well-heeled poetasters, mistaking their ease of life for true refinement. Verse turns his mind to higher things, and he is smitten by a young school-teacher, Angela. He goes bankrupt trying to impress her, and he still runs up against the barrier of culture. On one occasion he invites her to a soirée. At dinner he revels in his own repartee and thinks he has made a cultural coup by comparing his wife's cooking to that of Vatel, Louis XIV's chef. "He looked toward Angela, happy with his prodigious memory, proud of his knowledge," only to find her correcting him: Vatel was the Prince of Condé's cook, not the king's. Embarrassed by his *faux pas*, he ushers the guests to the parlor where they listen to the "Blue Danube" in "almost re-ligious silence" on a radio bought on credit.

In the following weeks Fernando's passion is inflamed. He writes love let-ters and poetry to Angela, praising her intelligence. He is not favored with a response. Desperate for her attention, he contrives an outing to the club where all the chic people go, spending his last pennies doing so. There he and Angela run into Doutor Claúdio, a polished lawyer, renowned poet, and ac-claimed critic. Fernando and Claúdio have drunk together several times in the past, ostensibly as fellow poets plumbing the depths of the human soul. But Fernando has always felt at a cultural and intellectual disadvantage. Shortly after meeting him, Angela falls for Claúdio. Fernando's life unravels. First he loses Angela. Then he discovers that Claúdio had merely been kind in praising his poetry. His wife, a woman from the interior who thought she was moving up by marrying a big-city bank employee, leaves him. The bank fires him for being an agitator and a bad worker. He dies.

Piercing the fog of melodrama enshrouding this story, we can perhaps make more concrete, or at least personal, the anxieties, aspirations, and am-bivalences of collar-and-tie life in Brazil's big cities in the early 1940s. In this book the manual-nonmanual divide is never explicitly mentioned. Social distinction is coded through culture. The quest to be culto, however, is a tor-tuous one. Unsatisfied with the modest status of bank employee, Fernando believes that only culture can redeem his miserable life, for only cultural re-finement will make Angela love him and Claúdio respect him. His fevered imagination conjures the ideal as a kind of meritocracy; anyone can become culto through knowledge, polish, and acquired spiritual sensitivity. He fails to understand that his circumstance effectively precludes him from attaining this dream in all but the limited sense of being a cut above workers because of his respectable job and his smattering of self-inflicted cultural knowledge. The final realization that he cannot compete with Doutor Claúdio's cultural repertoire, and the money that makes it possible, ruins him.

An easy interpretation of this tale would suggest that Fernando simply took the ideal of being culto too seriously. When white-collar associations urged "general culture" upon their members, they were adopting a pragmatic strategy of appropriating the cultural mantle of those above against the cold winds from below. Individuals of modest seriousness might attend classes, frequent the library, check out records; little more was required. On this view, Fernando simply got carried away. But Pacheco's book may point to another consideration. The ideal of being culto, as represented in the novel and as articulated by white-collar individuals and associations in the 1930s and 1940s, implied a kind of upward leveling. This was perhaps especially true for the vast bulk of middle-class people who lacked university training. For them general culture could, in principle, be obtained by reading the right books, listening to the right music, attending the right plays, showing up at the right cafés, all of which were increasingly available through white-collar associations and a growing consumer market for cultural goods; they invested limited time and money in a manner that would best equip them to confront a social world in which a patina of culture kept the *inculto* (uncultivated) at bay. Most probably never expected to transcend their station through culture, as Fernando hoped he might. The meretricious equivocality of what it meant to be culto, however, at least allowed them to imagine a kind of moral equality with those above them, in contrast to the strict hierarchical separation they saw between themselves and those below.

The Rewards of Work

The experience of work seems to have reinforced the hierarchy of nonmanual over manual and culto over inculto among the men who earned their livings in the collar-and-tie sector. At a basic level geographic separation between the locales of manual and nonmanual work could play an important role. With the emergence of large factories manual workers often traveled to or lived in sooty industrial districts wholly distinct from the glittering downtowns of Rio de Janeiro and São Paulo. Banks, large commercial firms, retail stores, professional and government offices—all were located along broad avenues regularly swept clean by public workers. These work places were often within easy walking distance of restaurants, newsstands, bookstores, cafés, and the other amenities of urban life.

The split was captured in a 1944 *Correio da Manhã* article on the neighborhood of Brás, which encompassed a large factory district in São Paulo. The River Tamanduateí, said the article, allowed those who lived and worked downtown to be "totally unaware" of the "anonymous workers" of Brás, who consumed their youth in the "furnace and looms of the factory."[69] And yet, the Tamanduateí was often enough crossed in both directions. Collar-and-tie clerical, professional, and administrative personnel worked in offices at the plants. Manual workers labored in small shops, domestic service, and the numberless subaltern positions in the center. So a sharp divide was doubtless more symbolic than real.[70]

Far more than geography, the nature of white-collar work itself and what it required of those who performed it separated middle-class from working-class people. A first obvious distinction was appearance. Among factory and unskilled workers personal appearance was largely irrelevant to their work. Factory work was dirty, uncomfortable, unpleasant, and often unhealthy or downright dangerous amidst fumes, heat, and poor ventilation. Collar-and-tie work was, on the whole, lighter and cleaner than manual labor; pens, adding machines, typewriters, paper, file cabinets were the tools of office work, whatever the nature of the final product. Moreover, such work was often performed in tolerably pleasant, orderly surroundings and generally demanded a certain decorum.[71] As a result, collar-and-tie employees, from bank and commercial clerks to salesmen, to public functionaries, to professionals, were expected to wear long-sleeved shirts and ties (*colarinho e gravata*), presentable shoes, and oftentimes a jacket.[72] Overall presentation, then, was crucial to securing and maintaining a collar-and-tie job. Indeed, want ads for office jobs throughout the 1930s and 1940s regularly referred to the importance of an applicant's "good appearance"—a broad concept that included "the manner of dressing, of speaking, of acting . . . in addition to physical traits, especially the color of the skin, of the teeth"—suggesting a class- and color-based test for certain kinds of jobs.[73]

Racial attitudes crucially inflected the manual-nonmanual hierarchy. The issue was rarely discussed in the publications of collar-and-tie employees and professionals, but census data, summarized in Table 3, indicate a close association between darker skin and manual labor.

Blacks and mulattos of all shades confronted great resistance from employers. They rarely landed jobs in the commercial sector because appearance mattered, and good appearance was something "people of color could not have," as one employer noted. A shopkeeper in São Paulo who catered primarily to a middle-class clientele lamented the fact that he "was obliged to turn away intelligent young women with diplomas" just because they were *mulattas*.[74] The greatest opportunities for those of darker skins to move out of manual labor were in government employment, where nevertheless most worked as orderlies, doormen, and messengers, not the kinds of jobs likely to vault them into respectability.[75]

TABLE 3

Occupational Categories by Race, Rio de Janeiro, 1940

(Percentages of whites, blacks, and mixed-race workers)

	White	Black	Mixed-race
Agriculture	52	25	23
Extractive	60	25	15
Industry	66	16	18
Transportation	70	11	19
Services	76	9	15
Commerce	86	5	9
Banking	93	2	5
Liberal professions	85	4	10

SOURCE: Pinto, *O negro no Rio de Janeiro* (1953), 84–85.

Prejudice was woven into the fabric of a competitive system. Whites vying intensely with each other for respectable jobs did not want to face blacks and mulattos as well. This was true especially of whites on the lower rungs of collar-and-tie respectability, for it was there that mulattos made what headway they did in a competitive market where the power of patronage had weakened.[76] An unspoken discrimination against those of darker skins coincided with the interests of hard-pressed collar-and-tie whites or near whites who were trying to assert hierarchical status against those below them, including those with darker skins.

If pushed, most whites or near whites would probably have denied the existence of racial discrimination, or at least systematic racial discrimination, in the labor market. The perception was widely held that mulattos had always been able to move up the social scale if they knew the right people or were well qualified for their jobs, just like anyone else. According to contemporaries, those who did not had only themselves to blame for failing to capitalize on opportunities. Most black and mulatto elites, who through patronage or pluck had succeeded, appear to have agreed, at least publicly. To do otherwise would have been to diminish their own accomplishments and potentially disrupt their relationships with patrons. One wrote in the late 1920s that "race prejudice does not exist . . . the nation is not to blame for the state of Brazilian blacks." Another shrugged off casual discrimination because it was "bound to happen, what with all the classes and individuals in search of advancement these days."[77] White collar-and-tie employees and professionals would surely have agreed; it allowed them to reap the rewards of hierarchy while subscribing, *sotto voce*, to a doctrine of equal opportunity for the races.

Collar-and-tie work differed from most manual labor, and especially from factory work, in the level of supervision and work-place order. Industrial workers labored under direct surveillance and were subject to the "collective discipline" of whistles, guards, and inspectors and the rigor of assembly-line mechanization that imposed rhythm and pattern on factory work.[78] White-collar employees, by contrast, bore substantial individual responsibility for the outcome of tasks performed and were supposed to accomplish them largely without direct oversight. Public servants undertook bureaucratic tasks, bank employees counted money and made small decisions, teachers led classes and graded papers, labor lawyers heard and decided cases, salesmen sold merchandise, journalists wrote—all "without a boss watching."[79]

Which is not to say that collar-and-tie employees went completely unsupervised. Yet the oversight differed from that to which factory workers were subject, because it was not as direct and because the work was not as easily controlled as assembly-line labor. Bank employees were routinely monitored and their accounts checked by higher-level employees, but they retained considerable individual discretion over exactly how and when to reconcile their accounts. Government experts spilt considerable ink in the late 1930s and early 1940s trying to devise ways to control public functionaries, who were notorious for frequent illnesses that caused them to miss work, for taking extended lunches, and for ducking out of the office early at the end of the day.[80] The tone of persuasion rather than repression bespeaks an attempt to instill a sense of dignity in and responsibility for work rather than an effort to subject the employees to ever greater levels of supervision.[81] It also suggests that collar-and-tie work implied considerably greater control over day-to-day work lives than was true of the many who labored in factories.

For those in managerial positions this control took the form of actual authority or ascendancy over social inferiors, or even social equals. Managers were generally sandwiched in the middle of work-place hierarchies. Sr. Oscar, aide to the director of a São Paulo pharmaceutical company in 1950, monitored the performance of section heads and their manual workers, settled disputes among sections and between workers and their foremen, hired and fired, and reported back to his own boss on the details of day-to-day operations.[82] Sr. Oscar's job may have been one of greater responsibility and thus of privilege and distinction than most. In essence, however, it appears to have differed little from the positions held by tens of thousands of managers and supervisors in industrial, commercial, and banking concerns large and small and in public offices throughout this period.

Managers were only the most obvious examples of the growing number of collar-and-tie employees—schoolteachers, government labor lawyers, and social workers—in positions of immediate superiority vis-à-vis social inferiors at the work place. Discretionary powers engendered a strong temptation to lord hierarchy over social lessers. Some were quick to succumb. One young lawyer who worked for the state Department of Labor in Rio, for instance, was accused by low-level commercial workers of acting as though he were an "employer" and of behaving high-handedly with those who came before him to plead their cases.[83] Such haughtiness may well have been endemic to public functionaries, a perquisite of professionally drab positions. In fact, a public opinion survey conducted in 1946 indicated that poor people in general were treated shabbily by bureaucrats in government offices, whereas the well off were better attended to—not so surprising a result in a culture of patronage.[84]

Collar-and-tie employees and professionals were themselves subject to workplace hierarchies. Many doubtless balked at the bridle and resented their lack of power. This aspect of everyday life they shared with manual workers. The almost neurotic Fernando in Pacheco's novel *Bank Clerk* is the perfect evocation of the abiding anxiety consciousness of subordination could cause. This was probably especially true of lower-level, younger employees. As a mother counsels her stenographer daughter who daydreams of being a teacher, "Poor people must be careful. . . . A person becomes distracted or falls asleep. He arrives at his work late—the boss protests. . . . By the time he turns around, he's out of a job."[85] Perhaps women especially had reason to worry. Typists, file clerks, and stenographers were so plentiful that bosses could easily replace them. Moreover, male bosses appear to have retained a deep suspicion of female employees. For instance, efficiency experts in the public service complained that women talked too much on the phone and generally adhered to the "law of minimum effort."[86] Only in areas considered an expression of a nurturing temperament, such as teaching and social work, were women allowed to work "without a boss watching."

Many collar-and-tie men, by contrast, enjoyed a luxury unavailable to most manual workers: they could imagine a relationship to the boss akin to a voluntary arrangement necessary to the proper functioning of organizational life. More often enunciated than realized, the ideal was captured in a 1950 report arguing that lawyers, even those working for salaries, "exercise an eminently intellectual activity," so that on-the-job "subordination is not the same as that to which the manual laborer is subject, because the assistant, through his studies and knowledge, can impose himself upon the esteem of the boss, without thereby violating the obedience with which he is charged."[87]

In other words, "intellectual workers" could see themselves as possessing certain cultural capacities that somewhat attenuated perceived differences between themselves and their bosses. Thus, accountants wanted to be "friend[s] and assistant[s]" to their bosses, rather than merely servants.[88] Mid-level bank employees could aspire to be within a common "sphere of familiarity [*intimidade*]" with their employers, "notwithstanding the protocols of hierarchy" and a duty of "serviceability."[89] Obedience, after all, did not imply a "loss of personality"; rather, said a bank employees' publication, "what prevails in this case are the discreet manifestations of the spirit of sociability that must emanate from any man who would consider himself educated. He who attunes himself in this way to his supervisor establishes by the spontaneity of his manners an obligation of moral reciprocity."[90]

Nor was this merely the reciprocity of an inertial paternalism. The mutual obligation contemplated here was grounded as much in education and social position, impersonal links between rough equals, as in the personal connections characteristic of patrons and clients. This ambiguity of obligations deeply etched work life. Male collar-and-tie employees, depending on individual circumstance, had a means of reconciling the tensions inherent in the economic dependence and subservience of employment situations. They could preserve individual dignity by insisting that, within the "protocols of hierarchy," cultural capacities and the status of culto rooted a relationship of rough moral equality with those above them. There was no guarantee, of course, that bosses would see things the same way.

In a similar vein part of the effort to dignify collar-and-tie work involved the growing sense that work could and should be rewarding, valuable, and important. Not only lawyers but also public functionaries and advertising men wrote rapturously of the "nobility" of their work and of their high social function.[91] A 1946 manual for teachers called teaching above all a "pleasure" performed by people who "love their work" and were "relatively unconcerned with pecuniary gain."[92] A bank employees' publication and an accountant referred to the dignity of their professions and the important honor and responsibility they had to serve the public well.[93] One bank employee was explicit about how work could dignify him against those in other classes. "It is good to be useful," he wrote. The "depravity of the upper classes and the degraded classes is their failure to work."[94] Army officers too urged the importance of work, "for it is the profession that elevates the individual's moral life," giving him a clear understanding of his "social function, and thus of his duties."[95] A *Vida Doméstica* article entitled "Happiness" eulogized work as a "stimulus to life, glory, happiness, and consolation."[96]

Byron Freitas, a government functionary and writer on issues of public service, provided perhaps the best summary of this attitude toward work, which he saw as of relatively recent vintage in Brazil. In a treatise on personnel administration, drawing on his experience in Brazil and his familiarity with management theory taking shape in the United States, he warned readers—would-be upper-echelon private- and public-sector managers—that they could not afford to ignore that "professional work today exerts a much more profound influence than ever before." Professionals now wanted to "feel a certain satisfaction" in their tasks, which would lead them to "a kind of perfect psychological equilibrium" in which work would become a "moral necessity." The resulting "sense of euphoria" would allow them to succeed and "aspire to a higher social position."

The author recognized that this "euphoria" and the success and aspirations it could foster were not universally felt in the collar-and-tie sector. Many people had little real interest in their work, he observed, "In such situations, the 'profession' becomes simply a job for pay, incapable of stimulating the individual constantly to improve himself."[97] For such people, work held few spiritual, intellectual, or moral rewards. Novels intimate at this hidden transcript. Fictional bookkeepers, bank employees, low-level lawyers, and bureaucrats live out lives of deadening routine and "lethargic serenity ... listlessly await[ing] retirement and death."[98] Still, though the notion that work could be dignifying was a more realistic hope for certain white-collar occupations, such as the liberal professions and teaching, than others, such as commerce, good work as an enunciated value was more widely available to collar-and-tie people than at any previous time.

BY THE 1950s the central symbol and reality of urban Brazil's social hierarchy was work. At the most fundamental level social position depended largely on whether one performed manual labor or could claim to belong to a nonmanual occupation recognized as culto. In Hutchinson's

1956 study of occupational prestige São Paulo university students ranked doctors, lawyers, and priests, followed by managers, journalists, *fazendeiros*, teachers, accountants, public functionaries, shopkeepers, expediters, office clerks, and traveling salesmen in the top half of a list of thirty occupations. The bottom half included manual occupations, lumping low-level clerks and chefs with mechanics, carpenters, waiters, stevedores, and garbage collectors.[99]

In some regards Hutchinson's findings are hardly surprising, for the manual-nonmanual distinction and the insistence that culture conferred status were not new in Brazil or elsewhere. However, these old notions came to play a novel role as the idea, experience, and representation of class emerged after the turn of the century. White-collar associations led the way through their publications. This did not imply broad solidarity cutting across occupational lines. On the contrary, associations acted largely independently of each other, though hardly in isolation. Like-minded rather than cooperative, all drew on the same criteria, which one Brazilian observer claimed as the defining qualities of the "middle class"—the "cultural criterion, that is, education beyond grade school," and a "professional criterion, in the sense that their work is not corporeal or mechanical."[100] Although not a broad-based, middle-class movement, the various individual and associational bids for social recognition marked a dramatic departure: hierarchy affirmed, renewed, and challenged through collective, institutional means rather than through patronage and personal relations.

Hence the ambiguity of the process. Seeking a stable social order, collar-and-tie individuals and associations blended ideas regarding the modern division of labor with deeply rooted Brazilian traditions that allowed some people to raise themselves above others by disdaining manual labor and privileging culture. In so doing they helped to define the social place of manual workers. As they did for women, the vast majority of whom were not directly involved in the collar-and-tie labor market that defined respectability for their husbands. But it was not only a matter of setting themselves off from those below. Reflecting an ethos that was quickly gaining currency, collar-and-tie associations treated culture as a kind of capital that could be earned by investing in education and competing in the labor market. Individuals possessing little property or wealth could thus imagine that their lives differed only in degree from those with money. Of course, this could only be a tenuous identification, since money was so deeply implicated in what it meant to be culto, as the fictional bank teller Fernando discovered only too late.

Still, nonmanual work and the claim to culture, though coarse, represented practical criteria of distinction by which collar-and-tie people could recognize one another in everyday life through manner of dress, "overall appearance," proper speech, and schooling. They gathered in clubs, theaters, restaurants, and other social settings effectively closed to the working class.[101] They might aspire to be known for their "notably high mental level, with broad general knowledge, good manners, and a solid base of general culture," but mutual respect and social mingling did not preclude the fine discriminations made possible by close attention to cultural acquirements and credentials.[102] Faculdade graduates could look down their noses at those with only secondary-school educations, who might lord it over those who had not finished secondary school, who could at least know themselves superior to the humble clerk with barely more than a primary education, who could distinguish himself only from manual workers, though he might earn less than a skilled craftsman. The common thread of this experience was neither an organic solidarity nor a shared struggle, but an individual drive to put as many people below oneself as possible.

Yet hierarchy might also be used to restrain those who sought to rise too far. In Almeida Fischer's 1950 short story "Suspicion" a public functionary punctures his boss's arrogant pretenses by giving him exactly what he wants. After being ordered about by his supervisor in a particularly imperious way, the functionary fawningly refers to the man as doutor. In this way he was able to "avenge himself. That 'doutor,' said with emphasis and heard by the whole office, calmed him down. Everyone knew that 'seu' [a term of address, like mister, used with first names] Rogério had never been a doutor and that his major disappointment in life was not having obtained the title, even though he had exerted himself to do so as a young man."[103] Here an appeal to hierarchy served the purpose of enforcing a rough equality among those divided only by lines of authority, not culture, even as it bolstered the very idea of hierarchy as a defining feature of social life.

This complex calculus of social location was the product of a more fluid relationship among individuals in a competitive culture. Opportunities for advancement, while growing, could not be taken for granted. To set themselves apart from those below, white-collar men subverted hierarchy vis-à-vis those above. Once culture could make the man—and only very occasionally the woman—the elite monopoly on culto status was broken, transformed into a trait that anyone with the right education and job could claim, at least in principle. For the most part elites now had only their money and access to patronage—their power—setting them off from what seemed to be throngs of upward strivers.*

Hutchinson's study of São Paulo university students hints at how far this process had gone and how closely connected it was to the emergence of a middle-class identity. The same university students who had drawn a sharp line between manual and nonmanual work also overwhelmingly identified themselves as middle class, rather than as upper class or rich, bourgeoisie, liberal professionals, poor or proletarian, or other classes.[104] There is no shortage of reasons why students might choose to identify themselves as middle class to a British researcher, not least among them that they may have thought it was what a foreigner would want to hear. There might, in other words, have been a bit of *para inglês ver"* (for the English to see) in this.† Nevertheless, Hutchinson's results point to the consolidation of a class society in Brazil: Where once university graduates had been able to imagine themselves elites for being doutores—indeed, would have demanded it—by the 1950s they could easily locate themselves within a taxonomy of class, and the idea of the middle class, for all its tensions, was sufficiently elastic that both the likes of Ribeiro's clerk and Hutchinson's university graduates could invoke it.

---

*It is worth noting that Sérgio Buarque de Holanda in his *Raízes do Brasil* of 1936 argued that this had always been so in Brazil. Portugal's ancient nobility, he wrote, had at various times achieved predominance, without ever managing to constitute itself a "closed aristocracy." As a consequence, the hierarchy carried to Brazil starting in the sixteenth century had never been "rigorous or impermeable," but subject to a ceaseless reckoning of privilege and place. Nor was Brazil fertile soil for the making of a more hierarchical principle, given the instability and opportunities of social and economic life in the New World. Thus, personal prestige, argued Holanda, had long maintained a certain independence from "inherited names," so that Brazilians (and other Ibero-Americans) were, in fact, "legitimate pioneers of the modern mentality," knowing as they did before other Europeans that the nobility was not closed but open to change and renewal from below.

†This is the sense that Brazilians, when interacting with outsiders and particularly with outsiders from Europe or the United States, respond by trying to live up to the expectations they want foreigners to have of them and so diminish the distance between themselves and outsiders. Of course, as much as anything else this is mostly an effort to identify with such expectations, at least when facing a foreigner. See Fry, 17–18. The phenomenon of *para inglês ver* suggests the perils of thinking about Brazilian reality as though it could be insulated from implicit and even explicit comparison with other countries, particularly those widely thought to embody successful modernization. The experience of living one's life as though in relation to a projection of modernity based on a screenplay already written has been integral to Brazilian life in the twentieth century.

4

Struggling and Aspiring

IN 1951 PROFESSOR WAGNER Vieira da Cunha understood that Brazil was undergoing profound change when, in his tenure essay for the University of São Paulo on that city's recent breakneck modernization, he wrote, "Current society tends to a 'regime of free competition,' which has given rise to great uncertainty and insecurity among individuals." While the study did not specifically address the middle class, Da Cunha's conclusions limn a social world of competition among nonmanual employees. Historically, he said, individuals had enjoyed limited opportunities for social mobility in Brazil. Now that there is economic and educational "competition among individuals . . . the struggle for position is general," a consequence of the fluidity and indeterminacy of life in a competitive social order.[1] For those in an emergent middle class the ability to distinguish themselves from *inculto* manual workers had come to be mediated by market relations, though not market relations pure and simple. Alongside a growing tendency among employers to choose employees on the basis of experience and credentials, personal relations remained a vital reality in hiring and promotions between 1920 and 1950. Of course, middle-class people had no monopoly on "uncertainty and insecurity." More than in other social sectors, however, their aspirations and anxieties appear to have been rooted in the hope of rising and the fear of falling and in an unresolved tension between merit and patronage.

Secrets of the Market

In 1931 a group of beaming, serious young men in ceremonial regalia heard accountant D. J. Stamoto issue a stern warning in his commencement address at the Alvares Penteado Commercial School in São Paulo.

"Whether he wants to or not," Stamoto intoned gravely, "every man must involve himself in business, must look to the material side of life. *Today we all do business.* Modern life is characterized by commercial expansion, by the struggle of interests."[2] It was a defining moment for the class of '31. Theirs was a good school with a solid reputation. They had studied hard over the previous years. Many of them had stinted themselves of ease to obtain their degrees. All had dreams of success for themselves and their families. But what had Stamoto meant when he said that "today we all do business?" More to the point, what might the young graduates have understood him to mean?

The experience of an anonymous 23-year-old graduate of Alvares Penteado is suggestive. After leaving school in 1933 or 1934, he worked at several firms in São Paulo's commercial district, the Triângulo. Toward the end of May 1936, having gained valuable skills, he was ready to take the next step. He bought an advertisement in the classifieds of O *Estado de São Paulo*, São Paulo's main newspaper, "offering" his services as an "office assistant."[3] In composing the brief notice, this young man carefully deployed his two big selling points: he held a diploma from the Alvares Penteado, which, though no longer so rare, was an accomplishment most still could not boast, and he had experience in a number of good firms. His ad ran first on Thursday, May 21, again on Saturday, and then finally on Sunday, May 24. He knew that few people advertised themselves in this fashion. On any given day there probably were not more than fifteen such ads. But anything was worth a try.

The other option, this young man knew, was to scour the "employees sought" section of the classifieds, to see which companies might be looking for an office assistant. Several ads had appeared in May. None had panned out. Perhaps others looking for similar work had taken them. The week his ad ran a number of other office employees had done the same thing. One of them was an office supervisor and claimed to have accounting skills and languages. Another was a British subject who spoke fluent German and had experience at a "large North American concern."[4] Languages and experience in foreign firms were invaluable, and the Alvares Penteado graduate surely felt the pressure of anonymous others competing for the same jobs. More supervisors, bookkeepers, office assistants, accountants, and salesmen than ever before were offering their services; even women were beginning to take some of these jobs. Too many, it must have seemed, boasted diplomas, language skills, and experience. Still, he may have consoled himself, for those who knew how to take advantage, the opportunities were considerable. So perhaps he paused wistfully over the ad in the Sunday, May 31, edition for a manager at a foreign firm.[5]

We cannot know what became of this young man. His ad ran for three days and did not appear again after May 24. Maybe he could not afford to run it any longer. With luck he withdrew it, having found a good job that set him on a path to the success he envisioned: something in the growing insurance or advertising industries or a position as office manager in a factory or perhaps as an accountant with a firm. Just as likely he had to settle for much less, faced with the competition of thousands upon thousands of others—hence the "great uncertainty and insecurity" of which Da Cunha was to speak in 1951.

A survey of the classifieds suggests what this fellow was up against. Where the number of jobs advertised in *O Estado de São Paulo* averaged 11 per Sunday in May 1932, by 1940 the average had risen to 44, and by 1950 the number had soared to 250. Where the positions listed in the early 1930s were limited to bookkeepers, accountants, governesses, and the occasional "office assistant," later ads ranged widely, seeking liberal professionals, managers in commerce and industry, advertising men, salesmen, accountants, scientists, librarians, industrial chemists and engineers, sales managers, interpreters, office managers, and countless "office assistants," virtually all in the private sector. There were a few ads for skilled manual workers, carpenters and electricians, and high-level master workers, such as metallurgists who knew a production process and the shop floor well enough to be foremen. Ads for unskilled manual laborers appeared infrequently and took the form of a general call for workers at a given plant rather than the individualized ads of white-collar positions.

Despite their variety, these ads clustered at the lower end of collar-and-tie responsibility, prestige, and pay. Some advertised dead-end jobs suitable only for young people, often part-time students or women temporarily in the work force. Others, though low-paying, were touted as entry-level positions, "jobs with a future" for the "ambitious and competent."[6] Advancement to "higher positions" was implied in countless such ads during the 1940s. How much was hyperbole and how much honest representation is hard to say. Those referring specifically to a career ladder may often have been genuine. By 1950, however, everything from office boy to factory manager could be a "job with a future" in the classifieds, and the phrase may have become little more than a catch-all to draw the eye of ambitious and competent applicants. Yet even as a slogan it reflected a widespread mindset of upward movement, competition, and market behavior of relatively recent origin.[7]

This lends insight into how the Alvares Penteado graduates may have understood Stamoto when he said that "today we all do business": beyond the obvious point that many of them would work in retail, industry, or services, Stamoto's monition implied that collar-and-tie employees would have to act *as businessmen* with regard to their own economic lives, "offering" their services in constant competition for scarce jobs with others.

To lowly and even not-so-lowly office, bank, commercial, and government employees a competitive labor market was nothing new; the petty collar-and-tie sector had been crowded and unremunerative since at least 1900. After 1920 the struggle had become more general. Just about "everyone," worried one white-collar publication in 1935, aspired to some "little government or bank position," from the immigrant's son with a primary education to the university graduate who could not retain a clientele or obtain a sinecure in the public bureaucracy.[8] Night schools and correspondence courses were springing up, and more people than ever before were attending graduation ceremonies and seeking positions of responsibility, respect, and reward in business, finance, government, and the professions and, failing that, settling for substantially less, so long as it was nonmanual work.

The cultural divide between manual and nonmanual work loomed large in white-collar job choice. Men preferred nonmanual jobs, even if they paid less than some manual jobs might have—and even if they were usually performed by women. According to an association of women teachers, men with some schooling who had "failed in life, who had seen their plans frustrated" often went into primary-school teaching because they "disdained manual work in factories and shops."[9] To these men status and class brooked far larger than the division between sexes. In the same vein at a 1945 congress on medical and social problems in the postwar period, Dr. Flaminio Fávero blamed low salaries and unemployment among doctors on the deep and broad "contempt for manual work, there being a greater attraction for work of an immaterial sort."[10]

Indeed, the generalized jostling for social position led many practitioners of the more prestigious professions to fear they too lived under a regime of raw competition that had made their work a mere "commodity."[11] Of the many explanations offered for intensified contest within the professions, one predominated, the press of the socially ambitious. Already by the mid-1930s doctors and lawyers commonly complained that the *faculdades* were "overproducing,"[12] and in Rio the director of an association of private schools noted that there were four times as many teachers as positions.[13] An ad for the Brazilian showing of Warner Studio's *Gentlemen Are Born* (1934), an American film about a poor young man who graduates from medical school and cannot find a job, hints at how general the problem was perceived to be: "We thought the diploma would open up the world to us, that everything would be so easy . . ." said the ad, wistful ellipsis indicating that it was anything but.[14] In a somewhat more alarmed tone a 1941 report on the legal profession repined the "unbridled competition" among lawyers since the "differentiation of the middle class within the social order."[15]

Signs of keen economic competition were pervasive. Recent graduates from the faculdades rarely succeeded in setting up practices of their own. Young lawyers often underwent difficult and financially lean three- or four-year apprenticeships to attorneys of established reputation. They typed, ran errands, did the dirty work, and usually earned miserably or not at all for their pains. So dismal were their prospects as independent professionals that many law faculty graduates, according to one account, had to move from homes to smaller apartments, fire the cook and washing woman, eat less, and stop smoking.[16] The ambitious, lucky, or well-connected might, after several years, attempt to build a practice by offering their services free of charge to organizations where they could make contacts for the future, such as the journalists' union, the press club, the union of newspaper salesmen, and other such groups. A multitude of less-fortunate lawyers crowded the records and notary offices. They tussled with "false lawyers" and the *rábulas* with some legal training but no license to practice for small matters shrugged off by more prominent professionals.[17] Doctors and dentists often were no better off. They competed not only with fellow professionals but with charlatans who worked on commission for druggists or prowled for patients in the outer darkness of medical practice.[18]

More commonly secondary-school- and university-trained professionals unable to establish practices of their own sought salaried employment in the private or public sectors. They might hire out to a firm, apply to one of the unions or associations emerging with the new labor system of the 1930s, or seek a post in the public service. Collar-and-tie types vied for these positions fiercely. A doctor in the mid-1930s described the physician's life in terms of the "impossibility of securing a clientele that [would] allow him to sustain himself and his family." His only option, said the author, is to compete for "any position, however small the salary." And one is not enough, so he seeks a second and a third, "picking up crumbs" in an effort to make ends meet.[19] Lawyers, journalists, and teachers faced the same problem, for they were "generally poorly paid because of the great competition," as a *Diretrizes* article bluntly noted in 1934.[20]

As a result, young men were often forced to seek employment outside their area of specialty. The founders of an association for accountants and bookkeepers in 1935 worried about the "frightening" growth of the profession in recent years. In Rio alone there were thousands of accountants and bookkeepers, all looking for work, forcing salaries down and unemployment up. A Rio newspaper reported in 1935 that many credentialed accountants were having to abandon the profession and go into sales or insurance or even become office clerks.[21] Graduating pharmacy students were warned in a 1942 commencement address that "very few of you will actually practice pharmacy" but will instead go into "other arenas of the day-to-day struggle."[22] By the early 1940s it had become common for lawyers to work as journalists, bureaucrats, and even police investigators.[23] Doctors faced the all-too-thinkable prospect of ending up "bank employee-doctors, bureaucrat-doctors, musician-doctors, telegrapher-doctors," men who clung to the prestige conferred by their training and diploma though they might work shoulder to shoulder with others of more modest cultural attainments.[24] Many, doubtless reluctantly, would have agreed with *O Cruzeiro*'s assessment that "the university diploma is not the magic lever that once conquered the world! . . . Very quickly it is forgotten at the bottom of some drawer and the doctor, lawyer, engineer go to work in commerce, in public offices."[25]

The public sector played a key role in the economic lives of collar-and-tie employees of all types. Ten of thousands signed up for civil-service examinations after reforms in 1938 made them fairer. At the same time uncounted thousands wrote letters to potential patrons begging help. Oftentimes public employment was a last resort for those who had failed in some other area of life. Sr. Siedler, who by his own admission had enjoyed better-than-average success in running a small jerked-beef company in Rio Grande do Sul, wrote to a high government official in 1941, 1943, and 1944 asking for a government post, perhaps a position at the newly created National Meat Institute in Rio, where he could use his accounting skills. His business had gone sour, and he was now "poor and unemployed."[26] Others faced the same prospect right out of secondary school or faculdade, so that many newly minted graduates saw public employment as a first resort. An architect put it facetiously but with the bite of reality: "With the diploma he receives upon finishing his studies, the architect has the right to opt between two basic destinies: to die of hunger or become a public servant, [for] it has been said that Brazil is the country in which there are two kinds of people, public functionaries and those awaiting an opening" in the bureaucracy.[27]

Though exaggerated, the point is clear: government employment served as a kind of guarantor of collar-and-tie status, often when other options had fallen through. Especially in Rio. A 1946 survey of social and political attitudes concluded that the Carioca "middle class" suffered under an "illusory sense of well being" because of the large number of government jobs available.[28] Of the "dozens of recent graduates fill[ing] the anterooms of the [federal] ministries," the fortunate found jobs in their specialties and were able to build respectable careers, educate their children, and look forward to retiring with livable pensions.[29] Others took temporary jobs unrelated to their training and worked toward the day they would be able to obtain a permanent government post. Journalists, for instance, were notorious for their revolving door to the public bureaucracies. They would work at government jobs during the day for five or six hours and then go to work after hours as editors, reporters, writers, or admen at newspapers or magazines.[30]

This was a common pattern among collar-and-tie employees. Dr. Oswaldo Orico worked from 11 A.M. to 5 P.M. at the Ministry of Education and Health as director of the Division of Extracurricular Education and from 7 to 10 P.M. as the night principal at the Ginásio Copacabana.[31] Throughout the 1940s many public functionaries made ends meet by responding to newspaper ads for *bico* (off-hours pick-up work).[32] Even liberal professionals did so. Indeed, moonlighting was perceived to be so prevalent by 1950 that the Order of Lawyers in São Paulo asserted that the "real reason" liberal professionals worked short hours in government offices was so that they might work outside their public-sector jobs, which made it possible for the government to pay them less.[33] The importance of the public-service option to white-collar men is apparent also from the outcry accompanying the government's decision to hire women as bureaucrats. In the early 1940s, for instance, a group of university students sent a long petition to President Getúlio Vargas asking him to exclude women from the ranks of public functionaries.[34] While they doubtless yearned to establish practices of their own, they knew only too well that they might end up in government jobs.

Compared with those who worked in the established occupations of medicine, law, and teaching, those in newer professions had a somewhat easier time of it during the 1930s and particularly the 1940s. According to a contemporary student of the matter, statisticians, certain engineers, advertising experts, high-level accountants, and especially administrators enjoyed a "privileged position in the labor market, so great is the demand" for their services.[35] Firms and companies maintained close contacts with the faculdades producing the new breed of professionals and competed for the preference of recent graduates, promising career advancement and good salaries by standards of the day.[36] Those who could combine technical with managerial skills commanded great advantage.[37] Not surprisingly some were more sanguine about the rigors of competitive life in the white-collar labor market than more hard-pressed *confrères* in government and the traditional professions. A young advertising man gushed in 1941 that his profession "infuses life and excites people," an effect of which was to make them "more dynamic, to give them enthusiasm for work, for the struggle for life. 'Struggle for life' of the North Americans? I would say instead, 'struggle for comfortable life.'"[38]

Insight into the changing meanings of this struggle for life can perhaps be had from an unlikely source, advertisements for health tonics. By the 1930s such tonics had been around for at least a decade. During the 1920s, however, they were advertised primarily as catholicons that could enhance physical performance or appearance. A 1920 ad for Biotônico, for instance, promised to make men vigorous, women beautiful, and children robust.[39] As late as 1934 an ad for Nutrion pledged only to reinvigorate the weak and increase the resistance of the strong.[40] Reflecting the heightened economic and social significance of "intellectual" work, ads after the mid-1930s hawked these tonics as elixirs that could ensure cerebral vigor and sharpen the competitive edge for those involved in collar-and-tie work. Against a background of a man in a suit sitting at a desk, looking thoughtfully at documents, with trains, planes, factories, and cities whirling about him, a 1937 ad for one of these nostrums admonished: "In the turbulence of modern life victory goes to those with strong brains! NEUROBIOL—Tonic for the Brain."[41] Another 1937 ad advanced a similar claim: "Winner—That's the title everyone wants to have, but not everyone knows that force of will, by itself, is not enough. To win one's muscles and brain must be vigorous. This can be accomplished by using the powerful tonic VINOVITA."[42]

Later ads focused on restoring the organism sapped by competition and overwork. Among others, they had in mind the 259 Rio bank employees in 1942 who, according to one publication, suffered from "bank clerk's psychoneurosis," which "affected the functioning of the brain, caused fatigue, made it hard to concentrate, caused headaches and irritability."[43] Thus, in 1945 Seducamol promised "Control over your nerves!" "In today's agitated life, every daily activity demands control of the nerves—just like acrobats in their risky exhibitions. Students, public functionaries, housewives, etc., must all have perfectly equilibrated nervous systems—free of irritability, insomnia, and neurasthenia."[44] Fosfatos Horsford was the perfect answer in 1945 and 1946 to "nervous exhaustion" and "tired brains"; its users would "feel a new inclination to work, not feel mental laziness and not suffer from memory loss."[45]

These advertisements were not meant to be faithful descriptions of social reality. They sought to sell a product that depended on convincing people that they could sharpen their competitive edge or recover from tired brains by using these tonics. Moreover, Brazilian copywriters, whether or not employed by foreign ad firms, took their direction from American magazines and freely borrowed techniques and even motifs. Still the ads represented the competitive experience in collar-and-tie terms just when the ranks of collars and ties were growing. These words and images, in turn, contributed to the atmosphere of economic and social competition that was coming to characterize middle-class life in Rio and São Paulo. By focusing on brains and nerves, the ads reflected and reinforced the growing sense of a middle place in the social order; between the poor who worked with their hands and the rich who cared only about money were those who could imagine succeeding "through intelligence, through knowledge," as one novel of the middle class put it in 1949, for "even if they could never be rich, they would have knowledge."[46]

Of Merit and Pistolão

By 9 A.M. the lines had been forming for an hour. Over a thousand people waited patiently outside a Rio de Janeiro testing center in an "atmosphere of order and happiness and with no need for a policeman to be present."[47] It was Monday morning, May 27, 1940, and roughly 1,300 men and women had shown up to participate in a *concurso* (competitive examination) to determine who would get jobs with the federal government. Many of them had been preparing for months, attending commercial cram courses and smelling of the lamp from late-night study. Once inside the center they sat down at individual desks, lifted their pens, and began to answer questions on law, administration, accounting, history, Portuguese grammar, geography, statistics, and bureaucratic procedure. Working silently toward their dreams of respectable "intellectual" work and material security, they were the pool from which a new breed of government functionary, those chosen exclusively for their qualifications, was to be drawn.

The advent of concursos for large numbers of federal, state, and even municipal collar-and-tie careers represented a fundamental shift in the fortunes of those within Brazil's emergent middle class. Enthusiasm for the tests was unbounded. Between 1937 and 1944, the heyday of competitive public-service examinations, nearly 170,000 Brazilians took part in more than 1,600 written and oral tests of specialized knowledge and general competence for admission to federal employment.[48] Many more participated at state and local levels. The concurso phenomenon was widely hailed as proof of the "democratization of the public service." In stark contrast to a patronage system dating back to the nineteenth century, the new concurso regime emphasized merit.[49]

Detractors saw in the multitudes of exam takers an indecorous and "extraordinary competition" for public posts. Supporters looked beyond the numbers. Responding to criticisms of an oversubscribed 1940 examination for government office clerk, a defender insisted that there was no unseemly "race" for public posts. Rather, some candidates were simply seeking to "improve their situations," a perfectly natural and commendable desire.[50] Others merely wanted to gain some experience at minor government posts as stepping stones to higher aspirations. Others still took the exam to train toward the more difficult test for administrative officer. Those who succeeded, assured the government's civil-service journal, would enjoy an "enviable moral position, a sense of intimate satisfaction and social respectability."[51]

The concurso's achievement, according to most contemporaries in the late 1930s and early 1940s, was that it tended to undermine the patronage system based on the *pistolão* (letter of recommendation). Throughout the 1920s and early 1930s resentment against patronage had smoldered. For example, Paschoal Lemme remembered the bitterness with which his parents opposed his decision in 1923 to become a schoolteacher. At the time most teachers were appointed through connections, and his immigrant parents felt the pistolão "not worthy of a Lemme."[52]

Mordant humor tells the same story. A 1927 cartoon pictured a job applicant, hat in hand, shoulders stooped, an archetypal caricature of abject subservience, speaking to a government minister: "I am the brother-in-law of congressman Zebedeu, and I want a place in the . . ." He is interrupted by the minister, who responds: "Excuse me, we haven't even gotten to the cousins yet. Come back later."[53]

Some simply ranted. "Who says the pistolão is dead?" asked a widely read magazine in 1937. "The little beast has seven lives, like the cat. . . . It would be easier for the whole of Brazil to pass through the tunnel at the *central* [the main train station] clenching a pistolão, than for a saint to try to enter the kingdom of heaven without help from his *padrinhos* [god-fathers]."[54]

Reform came in 1938. White-collar organizations had railed against patronage throughout the early 1930s. On paper they favored "impersonal processes" for judging "level of culture and general knowledge" in hiring.[55] Had not the Revolution of 1930 come to power promising "concursos for everyone down to the doorman," as one doctor framed the issue in 1936?[56] Responding to this clamor and desiring to "modernize" Brazil's civil service, federal policy makers instituted a regime of fair examinations. Once it was in place, officials were quick to assert that patronage had been eliminated root and branch and that a system of pure merit reigned where none had existed before. A 1940 article by a public functionary exemplified the rosy assessment: "Today, happily, noble blood, hereditary succession, vouchsafing, and political pressure no longer have any influence, that is, they no longer exist, having ceded to the guarantee of law, of morality, of merit, and of administrative composure, where order, administrative morality, and intelligence are the only criteria that matter."[57]

This was not mere cant. After 1938 more people were admitted to public service on the strength of their demonstrated competence than ever before.[58] Test conditions were rigorously controlled, examinations were graded blind, and the identification of scores was done in a public place. The scrupulous fairness of the tests engendered considerable pride among those who took them. Some began to talk of a "career civil service" like the ones in France, England, and the United States.[59] Those in higher-echelon positions who announced publicly that they would abide by the results of concursos rather than patronage were applauded.[60] Even in the private sector there were pressures against patronage, at least for white-collar jobs entailing individual responsibility.[61]

Rumors regarding the demise of the pistolão after 1938 were premature. The reforms were neither complete nor irreversible. In 1944 columnist Frederico Lane noted that despite a growing insistence on "impersonal norms of selection" too many people were still being chosen the old way.[62] Federal posts were frequently filled by temporary employees, *extranumerários*, who were not required to participate in concursos. At any given time they constituted a majority of public servants, thereby leaving open a huge field for patronage appointments. In addition, while the concurso system made some headway at state and municipal levels in Rio and

São Paulo during the 1940s, many functionaries continued to be filtered through the fine mesh of patronage.

Perhaps more important, the concurso appears to have become an object of political struggle after 1945. The number of concurso candidates peaked in 1943–44 and dropped off significantly after President Vargas's ouster in 1945. It soared again with his return to power in 1950 and plummeted to nearly zero after his suicide in 1954.[63] Vargas, though hardly above patronage, saw the concurso system and merit-based admissions to the civil service as means of garnering support among collar-and-tie employees and professionals. His opponents quite nakedly resorted to patronage to secure their base, in the process undermining confidence in a system of merit.[64]

Thus, whatever changes and struggles were taking place at the level of official policy, reliance on connections continued to inform the expectations, anxieties, and strategies of collar-and-tie people negotiating the job market. It was still common in the 1940s for bank employees to marry the daughters of *fazendeiros* in the hope that a father-in-law could pull strings in behalf of family members.[65] In a world increasingly competitive and meritocratic, they and others would have understood the burlesque truth of lawyer Marco Tullio's statement that "the pistolão is more or less the perfect means of getting something," though they would perhaps have chuckled uneasily at his jest that the pistolão was a "right, not a favor."[66] The very fact of such a spoof suggests that the anatomy and culture of *pedido* (a letter from a client requesting a patron's help) and pistolão bear examination.

Letters to high government officials during the 1930s and 1940s reveal no single model for a pedido. Some writers sought favors from a patron who had helped them or family members in the past. Napoleão Bolivar de Araripe Sucupira wrote to Minister of Foreign Affairs Osvaldo Aranha in 1945 worried about his "always uncertain future" as a commercial employee. Carefully separating personal from impersonal criteria, he said that he was sure Aranha would be willing to help him obtain a public post, "not so much for any individual merit of my own, but in consideration of your friendship for my father."[67] Others claimed social credentials and simultaneously asserted family connections, though frequently it must have been a stretch on both counts. For example, in 1941, while claiming "no credentials" of his own, João Bittencourt, a postal employee, identified himself as being from a family with an historic name, "which has done nothing for me to date." His mother was daughter of the Baron of Paranapiacaba, a relative of the Andrades, who were relatives of Aranha's family. He wanted a job to supplement his income and thought perhaps

Aranha would be able to obtain something for him at one of Rio's casinos.[68]

Some simply sought favor from the powerful and well placed. They wrote for a variety of reasons. Most said it was because they had heard that the potential patron was generous and caring and had a good track record of attending to employment requests. Virtually all said it was because they were desperate. People from smaller cities frequently requested protection from potential patrons they did not personally know.[69] As one pedido writer from Fortaleza put it: "I have not met you, but I take pleasure in trying to do so now."[70] In these letters the interplay and tension between impersonal norms of bureaucracy and the more personal ones of patronage were palpable. Older people could find a lifetime of habits too hard to break. Alvaro Henrique Bouson, an administrative official with the postal service, wrote Aranha in 1938 from Florianópolis asking for a promotion to section chief. Bouson knew of the reform but insisted that he was not addressing himself to the minister "with the intention of trampling other people's rights; rather all I ask is for the protection of a great Brazilian and the recognition of the services an old functionary has rendered."[71] Others claimed personal attention by indicting the concurso system. Antônio Cunha, a lawyer in the interior, wrote Aranha in 1938 requesting "any position" for his son, whom he had advised not to participate in the concurso, since for a career as police detective there were always "preferred candidates."[72]

Finally there were those who actively truckled to potential patrons. Writing from Rio Grande do Norte, Adalberto Tavares dos Santos Lima reported in a letter to Aranha that his five-year-old daughter referred to Aranha as her "new godfather" and kept among her toys a framed picture of Aranha clipped from *Vida Doméstica*. She keeps saying that "my godfather is the greatest man in Brazil." And by the way, said the father, I would like to move to a "first-class state in the South," preferably São Paulo. Those with patrons had already made the move, he noted; even though the government says there are new criteria, the fact is "we live in a political regime and only with politics is it possible to get anything."[73]

Among those aspiring to collar-and-tie employment in the big city, the pedido appears to have been little more than a stratagem alongside other expedients for facing what one letter writer, a lawyer, referred to as the "extraordinary intensification of the struggle for life" in São Paulo.[74] Thus, and especially before the reform of 1938, competition for respectable employment could prompt a morbid opportunism. In June 1936 a father wrote to Getúlio Vargas from Lapa in Rio on behalf of his son, noting that a particular municipal water and sewers engineer had died the day before, leaving a vacancy. The petitioner's son, in whom the Baron Ramiz had taken a great interest, was number one on the list of people up for the next vacancy. Would Vargas make sure he got the job?[75]

There were always a few whose family backgrounds commanded attention from politicians such as Aranha. More common were those lacking "family resources." Waldemar Augusto Machado, 23, asked Aranha to help him obtain a post "that will assure me a remuneration that will allow me to make a future and a home, as all those my age desire." At the time of writing he was an accountant with a degree from the Superior School of Commerce in Rio, who claimed to translate English and Italian. For the last two years he had been working at a commercial firm in Rio, typing, bookkeeping, and writing business correspondence. He felt underpaid.[76] In another case Clementino de Moura Beleza wrote Aranha in 1944 concerned above all with making a living and maintaining social position. Discerning no fine line between patronage and merit and fearing the worst, Beleza hoped that Aranha would intervene to make sure he was "approved" in a recent concurso for a government job.[77] José Pinho Corrêa Netto wrote in 1949 because, while he liked his job in Rio as an insurance adjuster, he lacked a patron within the company. He was at a serious disadvantage vis-à-vis all of his colleagues who had sponsors. A word from Aranha to the right ear, said Corrêa Netto, would resolve the matter satisfactorily.[78] Beneath this air of casual confidence lay the knowledge that patrons were fickle. Currying their favor could be like playing the lottery, even if they were personal acquaintances, which increasingly they were not.

Anxiety was palpable in most of the letters: fears of falling into poverty, of not being able to make ends meet, of not being able to finish school. Supplicants quavered with the dread of rejection, or worse, of simply being ignored. In Érico Veríssimo's novel *Crossroads* João Benevolo, an unemployed commercial employee, after considerable prodding by his wife, swallows his pride and importunes his old boss for help in getting a job. At the end of the interview the boss wishes him well and gives João a pistolão addressed to another businessman who owns a factory. Knowing that he has sent João off to a manual-labor job, the boss adds insult to injury by telephoning the businessman after João has left the office. Telling him to rip up the letter, he adds, "The fellow doesn't interest me in the least."[79]

If patronage implied dependence on the caprice of those above, it was not always a wholly one-way affair for those in the social middle. Managers, administrators, and public functionaries could become part of patronage networks at their places of work. Linked to patrons, they could enhance their position by broadening connections with potential clients below them. Thus lawyers, bank employees, accountants, and doctors might very well attest to the moral probity of an applicant to one of Rio's or São Paulo's many social work schools who, once employed, would have a reciprocal obligation to their recommenders.[80] Or these same professionals might seek relations with others at more or less their level who perhaps someday would be able to introduce them to other potential patrons. Connections were like diplomas, part of the arsenal for confronting a competitive social order. As work was becoming more meritocratic and market-oriented, pedido and pistolão continued to be a strategy any collar-and-tie employee might pursue.[81]

Women were no strangers to the gentle art of the well-tempered pedido. Throughout the period women commonly wrote on behalf of fathers, husbands, sons, and other male (and female) relatives.[82] The subservience implied and played up in any pedido was more or less the same whether the writer was a man or a woman, though in some sense it was easier for women to assume the role of abject dependents. In a society recognizing the validity of such requests, a wife's connections could be as important to family survival as a husband's and a source of domestic power in their own right. But women did not make requests solely for others. Those who sought jobs on their own behalf understood as well as men that a pistolão could be "an essential factor in achieving" one's goals, as Maria da Gloria observed in a letter to Aranha in 1948.[83] Even so, the idea of merit may have been specially implicated in women's limited emergence from the home into paid work during these years. Many women found their way into public service, chiefly because they were officially welcomed there after 1938. Over the anxious murmurings of men who felt threatened in their jobs, the federal government heralded women's inclusion within the ranks of public functionaries as a "victory of the system of merit."[84]

As part of the normal course of collar-and-tie life, then, patronage vibrated in constant tension with the notion that effort and talent were to be rewarded above all. In 1944 one pedido writer, an engineer from Niterói, across the bay from Rio, described himself as a "self-made man" who now needed Aranha's help in order not to remain a draftsman all his life.[85] This petitioner clearly understood the difference between a system based on merit and one based on patronage. At a more general level merit-based concursos were a welcome ideal, though people rarely hesitated to take advantage of a patronage relationship when the opportunity called or need demanded it. Still, resentment against the pistolão never again burnt itself out. In good measure this is because the issue became part of partisan political struggle after 1945. Aside from continuing complaints against patronage by professional associations, perhaps the best evidence of continued vexation is, once again, humor.[86] In 1952 the second edition of a tongue-in-cheek treatise purported to lay out the philosophical and jurisprudential principles for the dispensation of patronage.[87] By blending the personal and political criteria on which the pistolão was based with impersonal and bureaucratic mechanisms of the law, Marco Tullio's satire highlighted the fundamental paradox of social competition during this period and reminded readers that politics was always just beneath the surface of everyday lives.

The implications of this ambiguity are arresting. Those in an emergent middle class understood that in the new Brazil, as in Europe and the United States, economic and social competition was supposed to be meritocratic. White-collar associations proclaimed merit as an ideal continually throughout the period. Yet in the context of a society so long saturated with patronage, the anonymity implicit in merit-based job decisions may have grated. In this regard the words of 23-year-old law-school graduate Mário Natal e Silva are telling. In 1944 he wrote to Aranha complaining that he had not been able to find a job appropriate to his social station. He asked to be appointed director of a public agency, "lest, over the course of the years, my family's name be forgotten completely, and I fall into the middle classes."[88]

More was at stake here than just Silva's need to earn a living. In his mind, to be middle class was to be nameless and anonymous. Compared with the small world of eminences who belonged to a superior realm of personal and strategic connections, middle-class people inhabited a competitive universe in which family and friends might only incidentally be of help. Constantly on the lookout for a helping hand, collar-and-tie people increasingly sought patronage impersonally, from superiors who did not know them. For while they wanted to succeed on their merits, collar-and-tie employees and professionals chafed at market anonymity and were sensitive to the possibility that friendship or the influence of the powerful could propel them as far as or further than their skills and talents. They knew only too well that, even in a supposedly meritocratic world, promotions and raises often depended on their ability to "adulate" their superiors.[89] Perhaps this was why Dale Carnegie's *How to Win Friends and Influence People* went through fifteen Brazilian editions between 1939 and 1950.*

Education—The Gateway to Everything

Notwithstanding the persistence of patronage, collar-and-tie people were coming to see education as the surest means of betterment. Valentim Bouças, a successful São Paulo entrepreneur, warned the 1934 graduates of the José Bonifácio Commercial School to husband their "knowledge" as they would "capital," urging them to "care for and increase it," "because today's world will not bear mediocrities."[90] Writer Genolino Amado noted more pointedly in 1940 that the "common man" now feels "obliged to learn more, to prepare himself for life and its competitions . . . to train for work." Whether in concursos, private firms, or institutes, said Amado, "competition of all sorts in the areas of commerce and public service requires of petit-bourgeois youth just starting a career a higher level of preparation in foreign languages and in the most varied modern subjects."[91]

Demand for education exploded during the 1930s and 1940s. Primary-school enrollment for all Brazil increased by over 100 percent between 1935 and 1950, surpassing 5 million, about 40 percent of school-age children. In the same period secondary schools, the training ground for white-collar employees, expanded between 250 and 300 percent, reaching nearly half a million in 1950, perhaps 10 percent of fifteen- to nineteen-year-olds.[92] In Rio alone the number of secondary schools more than doubled between 1935 and 1945, and the number of students nearly tripled to 54,000.[93] Thousands of young men and women made great sacrifices to obtain degrees from the Alvares Penteado and other commerce schools, from a variety of general-studies secondary schools, and from dozens of normal schools.[94] Mothers now told their sons that "he who does not study is worth little."[95] Indeed, as late as 1954 one critic in the government thought simplistic the notion, clung to by many parents, that secondary school was the "magic key" to success.[96]

---

*In many ways Carnegie's book may have been right at home in Brazil during these years. One historian of the United States has characterized the book's message as representing a "strange kind of individualism for individualistic America," for it suggested that "the way to get ahead is to *make* other people feel important" (Susman, 165). This is precisely the art of the *pedido*. Little has been done in the American historiography to pose the question of Carnegie's "strange kind of individualism." Rather, it is still common, and this is also true for the Latin American historiography, to minimize the role of asymmetric reciprocities in social and political life.

Higher education also grew. The number of officially approved faculdades in Rio and São Paulo rose from 200 in 1935 to nearly 300 in 1945.[97] University enrollments across the country, stagnant through most of the 1930s, more than doubled between 1940 and 1950, approaching 50,000.[98] Perhaps more important, university students were no longer just the sons of fazendeiros or of well-to-do families. According to Hélio de Almeida, president of the student association of the University of Brazil in Rio, by 1940 "everyone" wanted to study and become an engineer, doctor, dentist, lawyer, *doutor* in something, since "the bachelor's degree is the gateway to everything."[99] Many of these students worked their way through school as journalists, public servants, commercial employees, and bank clerks. For parents the cost of a child's education was becoming an indispensable element of the expectations that went along with a collar-and-tie salary and social station.[100]

The supply of degree holders in the white-collar job market ballooned. Between 1940 and 1950 the number of people in the city of Rio and the state of São Paulo holding an educational degree beyond grade school increased from about 250,000 to nearly 650,000 and rose in every occupational category. In Rio 17 percent of people older than fifteen and close to one-quarter of all whites over fifteen had secondary-school or university degrees.[101] This could only mean greater competition for all in the collar-and-tie employment market. Minimal educational competence was no longer adequate to secure a decent collar-and-tie job by the 1940s. Those who could not meet the new strictures of the market or who labored in jobs requiring little education faced financial difficulties and eroding status.

Such insecurities help account for the ceaseless complaints in professional publications and general-audience magazines about the miseries of recent graduates, who were having a tough time landing jobs worthy of their talents and training—and their social status. They also explain the shock of indignation that ran through lawyer J. J. de Gama e Silva's article when recounting the story of a mere chauffeur in Bahia who, having claimed he was a doutor, practiced as a lawyer, then became a police investigator, and finally ended up as director of the prison in Bahia, despite the fact that he had a criminal record rather than a diploma.[102] One senses in Silva's piece not only a concern for protecting the profession against opportunists and charlatans but also a frustration that one so uneducated and socially unfit for "intellectual" work had gone so far. After all, if the prestige of a university diploma remained high, by the mid-1940s it was becoming less a symbol of social elevation than a prerogative of which only strictly professional advantages could be derived. A chauffeur who could pass for more represented a threat to the idea that educational credentials could effectively safeguard status claims.

The felt need to gain marketable skills through education was not limited to those who could afford full-time study. The federal public service instituted a variety of educational programs for its functionaries, and in the second semester of 1941 10,400 ambitious public employees enrolled, knowing that to compete for the better posts one had to have a degree or an area of expertise.[103] To meet the demand for exam preparation, magazines regularly advertised dozens of study aids for official concursos covering Portuguese grammar, mathematics, accounting, law, banking, good writing, editing, and myriad other subjects.[104] "Professor" A. Tenonio d'Albuquerque was one of the big names in study guides and by 1945 had personally prepared over 1,000 candidates for examinations, according to one ad.[105] Nor was it unknown for private firms to sponsor their better white-collar employees in courses outside work so that they might "improve their total status, that is, rise in the social scale."[106] At a more modest level correspondence courses promised to improve the chances of their students. The Brazilian Universal Institute of São Paulo, for instance, urged people to "assure your future" by studying architecture; mechanical, artistic, or fashion design; accounting, typing, stenography, and office assistant skills; English and Portuguese through the mail. "Declare your economic independence and improve your professional and intellectual 'standard,'" said one advertisement. *"Life, wherever one goes, is dictated by a biological law: He wins who is strongest."*[107]

Minister of Education Gustavo Capanema focused on the relationship between educational competence and the life of competition in a speech to students at Rio's University of Brazil in the late 1930s or early 1940s:

> Wherever you end up, you will win only if you are truly competent. . . . Do not expect to succeed in life through favors from friends, or by the protection of the powerful, or by getting lucky. All that will fail. The only thing that won't fail is the vigor of your intelligence and your virtue. The only thing that won't fail is your own power. Prepare yourselves for the struggle. Be strong. And know that strength comes from one source: study.[108]

Capanema's exhortation to meritocratic self-reliance doubtless resonated among the students. They were well aware of the challenges facing them after graduation. Most probably would have been pleased to make their own way. They also knew that there was as much ideal as reality in the minister's words. Perhaps patronage's glory days had passed, but it remained a crucial fact of life that rugged individuals could often make it only with the help of others.*

Hope of Rising, Fear of Falling

What will your son be tomorrow? A lawyer, engineer, doctor, or . . . ? His future depends on the present—on his capacity to dedicate himself to his studies. It depends on the energy that Tônico Infantil provides children's organisms. . . . Tônico Infantil will allow your son to be an exemplary student today . . . and tomorrow a real man.

This advertisement for an infant brain tonic ran in 1948.[109] The angst on which it played was by no means limited to the middle class.[110] In modernizing, market-oriented societies, concern for the future is not the preserve of any one group. It is shared among all those who make their lives in a competitive social order. What this ad did, however, was universalize a common experience from a particular perspective: the emphasis on studies suggests that it was aimed not so much at the rich, whose property, assets, and connections cushioned their relationship to the market economy, or at the poor, who could rarely afford to send their children to school, but at those in the middle who dreamed of their sons becoming doutores, knowing there was no guarantee.

Orientation toward the future was hardly new. Immigrants had aspired to financial independence through the ownership of small shops for decades, and their sons and grandsons had long champed to become doutores. What changed during the 1920s, 1930s, and 1940s with the broadening of educational and employment opportunities was that large numbers of men in collar-and-tie occupations began to imagine they could improve their circumstances during their own lifetimes. White-collar publications began to urge readers to "always try to move up a little more" and to "day after day seek to better [their] situation."[111] Often the powerful told collar-and-tie employees and professionals precisely what they were

---

*This raises the issue of how individualism should be understood in Brazil and elsewhere. Recent anthropological work suggests the possibility of talking about an individual who is never outside a web of social relations with others, upon whom economic, social, and political fortunes depend. If this seems at odds with more conventional notions, it may be because Europeans and Americans—and especially the latter—have tended to accept at face value the notion that there really can be such a thing as a radical individual apart from webs of social relationships. This may be as much a reflection of ideology or of taking certain categories for granted as of historical reality. See Matta, 137–97; Velho, 67–78; Hess and Matta, 270–91.

primed to hear. In 1936, for example, the graduating class at the Normal School of Commerce in Rio applauded mayor Pedro Ernesto Batista when he concluded, perhaps somewhat optimistically, that "it is now possible to see the commercial career as a field propitious to aspirations of individual prosperity."[112] In the same vein pedido writers spoke of wanting to "advance," "improve their standard of living," and "little by little rise to new posts."[113] Byron Freitas, a student of public and private bureaucracies and personnel management, wrote in 1945 that a central element of modern professional life was a desire "to succeed in a career and aspire to a higher social position."[114]

Implicit in the hope of rising was the fear of falling, as public functionary José Moacir de Andrade Sobrinho understood. He explained in an essay how he had put off marriage until he could resolve his financial situation "within the limits of comfort and tranquility which [he and his fiancée] had planned, so that we would not fall from the social level of our dreams, of our aspirations."[115] A delicate blend of material comfort and social status, Andrade's future was one easily ruined by haste or lack of care.

This fear found expression in the advertising integral to the emergence of a consumer culture after 1930. Advertisements for refrigerators, radios, victrolas, soaps, shaving cream, and cosmetics made a public spectacle of status anxiety through the staging of consumer desire. An ad campaign by the Sul América insurance company throughout the 1930s and 1940s is a beacon in the fog of advertising that settled over Brazil's larger cities during these years. Text and images from the decade-long campaign neatly reveal diverse aspects of the collar-and-tie market experience: competition, status anxiety, generational mobility, the importance of education in negotiating the modern world. At the core of the message was the idea that individuals could control their own and their family's future for better or worse.

A good example is an ad that ran during much of the 1930s. It showed a young, ragged, barefoot boy hunkered down to shine the shoes of a knee-stockinged boy in shorts, jacket, and tie, with books under his arm. The text read:

> Which of them is your son? One of them has everything: books, nice clothes, entertainment ... boots to be shined. The other, an unfortunate soul, often does not even get a crust of bread. This kind of thing happens every day on the street corners, always with different characters!
>
> A life insurance policy would have made the other child happy, if only his

parents had taken precautions. Anyone can afford this policy. By economizing just a little bit at a time, you can guarantee your son's education and future.[116]

The improbable assumption here is that the shoeshine boy was the son of moderately well-off parents who had lacked the foresight to provide for their son's education, condemning him to a life of penury and subservience. The advertising strategy, crassly executed, sought to arouse anxiety and guilt in parents by calling their attention to the frightening possibility that their sons could just as easily end up shining shoes as being secure professionals. This was a view of the economic world entirely denuded of personal relationships on which to fall back. In this ad even little boys were alone in the struggle for life.

With minor variations the same ad ran in white-collar publications well into the 1940s. The bootblack became a mechanic or a factory worker or a bellhop. He was neither black nor mulatto, as likely so many bootblacks were, for the boy had to be white to sustain the drama of social decline. The other boy was invariably destined for school and ultimately a respectable career in medicine, business, science, or law. Almost always the father was to blame for the son's failure:

> His father made him lose his opportunity to be something in life! With each passing day, the struggle for life is getting harder. Today, competition is a harsh reality, and not only in business but in the field of knowledge as well. The strong, the educated and the capable always win! . . . How would you like it if your son was a stepping stone for others?[117]

Only fathers and sons faced the dilemma. In the spectacle of advertising, mothers and daughters did not directly enjoy the benefits and only rarely bore the burdens of raw economic competition. They did experience them indirectly, for a stay-at-home wife was part of the ideal for collar-and-tie employees and professionals. This was a vision rooted in Brazil's patriarchal past harnessed to a new meaning: one sign of a man's success was the ability to keep his family as far away from the competitive arena for as long as possible. Middle-class women could stay home and children could go to school, unlike so many women and children in working-class families. Sul América was attuned to this anxiety as well, running an ad in which a woman and her children are evicted from their home because her deceased husband had lacked the foresight to buy life insurance. Across the threshold of her husband's death, this ad suggested, was the brute fact that she would have to work to support herself and her children, facing inevitable social degradation.

By the mid-1940s crude appeals to status anxiety softened to a vaguer sense of planning for the future and gradually improving one's standard of living. It was as though the seeds of disquiet sown in the 1930s had taken root and no longer needed constant watering. The Federal Savings and Loan Company of Rio de Janeiro pictured a family—here, finally, a calmer husband could appear with wife and small daughter—looking off into the middle distance. The father is in a double-breasted suit and tie. Mother and daughter are well, but not flashily, dressed. The text speaks vaguely of "plans for the future . . . realizing your plans for TOMORROW," with little sense of the angst and recriminations of earlier tableaux.[118]

These ads must be considered with caution. They almost surely exaggerated the "uncertainty and insecurity" of white-collar life. Still, text and images yield clues to the dilemmas of the middle-class condition. The future was dissonant; beneath a major key of hope and aspiration was a minor key of anxiety and fear. The implicit, invisible audience was neither the rich, who had nowhere to rise and whose resources generally preserved them against the dread of rapid downward mobility, nor manual workers, whose circumstances precluded a realistic and widespread expectation of betterment. Rather, these ads targeted those who walked a razor's edge between rising to genuine security and falling to a social level symbolized by the manual worker: the bootblack, the bellhop, the mechanic, the assembly-line worker. Moreover, modeled as they were on American techniques, the ads were a further means by which Brazilian magazine readers came into contact with the ideal of a prosperous, middle-class modernity.

The story of Pedro Nunes is intimate evidence that advancement was possible even for the quite ordinary. A native of the state of Alagôas, he had attended school and then obtained a diploma in typing from the Remington School in Maceió. His first job was at a German import-export firm, where he typed ship manifests and arrival notices. After finishing secondary school in 1929, he sold subscriptions for a local newspaper and subsequently became an editor. This experience sparked an interest in the growing field of advertising. In 1932 he decided to try his luck in Rio. Through his father he secured a pistolão from Costa Rêgo, ex-governor and ex-congressman of Alagôas and a columnist at Rio's influential *Correio da Manhã*. The letter introduced him to the owner of A Capital, a well-known retail store on Rio's fashionable Rio Branco Avenue. Reflecting later on the ambiguous role of patronage in the lives of collar-and-tie employees and professionals, Nunes said that while he had always thought of the pistolão as a "demoralizing institution," it often gave results, as in his case.

At A Capital, Nunes typed, handled correspondence, composed advertisements, and learned about the retail business. In the mid-1930s he left the store with an associate who was opening a new men's furnishings shop; Nunes took charge of the advertising and credit departments. In the early 1940s he was asked to take over advertising at a respected Rio department store, A Exposição. This was a crucial moment in his professional development, for it was here he learned about merchandising and marketing. He remained at A Exposição for much of the 1940s, sharpening his skills by taking courses in retail sales, administration techniques, and public relations. In 1948 Nunes moved to the Rio branch-office of a large American advertising firm, McCann-Erickson, where he was put in charge of the radio department. From the "advertising men" at McCann he learned how to plan and carry out a full-fledged ad campaign. In the early 1950s he did a two-year stint at another large retail concern, Galeria Carioca, where he was offered a considerably larger salary to set up a "house agency" and act as head of sales and advertising. After Galeria Carioca he moved to São Paulo to head up sales and advertising at Lojas Garbo, a highly regarded men's clothing store.[119]

In capsule form Pedro Nunes's trajectory represented the middle-class dream of professional success. There was nothing unusual about him. He hailed from a small state far from Rio and São Paulo. He had obtained only a secondary-school education, though he had augmented his skills subsequently. He had resorted to patronage to make his initial move from Maceió to Rio. He had had the good fortune to fall into the emerging advertising industry when it was still possible to be self-taught. Hardworking, knowledgeable, and likable, he succeeded largely by his own efforts. Most did not advance so far. But stories such as Nunes's were common enough to be the basis for genuine aspirations.

Virtually all collar-and-tie occupations offered opportunities for advancement along a career line, at least in principle. This premise underlay public service, bank work, and other private-sector hierarchies. The logic was that employees in these areas would advance in the course of professional life to higher pay and greater responsibility, up to a point. Over time greater expertise and better skills all made one more salable in the collar-and-tie labor market. Those with ambition and talent (and oftentimes connections) would succeed. Such were the "upper-floor" employees in banks, the public functionaries who moved to the top of lettered career ladders, the teachers who with experience were paid more or moved into administration, the office employees who in time became managers or branched off into other business-related services, and the managers and professionals in industry and commerce who, as they became more expert, commanded greater responsibility and better salaries. Young lawyers, doctors, and engineers may have been poorly, at times miserably, paid, but they were at the beginning of careers that promised better, even if the promise was often emptied of meaning as they settled into bureaucratic posts where they felt their talents wasted.[120]

Indeed, all could not be accommodated. There always seemed to be many more potential climbers than narrow career ladders would bear. What of the ex-tailor, accountant-with-diploma who in 1936 was working for an "important firm" in São Paulo and wanted a job in "feminine fashion?"[121] What of Rubens Siqueira, who barely missed the cut in a 1940 concurso for administrative official and was turned down cold when he asked that his test be regraded?[122] What fate the countless office assistants who responded to numberless want ads in Rio's and São Paulo's newspapers during the 1940s? What became of the growing numbers of university-trained professionals who could not mount practices of their own and who so often could not land decent jobs? It is hard to do anything other than speculate.

Common must have been the humble employee who did not rise, the individual who did not make the grade in the concurso, the young man who could not afford to study, or the one who could not obtain a pistolão at the perfect moment to launch a new and more lucrative career. Many undoubtedly despaired at the instability and tedium of bank and bureaucratic jobs, in which promotions came slowly or not at all, and in which *empistolados* (those with pistolão), sometimes with lesser skills or intelligence, took plum positions. Many collar-and-tie people surely ended up like Dona Lola's children in the novel *There Were Six of Us* or sensitive Noel and his girlfriend, Fernanda, in *Crossroads*: all nurtured dreams of respected careers in medicine, law, engineering, teaching, and writing only to find themselves in bank work, commerce, shopkeeping, and office work, which by any stretch of their imaginations was better than manual labor.

There were those who could not avoid manual labor, especially blacks and mulattos. While it was not unusual to see mulattos in public service by the 1940s, they faced high barriers to professional and social advancement in most areas of the economy. Illiterate and relegated to manual labor, most darker-skinned Cariocas and Paulistanos had little hope of improving their situations. Even when they possessed the requisite skills, employers in the collar-and-tie sector remained reluctant to hire them.[123] They were thought unfit to deal with the public as clerks, not responsible and honest enough to work as commercial employees, and insufficiently orderly in their thinking to perform office work.

As a result, darker-skinned Brazilians usually did not take collar-and-tie jobs. Though talk of race was generally muted or disguised, white skin or something close to it was a *sub rosa* requisite of most white-collar employment. Dark-skinned applicants were rarely turned away explicitly because of race. Instead, a black or dark-hued mulatto candidate for a job might show up for an interview and be told that the spot had just been filled or that it was for some other reason no longer available. He might be offered some menial task, not the job advertised. This was the case of a young journalist with a secondary-school diploma who went to interview for a newspaper job armed with a pistolão. He was told that he could work in the news room, but only sweeping the floors, notwithstanding his qualifications.

When a mulatto or occasionally a black did obtain a decent job, an occurrence common enough not to be remarkable, his prospects of rising often were limited by the racial attitudes of coworkers. A subchief of a division within the postal service was temporarily made head of division while his boss was away. During his brief tenure as chief, he found that white employees refused to recognize his authority. When career advancement depended on the goodwill and attention of coworkers and bosses, darker-skinned Brazilians were at a distinct disadvantage, often watching lighter-skinned colleagues pass them by.[124]

Some nonwhites did advance. While their numbers remained small, Carioca mulattos in 1950 were three times as likely to have a secondary-school education as darker-skinned blacks and twice as likely to be employed in a white-collar job, according to the census.[125] This is largely because skin color could be subsumed to upward mobility in certain instances. In short, money (and connections) *could* lighten socially and professionally. A light-skinned mulatto might get the right breaks and rise to a point at which he could insist that he was socially white. This was largely a willing illusion maintained by a culture that conceived of race in terms of shadings of skin color. Yet such a person would always have been at risk of having the veil of illusion drop, exposing him (or her) to the subtle and not-so-subtle discriminations to which nonwhites generally were subject during these years.

All of this during a period in which white Brazilians with education and credentials appear to have been making headway in precisely the positions closed to nonwhites. Two researchers, one in 1953 and one in the early 1960s, concluded that upward mobility from the "lower class" to the "middle class" was substantial from the 1920s to the 1950s.[126] According to one of these, "newly differentiated occupations," especially white-collar ones, accounted for nearly half the change, a consequence of "modifications in the structure of status."[127] If correct, this bolsters the conclusion of a widely held sense of individual advancement during the 1930s and 1940s.

Only a very few collar-and-tie people ended up like the fictional Júlio in *There Were Six of Us*, who rose from precarious middle-class beginnings to great wealth, and Torquato in the novel *Middle Class*, who went from traveling salesman to wealthy shoe factory owner, realizing his dream of "making money, prospering, becoming someone, triumphing."[128] Others finished like Torquato's brother, who abandoned a comfortable if tedious existence on the *fazenda* for the uncertainties of the city and a minimal job in public service. Yet, in the end, the vast majority probably lived neither extreme. There were never enough jobs to satisfy all who sought them. So people struggled to make lives as reasonable as circumstances permitted. They got so far and no further in their careers and standard of living, relied on the social advantage of being brain- rather than hand-workers, of being light-skinned, hoped that they would be able to give their children an education and a solid career, afraid all the while that it might come crashing down around their ears.

"IT SEEMS EXTRAORDINARY the extent to which the competitive spirit has penetrated all our activities," wrote João Lyra Filho in his rambling 1942 book, *Problems of the Middle Classes*.[129] Or as a character in Democrito de Castro e Silva's novel *Middle Class* notes: "Now it is up to each individual to make the most of his luck and try to live."[130] Never before in Brazil had anonymous employment markets and a sense of generalized competition been so central to social life, though competitive lives mixed market and nonmarket strategies.

The symbolic and experiential core of these lives was the tension between merit and patronage. Announced and widely touted by white-collar associations and the state after 1930, merit came to be an ideal available to all who labored in the collar-and-tie sector. At the same time these employees and professionals negotiated the circuits of patronage on an everyday basis. They lived simultaneously the desire for an equal opportunity to succeed according to their abilities (failure was rarely mentioned in this context) and the ethic and practice of a hierarchical arrangement in which success depended on attention and help from superiors. Everyday life thus produced a volatile mixture of the egalitarian assumptions underlying a meritocratic market economy and a practice in which people might call on the solidarity of friends and family or reaffirm hierarchy by bending knee to superiors. One of the consequences of this situation was that any organic sense of relationship among hierarchical unequals was now definitively subordinated to the need to "earn a living, to win in life" on one's own.[131]

The day-to-day significance of the possibility of upward mobility for middle-class people, then, probably had less to do with an expectation of vaulting to empyrean social realms than with maintaining a vague sense of moral equality with those above. The tension between merit and patronage had a key role to play. Merit allowed those who could imagine moving up to place themselves on the same moral plane as those above, perhaps even higher, since they would have made their way without help. Young Carlos in the novel *There Were Six of Us* understands that "Father is not rich today, but he could have an opportunity and end up rich." His mother "lifted her eyes from her work, proud at that moment to hear him use the word 'opportunity' so well; I thought that few children of his age would know what it meant."[132] For those who did not succeed, patronage provided a handy explanation, as so many pedido writers understood:[133] if others rose, it was because they had padrinhos, not because they were more meritorious.

Few paused to notice the incongruities of their circumstance. Most collar-and-tie employees had other concerns, principally what Lyra referred to as the "hope of rising" and "fear of falling." But Lyra seemed to treat these possibilities as more or less equally likely, two sides of a fair coin. In his paper entitled "The Meaning and Value of the Middle Classes," delivered at a 1940 conference, Tito Prates da Fonseca suggested otherwise. He defined the middle classes as a "heterogeneous" group "joined in the ambitions rooted in their social position, from which they do the utmost not to fall. The intention not to lose position is stronger ... than their aspiration to climb into a higher social class. Their unifying axis is this intention."[134] Perhaps this is not so difficult to understand. In a tight competitive arena most recent arrivals to middle-class status—whether risen from below or fallen from above—may reasonably have sought to secure their position rather than try to rise into the "upper class." The distance from respectability to degradation, after all, as the Sul América ads suggest, was seen as enormous and unrecoverable. Middle-class people might dream of living in expensive mansions, but when they woke, the cold fear of falling gripped them, for in the struggle to secure a decent life that might allow certain comforts, they knew few guarantees against slipping below their level.

5

Keeping Up Appearances

Bᴇ 1920 ᴛʜᴇ ᴜʀʙᴀɴ ᴇʟɪᴛᴇ of Rio de Janeiro and São Paulo had been sampling the market for consumer goods imported from England, France, and the United States for well on 30 years. Ladies and gentlemen toward the turn of the century made a point of adopting the latest English and French fashions, whether or not suited to the climate. Women swaddled themselves in layers of undergarments, wore heavy dresses, and faced the world through a mask of makeup that ran in the heat. Men sported woolen coats and starched collars over long-sleeved shirts and woolen pants, even in Rio's sweltering summers.[1] After 1890 coffee wealth and a rising tide of imported manufactured goods gave elites further means of signaling their privilege. The transformation was profound. The point now was not so much to own particular goods, but to be seen sampling the vast cornucopia of manufactured goods produced by European and American industry and to display them conspicuously.

From the 1920s onward the acceleration of national manufacturing and the cheapening of mass-produced imports brought greater numbers of moderately well-off Brazilians into intimate contact with consumer markets. Neither rich nor poor, these new consumers readily understood that ongoing participation in a consumer culture could connote social difference. They also realized that modest means limited their capacity to consume. Unable to match elites, middle-class people had to find ways of tailoring consumption to their economic and social situation. The cutting and stitching of this compromise took place in middle-class homes, principally by *donas de casa* (housewives) who lived the everyday dilemmas of promise and limitation.

"Given the Social Level to Which We Belong . . ."

As during the 1920s middle-class people lived under an inflationary cloud after 1930. Following a small decline in the early 1930s, the cost of living rose steadily to 1945 and dramatically during the late years of World War II; the cost of servants doubled, the cost of food tripled, the cost of clothing quintupled, and general household expenses sextupled.[2] White-collar associations complained bitterly that "the budget for a middle-class family" was out of control.[3] Salaries were so "completely out of whack," complained one article on the plight of public servants, that "middle-class" families could no longer "dress decently, educate their children, balance their expenses."[4] In the mid-1930s some feared that it was now only "a myth to hope for a higher standard of living."[5] Hard-won collective salary "readjustments" promptly evaporated under the heat of inflation, sweating the "so-called middle classes . . . of jacket and tie" perhaps even more than "proletarians," according to a bank employees' publication in 1938.[6] Debt and cash problems forced many husbands to work more than one job and encouraged wives to work outside the home. By war's end many worried that large numbers of middle-class families verged on an "ominous degradation" if the imbalance between salaries and the cost of living was not redressed.[7] One market survey from the period cut to the quick: "Very soon the middle class will be supplying industry with a large number of skilled workers."[8]

This was the dread that stalked those who thought themselves above the lower orders but knew themselves insecure. White-collar associations dramatized the situation by highlighting instances in which collar-and-tie employees and professionals earned less than social inferiors. In 1939 a bank employees' union in São Paulo fired off a memorandum to the minister of labor and industry on behalf of "bank employees, public functionaries, and the middle class in general that lives from monthly salaries." Their situation was so bleak that "in São Paulo one very frequently finds hundreds and thousands of manual workers [*operários manuais*] who earn higher salaries than many mid-level bank employees, and even more than some chiefs of section of various well-respected banks."[9] The shock of revelation, they assumed, would bolster demands for permanent salary hikes.

Claims of this sort were doubtless calculated to have maximum effect on the politicians and state agencies able to address the salary problem. As such, the accuracy of these statements is less important than the image of well-scrubbed, reasonably educated, middle-class men who earned less than some janitors, doormen, stone workers, or soccer players who were said to earn more. In other words, financial insecurity, far from attenuating the distinction between middle and working classes, reinforced it. Middle-class people had something to lose—which accounts for their anxious ululations. They understood that respectability, while not exclusively a matter of money, depended on a reasonable salary. And except at the lowest occupational rungs or when salary adjustments lagged behind cost of living, collar-and-tie salary earners did on average earn better than the vast majority of manual workers.[10]

A series of market surveys conducted by the Brazilian Institute of Public Opinion and Statistics (IBOPE) confirms this conclusion for the immediate postwar period. These studies divided the economic and social world into three "classes": A, B, and C, where the A's comprised "rich" families, and the latter two were referred to as "middle class" and "poor class." This classification scheme went far beyond mere income designations; it revealed a whole theory of social differentiation. IBOPE researchers explained it this way:

> Our division of the sample into three socioeconomic categories was done according to the criteria of economic situation, social position deriving from the occupation of the head of family, level of culture, greater or lesser use of home appliances, such as electric waxers, vacuum cleaners, refrigerators, neighborhood, etc. The classification is, to a certain extent, arbitrary but based on considerable prior experience. Nevertheless, the criterion of material well-being was not decisive. Between two families, one headed by a worker and the other by a magistrate, both with approximately the same income, we chose to classify the former as a "C" and the latter as an "A" or maybe a "B."[11]

We cannot simply take IBOPE's "middle class" at face value. In most of these studies the sample represented A, B, and C groups in a 1:3:2 proportion, suggesting enormous variability of income and occupation among the B's. Still, the studies permit some firm impressions regarding the relationship between middle-class status and income.

In considering Table 4, it is important to note that workers, as a 1943 article put it, perhaps somewhat dramatically, did not so much live as "balance themselves for a while between life and death."[12] Contemporaries knew of and often commented on the wretchedness of working-class existence in São Paulo and Rio. Workers generally lived crowded together in *cortiços*—"beehives" of small, irregular dwellings, usually without plumbing, always without privacy—chronically short of food, perilously close to the margin of survival.[13] So, while in purely monetary terms B's

TABLE 4

Monthly Family Incomes, Rio and São Paulo, 1946

Study		A	B	C
July 1946 (São Paulo)		Cr$ 14,286	Cr$ 4,549	Cr$ 2,456
Oct.–Nov. 1946 (Rio de Janeiro)	Only head of family working	Cr$ 10,708	Cr$ 4,737	Cr$ 1,565
	More than one family member working	Cr$ 15,238	Cr$ 5,453	Cr$ 2,101
Nov. 1946 (Rio and São Paulo)	Rio	Cr$ 12,030	Cr$ 4,958	Cr$ 2,462
	São Paulo	Cr$ 17,000	Cr$ 5,531	Cr$ 2,250

SOURCE: IBOPE 11; IBOPE 12; IBOPE 14. For purposes of comparison, the cruzeiro amounts may be converted to dollars at Cr$18.5 to US$1.

were closer to C's than to the richer A's, a point of abiding concern among IBOPE researchers, the social distance between typical C's and typical B's was that between lives of bare survival and lives of modest material aspiration beyond merely keeping body and soul together. By the same token, the distance between A's and B's was also great, for it represented the difference between a life of relatively secure ease and at times luxury and a life of budgetary uncertainty and limits.

Many middle-class families confronted these limits by having women work outside the home. As a bank employees' publication noted in 1938, "The wife, whether she wants to or not (I speak, naturally of the middle class) must work, helping her husband or whoever supports the family— because with the growing cost of living, salaries of breadwinners are generally not enough."[14] Nor was it unusual for unmarried daughters to work outside the home. And though women remained a minority of collar-and-tie employees and professionals, specific occupations underwent sea changes. By 1940 three-quarters of all public elementary-school teachers in Rio and São Paulo were women, and by the late 1940s as many women as men, or more, were employed as retail clerks in Rio.[15]

Salaries declined whenever women entered an occupation in substantial numbers. Male heads of family found it ever more difficult to establish careers in commerce and teaching that would permit a middle-class lifestyle. A 1948 article in *O Cruzeiro* concluded that commercial employees were among the "socially diminished sectors . . . of the middle class" who could barely provide their families the "degree of comfort" they needed.[16] In 1947 a majority of men employed in Rio commerce was under 21, and only 15 to 20 percent of all men employed at commercial jobs were mar-

ried.[17] Most commercial employees, especially retail clerks, did not expect
to support families on their salaries alone. Yet the desire to maintain or
enhance middle-class status was a principal reason women had begun to
take up such jobs in the first place. This problem was exacerbated by the
growing numbers of lower-class men and women seeking clerking and retail jobs previously closed to them. However tenuous a perch low-level
commercial employment represented for middle-class people, many in the
lower orders saw it as an opportunity for upward mobility. In one poll 75
percent of job-hunting industrial workers said they would prefer to work
in a store or an office over a factory.[18] By contrast, young middle-class
men and women took to commercial work as part of an effort to maintain
status.[19] So as the supply of literate, primary-school-educated young people grew, commercial employment became a boundary zone between
manual and nonmanual work, populated by supplemental and marginal
middle-class earners alongside comers from the working class, particularly women. In this borderland the aspirations of those who sought to rise
and the anxieties of those who feared they might fall became entangled.

Nor were commercial employees the only ones stricken with angst over
their standard of living. Most liberal professionals, from doctors and lawyers to accountants and engineers, were described as poor compared with
the small number of well-heeled private practitioners who remained the
envy of all.[20] A cartoon that appeared in São Paulo's main newspaper in
1946 suggests this apprehension was widespread: two men in suits and
ties are talking to one another in a cramped apartment living room. One,
"the optimist," says, "If things go on as they are, we'll end up begging in
the streets." "The pessimist" responds, "From whom, my friend? From
whom?"[21]

The fear that made this cartoon possible led collar-and-tie associations
and individuals to insist that middle-class people were entitled to a certain
standard of living, "given the social level to which we belong."[22] The
"middle class," wrote one public functionary, needed to maintain a high
"cultural level" and "by dint of his social and economic condition, [the
middle-class man] must dress decently and educate his children."[23] Otherwise, winced a bank employee, it might be impossible to "resist . . . the
circumstances that push us down."[24] Such statements amounted to an argument that market forces alone should not be allowed to determine social standing. Rather, an irreducible sense of hierarchy rooted in "moral
and intellectual capacities," "social responsibilities," and "inherent decorum" should be maintained in relation to the lower classes.[25]

Claims of privilege over ordinary workers bespeak a vivid insecurity among "middle-class" people that they might "slip back to the lower levels."[26] The opinion magazine *Diretrizes* made the point by implicitly comparing the Brazilian with the American middle class. In 1941 it ran a translation of Eleanor Roosevelt's "Message to the Middle Class," which originally appeared in New York's *Pic* magazine.[27] Roosevelt began by pointing out that she did not like to talk about "class," as classes did not really exist in the United States (and by *Diretrizes*'s implication, in Brazil). Nevertheless, she identified middle-class Americans as those who, "because of their social condition, feel obliged to dress well and spend more time on their education," at times even going into debt in order to finish their studies. Worse still, she continued:

> Within the middle class, more than in any other class, prevails the instinct for imitation. . . . In the middle class (unlike the rich and the "lower class"), almost everything is done with attention turned toward the neighbors. At times I think that if everyone understood that the most important things are the realities of life and not material appearances, the drama of the middle class would lose much of its intensity.

Precisely what the editors at *Diretrizes* sought to accomplish by publishing this piece is not known, but it resonated with other characterizations of the Brazilian middle class and may even have comforted Brazilian readers who could at least imagine that their situation was no worse than it was to the north.

Diretrizes was not alone in depicting middle-class people as being uncomfortably wedged in the middle of a social order, living "a tight life, with greater aspirations than the proletariat and without the ease of the high and fat circles."[28] Public opinion researchers saw this as the middle class's defining tragedy: "[They] yearn for a better representation and struggle desperately to keep up appearances. In this sense, we judge the situation of workers to be better, for they do not have greater social obligations."[29] Or as one commentator worried, the middle class's surrender to the "bourgeois spirit" of materialism threatened to upset the "proper balance between economic possibilities and standard of living," which could only lead to lives "tortured by the desire for ostentatious exhibit."[30]

Admiration for, or perhaps envy of, the rich entwined with deeply felt resentment toward them. A striking example is Júlio, the respectable commercial employee in Sra. Leandro Dupré's novel *There Were Six of Us*. Through much of the story Júlio more or less constantly criticizes the rich in general and his wife's aunt in particular. He sees them as egoists who never do anything for friends or family. All they care about is "themselves, themselves, themselves." "You can't count on any of them," he splutters when the aunt declines to lend him money, an accusation of special disquiet in a society so long organized around family ties. Yet Júlio also understands he must remain on good terms with the rich, most especially when they are family. So when he and his wife receive an invitation to an elegant ball at the aunt's house, they are forced to spend the children's clothes money to outfit themselves properly. Júlio complains bitterly as he dresses that all the rich are good for is to make "poor people spend money."[31]

The longing for a better representation, then, was likely less a conscious effort by middle-class people to imitate the rich than an imperative not to be confused with the working-class poor. Hence the frequent allusions to indebtedness among collar-and-tie employees and professionals. One publication referred to the marked "tendency to financial bohemianism" within the middle class. Young bank and commercial employees, public functionaries, and struggling professionals were especially susceptible to the "seductions credit," one author lamented, since they tended to see debt as necessary to maintaining "social and economic condition."[32]

A family budget detailed by a public functionary for himself and his wife sheds light on what it meant to keep up appearances.[33] Rooted in assumptions regarding his "social standard," José Moacir de Andrade Sobrinho described his fixed monthly costs, from rent of a "very modest" house to a single live-in maid, groceries, utilities, milk, toiletries, pastries, and transportation. He then went on to detail the couple's necessary yearly expenses for clothing and accessories. For his wife: 6 dresses, 12 outfits, 1 "robe manteau," 10 pairs of hose, 6 pairs of shoes, 5 hats, 3 purses, 2 pairs of gloves. For himself: 2 ensembles, 2 suits, 12 pairs of pants, 12 shirts, 18 pairs of socks, 24 handkerchiefs, 12 button-on collars, 2 pairs of shoes, 6 ties, 2 fedoras, 2 straw hats for summer, 6 pajamas. Prorating yearly expenses and adding in medical, dental, and pharmacy bills, entertainment, books, magazines, and income taxes, he came to a "very reasonable" budget of 1,945 mil réis a month in the mid-1930s. Clearly, this government bureaucrat did not count on being rich. He hoped to do well enough that his wife would not have to work outside the home, the mark of a man who could truly provide for his family. He expected to eat fairly well, evidenced by the daily kilo of meat budgeted for the two of them, at a time when workers were getting by on less than 100 grams a day.[34] He took it for granted that they would dress well.

While Andrade had every reason to pad his numbers, so long as they appeared to be in reasonable proportion to his social place, his budget was not dramatically out of line with other estimates of middle-of-the-road salaries during the period. His calculations, thus, are more useful as an indicator—"utopian," as the author himself admitted—of middle-class aspirations and of what a "reasonable" standard of living meant to middle-class people, even those who might not attain it. Above all Andrade appears to have imagined for himself a life of relative comfort rather than assured ease. He anticipated working for the rest of his days and wanted only to provide for his family in accordance with his social standing.

The yen for a secure social position defined the expectations and aspirations that, in the broad, distinguished the material lives of middle-class families from those below. Housing was a crucial aspect of middle-class life. Studies conducted during the 1930s indicate that the vast majority of working-class homes had fewer than four rooms. One sociologist found in 1940 that nearly 90 percent of manual workers' homes lacked indoor plumbing, roughly the same percentage shared a kitchen with nonfamily members, and over 50 percent of these abodes were dirty and overcrowded or utterly lacking comfort.[35] In poorer dwellings beds, hammocks, chairs, eating table, and stove were often jammed into a single room.

While systematic studies do not exist for the middle class, novels centered on middle-class homes offer a glimpse of the differences. One novel described the "modest house of a bank employee," with the "six rooms demanded by his social position": a small parlor for guests, with stuffed chairs and freestanding ashtray; a dining room, decorated with cheap paintings and a reasonable radio; a small area for the maid; two bedrooms; a kitchen; a bathroom.[36] The more fortunate presumably did better than this, but all could dream of attaining the security of a bought-and-paid-for home. In fact, IBOPE surveys indicate that even in the mid-1940s not more than a quarter to a third of B's owned a home in Rio and São Paulo. Yet half said they had plans to buy one.[37] Everyone else lived in rented houses or apartments, some by choice, some not. Even here the difference between B's and C's was apparent, the former spending just short of three times on rent what C's did.[38] Moreover, apartment dwelling could mean a step up in status, as suggested by a report on the "middle-class invasion of Copacabana" in the late 1930s.[39]

Servants stood as a second difference between typical middle-class and working-class budgets. Working-class families rarely had maids. In respectable collar-and-tie families at least one servant appears to have been de rigueur.[40] This was more than just a matter of having someone to clean the house. It meant that middle-class men and women could project to the world the fact that they were free, at least symbolically, of the most degrading manual labor involved in running a household. Moreover, for a majority of middle-class men the presence of a servant meant that however much they were subject to bosses, or social superiors outside the home, they could at least return at the end of the day to a situation of dominance over a (sexual, class, and often racial) inferior who owed them even more deference than their wives. In the case of middle-class women the presence of a maid served to reinforce traditional lines of authority and social privilege, according to which certain people could employ others to do the heaviest and most undesirable work around a house.

Much more was bundled up in this relationship between dona de casa and servant than merely the issue of who performed what work. In 1930 Cassilda Martins wrote an article opposing the idea of sending young, lower-class women to special home economics courses to be trained for domestic service.[41] The danger, according to the author, was that well-trained servants would "overwhelm" their employers with "technical and professional superiority and rising salary demands." If servants rather than housewives became experts in the art of housekeeping, housewives would "not be in charge of [their] own homes." Rather, they would be "dominated, ruled" by their servants, because their "young authority" would not be rooted in "understanding the problems of their calling." Fear of inversion is palpable and speaks volumes of just how central the employer-servant relationship was to middle-class life. Indeed, an abiding concern for projecting authority over the maid may be one reason feminism made limited headway in Brazil during these years; a satirical article hinted in 1935 that feminism's egalitarian impulse might too easily undermine the authority and position of ordinary donas de casa who were not prepared to give up the privilege of being *patrôas* (female bosses).[42]

Clothing expenses constituted a further point of difference between middle- and working-class budgets. Poor people, as a rule, owned little beyond the strictly necessary. According to a 1945 study, a "typical" working-class woman might have two or three pairs of shoes, four dresses, five pairs of hose, and several changes of underwear. One-third of working-class men surveyed had only a single jacket, most had only three or four pairs of trousers, and few owned more than two pairs of shoes.[43] At best they might have one Sunday outfit. By contrast, those with pretensions to respectability had long attached great significance to their manner of dress (as Andrade Sobrinho's clothing budget suggests) and considered it part of their obligations to garb themselves decently.[44] At times they spared no expense. Pacheco's (in this regard just barely) fictional bank employee saddled himself with debt in order to keep his family "well attired" in accordance with their "social milieu," for the inability to dress well was a sure sign of financial emergency.

New ad techniques reinforced sartorial "elegance" as a badge of respectability. Advertising copy and tableaux portraying dance and dinner parties, casinos, theaters, and clubs emphasized the importance of always dressing for success, at work as well as play. Magazines aimed at women ran advertisements for sewing machines and sewing courses tempting housewives and women who worked outside the home to create their own fashions and look "modern and elegant" without bearing the expense of a clothier.[45] *O Cruzeiro* ran fashion columns encouraging women to spend a great deal of time and as much money as constrained budgets permitted planning their wardrobes. These inducements appear to have worked; in 1946 IBOPE found that B women in São Paulo spent three times what C women did on clothes, though B's earned, on average, only twice what C's did.[46] Middle-class men were not subject to the same barrage of advertising as women, though employers and general culture made it clear that they were expected to dress respectably for work and social occasions.

"Culture" was a further expense marking the budgets of middle-class families. These costs took the form primarily of newspaper and magazine subscriptions and books. Since these items, as public functionary Andrade Sobrinho put it, were "indispensable to the cultivated man," it is no surprise that B's in São Paulo devoted nearly 5 percent of their tight budgets to buying printed reading material, compared with roughly 3 percent for A's and 2 percent for C's. Books appear to have been particularly important to middle-class families. According to one IBOPE study, B's spent the same amount of money on books as did A's (though they earned only a third as much) and more than seven times as much as C's. Books were an attractive investment, for they served two functions. Their presence in the home reflected a certain level of refinement. At the same time they provided entertainment. Advertisers played on both themes throughout the 1930s. Encyclopedias and the classics were available on installment for those who wanted to display their erudition in conversation or on the bookshelf. Monthly publications such as *The Detective—Magazine of Thrills* kept people up nights with the derring-do of American and Brazilian gumshoes.[47]

Finally, education, a traditional expense, loomed far larger during this period, often straining family finances. Working-class families were fortunate to keep children out of the work force long enough to finish primary school; they almost always lacked the means to send children to secondary school.[48] Middle-class families, by contrast, understood that education and training beyond grade school were indispensable to professional success. They saw education as absolutely essential to survival and made sacrifices in other areas, notably entertainment expenses, in order to afford school.[49] IBOPE reported in 1946 that the typical São Paulo B family dedicated 5 percent of its budget to schooling and books for the children, where A and C families spent no more than 3 percent.[50] According to the study, B's outspent C's five to one on schooling their children—largely because middle-class families sent their children to private schools—suggesting simultaneously the enormous educational deficit suffered by the poor and the importance of education for the middle class.[51] Andrade Sobrinho's budget bolsters the point. He itemized the lifetime costs of educating his children, including tuition for a private secondary school, uniforms, books, travel, some kind of university preparatory course, and university study, as part of his long-term budget. In fact, the *faculdade* remained beyond most people of moderate incomes during this period, but secondary school was a common expectation by the 1940s for those who sought to give their children a leg up in "the struggle for life."[52]

"There Are Always More Things to Buy and Consume"

While traditional household and personal consumption intensified after 1920, in the widespread availability of consumer durables—radios, record players, household appliances, wristwatches—glinted the dawn of a consumer society in Brazil. The seeds of the new mindset had been planted after World War I, when industrial expansion and urbanization began to displace household production to a market for goods and services. Elites were the first to integrate their habits into the logic of the consumer marketplace, enticed by the arresting images of modernity issuing from New York, London, and Paris. The middle class followed, quickly increasing their desire for consumer delights that were ever more common and affordable.

Mass advertising made its debut on the radio and in such general-circulation magazines as *Vida Carioca*, *Revista da Semana*, *Vida Doméstica*, and *O Cruzeiro*, widely read among middle-class families. Stress was on things "modern." In 1928, for instance, *O Cruzeiro* broke with the stuffy, elite-oriented weeklies of old and announced itself the harbinger of a modern Brazil. Amidst images of soaring skyscrapers it vowed to leave behind the "ruins of colonial Rio" and instead "promote progress."[53] In 1930 this daring new publication speculated that by the year 2000, Rio would be a city of 14 million dotted with skyscrapers. Hydroplanes would skim across Guanabara

Bay and private planes would land on the tallest buildings. Throughout the 1930s the magazine experimented liberally with novel reporting and advertising techniques sweeping the United States and ran features bespeaking modernity. By 1941 *O Cruzeiro* had become the magazine of choice among middle-class Brazilians and proclaimed itself "the magazine that accompanies the rhythm of modern life."

Foreign manufacturing companies participated in the cultural shift more directly by insistently characterizing their products and the people who bought them as modern. General Electric announced in 1932 that it was opening a store to sell its "domestic marvels" in Brazil, because "modern homes, the homes of families where the idea of comfort is linked to thrift, cannot fail to be in contact with General Electric Stores."[54] More than a decade later it continued with the same theme, stressing that "electric servants"—radios, refrigerators, and toasters—were bound to "increase the comfort and happiness of life."[55] Similarly the Ford Motor Co. not only sold cars but offered "true bumper to bumper modernism."[56]

This sort of advertising was the single most important vehicle for diffusing an ethos of consumption and indirectly a sense of imminent progress. Ad agencies proliferated after the mid-1930s.[57] J. Walter Thompson, Standard Propaganda, McCann-Erickson, and two or three dozen other ad agencies, foreign and Brazilian, opened in Rio and São Paulo during the 1930s and 1940s.[58] As was true in other countries, ad men approached their work with an almost missionary fervor.[59] One agency said that the purpose of advertising was to "create needs, awaken desires, understand, deepen, exploit, and consolidate markets" as part of an ongoing effort to "create new habits [and] stimulate the demand for comfort and civilization."[60] This project found expression in glossy magazines, such as *O Cruzeiro*, where advertising copy and images reflected the lifestyle of modernly prosperous, though by no means rich, middle-class families enjoying the fruits of a consumer economy.

Advertisers, manufacturers, and economists declared themselves sanguine about the coming era. One ad firm gushed over the "enormous possibilities and opportunities" awaiting Brazil's "great industrial transition."[61] Collar-and-tie organizations eagerly joined in the hosannahs, chorusing that individual fates were linked to the expansion of "internal markets," to "economic progress," to "intensive industrialization," and above all to "rising standards of living" and "large consumer markets."[62] The influential opinion magazine *Diretrizes* spoke in glowing terms of the "coming civilization of comfort and well being for everyone; a civilization in which everyone would, in fact, have his little portion of happiness."[63] At least as imagined by advertisers, middle-class employees, and opinion makers, modernization was to be a process leading to the material uplift of all Brazilians.

Available evidence hints at what IBOPE researchers characterized as an "almost imprudent optimism" by war's end. A survey conducted in 1946 found that 54 percent of those polled believed Brazil was headed for prosperity, while only 18 percent thought the country was headed for crisis. B's expressed the highest confidence, followed by C's and then A's.[64] This hopeful outlook seemed to clash with an underlying mood of financial instability rooted in the inflation of which collar-and-tie associations complained so bitterly throughout the period. These sentiments were not so much inconsistent as in tension, reflecting the predicament of promise amidst crisis that had characterized middle-class social and economic life since the 1920s.

Whatever the overall mood, the allure of products symbolizing modernity was considerable and quickly came to be linked to social standing. In 1944 the author of a paper on progress and living standards argued that a "dignified" lifestyle implied the use of radios and sewing machines, "indispensable products that progress was furnishing."[65] The radio provides perhaps the best example of this process. Though ownership of a radio set was a privilege of the rich during the 1920s, by the early 1930s middle-class families began to afford them. In 1931 E. Monteiro Barros, president of the Union of Commercial Employees, proudly announced in a speech to members that he had a radio in *his* home, "as is the case for any person of good taste."[66] It was almost as though he were responding to the ad that ran in *Vida Doméstica* in May 1931: "Still without a radio ... How come?"[67] Throughout the 1930s the aspiration to own a radio ballooned. A 1932 ad touted the Erickson 313VX as "a radio for the home: modern, economical, sonorous, within everyone's reach."[68] In 1935, heralding a new section devoted to radio programming, *Vida Doméstica* proclaimed that radios were now in all "modern homes."[69] Advertisers sought to connect radios to a sense of elevated social status. A Philco ad in 1937, for instance, pictured a gathering of distinguished-looking people in evening gowns and dinner jackets, sipping champagne in a spacious and well-appointed living room, sitting around a wooden cabinet with large speakers, marveling that "It's just like being at a concert."[70] By 1940 Andrade Sobrinho included a radio in his budget as the "next big expense" after rent, servant, clothing, and culture, because it was "an indispensable resource of modern life."[71] Between 1944 and 1950 the number of radio stations in Brazil tripled to 300.[72]

This deepening sense of having to own certain "modern" things—radios, but also refrigerators, telephones, mass-produced area rugs, typewriters, sewing machines—signaled a transformation in the social meaning of consumption; the very idea of "need" was changing just as purchasing opportunities were expanding dramatically. More and a greater variety of things became available to a larger mass of people than ever before. João Lyra Filho in his 1942 book on the middle class claimed hopefully that the growing demand for manufactured products was creating "a general incentive to those industries producing goods within the immediate reach of the middle class, including houses, cars, radios, and wine."[73] In 1943 an article in *Diretrizes* noted that a "sense of comfort is a characteristic of the American [United States] civilization that is having a great influence among us, an influence that will only get stronger in the near future."[74] By 1945 an advice book for donas de casa had deemed floor waxers, radios, vacuum cleaners, and sewing machines acceptable wedding gifts.[75] A year later IBOPE researchers concluded that those who possessed these articles would buy newer, modern ones over the years and were likely as well to own "a thousand other useful things, from perfumes and beauty products to canned soup and toasters."[76]

The growth in consumer culture was hardly a secular trend. It was intimately entwined with the social, economic, and political forces that were remaking Brazil during the period, as evidenced by the history of São Paulo's huge department store, Mappin.

Founded in 1913 by British importers, Mappin had until 1930 catered exclusively to São Paulo's coffee aristocracy, which had money to burn on expensive imports from London and Paris. It was self-consciously elitist and while the coffee economy boomed had no incentive to the contrary. The collapse of coffee exports during the late 1920s and early 1930s and the ousting of the Paulista elite from political power in the Revolution of 1930 presaged thoroughgoing change. Over the following decade the store passed into Brazilian hands. New management adjusted to the conditions of a modernizing Brazil by reorienting Mappin to a more popular clientele. Where previously the subject of price had been taboo, after 1932 the store began to tag all of the articles appearing in its lavish display windows. It innovated sales techniques unknown in Brazil, such as catalogue and telephone orders, and liquidations to clear stock for a new season. Starting in 1934, it helped to popularize radios, selling on installment, the only way a bookkeeper could afford to buy a device that might cost more than his monthly salary. The size of the emporium, the diversity of the goods, and the care given to sumptuous presentation dazzled those who were used to the more jumbled aspect of traditional commercial houses. Here, as one newspaper raved, "the impeccable lines of the latest models stand out, products of a healthy and attractive modernism."[77]

By 1940 São Paulo's premier department store was no longer an exclusive preserve of the rich. The elite continued to meet at the Tea Room and increasingly at the American Bar, but the store found itself under competitive pressure to broaden its appeal still further. The revolving doors and thick carpets that had sealed the store from the street were removed so that passersby would not be intimidated from entering. A wartime shortage of imported goods, the store's lifeblood since its founding, led to the inclusion of a growing array of nationally produced items that were winning a considerable following. Managers ran down the store's stock of Rosenthal porcelain and Cristolfe silver service in favor of Nadir Figueiredo's china and Wolff stainless. In 1943 Mappin announced a sale on a new collection of rugs, "the authentic pride of Brazilian industry." After the war home appliances became big business and even in that area of manufacturing, cheaper national brands began to gain a market against foreign imports. In 1948, responding to stiff competition from other retailers, including Sears Roebuck, Mappin began to feature off-the-rack apparel, much of it locally produced. By the mid-1950s the store's advertising manager summarized the changes of the preceding two decades: "Mappin took the care and had the ability to come down a few steps in status without falling into vulgarity or losing its name."[78] It had turned its attention to a consuming middle class that made up in volume the financial freedom it lacked in comparison to the store's earlier elite clientele.

These more modest consumers found credit ever more readily available. Well-known stores in Rio such as Parc-Royal, Casa Yankee, and Casa Bastos banded together in 1930 to form a credit agency. The idea of buying now and worrying later was nothing new to cash-strapped middle-class families, who had long borrowed money at usurious interest rates to support their standard of living. Credit simply reinforced and institutionalized the impulse. In the mid-1930s the Sul América insurance company sought to persuade potential customers to buy the "policy that demands no sacrifices," because it would enable them to "spend and spend" without a worry for the future.[79] By 1940 *O Cruzeiro* had run an ad barking the advantages of freely available credit: "If what you have at the moment is not enough, buy anyway. Your credit is worth gold."[80] In 1944 *Reader's Digest*'s Brazilian subscribers were told by an American author that they could "live beyond your means . . . luxuriously on a small income."[81]

Many heeded the advice. An IBOPE study of the earning power of *O Cruzeiro* readers in Rio and São Paulo provides a snapshot of consumption patterns in the early 1940s.

TABLE 5

Consumption by Social Class, Rio de Janeiro and São Paulo, 1946

(Percentage [range] of Class A, B, and C magazine readers
owning indicated items, 1946)

	A	B	C	Pct. of total
Automobile	61–77	10–17	0–4	14–26
Telephone	72–100	35–72	8–31	34–63
Refrigerator	62–100	26–39	0–5	21–57
Radio	96–100	91–98	78–84	90–95
Record player	46–62	21–43	3–14	21–41
Vacuum cleaner	61–86	22–36	0–9	24–41
Electric waxer	85–100	56–59	6–16	45–56
Washing machine	0–6	1–3	0–1	1–3

SOURCE: IBOPE 14.

Table 5 contains two crucial points. First, it shows that B's were much more likely to own modern household appliances than C's. Moreover, certain products implied ownership of others: one did not buy a vacuum cleaner without owning rugs, a floor waxer was pointless without tile or parquet floors, and a record player was useful only if one bought records. At the same time A's far outspent B's on these products. The percentages among A's suggest that high-income families went in for pricier models and were likely to own all or most of these items, while middle-income families had to be much more careful in choosing which ones to invest in and frequently had to buy on credit.[82]

The table also suggests the inherent instability of status claims based on the ownership of a particular product. For example, in the mid-1930s the radio had widely connoted privilege. By 1946, when the study was carried out, they had become so widely available that radio ownership, in and of itself, no longer set one off from one's lessers. In short, even at this early stage the logic of consumerism, the constant pressure to own the latest model, the fanciest style, or the newest gadget in order to keep up with peers and ahead of those below had already taken root.

Consumption heavily accented class relations. IBOPE frequently performed marketing surveys polling only A's and B's, excluding C's because they were thought to be outside the market for products such as tires, apartments and houses, perfumes, deodorants, electric floor waxers, and fountain pens. No less significant, the day-to-day interplay of heightened material expectations and severe budget constraints appear to have deeply touched inner life. IBOPE studies offer a glimmer of what was happening.

In late 1944 the organization conducted a study for Casa Canada, an upscale woman's apparel store in Rio.[83] In interviews probing attitudes toward the store, 300 women mentioned ninety-nine other fashion stores, suggesting something of the importance middle- and upper-class women attached to clothes shopping. In the case of middle-income women (the B's), however, Casa Canada was a place for active dreaming; while only 5 percent believed its prices were reasonable, 75 percent admitted stopping at the store's window displays. This proportion is striking only because less than a quarter of A women and less than 2 percent of C women paused to window shop. The former knew they could enter and buy and so did not waste their time at the window. The latter knew they could neither enter nor buy and so did not waste their time dreaming. Something in this image of a middle-class housewife breaking stride at Casa Canada's display window, longing for something beyond her reach, sighing and returning to the grocery shopping for which she had left home in the first place, bespeaks the constitutive dilemma of middle-class consumption, always wanting more or better than a limited budget would bear.

Another IBOPE study makes a similar point. Surveyors queried A and B (not C) consumers in São Paulo about plans for home ownership. Nearly half of B's who said they intended to buy a house indicated that they would need a garage, though less than a fifth owned a car. Noting that some might want to use a garage as a storage space or to enhance the value of the home, researchers concluded nevertheless that "many are merely hopeful or confident that they will soon be able to own" a car to put in it.[84]

Modern products, in short, held many in rapturous thrall. In São Paulo more B men said they remembered an advertisement for Firestone tires than A men did, 52 to 50 percent, as though they were so fascinated with the idea of owning a car (few actually did) that they paid close attention to advertisements featuring cars and products related to cars.[85] In Rio de Janeiro more B than A men claimed to know General Motors brands and products, 63 to 58. They named a long list of electrical products they believed were produced by GM; as it turns out, they were confusing GM and GE.[86] The point remains that they appear to have been attentive watchers of ads, ever seeking new consumption opportunities within their financial grasp or, at least, their imaginative horizon. The mindset of this budding consumerism was summarized pithily in an IBOPE study on the living conditions of commercial employees in São Paulo: "There are always more things to buy and consume, there is always a desire to better one's standard of living."[87]

This desire may well have become entwined with another. In his column "Eve Without the Rib" for *O Cruzeiro* in late September 1946, the pseudonymous columnist "Adam Jr." commented on the consequences of "Progress" in Brazil.[88] Caustically criticizing feminism in Brazil and abroad, Adam decried recent developments on the amorous front. Once upon a time, he said, women married men for their dignity, bravery, intelligence, or generosity. Today, he snarled, they marry the number of cylinders his car has, how many home appliances he can offer in the apartment, and how many radios and record players he can obtain for the marital household. Of course, it is an open question whether Brazilian women were more conscious of material well-being in choosing husbands than they had been in the past. Still, it is significant that Adam—and others— should have identified the pressure at all, for it suggests, at a minimum, that male breadwinners were now conscious of and increasingly insecure about the intimate importunities of a consumer culture.[89]

"Home Is the Small World of the Family"

Concerns over the social effects of consumption were of a piece with growing tensions between men and women and broader worries over a "degradation of customs" in family home life. As early as 1924 *Vida Doméstica* condemned the "feverish pace of modern life in a large city" and proposed that women "be educated in the worship of the home."[90] Initially this criticism was leveled primarily at well-to-do women. With too much time on their hands the daughters of the rich were abandoning their domestic responsibilities for the allures of jewelry, telephone calls, and chauffeur-driven shopping trips. But by the mid-1930s critics felt that even the more modestly placed were in danger. One article argued that home life was dissolving because comfort, once a privilege of a few, had in recent times become a possibility for many.[91] Another rued the passing of family get-togethers in favor of beach outings, theater, cinemas, tea houses, clubs, shopping, and strolling around downtown, where the rich set the style and others strove to imitate.[92] "Life runs in the street," said an author concerned for the middle class. "Family life is not something about whose fate we can afford to be complacent."[93]

The perceived threat to home life met with a considered effort to reinforce family traditions. Magazines widely read within the middle and upper classes, and especially by women, railed throughout the 1930s and into the 1940s against a sinister modernity that was disrupting the family. Catholic conservatives, among them women, argued that women should close ranks against the "violent incursions of radical modernism," which "authoritarian men" and "conformist women" had promoted at the expense of an "ennobling life" anchored in the home.[94] Critics insisted that the home as "sanctuary" could "resist the penetrations of modernism" only if presided over by the "gentle hands of a woman" and "ruled by a paternal intelligence."[95] Women should remain the "central pillar of the home," "firm guardians of the traditions of the family."[96] Government too addressed the issue, passing edicts that in rhetoric, if not in practice, sought to preserve and protect the woman's role at home. According to the labor ministry in 1942, it was neither "convenient nor desirable" for women to seek outside employment, because it undermined "family unity and morality."[97]

These statements do not prove that middle-class women took conservative admonitions at face value. They do indicate that women faced alternative and conflicting ways of understanding their social roles. Certainly, many women were attracted to aspects of so-called modern life. Women who worked outside the home may have done so out of necessity and only for brief stints, but this was not inconsistent with a desire to experience the wider world. Movies, car rides, fashion, romance and detective novels, magazines, radio, shopping, samba, and dancing—all were newly available to young women. Incomes of their own and new opportunities for privacy made young women more independent of parents and led to conflicts over their relationships with young men. The latest fashions and the ability to buy them tempted their vanity and their pocketbooks. By comparison home life could seem "boring."[98]

Still, there is no warrant to conclude that middle-class women wholly rejected a domestic role. Work outside the home was usually temporary and often unappealing. Most jobs open to women offered little room for advancement, quickly became routine, paid poorly, and at times subjected them to "liberties" from bosses and male coworkers.[99] For every Fernanda in Veríssimo's *Crossroads* who dreamt in vain of leaving office work to become a teacher, there were probably several young women who preferred the role of wife and mother that had been expected of them since birth. As wives and mothers they became living symbols of home and family, "queens, sagely ruling over their little kingdoms."[100] They were charged with the important responsibility of maintaining an orderly home, seeing to the education and moral character of children, balancing accounts, ensuring spiritual repose for their hard-working husbands, making themselves beautiful, and upholding the greater interests of the nation.

Moreover, most middle-class women probably faced considerable pressure and incentives not to seek paid work. "In the ideal family," as one advice manual for donas de casa put it, "the woman should not exercise a paid profession outside the home."[101] As much as anything this was a matter of status and class, for among the "proletarian classes" the whole family commonly worked.[102] And even if they did work outside the home, women were still responsible for managing domestic affairs, so that an outside job meant a double shift. In other words, despite breezes of change, home life stood fast as the defining experience for middle-class women during this period.

Yet as the fact of a backlash suggests, home and family life had already changed by the early 1930s. Nowhere was this more obvious than in the sphere of consumption. Advertisers had been targeting women since at least the 1920s. In the 1930s what had been sniper fire became a frontal assault. Advertising was directed increasingly at women in their role as donas de casa who controlled domestic budgets. In September 1937's issue of *Vida Doméstica* an advertising agent explained the logic of appealing to the "eternal female" in publicity. Women read most of the ads in magazines, he said, and made the greatest part of all purchases. They, after all, were primarily concerned with the comfort of home and family. Even for exclusively male items, insisted the author, the woman's direct or indirect influence over purchasing decisions was determinative.[103] Recognizing this fact, newspapers sought to attract advertisers by claiming that "the woman is the buyer par excellence."[104] IBOPE researchers took women's attitudes perhaps even more seriously than men's in their market surveys in the mid- and late 1940s. As of the 1930s modern consumption entered Brazilian culture through the front door of the middle-class home in the arms of housewives.

This represented a shift from earlier times. Before 1920 most household necessities had been peddled door to door by suppliers or salesmen. Otherwise the maid went to market. These experiences were routine and personal, and advertising was all but irrelevant to the demand for products. Even clothing was not sold through a consumer market, as women, except those who could afford to import fashions from abroad, were expected to sew and embroider that which they did not have made by a seamstress or tailor. Marketplace savvy simply was not part of the job description for most donas de casa.

World War I marked the beginning of a transformation. By the 1920s as the quantity and variety of goods offered for sale grew, women found themselves faced with new opportunities and new dilemmas. Their challenge, according to one ad, was to assure the "greatest economy and maximum comfort in the home," through prudent spending and house-keeping practices.[105] Provisioning a household was no longer just a matter of paying the peddler or supplier who came to the door. As a 1945 advice manual remarked, "knowing how to buy is an art. It is indispensable knowledge for every dona de casa."[106]

Attuned to the times, advertisers competed for women's attention through the images projected in advertisements: women in cars, women as beaming homemakers, women as bosses to their servants, women confi-dently negotiating the world outside the home, women as slinky, inde-pendent, and self-assured (though as often as not on the arms of men). These advertisers understood that homemakers made myriad mundane decisions for the household each week. They assumed that wives could in-fluence husbands to purchase a wide variety of modern products, such as electric floor waxers, rugs, radios, record players, and cars.

Nor were advertisers blind to the possibilities of appealing to women's vanity. Anywhere from half to three-quarters of the ads run by O *Cruzeiro* in the late 1930s and early 1940s featured health and beauty products. Women were told to be slim and energetic, because "fat women lose their attractiveness," to regenerate their nervous systems, to firm up their breasts using Russian Paste ("for the first glance is to the bosom"), to douche themselves, to heighten their powers of seduction using Colony Skin Milk, to cultivate the "perfect body," to brush their teeth with Col-gate so that they could "captivate a lieutenant," to use Regulator Xavier, the key to happiness in "this century of dynamism and progress" and the only solution to premature aging, to make themselves beautiful through makeup and clothes, for "women have an obligation to be pretty," lest they be unable to snare a man or their husbands become indifferent to their charms.[107]

The ability to purchase and use certain beauty products seems to have been a further point of separation between middle and working classes. Whereas three-quarters of B women responding to an IBOPE poll claimed to read O *Cruzeiro* on a weekly basis, only 40 percent of C women did.[108] According to the researchers, most of the 60 percent who did not read the magazine could not afford it. The many lower-class women who read magazines like O *Cruzeiro* probably harbored no real hope of buying the products advertised, and those who did not read magazines simply ig-nored or suppressed the desire for things they could not have. Market studies offer some support here: IBOPE limited its research on perfumes and deodorants to A and B women.[109]

While the market for consumer goods represented a new development

and altered established patterns and relationships, it simultaneously reinforced certain aspects of the patriarchal family. As depicted in advertising
copy and images, women were far more often wives and mothers than
professionals. Ads for "regenerative wines" claimed to restore strength
sapped by the hard work of keeping house. Beauty products were hawked
with an eye to individual vanity, though also as part of a responsibility to
husbands and an aid to marital bliss. Home appliances were practical,
conferred status, and symbolized progress all at the same time.

Even so, in many of these ads women bore a quality of independence
and autonomy in their roles, suggesting that all was not as it had been.
New consumption patterns were altering the balance of power in domestic affairs.[110] The middle-class economic dilemma—how to purchase modern products, send children to the right schools, rent or buy the proper
house, afford a maid, clothe the family appropriately, and otherwise keep
up appearances in the face of inflation—made it imperative for families to
establish priorities and adopt prudent practices. Donas de casa were in a
position to do so and thus were a pivotal force in defining and maintaining
the middle-class home. Dona Lola in Dupré's *There Were Six of Us* is emblematic. She worked hard to keep her home orderly and presentable,
made sure the children were properly groomed and attended school, did
what she could to make her husband comfortable after work, and labored
late into the night making bonbons on consignment for a little extra
spending money.

There was no uniform method employed by all donas de casa. As had
long been the case, housekeeping was learned by osmosis and example
during childhood. Practices varied from family to family, and some
women were undoubtedly better at it than others. Nevertheless, we can
get some sense of what was at stake in housekeeping and some inkling of
its broader social meaning by closely considering housekeeping advice
purveyed in manuals and magazines after World War II.

Books such as Isabela Serrano's *My House* and *Notions of Home Economics* and Marialice Prestes's *Problems of the Home* effectively summarized advice scattered across various general magazines.[111] For the most
part these books were fairly mundane. Chapters covered the minutiae of
home hygiene: how to deal with refrigerators, stoves, and other new-
fangled home appliances, how most frugally to use and mend clothes, how
to prepare and conserve food, how to keep household accounts, how to
deal with the servant, and how to rear children. But there was also an ideology of domesticity hidden in their pages. In Serrano's *My House* the
dona de casa was the dominant personality in a small domain that re-

quired her to be at one and the same time a partner to her husband, a worker in her own right, and the employer of a servant whose job it was to perform the most unpleasant and routine tasks around the house. The dona de casa was responsible for ensuring the cleanliness of her home, the healthfulness of her food, and the moral rectitude of her children. She was charged with creating and maintaining a pleasant and alluring environment by ensuring harmony and coordination of furniture, rugs, and colors. Superficially this seemed to codify a fairly traditional understanding of the home. As Serrano understood it, home life was the sweet and heavy charge for which society had destined women, "a somewhat more obscure life" well worthy of being cherished.[112]

Yet this formulation betrays a glimmering recognition of a changed social order. Serrano conceived of the home as a husband's place of repose and regeneration, a refuge from the harshness of a competitive world outside the domestic cocoon. Husbands worked long hours, often at unrewarding jobs and under the thumbs of demanding bosses, to provide for their families. They deserved some pampering when they got home: "The man works, struggles for life and, sometimes, returns home worried and nervous. He must find at home a tender and patient wife and a tranquil atmosphere, so that he can go back to work the following day rested and calm, and be happy to have stayed around the house."[113] What is interesting about this view of the domestic sphere, and the woman's role in it, is that its stated rationale was economic rather than patriarchal. According to these manuals, a wife owed her husband tenderness and patience rather than obedience. Her obligation was rooted in the family's broader relationship to a market economy rather than in some inherent duty to a patriarchal husband. Of course, traditional roles had not completely crumbled.[114] But if advice books and magazines are any indication, they were changing in subtle ways, accommodating rather than negating market forces.[115]

On this view, donas de casa had a crucial role to play at the boundary between home and market. Above all, their mission was to preserve "the small world of the family" by ensuring a "solidly settled economic base" through proper practices.[116] Occasionally, said these advice givers, women might work outside the home or take work in to help make ends meet, often by mending or tailoring children's clothes for richer patrons. Preferably, and more commonly, donas de casa were to control expenses and economize. Only then could the family's "moral, intellectual, and physical faculties" be assured of "normal development." The reason was obvious to Serrano: "Material privations affect the body and the spirit. Disappointments, worries about the future, poor nutrition all tend to irritate the individuals and are a powerful factor in domestic disharmony."[117]

Here we can see that the advice purveyed by these books and magazines ran primarily to middle-class readers. Without explicitly defining their target audience, manuals and magazines alike emphasized the importance of frugality for those caught between the ease of ample resources and the wretchedness of working-class poverty. The "frugal woman" could work wonders in dressing her children by altering adult clothes. The "frugal woman" did not throw old socks away but used them as rags or gave them to the poor. Leftovers did not have to seem like leftovers. Homemade dresses did not have to seem homemade. Elegance could be achieved by using "few jewels, much simplicity and extraordinary cleanliness."

Nor was this merely a mandate for unavoidable belt tightening. Serrano and Prestes, echoing the magazines, presented thrift as a virtue to be pursued with industry and discipline. Serrano stated the point succinctly in *My House*: "Thrift should be the normal regimen of all homes, rich or poor. ... There are people who claim that thrift is proof of inferiority. Others refuse to economize in order to appear rich. These ideas are gravely mistaken." She went on to chastise women who spent "hours and hours" beautifying themselves, neglecting their children. These women should not ignore their appearance, of course, because their "social condition" demanded more of them than of "working-class women or women of the people." Nevertheless, Serrano attempted to persuade her gentle readers against excessive exhibition and vanity, too often the result of caring more for what neighbors said than for the family's comfort. The same rule applied in personal relations: "The first quality of a truly refined person is simplicity, absence of affectation. Pedantry, artifice, exaggeration bespeak an individual who does not feel at ease in a polite environment and who, as a result, pretends to qualities he does not possess."[118]

In response to those who might envy the showiness of the rich, Serrano noted that rich families were often "unbalanced." By pursuing luxury, "people of greater resources" violated the cardinal rule of domestic economy, "equilibrium in family finances." This impoverished their spiritual and moral lives, denying them a "normal life" and any real sense of "distinction and elegance."[119] Accordingly, she censured women who worked outside the home to pursue "condemnable luxury and superfluous display." Wealth was not necessary to happiness, for even "modest lives" could be happy. There was instead a "middle way, a minimum necessary so that the family can maintain itself with decency."[120]

In Serrano's idealized view of the domestic sphere order, discipline, and equilibrium were the shibboleths. Religion, she insisted, was indispensable, though principally as a standard of right conduct.[121] Homes in which these traits reigned, through the heroic efforts of donas de casa, enjoyed comfort, tranquillity, stability, and a "sound morality." "Order is a treasure," wrote Serrano. "In the well-cared-for home, things take on greater value, everything is elevated and one has the impression of comfort, security, and elegance."[122] Or as one magazine put it, "It is precisely in the intimacy of the home that the order or disorder of our spirit is revealed."[123] The homes of the rich knew only disharmony, disorder, and disorganization, concluded Serrano, for while the poor could not help themselves, the rich were given over to ostentation, rending the harmony of their homes, and producing disordered children.[124]

The most striking aspect of this language is the sense that people of moderate means could create home lives morally and spiritually superior to those of the "capricious" rich.[125] In these manuals order and discipline were interior traits attained through hard work and application rather than through money. What mattered was the "psychological state of the individual," not possessions; thus Serrano counseled her readers to be "optimistic and try to see the world through the prism of good spirits. Happiness is to be found within, not without."[126] This was best done at home, a space, as much imagined as real, set off from the turbulence of economic competition, politics, and class struggle outside. For in Serrano's words, the home was a refuge where the family could "choose its relationships, determine its own program for life, and ensure the proper upbringing of children by avoiding futile and pernicious contacts with society."[127]

The importance of the advice proffered in these books and magazines is not that it somehow represented a more authentically middle-class conception of life. Many persisted in their "instinct to imitation," not infrequently eschewed frugality, and often ignored well-established traditions. Still, it would be hard to deny what was implicit in the advice itself: that middle-class families faced a real dilemma in how best to maintain a respectable home under the constraint of tight budgets. In this way housekeeping advice laid bare the inner tensions of middle-class economic and social lives and at the same time provided donas de casa with a model to ground their domestic world amidst a swirl of desires and fears. As in Sra. Dupré's novels, husbands doubtless became angry, despondent, and drunk when they could not advance another rung in their careers, families lived in fear of losing the house, sons longed for great wealth or contented themselves with modest aspirations. And long-suffering women like Dona

Lola tried to hold the outside world at bay through hard work, will, and sacrifice, embodying the ceaseless drama of people who seemed never quite sure of themselves.

Despite, or perhaps because of, this insecurity the home was also where middle-class people learned to recognize and negotiate social difference and distinction. Serrano stressed the imperative of knowing proper rules of etiquette, manners, and social conduct and of understanding where different people were placed "within the social hierarchy."[128] Similarly, columns in women's magazines taught readers "social rules," so that they would know how inferiors should address superiors and vice versa, suggesting confusion over social place.[129] While this meant that middle-class people generally owed a certain deference to their superiors, it also meant that their intermediate position in the hierarchy was relatively secure vis-à-vis those below them. Thus, if the housewife who "work[ed] hard, roughening her hands, cooking, etc." had to be told not to "feel shame before the great ladies of society," she could at least demand deference from her servant.[130]

A soap ad that appeared in O Cruzeiro in 1950 intimates the stakes in this relationship.[131] A dark-skinned women in typical Bahiana dress sits on a stool in the kitchen. On a step ladder the white dona de casa holds a jack hammer to the top of the servant's head. A large caption reads: "Soft water on hard stone. . . . " Below the text continues, "If your maid doesn't know how to read, she will at least know how to recognize figures. Teach her, repeat to her, insist that she buy legitimate PLATINO soap, the only one that has a 'system of compensated alkalinity,' with the picture of the lighthouse stamped on the bar."

All that separated as well as joined middle-class employers and their servants is set out in this ad. The maid is illiterate and depicted as none too bright. Black and dressed in the traditional garb of a Bahiana rather than a uniform or clothes more practical for the dirty work of cleaning, she is an emblem of a backward-looking, African, and therefore unmodern Brazil. The dona de casa, on the other hand, white, literate, and well dressed, wields the tools of modernity to crack open the hard head of her social inferior, an act that violently inflects the injunction to "teach" the maid how to buy the proper, scientifically adjusted soap.

This tableau hints at the tensions inherent in the middle-class dona de casa's role as employer of a maid. On the one hand, race, class, and modernity were tightly knotted with the intimacy of home life, where the markers of an unstable hierarchy favored the employer over the servant. Beyond obvious racial and class advantages this symbolic dona de casa is a partner in a modernizing project through her traditional relationship to the maid. Yet by employing a jack hammer, she is engaged in manual labor, which devalues her contribution vis-à-vis more respectable, nonmanual work performed by the husband, whose income pays for the maid as well as the soap. Moreover, despite her social ascendancy over the servant, this dona de casa could not escape being seen to be a woman of modest means—as evidenced by the fact that she could only afford to hire a black maid rather than the white servants preferred by elites.

Donas de casa's fierce intimacy with the fine workings of social difference put them in the position of presiding over the process by which children learned hierarchy. Sra. Dupré's fictional family in *There Were Six of Us* reveals some of the subtle ways this message could be communicated—and garbled. In one instance older brother Carlos upbraids the younger Alfrêdo and tattles on him to their mother when he finds out that Alfrêdo's preferred friends are *moleques*, dark-skinned street urchins. Alfrêdo's obtuseness to so fundamental a division mystifies and troubles other family members. When Alfrêdo asks his mother if he can invite these friends over for dinner, twelve-year-old Carlos becomes apoplectic: "They don't even know how to eat at the table. I'll throw them out of here!"[132] In a gallant, if Quixotic, egalitarian retort Alfrêdo tries to defend his pals, insisting to Carlos that "they are as good as you are! Maybe better." In another instance Alfrêdo shows just how out of step he is with his family. When asked what he wants for Christmas, he first says a car. After his father explains, not without a hint of shame, that the family cannot afford a car, the lad asks for a soccer ball. His younger brother Julinho immediately censures him for wanting a gift to share with his little urchin friends. When finally Alfrêdo asks for a tool kit, his siblings all laugh at him and take up a collective chant: "Look at the mechanic. There's the mechanic."[133]

Alfrêdo could not reconcile himself to his intermediate position: he yearned for that which his family could not afford or would not accept. Signally unaware of the proper attitude to take in relation to social inferiors, he simply did not understand, as did everyone else in the family, why his choice of friends or gifts was objectionable. Or worse, if he did understand, he represented a willful challenge to the notion that hierarchical difference was an unquestionable element of the social order.

This same abiding sense of hierarchy could at times be turned against the middle class in very public and highly symbolic ways. A 1939 article in *Diretrizes* described Rio's carnival in sociological terms, comparing the "carnival of the rich" to the "carnival of the middle class" to the "carnival of the people."[134] The article situated middle-class revelry between that of elites, which erred only in being a bit too showy, and the more authentic carnival of "blacks, mulattos, and proletarians":

> If the carnival of the rich is a celebration—a celebration admirable for its good taste at certain elite dances, for a touch of malice, for a certain subtle disorderliness and above all for the magnificent beauty of the women among whom there are some surprising specimens of the human species in full splendor of capitalist grace—the carnival of the poor is more profound, oceanic.

In stark contrast, middle-class carnival was the celebration of "cheap costumes, yellow shirts, and sailors' hats" that had the "least tradition and creativity of them all." For the carnival of the "small property owner ... public functionary, commercial employee, or intellectual worker" indulged "the most facile poetry and the music of little marches and low-grade sambas, without any flights of fantasy, without any artistic creativity of any sort. The whole thing is made through very plain, flat, and mediocre improvisation, with a clearly middle-class content." As represented here, the middle class possessed few cultural merits, limited as they were by their resources and their inherently unimaginative tastes. According to this one author, at least, they had neither the money to display true refinement nor the spirit to create something truly meaningful. Incapable of reproducing elite culture, they were banished as well from the realm of the popular to a cultural limbo.[135]

IN DEMOCRITO DE Castro e Silva's novel *Middle Class* a young schoolteacher, Lúcia, decries the middle class as "an unhappy class, because it cannot be rich and must not be poor; those people are obliged to remain in the middle, unable to flee to the extremes. . . . The middle class is a horrible thing."[136] While these words flow from Lúcia's frustration at not being able to attend fancy balls where the better people meet, her exasperation is of a piece with the wider dilemma middle-class men and women faced during the 1930s and 1940s.

For Lúcia, to be middle class was to look in two social directions at once, above and below, in a context of promise and limitation. In the aggregate, middle-class people had disposable income, which enabled them to enjoy and aspire to many of the goods that, until recently, had been available only to the rich. In consumption, then, they discovered a further means of distinguishing themselves from those below. The material expressions of these aspirations were shaped by the torrent of advertising that flowed through middle-class lives in this period. The ads, the products they hawked, and the images they portrayed betoken a consumerist culture that compassed northward toward the United States without ceasing to be distinctively Brazilian. In other words, the consumption of manufactured goods represented the gearing of concerns for status in a hierarchical culture with the mechanics of mass-produced desire.*

Not surprisingly many got carried away. Having "learned to expect a higher standard of living than they can actually afford," as an American anthropologist characterized the Brazilian middle class of the 1950s, such consumers found indebtedness a common feature of middle-class life.[137] In this arena origins mattered little. Whether déclassé or recently risen, whether from the interior or from abroad, small victories were possible in a world where consumption was a form of competition. But the tug of war between small incomes and greater need strained lives. Pulled in two directions, middle-class Brazilians remained deeply insecure about their place in society. And so, in collective and public expressions they stressed the naturalness of their ascendance over the working class precisely because their position was so tenuous.

They strove to do so in the domain of home and family as well. Despite the growing number of women who worked at outside jobs, family and home remained the defining experience for middle-class women. The tight knot of market forces, straitened budgets, new opportunities, and concerns for hierarchy and status determined the middle-class dona de casa's lot: to work at the tangle, loosening here, cinching there, without ever being able to undo it altogether. By struggling to reconcile aspirations and budgetary limitations, by demanding deference from the maid, by raising children to recognize social difference, donas de casa, even in the face of growing gender tensions, were bound with their collar-and-tie husbands in a community of interests oriented to reproducing a middle-class way of life.

---

*This change cannot be likened to what Jackson Lears has called the historical process that gave rise to a "therapeutic ethos" in the United States. Lears's argument depends on a combination of a specific brand of individualism, a certain level of affluence, the deflection of religious sentiment, and the perceived collapse of a work ethic. See Lears. In Brazil the culture of consumption arose with the persistence of patronage amidst an ever more deeply entrenched market individualism, a rising appreciation for the virtues and indispensability of work locked in the same embrace with a disdain for manual labor, the continuing relevance of hierarchy in a social order increasingly infused with egalitarian expectations, and a distinct anxiety rooted in what I have called the predicament of promise amidst crisis. The contrast is not only a reminder that consumer culture, however universal it may at times seem, must be rooted in historical specificities. It hints as well that the culture of consumption, broadly understood, may be more complicated than examination of any one national experience permits.

Advice manuals and magazines suggest that donas de casa were the symbolic focus of an emerging sensibility regarding the role of home and family amidst the opportunities and dislocations of modern life and growing anxieties over the tensions of a class society. As market forces weakened the binding power of patriarchal authority, "habits of thrift" and "moral discipline" centered on the home became watchwords of an idealized middle-class life that continued to define women's roles in terms of their relationship to the home.[138] Notions of order, equilibrium, and morality may have been honored as much in the breach as in practice, but they were values middle-class people could take as their own by imagining that most working-class families, lacking resources, and most rich families, with too many, could never really live up to so high a moral standard.

6

Approaching the People

ON MAY 29, 1930, four months before the series of military and political upheavals that came to be known as the Revolution of 1930, *O Estado de São Paulo*, São Paulo's major newspaper, published a political manifesto. From exile in Buenos Aires, Luís Carlos Prestes, darling of the urban press, charismatic leader of the Prestes Column, which had tramped 25,000 kilometers through Brazil's backlands preaching revolution against the oligarchy and fighting the country's best generals to a running stalemate, broke with the liberalism that had defined his political stance as a spokesman for *Tenentismo* throughout the 1920s. Rejecting the "anodyne program" and "panacea" of reformism, he put class at the heart of his political analysis. Only a government of "workers," he wrote, was "capable of smashing the privileges of those who dominate."[1]

Many middle-class Cariocas and Paulistanos who had pinned their hopes on Prestes's earlier reformism were bewildered by his *volte-face*. Just months before he had declined to run for president under the Communist party's banner precisely because he thought their platform dangerous and too extremist.[2] Now he had taken up their cause. It was a betrayal of the first order. Alongside headlines about "Conflict between Capital and Labor in Germany" and reports about Stalin's growing influence in the Soviet Union, and in the face of a gathering social crisis in Brazil, editorials in the mainstream press registered their "surprise, astonishment, disappointment, and deception."[3]

Most Tenentes could not accompany Prestes on his radical path. Juarez Távora, one of Prestes's original comrades, set out his reasoning in an open letter responding to the May manifesto.[4] Távora denied the political relevance of class in opposing Brazil's entrenched oligarchy. He agreed with Prestes that "revolution" had to be more than getting rid of "bad men."[5] The system had gone wrong. It was necessary to "sanitize politics, eliminate the climate of corruption that envelops us." But, he added, the answer did not lie in "inverting the order of things—by the systematic annihilation of the bourgeoisie and the universal ascendance of the proletariat." The revolution was not to be a "privilege of one class," but rather a "common and universal heritage."

The exchange between Prestes and Távora stood for a wider debate within Brazilian society at the time—what role class was to play in politics. Prestes sought to establish class conflict as the fundamental premise of political reality. Távora stuck with the Tenentista sensibility that had taken shape over the 1920s, a universalist appeal to justice, morality, and reform. His position was rooted in a reaction against the oligarchy, not in an explicit struggle over the meaning of class in society. He rejected Prestes's dichotomous and conflictual vision of society in favor of "moralizing" a "corrupt" system to produce "social equilibrium." Claiming the moral high ground between contending forces, his political script called for a revolution of the undifferentiated "people" rather than of sharply divided classes.

This stance became the dominant ideological strain within Tenentismo after the October Revolution. Rhetoric, however, was not matched by political action. Before the revolution a promise of wider political participation had seemed reasonable and realistic, perhaps especially to those in an emergent urban middle class. The only possible counterweight to the power of rural *coronéis* to mobilize dependents on behalf of official candidates was the mass of voters concentrated in the cities. Higher urban literacy rates—by as much as three to one over the countryside—had the potential to make all the difference in an electorate limited to those who could read. After the revolution broader participation began to seem more risky. Ousted from political control, the Paulista oligarchy was far from powerless. They retained enormous economic resources and maintained a tight rein on politics in the countryside. The problem for the revolution's victors was to prevent the losers from regaining power. From their perspective the election of 1930, which had sparked the October Revolution, proved that an urban voting base was not yet enough to overcome fraud and vote manipulation in the countryside in national elections. In this situation open politics easily came to seem a threat to the new regime.

An editorial in *Correio da Manhã*, Rio's main newspaper, in November 1932 captured a further consideration militating against a broadening of political participation after the revolution. Among the Old Republic's many failings, intoned the paper gravely, was that its leaders had not understood a fundamental fact about modern society: "Where there is labor, where there is capital, there is, inevitably, the social question. It would be foolish to deny the fact."[6] And while the rest of the world had wakened to confront the issue, Brazil continued to sleep.

The urgency of this piece grew from the fear that organized workers might not prove as pliant as many had hoped. During the first half of the 1920s labor unions had been repressed into quiescence after the strikes of 1917–21. By the mid-1920s the labor movement had all but vanished from the streets and from the news. Newspaper readers through 1927 might easily have concluded that militant labor in Brazil had died in the cradle, mercifully strangled by firm police measures. The first hint this was not so came with a small number of strikes in Rio and São Paulo in 1926. During the next six years the number ratcheted up steadily: ten in 1928 to twenty in 1932.[7] To make matters worse, with the collapse of global markets, long lines of unemployed in the world's capitals were daily fare in Brazilian newspapers in the early 1930s. Communism seemed to be advancing everywhere, as evidenced by the actions of "terrorists" in Spain.[8] The specter of Bolshevism had even darkened Latin America's threshold: coup attempts in Chile and Peru portended the "nightmare of a Communist government on this continent."[9] At home tens of thousands of workers idled in Rio and São Paulo, nearly 2 million in the country as a whole. Foreign agitators and "political opportunists," said the newspapers, were preying on the Brazilian "working class," a "manipulable mass" easily seduced by dangerous pamphlets and books.[10] Corrupt elites exacerbated the problem through indifference and political infighting.

Politics after November 1930 consisted of efforts to resolve the dilemma of revanchist oligarchs and militant workers. By 1932 the consensus among antagonists appears to have been an indefinite suspension of democratic processes. In a sense it was an outcome implicit in the forces that had given rise to the Revolution in the first place, dissident elites and Tenentes who opposed the oligarchy and offered the possibility of broader political participation only grudgingly. Between 1930 and 1932 the political arena had become a free-for-all. Lacking a political base of their own and less experienced at Machiavellian maneuver than elites—whether victors or vanquished—the Tenentes gradually came apart. By late 1932 they were politically isolated. Individual Tenentes scattered to the winds. With them the only force to have represented middle-class interests and concerns, however obliquely and incompletely, dissipated.

Middle-class political experimentation during the 1930s was a reaction to this abandonment and to the growing perils of class. Would-be spokesmen for the middle class cast about for a formula that could fix their political role in a postoligarchic Brazil, a formula that would at once hold fast against a return of oligarchic rule, head off class conflict, and give representatives of middle-class interests a measure of influence. Any other resolution, they sensed, would push them to the margins of political debate—or perhaps force them to seek refuge there.

The Middle Class as "People"

Virginio Santa Rosa's *The Meaning of Tenentismo* emerged from this chaotic political situation. The essay represents a watershed in Brazilian political thought and discourse: it was the first analysis ever to explore the meaning of a major political event from an explicitly middle-class perspective and the first to impute meaningful political action to the middle class. While he was certainly the most explicit, Santa Rosa was not alone in his efforts to articulate what one historian has referred to as a "petit-bourgeois critique" of the Brazilian social order.[11] *The Meaning of Tenentismo* was part of a series of political and social essays published in the early thirties trying to make sense of postoligarchic politics.[12]

For Santa Rosa the key to the Revolution of 1930 was a new social and political force, the *pequena burguesia* (petite bourgeoisie). Stumbling over terms of unstable meaning, Santa Rosa argued that the emergent "middle class of the cities"—those who made their livings in the collar-and-tie occupations that had grown up with industrial and commercial expansion after 1900—were the driving force of Tenentismo. Together, "workers of the factories, rural laborers, the almost unconscious outcasts of the countryside," and the urban middle class made up the "masses, composed of the middle class and the proletariat." Recognizing the middle class's weak "associative spirit," the Tenentes had responded to an "imperious necessity" to represent the "urban middle class . . . possibly, their first political expression."[13]

Unlike the Tenentes and even their elite allies in the Liberal Alliance, Santa Rosa referred only infrequently to "the people." This was not merely a blindness to the role of inclusive language in drawing wide support. Rather, Santa Rosa's analysis focused on the petite bourgeoisie and middle classes as political actors unto themselves. By embracing what he characterized as an unpoliticized urban proletariat, a tutelary rural poor, and a politicized urban middle class within the term "petite bourgeoisie," Santa Rosa was able to articulate *the people* within the petite bourgeoisie rather than the other way around. In doing so, he placed the urban middle classes at the center of a populist project in which the people-as-petite-bourgeoisie actively sought its "political and economic rights."

The apparent equality among the various elements of Santa Rosa's "petite bourgeoisie" did not pass rhetoric. Whereas he saw in the urban middle class a group "joined by common interests" involving their work, status as consumers, "anxieties and aspirations," exclusion from the political system, and "economic subjugation" to "agricultural and industrial plutocracies," he dismissed impoverished urban and rural workers out of hand.[14] Rural workers were "uncultivated masses . . . incapable of understanding their own rights." As a consequence, the oligarchy had easily manipulated them in order to "crush the middle classes, suffocating their aspirations." He slighted urban workers by failing to mention the labor movement and by arguing for a "middle-class program equally distant from bourgeois and proletarian extremes." In practical terms this meant greater access to the levers of state power, a "moderate, petit-bourgeois capitalism" of professional associations, cooperatives, income guarantees, labor legislation, greater consumption opportunities, and an agrarian reform that would put an end to the *latifúndio* (landed estate).[15] Workers would benefit but they would not participate centrally in the process of political change. In short, Santa Rosa conceived a middle-class political project in terms of a broad coalition that included elements of the lower classes—"the fickle multitude that can be exploited"—by subordinating them to a politically mobilized and self-conscious middle class.

Santa Rosa harbored no illusions about the future of middle-class political influence. The oligarchy was formidable and the "urban middle class" too easily "bewitched by the illusion of democracy." Liberal democracy had been found wanting everywhere else in the world and in Brazil had never been more than a facade for oligarchic domination. Worse, said Santa Rosa, the "eternal confusion" of party politics might sow the seeds of an "anarchic future," like Germany's or Spain's.[16] Only a "new democratic mentality" of "organized public opinion" and councils of experts, he concluded, could bring an unruly society to heel by eliminating universal suffrage and representative bodies and with them political professionalism and the danger of social revolution.[17]

The historical meaning of Santa Rosa's essay must be parsed carefully. Certainly, he was not the spokesman for anything like a coherent, middle-class political movement. The importance of *The Meaning of Tenentismo*, rather, lies in its having identified the middle class as a category relevant to politics. Yet in the complex maneuvering and uncertainty of the immediate postrevolutionary years, efforts by middle-class people to assert themselves in politics would be, as Santa Rosa had feared, oriented along a new axis of political division, that between right and left.[18]

Wearied by the ineffectual politics of a two-year-old revolution that had promised much and delivered little, many who made their livings from the collar-and-tie sector were electrified when they read Plínio Salgado's manifesto founding the Brazilian Integralist Action (AIB) in October 1932. Son of a pharmacist and a schoolteacher, former member of São Paulo's Republican party, former supporter of the Tenentes, and author of two modestly successful political novels, Salgado proclaimed a set of principles that seemed directly to address the nation's gravest problems: the failure of politics old and new, national disunity, class struggle, the threat of "internationalist communism," imperialist greed, and a "bourgeoisie enraptured" by European civilization. Promising to restore "hierarchy, confidence, order, peace, and respect" through "authority," the manifesto proposed interior conversion through spiritual and moral evolution in lieu of violent upheaval.[19]

Salgado's message excited the imaginations of tens of thousands of collar-and-tie employees and professionals throughout Brazil in the years after 1932 and brought many of them into active, organized politics for the first time.[20] Many others who, after the revolution, had been cut loose from the patronage politics of the Old Republic, may also have found a political home in the AIB. Those who joined donned green shirts, wore a Sigma arm band (the sign of the integral), saluted with outstretched hand, attended rallies, heard fiery orators, marched in well-orchestrated parades, posted handbills, and engaged in running street brawls with communists. At the national and regional levels the leadership consisted principally of liberal professionals, writers, university professors, public functionaries, journalists, students, and middle-rank military officers. Small shopkeepers and collar-and-tie employees in the public and private sectors were also prominent in the leadership of local urban chapters. The rank and file generally hailed from the same sectors, with a predominance of middle-class types and about 20 percent urban manual workers.[21] By one estimate nearly 40 percent of the members had secondary-school educations, and one-quarter boasted a *faculdade* degree.[22] By 1934 the AIB claimed 180,000 active members, mostly in larger cities, and 300,000 to 400,000 by 1937. Though the number was probably closer to half that, Integralism represented the largest mass political movement in the history of Brazil to that time.[23]

Lists of occupations do not tell the whole story about those who became Integralists. Activists tended to be young—roughly 80 percent were under 35—and virtually all had occupations and levels of education equal to or exceeding their parents'. Most of the 50 percent or so who had risen above their parents came from small-property-owning, artisan, or petty collar-and-tie families, many of them immigrants a generation earlier.[24] In other words, Integralism's core constituency appears to have been young, upwardly mobile, white men with prospects in life.

Their desire to keep social distance between themselves and urban workers created a dilemma for Integralism's ideologues. Salgado, for instance, assured followers that despite the primacy of spiritual over material concerns, an individual member might legitimately "take advantage of the benefits made possible by growing technological progress and by the increase and prosperity of national production," since "aspirations of material well-being" were "just and unalterable."[25] Aspirations are one thing; reality another. Most of the rank and file were hardly miserable, but most also did not possess great property or enjoy power or prestige. A doctrine focused exclusively on their material situation could easily have fallen flat. This is one reason so many could respond enthusiastically to a political creed prizing intangible over material signs of success, one that called on them to judge themselves and others according to "intellectual and moral" worth rather than according to criteria of "greater or lesser fortune."[26]

Moreover, these were people primed for a spiritual message. A sizable majority appear to have been practicing Catholics who attended mass at least once a week and claimed that religion was of great importance in their lives.[27] Yet the hierarchical church remained ambivalent toward the movement.[28] According to Catholic intellectual Alceu Amoroso Lima, Integralists too often put their political loyalties above their religious consciences. At times, said Lima, Integralists had criticized the church itself for cleaving to a disguised form of liberalism. In light of the deep Catholic critique of liberalism, this was a gross exaggeration. Nevertheless, Lima and other Catholic writers skeptical of Integralism recognized its close affinities to Catholic social doctrine and assured professing Catholics that they might don the green shirt without risking priestly condemnation.[29]

The main contours of the Integralist program are well known: virulent anticommunism, nationalism as a means of unifying society and liberating Brazil from imperialists, a strong state to curb the excesses of partisan politics and avoid an extremist revolution, legislative representation by professional category (corporatism) in lieu of corrupt, "plutocratic" political parties, measures to protect the family and morality, spiritual revolution as the basis of a "true democracy" in place of a bankrupt liberal democracy, and distrust of capitalism as the basis for social order.[30] Most of these themes were not new, but never before had they been gathered under the banner of a political organization catering to the urban middle class. What grounded this cluster of attitudes and ideas was a vision of the relationship among social classes.

In his 1933 pamphlet *What Is Integralism?* Salgado located the middle class at the epicenter of the political universe, between "the money men, the men of great enterprises" and a dispossessed "proletariat." As against the "hatred" of these two classes for each other, a "cultivated and elevated spirit" rooted in "the intelligence and culture, the morality and spirit that create human dignity" enabled the middle class to stand above "petty quarrels, [turning] instead to the higher destinies of the human creature." The significance of this language is that it expressed social and political difference in class, though not exclusively in Marxist, terms.[31] Where capitalists had only their "interests" and proletarians only their misery, the middle class, because of its immaterial qualities—intelligence and culture, morality and spirit—was pure enough to bear an ethereal nationalism, to stand for the *pátria* (fatherland) as neither of the other classes could.

This idea of a lyrical middle class served a clear political function. Recognizing class as a fact of Brazil's capitalist society, Integralist ideologues insisted that the divide was, in fact, a deeper one between the civilized middle class, which sought to rise above greed and pettiness, and the soulless, immoral barbarians of capitalism on either side. Integralism aimed less at concrete political gains than at promoting "an internal revolution in each person, a transformation of everyone's way of thinking."[32] By absorbing class within an all-embracing "spiritual revolution" stressing moral over material change, harmony over conflict, unity over division, Integralism denied the legitimacy of class warfare. By identifying Integralism's central tenets so closely with the idea of the middle class, ideologues and orators could speak to a middle-class constituency without having to invoke the middle class explicitly.

This is what made it possible for Integralist leaders, like the Tenentes and Santa Rosa before them, to address "the people" almost exclusively without alienating their middle-class rank and file. Depicted as tutelary, the "working mass" was "oppressed, in agony, but without consciousness of its own moral dignity, oscillating in the demagogic winds blown by rebels and losers."[33] This was why working people could not be left to themselves in the political realm. They had to be led by those who could imagine themselves a cut above workers. Integralist ideologue Miguel Reale put it bluntly: "The people still cannot be allowed to intervene in resolving political problems, except perhaps as a source of the common ideal, but never with the powers of self-government."[34]

Nor was this merely a reactionary call to restore or preserve hierarchy, for workers' "incapacity" could, in principle, be remedied. Over time education would allow workers to participate more meaningfully in politics and achieve equality, not of condition but of stake in the nation. And so Integralist wives and daughters went into the *favelas* to teach poor people proper hygiene, morals, literacy, and national feeling, setting them on the way to meaningful political participation after a period of tutelage. Here "the people" were the broad masses of poor and working-class Brazilians who could not yet be trusted with political power, led by a virtuous middle class with no interest other than national unity.

While the rhetoric was meant to be inclusive, labor's place in the movement was carefully circumscribed by a middle-class outlook. Given the exploitation to which workers were subject, militancy was understandable, if unfortunate. Strikes themselves, however, were counterproductive, a consequence of the "red delirium produced by proletarian despair," wrote Reale.[35] As a result, labor organizations had no place in the AIB, since Integralism would pursue "social justice" on behalf of the working class. Workers should abandon militancy and dream of "rising according to [their] vocation and just desires. We intend to provide the means by which everyone can, through their capabilities, by their work and by their perseverance, always climb a little higher." Rather than the "cowardice" of communism or the "submission" of liberal democracy, said Salgado, "we teach the doctrine of courage, of hope, of love for country, society, life . . . for the just ambition to progress, to possess goods, to improve oneself, and to raise a family." Indeed, "it is possible even for the most modest worker to attain a higher financial or intellectual position."[36] The resonances with the everyday concerns of middle-class life were palpable. At the same time, the people were seen darkly through the thick lens of anticommunism. Workers might be pitied as individuals for the exploitation they suffered and respected for the work they did. As a class they were dangerous, because their innocent and untutored minds were easily turned to the unwholesome doctrines of Marx and Lenin. Communism was a "false mirage" that would require workers to give up family, dignity, country, and "spiritual aspirations." Integralism, by contrast, would secure "social justice" and reconcile workers to their place in society.[37]

This narrow and simplistic vision of the working class was paralleled by an unfavorable view of dominant groups. Where workers were dangerous because susceptible to "exotic doctrines," the "plutocratic oligar-chy" and the "bourgeoisie" were "egoistic" and "drunk on the endan-gered civilizations of Europe and the United States." The "individualistic" thrust of liberal-democratic capitalism had given rise to class struggle and communism, so that the upper classes were alienated from all that was good and honest about the "Brazilian people."[38]

Integralism proffered no easy solution to the problem of powerful, mo-nied interests. Education and literacy could turn the working class away from militancy. There was no comparable program of reform to combat economic elites. The only alternative was to create a counterweight to their power. Liberal-democratic practices were not an option, since elites had corrupted them. Only an inner or spiritual revolution against capital-ist materialism would suffice. But this could not be a revolution limited to the souls of middle-class Integralists. Rather, they would be the means by which workers, permanently mobilized as a political force, would come to embody the spirit of a more just and peaceful society. The perils inherent in such a project explain the tight entwining of the people, national con-science, and morality—the only strands of social experience the bourgeoi-sie could not control through money.

The tensions of Integralist ideology reflected middle-class insecurities and aspirations. The egoism of those above had pushed Brazil to the abyss. Integralism's answer was to make common cause with those below in the name of national progress and social peace, despite the risks of such a project. This could be accomplished if middle-class people would live up to Integralism's high expectations and if workers would accept their place in the scheme of things and abandon the politics of division. Only thus could a "people, strong and unified" be forged and the clanging discord of Brazilian society be harmonized. In other words, appeals to the people can be seen as part and parcel of an effort to confront the dilemmas of a class-divided society without accepting class struggle as the organizing principle of social and political life. Outside Integralism, the people were dangerous and unappealing. Within it a lyrical middle class could refine workers of their coarser qualities, transforming them into a spiritual counterforce to a degenerate ruling class.[39]

The political uncertainties that had given birth to Integralism remained unresolved by the mid-1930s. After defeat of the São Paulo revolt in 1932, a constituent assembly convened to draft a new constitution, one of the demands of the vanquished Paulistas. Debates went on for months. A final version received approval in early 1934. The new charter represented a victory for those who favored centralization over the loose federalism of the Old Republic. It also sought to address aspects of the social question by creating a system of corporatist representation within the broader framework of a liberal-democratic congress. Specifically, 350 state representatives were joined by fifty at-large deputies representing employers, employees, liberal professionals, and public functionaries. Employers and employees—of these, only a minority represented manual workers—took the lion's share of the seats, and professionals and functionaries were allotted three each.

Despite this effort to blaze a new path for Brazilian politics, the 1934 constitution showed the strains of an unsettled contest for political supremacy after the Revolution of 1930. The arrangement provided ample space for political maneuver by the still powerful coronéis who retained control over the rural electorate and by São Paulo oligarchs who had not given up on their effort to roll back the revolution. These forces combined to stymie reform. President Getúlio Vargas and his coterie, in turn, manipulated the corporate representatives to try to hold the coronéis and Paulistas at bay. The result was stalemate. Nor did passage of the 1934 constitution mark a dramatic departure from past electoral practices. The congressional campaigns of late 1934 and early 1935 were not only antagonistic, especially in races between pro- and anti-Vargas candidates, but marred by violence and fraud. Prominent leaders, such as Osvaldo Aranha, grew tired of the moil, accusing politicians of being "masochists and sadists."[40]

Amidst this political confusion and the frustration it engendered, a new organization took shape around a middle-class membership. Throughout the first half of the 1930s, except for the Communist party, the Integralists remained the only political organization to seek a mass following at the national level. This situation changed with the founding of the National Liberation Alliance (ANL) on March 12, 1935.[41] Though the ANL's program lacked Integralism's more systematic ideology, it promised that a "popular government" would "liberate" Brazil by nationalizing the assets of "imperialist" companies, put an end to Brazil's "feudalism" through agrarian reform, guarantee full personal freedoms, increase salaries, and, finally, create and enforce adequate labor laws.[42] The Alliance also declared itself the unrelenting foe of fascism and Integralism. It invited all Brazilians, regardless of religious, political, or philosophical persuasion, to join the popular struggle for Brazil's liberation.

This vague program won the enthusiasm of considerable numbers of middle-class people who felt excluded from politics and who had been searching for some form of independent political expression other than Integralism. One contemporary reported ecstatically that by May 1935 the Alliance's membership rolls were growing by 3,000 a day, or roughly 90,000 a month. Others reported even greater numbers of adherents, up to 50,000 in Rio just in the first few days of the organization's existence.[43] At the time of its closure by government decree in July 1935, a scant four months after its founding, the movement claimed around 400,000 members, though the most conservative available estimate puts the number at between 70,000 and 100,000 active, dues-paying members before being closed.[44]

In the aggregate the ANL's membership appears to have been similar to the Integralists', except that the proportion of workers among the *Aliancistas* was considerably greater. Best estimates suggest that in the Federal District and in the states of Rio de Janeiro and São Paulo over 50 percent of the Alliance's members were independent or salaried professionals, collar-and-tie employees, or students. About 40 percent were manual workers, though a fair proportion of these appear to have been independent artisans. Local chapters were usually organized geographically, by neighborhood in larger cities, or by municipality in the interior. Some took shape along occupational lines, as was the case for teachers and law professors in São Paulo, and stevedores, law and medical students, construction workers, typesetters, and doctors in Rio.[45] Working-class presence within the ANL was bolstered by close connections with a number of labor organizations, which sharply distinguished it from the Integralists, who did not welcome autonomously organized labor groups.[46] Like the Integralists, rank-and-file Aliancistas tended to be young, with 80 percent under 40 years of age. They were also overwhelmingly white and male.[47] The composition of the ANL's leadership was even closer to the Integralists'; the vast majority was drawn from the ranks of independent and salaried professionals and from among white-collar employees and students.[48]

A renewed crisis in middle-class personal finances appears to have been crucial to the enthusiasm with which the ANL was met between March and July 1935, the period of its legal operation. Deflation in the early 1930s had reversed by 1934, and the cost of living in Rio was rising, 15 percent in 1935.[49] Collar-and-tie unemployment, or the fear of it, appears to have been running high, especially among salaried professionals. Those who spoke for the ANL sought to put the crisis to good end. *A Manhã*, the Alliance's unofficial newspaper published in Rio, exhorted the "impoverished middle class of small shopkeepers and small farmers; the armed forces; scientists, technicians, teachers, liberal professionals, such as doctors, lawyers, engineers, and intellectuals, honest journalists, and students in secondary school and university" to become involved in the anti-imperialist movement alongside equally impoverished workers.[50] Other leftist newspapers did the same, identifying the "pauperized petite bourgeoisie" as a group to be mobilized and organized.[51] A publication aimed at young people issued a call to students who "felt suffocated by the strait jacket of misery and extreme privations to which they are subject, some impeded from attending school; others forced to interrupt their studies; all despairing of securing their future."[52]

Occasionally, this strategy of trying to identify the middle class with the working class through shared suffering was reversed, so that the working class was assimilated to a lifestyle of middle-class aspirations. The point was to suggest, both to workers and to middle-class people, that at bottom they had common interests, or at least common aspirations. For example, Brasil Gerson, a journalist for *A Manhã*, wrote a column in June 1935 entitled "Women on the Move," urging working-class women to join the ANL in liberating Brazil from imperialists and *latifundistas*. Once that was accomplished, he assured his readers,

> you will have your home with a radio and a bathroom, and the factories will be inviting and there will be good child care, where, while you work, the children will study and play and grow up healthy and happy, so that you will be proud. You will be able to go to the theater, to the club, to the cinema, because child care—very modern, very efficient—will be everywhere. Finally, you will be master of your own destiny and you will be able to study, enjoy yourself, and be happy in your family.[53]

Although the easy glide from anti-imperialism to child care and a lifestyle of assured comfort and independence assumed a certain naiveté on the part of working-class women, it does reveal something of how ANL ideologues and intellectuals conceptualized the working class in political terms. Alliance handbills, circulars, and newspaper reports only infrequently addressed the middle class per se. Much like the Integralists, the ANL generally directed its appeals to "the people," or "the Brazilian people." Handbills were never more specific about the term. *A Manhã* never went any further than to list workers, the middle classes, and the army as making up the people around whom the ANL's common front was to pearl.[54] The organization called for nothing more concrete than a "popular government" oriented exclusively to the interests of the Brazilian people. The ANL's political language, in short, was vague and inclusive enough to allow people from different social classes to see in it what they wanted.

The limits of this language and of the ANL's appeal are highlighted by struggles over whether the Alliance was to embody a moderate, middle-class reformism or whether it was to be the instrument of proletarian revolution. ANL propaganda had insisted from March to July 1935 on a "necessary clarification" that the Alliance was not a political party and had no affiliation with any other political organization.[55] In particular, ANL literature vehemently denied a connection with the Communist party.[56] Initially the Communist party went along. Eager to associate itself with the organizational potential of the ANL, the party hewed to a popular-front strategy between March and July, even denying that the ANL was a Communist organization.[57] As such, there was ample reason for the average shopkeepers, public functionaries, bank clerks, and lawyers who read the ANL's literature, followed its activities, and decided whether to sympathize or join to assume that the ANL was not a Trojan horse for the communists. The people, as characterized in the Alliance's propaganda, were not a matter of the organized, militant, radical working class bent on violent revolution. It was instead an expansive term that implied a nationalist, popular, "common front" without explicit distinctions of class, except in its bugle call to oppose latifundistas and imperialists.

The veil fell away as Communist activists became more aggressive in their efforts to seize control of the ANL. The turning point came when Luís Carlos Prestes, who had joined the organization in May, gave a speech at a Rio soccer stadium on July 5, 1935. Referring interchangeably to the people and to workers, Prestes sought to radicalize the ANL. He seems to have been less concerned with programmatic content than with tone and tactics. Except for two planks regarding unexceptional urban and rural workplace issues and one insisting that Brazil's Indians be given back land taken from them centuries earlier, Prestes's proposals differed little from the ANL's program, at the core of which was agrarian reform and anti-imperialism. What marked the speech and shocked so many contemporaries, and probably many of the ANL's rank and file as well, was that Prestes, an avowed communist since the early 1930s, urged the working masses to form up behind the ANL in order to oust Vargas's regime and install a popular government.[58]

Prestes's speech threw the ANL into turmoil. It had not been cleared with the Alliance's leadership, even though he claimed to speak for the organization. The mainstream press, which for months had been alleging that the ANL was a communist front, must have seemed prescient. In June 1935 Rio's *O Globo* had published a "subversive plan" supposedly intercepted from Moscow. According to the plan, which appears to have been a fabrication, revolutionaries intended to execute noncommunist military officers on the doorsteps of their homes in an immediate postrevolutionary purge.[59] After Prestes's betrayal moderate leaders of the organization, such as ex-Tenente Hercolino Cascardo, withdrew from the ANL, refusing to support a political organization dominated by communists. In essence, Prestes's soccer-stadium speech was the moment at which the political language of the ANL's popular struggle, open enough to accommodate a reformist middle class, became that of proletarian revolution.

Shortly after the speech the government outlawed the ANL and closed it down under a national security law passed earlier in 1935. The police stepped up repression, arresting hundreds. The organization was forced underground. Once submerged, the ANL quickly came under control of the Communist party, sparking a general exodus of moderate middle-class rank-and-file and local leaders. The Alliance ceased, thereby, to be a mass movement.[60] Fear of repression had much to do with why members quit the organization. The fate of journalist Amadeu Amaral became fairly common, and more important, commonly feared.[61] The secret police arrested him in late July for reading an ANL manifesto out loud to a group of friends at the Café Belas Artes in downtown Rio. He was held for 48 hours, pressed for the names of other ANL members, and threatened with exile to the far reaches of Matto Grosso, "where he might just vanish."[62] Such measures can only have had a chilling effect on many who might otherwise have continued to be politically active.

Repression probably was not the whole story. Aliancistas detained by São Paulo's Social and Political Police for questioning after the ANL's closure frequently insisted that they had participated in the organization only so long as it was legal and noncommunist. While these statements were produced in an environment of potential duress, affidavits of arrested Aliancistas contain nuances and distinctions hinting at a genuine limit beyond which many middle-class members and sympathizers of the ANL were not willing to go in their political activity.

Maurício Gertel, secretary of a local chapter in the state of São Paulo, claimed that he was not an adherent of "subversive doctrines," like communism and anarchism. Insisting that the ANL's program was one of "socioeconomic reform that would not abolish the federative republic," he indicated that he would be politically active only within the limits of the law. Twenty-five-year-old federal functionary Eduardo de Araripe Sucupira admitted that he had been part of the ANL but pointed out that he had abandoned the organization as soon as it was declared illegal. Augusto Pinto, a young collar-and-tie employee at the federal credit union office in São Paulo, testified that he stopped attending meetings when the Alliance was closed but also made the unnecessary admission that he would be active again if it were ever made legal. Many others offered similar statements, hinting at the surprise these people felt on being told that they belonged to an outlawed communist organization.[63]

The ANL's radicalization culminated in November 1935. Plans had taken shape for months among Communist leaders, including Prestes. Moderate voices had long since left the organization, enabling leaders to launch an insurrection to topple the government. Between November 23 and November 27, 1935, local military units of communist sympathizers rose up in Natal, Recife, and Rio de Janeiro waving the banner of the ANL in the name of proletarian revolution. There was some fighting, but what came to be known as the *Intentona* was snuffed out with celerity by the forces of order.[64]

The government's swift action was widely cheered. For example, a group of engineers chosen to serve on an electrification commission for central Brazil opened their report in the Engineering Club's magazine by "cordially joining the unanimous applause raised by all good Brazilians ... before the judgment, decision, and energy with which legal order was reestablished."[65] More significantly, there is no evidence of popular support for the rebels. By November most of the rank and file had abandoned the ANL. As a consequence, the Alliance was only a shadow of what it had been between March and July. Even those who continued to sympathize with it were caught off guard by the revolt and refused their public support, understanding that there was no point to risking the government's heavy hand.[66]

Beyond fear of repression, many who had sympathized with or joined the ANL during its legal phase may simply have been unwilling to affiliate with it as a radical, illegal, and subversive organization. The words of one leader attempting to exculpate himself from involvement with the ANL offer some insight. Roberto Sissón, ex-Tenente and founding member of the ANL, was arrested in early 1936 for his participation in the organization. In an open letter to Congress from prison, he sought clemency for himself and two others: "We are not communists, because within the national-liberation movement, we only meaningfully expressed the specific demands of the middle classes ... and all those who depended on them, in other words, the people of the cities."[67] He made more or less the same point in a long letter of explanation to the Navy in 1937: "Belonging to the middle classes, [we founders] defended their immediate interests. Now, our immediate interests are today common to all national classes."[68]

As evidence of Sissón's state of mind these statements are highly sus-
pect.[69] As clues to a fundamentally nonradical middle-class political sensibility they are tantalizing. Tellingly Sissón denied communist sympathies
by claiming to have represented the middle class rather than the working
class. He made "the people of the cities" dependent on and subordinate to
the middle class, which embodied the national interest. Drawing on a
widely shared characterization—the idea of the middle class as social balance wheel—he assumed that members of Congress and the Navy would
understand that middle-class people, by definition, could not participate
in a communist organization or revolution. That he had represented them,
Sissón argued, was proof that he was neither a communist nor a revolutionary.

Whether or not it was true of him, for the many collar-and-tie employees and professionals who joined the ANL during its legal phase, the Alliance's attraction seems to have been that it sought to articulate a broad-
based, common-front populism that could stump for reform while avoiding social upheaval. When a civil engineer, a teacher, a journalist, a maritime captain, a commercial employee, and an office worker in the electric
company in Rio, with the support of 30 former Tenentes, sought to reacti-
vate the ANL in 1937, they exulted that the "three months of the ANL's
legality marked in Brazil the greatest political event of our times." Without once mentioning proletarian revolution, a handbill they produced
concluded that the ANL had been above all a form of *civismo* (civic reformism) that had bubbled up from "all social strata who were victims of
imperialist oppression."[70]

Less explicitly than the Integralists, then, the ANL in its legal phase put
the middle class rather than the working class at the center of a political
worldview organized around the principle of national unity. Its politics
purposely hinged on a vague sense that the people were being oppressed
by the plutocracy and forces of international capitalism rather than on
any strong notion of class. Certainly Aliancista rhetoric was more sympathetic to labor unions than Integralist ideology. But this did not translate
into a widespread willingness to subordinate middle-class political sensibilities and interests, however inchoate, to a political project defined by
communists and oriented to what was widely perceived to be an organized, militant, and revolutionary working class.

At one level the political language and programs of Integralism and the
ANL during its legal phase amounted to rival, though not altogether dis-

similar, visions of how Brazilian politics should be ordered. In different ways both movements were uneasy with the very notion of class in the context of mid-1930s Brazil. As a result, ideologues articulated their programs not in terms of a middle class, but broadly, in terms of a rhetorically inclusive people. Both, moreover, shared nationalism as the basis for overcoming social divisions, an abiding sense of plutocratic and imperialist oppression, and an aversion to working-class revolution. Both held democracy as an important political value, though they diverged on its meaning. Integralists eschewed representative democracy, preferring a political system organized along professional-corporate lines within the limits of a strong state, suffused with a spirituality liberal-democratic capitalism lacked. The ANL's rhetoric seemed more positive about conventional democratic procedures. Yet its programmatic literature was guarded, preaching "broad popular freedoms of the people" without actually specifying a political form beyond "a popular government oriented solely by the interests of the Brazilian people."[71] Finally, both were possible because the Revolution of 1930 had disrupted the tight bond between patronage and electoral process that had tied so many—and especially civil servants—to the politics of the Old Republic.[72] Cut off from the empowering dependencies of clientage, some within the middle class sought other outlets for political expression.

Despite these similarities the two groups were sharply separated by the passions of the period. Integralists saw only communism in the ANL, Aliancistas only fascism in the AIB. Each played the bogey to the other, so that their mutual antipathy was as important to defining them, if not more so, as adherence to a specific set of doctrines, perhaps especially among the rank and file.[73] They differed most fundamentally on the issue of where the middle class fit into the class politics of Brazilian society. Put another way, they parted company on the political role of the working class. Judging by the Alliance's language, those who joined the ANL seemed willing to participate in a common project with organized workers, even if ultimately they were not willing to follow them into revolution. Most Integralists were unwilling to go so far. That these two groups came to divergent conclusions suggests not that the middle class was so hopelessly fragmented as to be incapable of political expression. It speaks, rather, of the contingencies and ambiguities middle-class people faced in finding a place in the politics of a class society cloven into warring ideological camps.

"Mere Politics"

Insight into the uncertainties of political experimentation among middle-class people comes from an unsigned letter to the ANL's newspaper, *A Manhã*, in 1935. The missive describes the writer's political trajectory from the 1920s to the mid-1930s. He cut his political teeth in late-1920s São Paulo by joining the São Paulo Democratic party (PD), a mildly oppositionist, antioligarchic group dominated by dissident elites in São Paulo.[74] After the Revolution of 1930 he left the PD, because, he said, it had begun to engage in just the kind of *politicagem* (chicanery or dirty politics) that had impelled him to support the revolution in the first place. From there he migrated to Integralism in the early 1930s. Their ideas of "strong government" and "nationalist ardor" seemed plausible responses to the "confusion of the country." He later abandoned the AIB when he discovered that Plínio Salgado had been a member of the São Paulo Republican party during the 1920s, the primary organ of oligarchic political rule in the Old Republic. He felt that Salgado could not be trusted because of this association, a reason bespeaking as great a concern for the corruption of Brazilian politics as for ideology. While reassessing his commitment to the green shirts, a friend who was disillusioned with the "joke [congressional] elections of October" 1934 gave him a copy of *A Manhã*, the ANL's newspaper. He liked what he read. Again he was drawn by their nationalism, though he was also impressed with their condemnation of totalitarianism, especially since the Integralist line "'against' the bourgeoisie, 'against' imperialism, 'against' bankerism" was so much sound and fury. Shortly thereafter he joined the ANL. He refused to sign his name to the letter, because he was an employee (from textual references, probably a bank clerk), and his boss was a "passionate" supporter of the Paulista oligarchy.[75]

This letter hints at the instability of political identification among those inclined to political activity in the late 1920s and early 1930s. It suggests that for many, politics and the decision to be politically active were central elements of the process by which they identified themselves and their place in Brazil's emerging class society. This anonymous letter writer was emblematic of the fluidity and contingency of middle-class politics during the 1930s. His trajectory also bolsters the notion that a core of concerns linked Integralists and Aliancistas—nationalism, the perceived need for political reform with order, the fear of extremism, a hazy sense of oppression—concerns that under circumstances other than those of the ideologically charged 1930s might have allowed greater middle-class political cohesion than in fact resulted.

The sort of enthusiasm for political engagement represented by the tens of thousands who joined the AIB and the ANL, among them the anonymous letter writer, became much less common after the mid-1930s. Closure of the ANL, fear of sweeping new repressive measures, growing concern over ideological conflict, and the dysfunctions of the political system dampened the passion for political experimentation and involvement. Increasingly the pressure was to "know nothing about politics, to have nothing whatever to do with politics," in the words of Antônio Lima e Silva, a small businessman who was detained and questioned for his links to the ANL in 1935.[76] After all, ANL activists were at risk of arrest, and the Communist party had taken control of the organization. Moreover, the inclusive political language of the early Alliance had given way to the combative rhetoric of proletarian revolution.

Yet, as one militant noted in August 1935, the Communist party was not ready to abandon efforts to woo the petite bourgeoisie away from their weak-kneed "national reformism."[77] Even after the coup attempt of November 1935 the left continued to pursue the grail of middle-class mobilization. In mid-1937 the left-wing press asserted that the "Brazilian middle strata" and the "enormous petite bourgeoisie" were "exploited and oppressed" and for that reason revolutionary.[78] In the late 1930s, despite all that had happened, the Communists remained convinced that "the middle strata are being mobilized."[79] Some middle-class individuals heeded the left's call to join the people's revolution. At least in the early 1930s it was a sufficiently common occurrence among young "petit bourgeois" and students that moderate and conservative political commentators pushed for greater government efforts to keep "intellectuals" off the revolutionary road.[80] By the late 1930s, however, the Communist party's dogged insistence that the middle class as a whole was on the brink of hoisting the revolutionary banner amounted to a gargantuan exaggeration or a breathtaking miscalculation.

True, many more collar-and-tie people than manual workers appear to have participated in the Intentona of 1935 or, more accurately, to have been arrested for participating in it. At least a thousand military officers, liberal professionals, and white-collar employees were swept up in the dragnet following the revolt. Even without including military officers, collar-and-tie types appear to have outnumbered workers among those detained.[81] Still, left-wing activists and sympathizers were vastly in the minority compared with those who did not participate. Shortly before the coup the ANL's newspaper was reduced to beseeching the "popular masses" not to "desert the streets."[82] When the uprising came, it shocked the wide public, prompting one magazine read within the middle class to refer to it as "a civil war, a fratricidal struggle, a class struggle."[83]

A sense of the fear abroad in the land can be had from another middle-brow Rio magazine, *Vida Carioca*, which congratulated the government for its alacrity in quelling the rebellion. It described the events of November at hysterical pitch: "The Intentona had a vast program of bombing, firing squads, arson, and massacres" that would have led to the destruction of "lives, homes, and property" and perhaps even "sackings and dishonor."[84] Hardly surprising, then, that the most immediate and far-reaching consequence of the Intentona was a dramatic shift in favor of the government and its repressive measures against communists and all other "extremists." In essence, after November 1935 Vargas had a free hand to repress not just the ANL but any group that appeared to threaten social order.

Integralism's exit from the political stage was more gradual than the ANL's. Taking advantage of the furor following the Intentona, the AIB mobilized members to run for office in local elections, enjoying some success. Even so, all was not well. Government police did not spare Integralists who conspired against the constituted order. And as Integralist demands became more shrill, the movement came under a cloud. Noncommunist voices began to speak out against the green shirts. The Democratic Student Union, for instance, opposed Integralism because they thought extremism on the right no more acceptable than extremism on the left.[85]

The movement remained viable through the mid-1930s nevertheless. By 1937 Integralist leader Plínio Salgado was claiming 300,000 to 400,000 militants in 4,000 cells across Brazil. To prove the point that Integralism was a political force to be reckoned with, he offered himself as a candidate for the presidency in the national elections scheduled for early 1938, predicting that he would garner half a million votes. He later withdrew. In his brief campaign he dwelt on familiar themes: the need for national unity, the corruption of political parties, and the dangers of communist revolution.

Two other contestants remained in the race: José Américo, Vargas's hand-picked man, and Armando de Salles Oliveira, the candidate of the liberal, largely fraudulent constitutionalism that had been practiced by the oligarchy during the Old Republic. The campaign ran fairly smoothly through early 1937 until Vargas and his advisors began to worry that Salles might actually win. Such a victory would have allowed the political forces that had been defeated in the Revolution of 1930 to realize their dream of regaining power. Around the middle of 1937 a rumor surfaced of a plan to "implant Communism in Brazil." Like the plot uncovered in 1935, the so-called Cohen Plan purportedly contemplated hundreds of political assassinations. Some in Congress denounced the plan as a fraud. High government officials and military officers insisted throughout that the document was real. In fact, Vargas was laying the groundwork to cancel the 1938 election and remain in power. By early November 1937 he had secured enough support among state governors that he was willing to proceed with the coup. The action was launched on November 10, 1937. No meaningful opposition materialized.

Integralists who had backed Vargas felt they were owed official recognition as the party of the new government. When Vargas refused, Salgado undertook a putsch of his own. It was easily put down. By late 1938 the AIB had been outlawed as the ANL had been earlier, and its members were being hunted down and arrested. The organization came under sharp censure. The opinion magazine *Diretrizes*, for instance, rebuked the Integralists for lacking a viable program and for being inspired by fascist models. Many Integralists, said the magazine, had "systematically abstained from thinking" and were no longer a "symbol of authentic nationalism, but a concrete expression of an exoticism that attracted weak spirits."[86] Well-known Catholic intellectual Azevedo Amaral found it disconcerting that Integralism had made such headway, "principally in the social strata where one could have expected greater resistance to propaganda and cheap drama wholly lacking an ideological position capable of impressing any beyond those of mediocre intelligence."[87]

How did the mass of middle-class people feel about the events of 1937? Nothing like a unified response is evident. Some doubtless feared its authoritarianism but knew they had no alternative to hunkering down and riding out this new storm. Most, tired of the political confusion since the Revolution of 1930, either heaved a sigh of relief or suspired nervously, hoping for a period of comparative calm. Perhaps the common denominator was a silent despairing of politics altogether. For even as Santa Rosa, the Integralists, and the ANL had sought to articulate a middle-class political position during the 1930s, a diffuse sense had persisted that politics itself—that is, contests among personalist factions, political parties, and divergent ideologies—was not capable of addressing Brazil's pressing problems.

By 1937 a disdain for politics and political process in Brazil had a long history. Plínio Salgado himself had quoted General Joaquim Osório Duque Estrada writing back from the battlefields of Paraguay that he did not recognize the legitimacy of political parties because they tended to divide rather than unify the nation.[88] In the 1890s Brazilian positivists—young lawyers, doctors, engineers, public functionaries, and army officers—echoed Osório's concerns, disavowing "political intrigue," especially the secret ballot and universal suffrage. Drawing on the writings of Auguste Comte, they favored a moral and political solution by which the oppressed "proletariat" could be integrated into society by an activist state guided by a nonpolitical, technocratic elite that would ensure order and progress.[89]

The positivist critique reverberated in the new century as frustrations with the political process began to take on an antioligarchic tone. During the Vaccine Revolt of 1904, much was made of the "low politicking" and "shameful electoral chicanery" that had characterized Brazilian politics since the 1890s.[90] During his civismo campaign of 1909–10 Rui Barbosa had acidly criticized the oligarchies that "usurp national sovereignty" for their own ends, claiming always that "elections are proceeding with the greatest normalcy."[91] Only a few years later Alberto Torres, a prominent political thinker and nationalist, argued that "politics, from top to bottom, is a mechanism alien to society, disturbs its order and is contrary to its progress" because politicians sought only to advance their own agendas, with no concern for broader issues.[92]

By the mid-1920s contempt for what one observer characterized as the "low, vile, indecent confusions of the business of politics" had reached a boiling point.[93] The Tenentes issued scathing indictments of the political process, referring in their broadsides to the "nepotism" of politics for personal gain, to the "satrapies" of those who sought to "choke" the Brazilian people, and to the "perversion of political customs" under oligarchic rule. Decrying "dirty politics," they called for "administrative moralization."[94] With the revolution's triumph expectations of genuine reform skyrocketed. Weekly and monthly magazines widely read in Rio and São Paulo applauded the "redemptive revolution" as a "breathtaking movement" that had liberated Brazil from the "clutches of a despotic and hallucinatory government."[95]

The Revolution of 1930, then, represented the convergence of a long-standing frustration with what was seen as a corrupt version of liberal-democratic political process and a distinct antioligarchic sentiment. As such, it held out the hope for genuine reform that would "republicanize the republic," as the Tenentes and dissident elites had summarized the reforms they advocated in the late 1920s. Yet by 1932 while the dust of revolution still swirled, significant doubts about the viability of representative democracy and a broad franchise were being raised. Rio columnist Tigres Bastos asked, tongue only partly in cheek, whether it might not be possible to "put an end to politics? Whoever did so would save Brazil."[96] Later in 1932 Rio's major newspaper, *Correio da Manhã*, editorialized that "Brazil does not live from politics, and to date owes its ruin to politicians who have inhumanely exploited it. Politics, among us, is the opposite of idealism, the negation of the patriotic sentiment and the spirit of sacrifice."[97] Essayist Virginio Santa Rosa also condemned the "eternal confusion" of party politics, which had been so disastrous for Brazil's embryonic middle class. In the same spirit commentator José Maria dos Santos noted in late 1932 that political parties in Brazil were so "unintelligent, interest-driven, and ineffective" that most Brazilians were at the point of concluding that nothing good could come of them.[98]

Integralism had been the first organized, sustained, and systematic critique along these lines. Liberal-democratic politics, said the Integralists, was nothing more than an "electoral comedy" in which "corruption was the rule" by which "monied parties" advanced narrow interests, "fractioning the nation" and leading to "classes struggling against classes." Socialism was no answer to the problem, since it considered society to be an "arena where Capital and Labor square off in a struggle to the death." This impasse could be broken, said Integralist writers, by abolishing political parties and limiting democratic suffrage in favor of a strong state run by experts. Only in this way could a "democracy of ends rather than means" "liberate workers and the petite bourgeoisie from the criminal indifference of liberal governments and save them from communist slavery."[99] From this perspective liberalism and Marxism shared a fatal flaw: both understood politics to be an arena of unceasing conflict and strife, where individuals and social groups vied for their interests against all others, heedless of the greater good. True politics, by contrast, was the opposite of conflict and division. Led by experts and honest elites, the strong, organic state, neither totalitarian nor liberal, would act not as the expression of aggregated individual wills but as society would act if endowed with a conscience of its own—precisely what Brazil's political system had never been able to do.

Within the ANL a gentler current of disdain for political process had also bubbled to the surface. ANL pamphlets disavowed involvement with political parties of any sort. While this was consistent with the effort to create a broad popular front, it also resonated to a growing frustration with politics as a whole. Aliancista literature and broadsides thus railed against "traditional politicians," "big bosses," and "coronéis" who had sold out to imperialism.[100] It is worth recalling that many of the ANL's founders—Roberto Sissón and Hercolino Cascardo, to name two—had been Tenentes, whose well-known sympathies for technical over representative government dated back to the antioligarchic struggle of the 1920s.

Collar-and-tie associations also expressed their frustration with politics throughout the mid-1930s. Most insisted that they remained above "partisan political contests" because "parties and political factions, with their ideologies, promise everything and deliver nothing."[101] In other fora collar-and-tie professionals complained that the promise of the Revolution of 1930 had been dashed by "mere politics," as an army officer put it.[102] As a consequence, said the vice-president of Rio's Engineering Club, "the middle classes" were experiencing the most "savage aspects of capitalist civilization."[103] There was ample reason for middle-class people (and not only them) to have lost confidence in the redemptive power of politics by 1937. Electoral reforms in the early 1930s had produced little change in actual participation and representation. The 1934 Congress, a cobbled-up hybrid of liberal and corporate representation, had resulted in deadlock. In 1935 the Communists had tried to take over the government and were proving difficult to eradicate. And in light of Italy's and Germany's situation Integralism's shrillness was increasingly off-putting.

Politics was balanced on a razor's edge. Notwithstanding the gloom, there was some hope in 1937 that the presidential elections scheduled for early 1938 might differ from past ones. President Vargas himself had promised a "free and healthy atmosphere" for the campaign. Rio's monthly *Vida Carioca* had taken him at his word and concluded that Brazil was moving toward "true democracy."[104] But hopeful confidence in the possibilities of open politics was short-lived. Old Regime forces had been regrouping throughout the 1930s. By late 1937 they appeared to be on the verge of restoration through the fraudulent electoral process against which the Revolution of 1930 had been a reaction. At the same time fears of communism reached new heights, especially after discovery of the Cohen Plan and its scheme to assassinate hundreds.

When on November 10 Getúlio Vargas canceled the January 1938 election, closed Congress, and outlawed political parties, the move met with little public opposition. In a radio address to the nation explaining the coup, Vargas blasted the "old as well as new parties ... which lacked ideological expression, and lived in the shadow of personal ambitions and local bosses, in the service of groups dedicated to booty and opportunistic alliances for low ends." Universal suffrage, he proclaimed, had become "an instrument of the bold and a mask poorly disguising the conspiracy of personal appetites and factious meetings." Glossing themes shared by Integralists and Aliancistas with the lacquer of modernity, Vargas argued that "democratic parties, rather than offer secure opportunities for growth and progress ... threatened national unity and endangered the existence of the nation." Traditional politics, he warned, was leading not to democratic solutions but to "violence and social war." For "political competition" among parties was giving way to the "incomparably darker prospect of class struggle." The only way to avoid this outcome was for Brazilians to put aside the divisiveness of partisan politics.[105]

The speech was a brilliant one, far more than just a boiler-plate justification for a personalist authoritarianism. It was a subtle blend of appeals to those who had lost faith in politics and feared class war, and soothing words for the "working classes," whose "just demands" could not be realized under oligarchic rule. It was, in essence, yet another effort to rally the Brazilian people against the power of the Old Regime. According to Vargas, the Estado Novo was a necessary and measured response to a specific conundrum of Brazilian politics during the 1930s, the threat that the old guard would regain power and the frightening possibility of class warfare.

Many within the middle class welcomed the change. Despite the promise of political reform, the middle class as a whole had gained little in the political infighting of previous years. Vargas's speech spoke to those who had become disillusioned with politics. In the weeks following the coup many collar-and-tie associations hailed the Estado Novo as a stroke of brilliant statesmanship. While most of these groups knew the importance of staying on the government's good side, there was open enthusiasm that someone had finally stopped the wheel of "political professionalism," which had made "our countrymen so indifferent to political activity."[106]

Early support for the new regime and its brief against politics was also evident in mass-circulation, middle-brow magazines. The popular Rio monthly *Vida Carioca* immediately heralded the "white revolution" as the "most sensational political transformation of the century." It had administered the "coup de grâce" to extremisms of both left and right and put an end to the "inconvenience of the multiplicity of political parties."[107] Less than two months later a commentator in *Vida Doméstica*, relieved that the old guard had not succeeded in retaking power, argued that "universal suffrage has lost its meaning among us" because "the parties had taken control of everything."[108] To those alienated from the political process the advent of the Estado Novo represented an answer to the quandary of how to steer clear of left- and right-wing radicalism and at the same time avoid the retrenchment of the old political elite. As a São Paulo commercial employees' monthly remarked in 1942, the new regime simply supplanted the "old democracy of parties," harmonizing "nonsensical antagonisms within a solution that has nothing whatever to do with a corrupt liberal democracy or with the totalitarianisms of right or left."[109]

Moreover, in the face of repression and widespread condemnation for extremists of all stripes, there was little reason for people to retain strong political loyalties, especially after 1937. Repression played a crucial role in dampening political enthusiasm. But after the experience of recent years many may have come to feel that extremism was simply beyond the pale. Carlos, the good son in Sra. Leandro Dupré's novel *There Were Six of Us*, perhaps stood for all those within the middle class who had tired of the febrile political passions of the 1930s. Integralism and communism, he averred in an argument with his brother, are identical: "They are both theories based on a single principle, a single essence, and the objective is the same: social confusion, conflicts, and failure. In the end they both lead to disequilibrium."[110]

Thus the outlawing of political parties may have been a matter of relative inconsequence to many within the middle class. For all the energy of the Integralists and Aliancistas most had never bothered with politics in the first place. Schoolteacher Paschoal Lemme may be emblematic of a widespread sentiment difficult to pin down. In his memoirs he stated forthrightly that, despite his leftist sympathies, he did not take active part in the politics of the mid-1930s. His two jobs, at the Secretariat of Education and Culture of the Federal District and at the Educational Inspector's Office of the State of Rio de Janeiro, "plus my family responsibilities left me no time to devote to other activities. But it was not just a matter of time, as I never had any intention of associating with a political party."[111] This statement is vague enough to bear any number of interpretations. Certainly, fear of repression and lack of time militated against political engagement. Yet perhaps there was more: Lemme's statement may also whisper of an irreducible aversion, born of historical experience, to participating in an activity, politics, that had produced only bitter fruit and been so long disdained.

EFFORTS TO DEFINE a place for the middle class in the political system faced enormous obstacles during the 1920s and 1930s. Brazil's middle class was not dealing from a position of economic or political strength. Without an independent base of power they could not be the confident business and commercial class of nineteenth-century Europe; they were much more like Europe's urban lower middle class between World War I and World War II—what English writer John Middleton Murry referred to as the most "completely disinherited section of modern society."[112] Lacking a history of participatory and partisan organization, they failed to build a political movement of their own. An ensconced oligarchy with enormous exclusionary powers and a budding industrial bourgeoisie monopolized political process. Thus it was that the young military officers who led successive revolts against the regime during the 1920s became the only political option, and many middle-class Brazilians supported them as best they could within the limits of the political straitjacket of oligarchic rule.

The Tenentes and later political organizations of dissident elites appealed to the people of Brazil's burgeoning cities as a counterweight to the rural electorate controlled by Old Regime political bosses. This meant seeking support from the expanding urban working class, whose militancy had rattled Brazilian society during the general strikes of 1917–21. The middle class, then, could emerge politically only in the context of a rhetorically inclusive people that made room for politically dangerous and socially inferior manual workers. Through most of the 1920s this presented no major problem, as government repression of the labor movement continued apace, even as the antioligarchic challenge grew.

The dilemma erupted after the Revolution of 1930 with the resurgence of labor militancy. For as the labor movement recovered its voice and as the Communist party maneuvered, wide segments of society, including most middle-class people, began to see in class conflict an overriding threat to a social order only recently freed from oligarchic rule. Integralism and the ANL represented middle-class efforts to articulate these anxieties politically. Like the Tenentes, both groups sought to use the people as a blunt instrument against the forces that loomed on either side. Nor were they alone in trying to do so: Getúlio Vargas's government was pursuing a similar strategy. And so the political meaning of the people remained sharply contested throughout the 1930s, available to anyone who could find the key to lock a definition into a particular political context. Vargas's genius was to recognize the quandary and opportunity of this situation and remake Brazilian politics in the process. In the end experiments groping toward an independent middle-class politics did not bear up under the whirlwind raised by this dilemma and Vargas's solution to it.

The final act in the broad-based alienation of middle and working classes opened after the coup ushering in the Estado Novo in 1937. Until that time the most urgent task of would-be ideologues and spokesmen of middle-class politics had been to establish a meaning for "the people" that would subordinate the working class to middle-class concerns, interests, tactics, and leadership. Vargas did just the reverse: he emphasized the political imperatives of the working-class-as-people.

By the early 1930s Vargas had already taken important strides toward locating workers at the very center of postoligarchic politics. In May Day speeches during the Estado Novo he addressed himself to working-class audiences with growing confidence, laying the groundwork for appeals to the labor vote during the 1945 and 1950 elections. Exhorting them to "cooperation and solidarity among social classes," he implicitly recognized workers as a collective force with a legitimate claim to political participation and enormous political potential, a rhetorical strategy not lost on workers.[113] Throughout the Estado Novo, workers wrote enthusiastic letters to Vargas praising his efforts on their behalf and gratefully accepting his equation of workers with the people.[114]

This gambit had profound effects. Responding to decades of pressure from sindicatos and anticipating future demands, Vargas's government between 1937 and 1945 elaborated the labor laws and set about articulating a populist discourse around urban workers. Those who up to the mid-1930s had variously imagined alternative middle-class populisms had failed. The middle class existed as a recognizable social group but lacked a clearly defined role in the political drama of postwar Brazil. As an engineer who lived through the period put it: "That was when Getúlio acquired the aura of father of the poor. Now, for people of the middle class, this didn't change anything."[115] But of course it did. For if during the 1930s the labor movement rose from the ashes of repression and found new voice and presence in politics and a kind of ally in Getúlio Vargas, and if old and new elites were able to take their place on the political stage, twenty years of efforts to approach the people on their own terms found the middle class uneasily situated in the unfolding drama of populism, more fractured and metamorphosing than many had hoped might be the case.

7

Collaboration and Indifference

A subterranean tremor approaches that will shake humanity. It is the struggle of classes. It is the ferocious battle between capitalism and the proletariat. . . . And woe unto us if we do not join together. We will be a dispersed
force, at the mercy of circumstances, subject to continual changes of direction, exploited by the interests of the moment defined by those who take
part in the struggle.[1]

These portentous words were spoken by Dr. Mario Azambuja in a speech
at Rio's Medical and Surgical Society in 1936. In uttering them, Azambuja
sought to galvanize the doctors of the society to join a *sindicato* (union).
He feared they were being left behind in a world that increasingly stressed
organized activity. Like so many collar-and-tie employees and professionals, the good doctor felt himself part of an excluded middle in a still-
unfolding class society defined by the conflict between adversaries.

He had reason to worry. Since the Revolution of 1930 labor unions, repressed and weak during the 1920s, had made a dramatic recovery.
Striking workers had forced themselves upon the attention of the state and
scrambled to take advantage of new legislation encouraging the formation
of state-sponsored sindicatos. Similarly, employers in the commercial sector and newly confident industrialists also sought the benefits of laws establishing a closer connection with the state. Bound together by their antagonism, organized urban workers, business, and the state were refash-
ioning associational life.[2] By contrast, collar-and-tie groups seemed in dis-
array. Federal civil servants' organizations had lost much of their clout
when the Revolution of 1930 brought an abrupt end to the politics of oligarchic patronage and electioneering. Most nonmanual employees continued to embrace dependence on paternalistic employers, which made it

difficult for them to salve the sting of inflation and low salaries. By the early 1930s, then, in the face of widespread economic insecurity, fear had grown among white-collar employees and professionals that they would be unable to defend their interests without organizations of their own.

This concern sparked a burst of enthusiasm for claims-making politics among collar-and-tie groups during the 1930s. Associations of bank and commercial employees, public functionaries, teachers, journalists, and salaried professionals pushed for salary "readjustments" from employers, and toward the end of the decade began to stump for government-mandated minimum salaries. They advocated job security and pensions, condemned the *pistolão*, and insisted on merit in hiring and promotion. Bureaucrats lobbied for access to public jobs. Liberal professionals struggled to impose educational and ethical requirements to root out unlicensed practitioners. Shopkeepers sought autonomy vis-à-vis "high commerce" and pressed municipal governments on matters of taxes, roving vendors, and employee relations. However much their specific agendas differed, collar-and-tie organizations faced a common complex of issues regarding the nature and purpose of associational life generally during the 1930s and through the Estado Novo: whether to be collaborative or confrontational in relation to employers and the state, what attitude to take in relation to working-class organizations and what political role to assume, and how to confront the conundrum of low participation rates—rarely above 15–20 percent in a given occupational category.[3]

"Everything Depends on Our Collaboration"

Urban workers and employers had begun to square off through representative organizations after 1900. Workers formed "resistance leagues" that grew increasingly combative through the 1910s as they sought better pay and working conditions for their members.[4] Business groups, incipient industrialists' organizations as well as import-export associations, gathered strength up to 1920, establishing closer connections with the state.[5] Between them men who saw themselves as a cut above manual workers but who felt they could not compete on equal terms with business interest groups began to experiment with associations of their own. Before 1920 these groups lobbied local, state, and federal government or businesses in the private sector, relying on contacts between well-connected members of the organization and people of power and influence in politics, the bureaucracies, and business.[6]

As economic crisis deepened during the 1910s and as patronage grew tighter, some within collar-and-tie occupations began to seek more effective means of defending their interests. With the example of militant workers before them, accountants in Rio formed a sindicato in 1917 and salaried doctors followed their lead in 1927.[7] Despite a more assertive stance these associations were not organized around a principle of resistance. Labor organizations' more defiant style grew out of the convergence of immigrant anarchism, political exclusion during the Old Republic, marginalization within the circuits of patronage, and miserable pay and working conditions. Collar-and-tie employees and professionals, while poorly paid and politically weak, had nevertheless long benefited from patronage. Their sindicatos bore the imprint of this experience, neither eschewing patronage altogether nor relying on it exclusively. The result was a style of collective action distinct from that of the labor movement.

A debate within the São Paulo Bank Employees' Association in the mid-1920s illustrates the deep uncertainty among collar-and-tie employees over the proper means and ends of collective action. Founded in 1923, the association struggled with whether to limit itself to "mutualist" objectives or constitute itself as a sindicato to act in defense of the "class."[8] One member worried that bank employees lacked the necessary "consciousness . . . matured by suffering and revolt" to form a sindicato. It made no sense to think of the association as an "organization of attack," he said in 1925, given that "all efforts beyond those of a purely beneficent society have not brought results."[9] A refractory stance would only undermine the association's more general mission of helping fellow bank employees through hard times.

More was at stake here than just a crude calculation of advantages and disadvantages. By dismissing confrontational tactics, this writer implicitly rejected working-class organizations as models for bank employees. His position won out in the mid-1920s, and the association did not become a sindicato until later.[10] Rio's bank employees came to the same conclusion, stating explicitly in 1929 that they would not be "a center of resistance, an organization antagonistic to banking interests."[11] Accordingly they encouraged high-level bank employees to join the association. Bank owners were only too happy to accommodate, seeing the association as a training school that would increase the supply of qualified employees, a view which dovetailed with employees' desire for career opportunities.

The terms of associational life underwent abrupt and sweeping change after the Revolution of 1930. During the Old Republic, government had typically responded to organized labor through repression; "the social question is a matter for the police" was the shibboleth among elites. The new provisional government departed radically from this practice. Now the labor ministry sought to coopt workers and draw their support rather than merely repress them. The primary instrument for this delicate operation was the labor law of 1931.[12] Workers were encouraged to form sindicatos, seek official state recognition, and have their slate of leaders approved by the ministry. In exchange the sindicato obtained a monopoly to represent local members of that occupational group before the state and employers. In a speech reprinted in the newsletter of a commercial employees' union in Rio, President Getúlio Vargas succinctly stated the philosophy underlying this solution to the social question. Because Brazilian workers lacked the "combativeness" of workers elsewhere, he said, and because capital and labor had never really been "belligerent," sindicatos should not be seen as "organs of conflict," but of "cooperation" with the "public powers."[13] On this view sindicalismo formed the core of a project that sought above all to defuse class conflict by promoting social harmony and controlling autonomous organization. And while militant workers were the primary target of this new tactic, the project impinged deeply on white-collar organizations as well.

For some collar-and-tie groups the new labor code offered a solution to the issue of whether to act as organs of collaboration or "organizations of attack." The 1931 law had two major effects on a number of collar-and-tie organizations. First, it strengthened their hand against employers, giving them greater bargaining leverage than before. Second, it allowed members of such groups to imagine they were collaborating with the government in maintaining social peace. The Union of Commercial Employees in Rio, for instance, saw the new arrangement as a measure for avoiding "impassioned intransigencies" between employers and employees. The union rejected the purely paternalist line of the long-standing Association of Commercial Employees, whose slogan was "Employee today, boss tomorrow." At the same time it emphatically denied being an "organ of struggle." Instead, it embraced the opportunity to be a "consultative organ to the government" and to meet employers as equals in a "humanitarian collaboration" that would "harmonize capital and labor."[14] This position stood in stark contrast to that of working-class militants—including utility, railroad, textile, and metallurgical workers—who were not as easily mollified by the government's apparent concessions. Though willing to strike strategic bargains, many labor militants perceived the demobilizing and repressive potential of the new labor code and railed against it throughout the early 1930s.[15]

Many collar-and-tie groups were openly receptive to the spirit of the 1931 labor code, though not without reservation. Even after registering with the state, for example, the association of São Paulo bank employees recoiled from calling itself a sindicato, opting instead for the ambiguous title Bank Employees Association of São Paulo—Syndical Organ. As one of the founders put it, the purpose of the association was to create a "calmer environment" for both bosses and employees, not to exacerbate social tensions the way it was said workers did through their sindicatos.[16] Associationally minded teachers in Rio's private high schools were nominally bolder, bearing the sindicato label without complaint, though they adamantly insisted on remaining a strictly professional organization, refusing broader political and ideological engagement. A small number of anarchists within the organization, seeking to radicalize "education workers" and free them from state control, foundered on members' refusal to stretch the limits of a proper professional association. Few teachers were willing to join a group not recognized by the government. Amidst ongoing efforts to consolidate their status as salaried, respectable professionals, fewer still were drawn to an organization that saw them merely as education *workers*.[17]

Some salaried doctors also saw advantages in official sindicalismo, the first among *faculdade*-educated professionals to do so. These physicians, compared with better-off colleagues in private practice, often earned niggardly salaries and enjoyed scant job security. Many were forced to seek employment outside the profession or string together several jobs to make ends meet. Despite status concerns they were willing to be seen as "intellectual workers" if granted the same protections as "manual workers" against the "parasitism . . . of bosses."[18] Yet more than merely immediate interests was at stake. In early 1932 Dr. Manoel de Abreu, member of the sindicato's executive board, applauded sindicalismo not only for its practical benefits but also because it would allow doctors to participate in efforts to end "the violent struggle among individuals" characteristic of capitalism and avoid "the violent struggle among classes" threatened by communism.[19] Not all agreed, however, that collaboration sufficed to advance their claims. Doubts that the state had their best interests at heart prompted some to adopt a more minatory tone. In early 1931 Dr. Gastão Ayres, at the First Congress on Medical Syndicalism, stated acidly that doctors' demands probably would not be met without resistance, specifically a "medical strike."[20]

A more sustained critique of this sort erupted from within the ranks of São Paulo's bank employees' sindicato in 1932. A band of noncommunist radicals sought to break with a leadership that had limited itself to seeking small concessions from the state. These dissidents wanted the sindicato to take a more independent stance. At roughly the same time the Communist party reversed its previous refusal to work with sindicatos officially recognized under the 1931 law. These two currents converged in 1933–34. Noncommunist radicals secured high posts within the sindicato and Communist militants took up positions of influence within the organization. The Communists apparently grasped the strategic advantages of an organization that could keep tabs on the flow of money and credit in Brazil's major financial and industrial center. Together these two groups challenged the *trabalhistas* who continued to favor state sponsorship. The split could hardly have been sharper. Trabalhistas argued that "class harmony" demanded the sindicato adhere to the principle of "mutual collaboration and not struggle." The radicals, Communist and noncommunist alike, employed the language of class conflict, pitting proletariat against bourgeoisie. Referring to their more conservative colleagues as "petit-bourgeois parasites," they explicitly identified bank employees as workers and began to raise the specter of a strike.[21]

By early 1934 this more aggressive political line had succeeded in winning over a considerable number of bank clerks to a more combative position. For the first time a strike among collar-and-tie employees became a real possibility. A number of factors contributed to this development. Between 1932 and 1934 large numbers of factory workers had struck in Rio and São Paulo. Many of these actions had achieved notable gains, especially in pay checks eroded by inflation over several years.[22] Salaries were a particularly sore point with bank employees, who by 1934 had experienced a 30–40 percent decline in real income since 1929 and had not been able to persuade government and employers to respond to their plight.[23] Moreover, since 1933 the sindicato had been in the forefront of a movement to promote syndical unity. By leading the drive to create the Coalition of Proletarian Sindicatos, it had brought many bank employees into closer political contact with what was widely seen as a restive industrial labor movement.[24]

When the labor ministry rejected demands for a pension institute and job security in July 1934, militant bank employees, under radical leadership, called the first nationwide bank strike. The walkout ran four days, paralyzed a large number of banks in Rio and São Paulo, and forced the government to muster the police to contain the excitable and secure order. Lasting until the government agreed to a compromise acceptable to the sindicato, the strike marked the first victory by collar-and-tie employees through a well-organized confrontation with government and employers.

It did not, however, represent all bank employees. Judging by the average age of sindicato members, the strike may well have been the action of young men at the beginning of their careers. Established employees at more prestigious banks may not have participated in large numbers. Their reluctance can be glimpsed by considering a report of what happened at the Banco do Brasil (BB). To be a BB functionary was to have considerable status and better pay than ordinary bank employees. Such advantages were not lightly endangered. Hardly surprising, then, that a newspaper reported that only 20 of 800 BB employees joined the strike.[25] This may have understated participation among BB employees, and implicit threats of reprisal doubtless kept many away. But it would be a mistake to discount the temper of people who felt secure and content in their jobs.

Radicals rarely made such headway elsewhere. No other collar-and-tie group mounted a major strike in the mid-1930s. Even so bank employees were not alone in facing challenges from the left. Within Rio's medical sindicato a cadre of self-avowed Marxists complained that the sindicato's leadership was not doing enough to defend doctors' interests. They were summarily expelled.[26] The following year a Trotskyite was elected to the presidency of the Rio de Janeiro Teachers' Sindicato. With the fear of communism running high because of the *Intentona* of 1935 and after being labeled a "Communist sindicato" in the mainstream press, the organization saw its members vote with their feet. By early 1936 all but 3 of more than 550 dues-paying members had withdrawn. Partly this was due to the fear of losing jobs; school directors often fired teachers who joined the sindicato.[27] In light of the rank-and-file's earlier rejection of an anarchist-led parallel organization it is likely that many members simply could not abide an organization run by Communists.

Fear of reprisal for sindicato membership was common during this period. A climate of generalized repression contributed to the disquiet. "Extremists" were harried under a new security measure, the "Monstrous Law" of April 1935. Thousands were arrested. The government's need to take a more forceful approach was clear; numerous labor strikes of 1934 and 1935 and the remarkable mobilization accomplished by the National Liberation Alliance threatened "social peace." Militants were apprehended, tried in military courts of special exception, jailed, and perhaps tortured. Emboldened by the government's heavy hand, employers appear to have undertaken a repression of their own, which spread beyond radicals to potentially anyone stepping out of line. In 1935, for instance, one

Dr. Granja was fired from his modestly paid position at the Portuguese Beneficent Society after he publicly supported demands by the sindicato for higher pay, though he himself was not a member of the organization.[28] In a 1938 letter to president Getúlio Vargas a doctors' group noted that employers "discreetly and silently prefer those who do not belong to the sindicato in hiring and promotion decisions."[29] Such practices were widespread within the collar-and-tie occupations.

Low-level repression of this sort, in an atmosphere of generalized suspicion against anything that smacked of extremism, had profound implications for collar-and-tie associational life through the mid-1930s. Many became all the more intransigent in defending peaceful tactics. For example, shortly after the wave of strikes that included the bank employees' walkout of July 1934 Dr. Silvio Boccanera reluctantly agreed that sindicalismo was necessary, though he hastened to add that it had to be "pacifist" and "oppose class struggle." The right to strike had to be protected, he said, "but the strike without hate . . . a peaceful stoppage that compromises with dignity . . . and recognizes that violence only breeds violence."[30] Otherwise, feared one teacher, the "coarse" masses might be swept away to "extremes and extremisms" by "ideologies."[31]

In some cases the explosive mixture of extremism, sindicatos, and repression opened deep rifts within collar-and-tie organizations. In late 1935 dissidents within Rio's Union of Commercial Employees began to employ the language of class conflict, referring to themselves as "proletarians" facing intransigent "capital." They wanted greater democracy within the organization and greater contact between the union and other proletarian groups. Fearing what they saw as the union's "most exploited and combative" members and concerned that the union not drift into the camp of manual workers, the union's governing board, composed of better-off members of the profession, swiftly put down the rebellion without broad protest from the rank and file.[32]

Among São Paulo bank employees the split ran deeper. In May 1935 a new organization emerged to challenge the left-wing directorate that had arisen during the strike of 1934. The Sindicato of Bank Functionaries, commonly known as Syndiké, took compass from "an absolute sense of order" to declare itself the implacable foe of combative tactics. While smaller than the original sindicato, Syndiké represented a group of bank employees equaling as much as 40 percent of the sindicato's membership.[33] Meanwhile the sindicato lambasted members of the conservative group as "individualists" who did not belong to a "real" sindicato, reserving special venom for what they saw as the Syndiké's gnathonic relationship to employers.[34] These more conservative bank employees probably did not think of themselves as toadies. Bankers did seek to manipulate the Syndiké, but the organization cannot be reduced to employer string pulling. Close examination of its publication reveals a distinct sensibility regarding the nature and purpose of collective action at variance with that of their more radical counterparts.

Leftist bank employees, said the Syndiké's journal, simply refused to understand that the pursuit of a career by "cultivated men" was a happy solution for many individual cases. Success was a matter of "always try[ing] to move up a little more," rather than of collective confrontation. What is more, young bank employees had a "debt of honor" with their employers, especially since so many of their superiors had started off as simple employees themselves.[35] Nor were members of the Syndiké merely puppets. In general, sindicalismo was a good idea, admitted the journal, but its defining purpose was to "settle conflict, and eliminate the harshness and bitterness of struggle," rather than to sow discord.[36] For while employers' and employees' interests were not identical, they were ultimately reconcilable. And so, in one breath Syndiké member and bank clerk Luiz André Costa could refer to bank employees as "proletarians" and wax eloquent on the importance of "keep[ing] up the struggle." In the next, mindful of "our dependence on the bankers," he could remind his fellow colleagues to eschew all ideologies, sectarian politics, and extremism.[37]

During the four years of the Syndiké's existence, the sindicato gradually moved toward greater collaboration. The Communists who dominated the sindicato's leadership resigned their posts in 1936 in favor of those willing to toe the government's line. They may have left because they did not want the sindicato to lose its official status to the Syndiké. The new governing council distributed a circular to its members, stating that the sindicato now intended to act "strictly within legal norms" to avoid "class struggle" by peacefully seeking concessions from the government. Making good on this promise, new bylaws prohibited strikes.[38]

Despite continued sniping, the two organizations established an uneasy truce and grew closer over the years. In 1939 they fused, repairing the split that had opened in 1935, though not without scars. Radical leaders hounded into hiding and its newspaper controlled by the labor ministry, the sindicato temporarily abandoned confrontation as the premise for its claims-making activities. For its part the Syndiké shifted to a somewhat more assertive stance vis-à-vis the government. Yet the revamped sindicato was a far cry from the one that had called the strike of 1934; with an eye to government censorship, the journal wrote not of struggle and demands, but of proper linguistic usage, manners, morality, and culture.[39]

In the face of the repressive backlash that closed the National Liberation Alliance, rounded up extremists, and beat back assertive organizations, the São Paulo bank employees' return to a politics of collaboration appears to have marked a general trend among white-collar organizations. The trajectories of the Union of Book and Newspaper Workers and Rio's Sindicato of Professional Journalists is instructive. Founded in the early 1930s, the union sought to bring press workers, reporters, and editors together in a broad-based organization. It had a tough time attracting reporters and editors to its ranks. Most appear not to have wanted to join an organization mingling manual and nonmanual workers. The sindicato was established in 1934. At first it too could not attract members. It began to grow only in 1935, when the union, dominated by communists and their sympathizers, took a "decidedly political" position against the government. At this point, whether they disagreed with the union's political line, feared repression, or were anxious to assert a narrower professional identity, journalists who had belonged to the union left to join the sindicato. The sindicato thereafter refused to adopt an antigovernment line or do anything that might justify repression against it.[40]

Other collar-and-tie organizations had similar experiences in the mid- to late 1930s. Doctors', dentists', shopkeepers', and public functionaries' groups all took refuge from a raging political and ideological storm in the lee of official recognition, agreeing that "sindicatos are no longer, as they once were, units of combat, anxious to strike back, but organs conscious of their purposes within the collective spirit."[41] Or as the Union of Civil Functionaries of Brazil put it in 1936, "Everything . . . depends . . . on our collaboration."[42]

The Estado Novo, midwifed by coup in November 1937, sought to enshrine these attitudes as a permanent feature of Brazilian political culture. Essentially the new regime set out to rationalize and institutionalize the labor schemes that had been taking shape since 1931. In practical terms three pillars were made to bear the weight of relationships among employers, employees, and the state: sindicatos, the labor courts, and the social security system. Sindicatos represented a group's interests before the state. Labor courts settled disputes that arose between individual workers and their employers. The social security system regulated employers' and employees' contributions to pension funds.

Although the labor ministry's attention was focused on working-class organizations, leaders of many collar-and-tie groups saw advantages in cozying up to the state during these years. Public authorities encouraged them. In a speech given on Public Servants' Day in 1938, government functionaries heard president Getúlio Vargas promise to end patronage and install a new regime of hiring and promotion through merit. He called on them to help remake Brazilian society by taking an "active part in the life of the state."[43] By 1939 the regime seemed to have taken official notice that "the stability of the middle class's way of life, which depends on a salary but enjoys a higher standard of living, is a requirement of the social order."[44] This solicitude for civil servants came at a price: under new legislation, public functionaries were promised job security, social security, and protection from the vagaries of political patronage but were barred from forming or joining sindicatos.[45] In effect this segment of the middle class had "given up its right to unionize." The state sought to ensure their collaboration through demobilization.

Other groups could not be controlled so directly. Nevertheless, in a variety of ways the Estado Novo accentuated the mid-decade emphasis on collaboration among collar-and-tie sindicatos. The incentive now, and the only realistic option for most of these groups, was to seek official recognition and lobby the state for benefits.[46] In this spirit a wide gamut of middle-class organizations proclaimed their enthusiasm for "permanent collaboration with the state" and its "corporatist" system as a way of promoting the "general happiness" that would defuse the "struggle of social classes."[47]

Beyond concrete gains the new system promised not only social peace and class harmony but also an escape from the messy and narrow confines of conflictual and partisan politics. A common refrain among collar-and-tie groups during the 1930s was that sindicalismo represented an alternative to "parties and political factions, with their ideologies, that promise everything and deliver nothing."[48] The Estado Novo took this view very seriously, as evidenced by the prominence Getúlio Vargas gave the matter in his speech on November 10, 1937, justifying the coup. It would be a mistake, however, to presume a monolithic collaborationism from statements of support for the Estado Novo. The period between 1937 and 1945 was one of censorship. Leaders of collar-and-tie organizations understood that the government's attention and favor depended on hewing to the official line of cooperation and social peace. Thus, it is impossible to conclude that sindicato members shared a uniform outlook. Those who disagreed may have left the organizations. Others may have stayed on but remained silent.

The language and practice of collaboration during this period is important for two reasons. First, with the exception of striking São Paulo bank employees in 1934, it represented the continuation of a sentiment expressed with varying enthusiasm by collar-and-tie sindicatos throughout the 1930s. This suggests that many members and leaders were perfectly content to cooperate with and take advantage of the Estado Novo. Second, there is no indication of a meaningful grass-roots effort among disgruntled members to maintain an alternative position. Some doubtless left in frustration. Others were forced out. But, in general, there appears to have been little resistance, and nothing like the factory commissions that struggled throughout the Estado Novo to keep organizational independence alive among industrial workers.[49] As such, for most collar-and-tie sindicatos, institutional collaboration with the government during the Estado Novo was not discontinuous with the period before 1937.

An election within the Sindicato of Professional Journalists of Rio de Janeiro suggests that collaboration with government during the Estado Novo was not solely coerced. In 1943, when the regime had already begun to face political challenges, two candidates ran for the presidency of the organization: Osório Borba, a young journalist who had been active in the organization for some time, versus well-known journalist André Carrazoni, editor-in-chief at a pro-Vargas newspaper in Rio. The campaign was a bitter one, in which Borba claimed to represent "journalists who were really employees," while Carrazoni (according to a Borba sympathizer) was "the candidate of the bosses . . . who did not represent the aspirations of journalists cum employees."[50] Carrazoni denied the charge, saying that his job was that of a "simple employee," suggesting that he understood the composition of the electorate he faced.[51]

For Borba supporters the fundamental issue of the election was whether the sindicato would collaborate with the state, "begging favors," or confront it in pursuing demands. Carrazoni stood for the proposition that the president of the sindicato ought to be "influential in official circles," which he certainly was. Detractors argued that he was not interested in "demanding and defending rights but in obtaining favors." As Borba himself put it, the lines were sharply drawn on the issue of "rights versus favors." When the votes were tallied, Carrazoni had won, demonstrating the strength of the collaborative sensibility and of patronage and clientage among this small sample of collar-and-tie employees.

Collaboration did not imply complete harmony among employers, employees, sindicatos, and the state. The government understood this and seems to have been less concerned with avoiding conflict than with channeling and dampening it. In 1939, for example, the doctors' sindicato in

Rio ran an article in its journal wailing that doctors were being "proletarianized" and were "coming to know the needs and afflictions that used to affect only workers."[52] Wringing this image for all it was worth, the journal hinted at the possibility that salaried doctors would seek a collective ruling against employers from the labor courts if the salary question was not soon addressed. Now that "the constitution has leveled medical work to that of the manual worker, it would not be humiliating" for doctors to proceed as other workers did. For all the bluster, the ultimatum appears to have been an idle one. Respectable physicians had little experience with the labor system, and most probably would have been humiliated stooping to the level of workers to air their grievances. In the end, despite the discord implied by saber rattling, these doctors were responding in exactly the way the new labor laws prescribed: rather than threaten a strike, they looked to mediate their conflict with employers through the state for broader as well as for their own interests.

Among the intangible rewards of collaboration was that collar-and-tie organizations could claim their members contributed to the common good. As an accountant put it in 1936: "Everyone is visibly preoccupied with stressing the importance of their activities, seeking to demonstrate in every possible way their relevance to the social organism."[53] Those most given to trumpeting the importance of their activities hailed from occupations that could plausibly claim to advance the public interest. Doctors, lawyers, engineers, and military officers commonly exalted their professions and insisted on the crucial role they could play in the nation's life. So too did teachers, dentists, bureaucrats, journalists, accountants, social workers, librarians, and advertising men.[54] Even after being barred from forming their own sindicatos, for instance, public functionaries for the state of São Paulo claimed to stand for "order and work, family morality and justice."[55] Occasionally, even shopkeepers and bank employees sought to show how their activities advanced the greater good.[56]

While it would be easy to dismiss these statements as cynical and instrumental—because concessions from the state could depend on an organization's toeing the official line, especially during the Estado Novo—or simplistic and naive, more was at issue. Workers might argue that they, rather than employers, actually produced society's goods. From a middle-class perspective, however, this was at best a political point about social justice, not an expression of their desire to serve society as a whole. By contrast, when collar-and-tie groups demanded recognition for the part their members played in society—even as they pursued their own interests—they saw themselves as making a different claim. Relying on the distinction between manual workers and intellectual employees, they imagined a higher role for themselves as they embraced the status quo (though not without some reservations) rather than oppose it.

From the 1920s to the 1940s collar-and-tie organizations elevated collaboration with government and employers above confrontation and conflict, just as the close link between patronage and politics was weakening. Rooted in an organizational legacy distinct from the "resistance leagues" of militant workers, this outlook appears to have crystallized during the 1930s amidst inexperience, fear of repression, and a sharp sensitivity to the implications of class conflict. More an abiding sense of the imperative to cooperate with constituted authorities than of loyalty to any specific government, these groups sought to hold themselves above the rising tensions that they feared might engulf Brazilian society. In terms of public pronouncements, they placed their faith in the "public powers," before which they would defend their interests and through which they would contribute to the greater good of the nation.

The remarks of a doctor from São Paulo at a medical congress in 1945, when the Estado Novo's power over sindicatos had faded, are emblematic. Dr. Alvaro Faria argued that while sindicatos had to fight for the betterment of "salary earners, public and private," they had to avoid the spirit of conflict, which pitted "group against group and class against class." Sindicatos, he said, had evolved "from instruments of struggle" toward "constructive ends," specifically, "consulting the interests of national capital as the basis of the economic and political emancipation of the people."[57] The key idea here was the extension of collaboration to a sense of participation in a broad national project of economic modernization that had emerged over the course of the Estado Novo. In Faria's vision the project's success depended crucially on class peace and concessions to "national capital." Few collar-and-tie sindicatos disagreed.

There were tensions within this outlook. Some groups, especially among liberal professionals, expressed their resentment against the government's hovering presence. They were willing to cooperate with government but did not want to be under such tight control.[58] Others felt poorly served by the system as it stood. The Bank Employees' Sindicato in Rio agreed in 1944 that "cooperation or harmony between capital and labor" was a goal to be pursued. But their words had an edge to them. Demanding "decent remuneration," the sindicato noted that "neither rigorous regulation nor the severe gaze of managers" could give "manual or intellectual workers" the incentive to work productively.[59] In the context of loosened state controls on organizational activity, this rhetorical willingness to associate themselves with workers—and with what a United States consular officer saw as a "growing restlessness" among them[60]—read almost like a warning or a threat.

São Paulo bank employees had already traveled this road. After the strike of 1934 they had remained wary of the state, much as had labor militants. While the sindicato hewed to the government's line during the Estado Novo, the experience of collective protest during the mid-1930s bequeathed bank employees a legacy that finally led many of them onto a different path from middle-class people generally. They signaled their choice by launching a nationwide bank strike in 1946, joining as many as 100,000 industrial workers in the wave of strikes that swept São Paulo early that year.[61] In doing so, they came to be identified with the labor movement and did not represent a viable model for the vast majority of middle-class employees and professionals, including at least half of bank employees, who preferred collaboration to conflict or remained indifferent to sindicalismo.

"Criminal Indifference"

In 1932 most commercial clerks in Rio wanted nothing to do with the Union of Commercial Employees. Rather than attend meetings to talk about their rights as workers, these young men, who worked at low-paying jobs under harsh bosses, primped themselves and stepped out to the dance clubs to prance and flirt the night away. Or at least that is how the union's publication explained the "criminal indifference" of most employees to its efforts to recruit new members.[62]

The union was hardly the only group to remark on the problem. Collar-and-tie sindicatos complained bitterly throughout the 1930s and into the 1940s of the difficulty they had in attracting members and galvanizing active support. São Paulo teachers griped about the "crisis of indifference" to their "efforts to congregate."[63] Doctors in Rio quoted Bertrand Russell to the effect that "the majority of men and women" went through life "accepting what is offered to them, without any great effort to think about what the moment requires."[64] Others spoke acidly of the "general skepticism" toward collective endeavor.[65] Still others lashed out against those who joined organizations with a purely "utilitarian idea, that is, concern for the immediate advantages" of membership with no thought to active participation.[66]

By the 1930s there were historical reasons why large numbers of white-collar employees and professionals might have been so skeptical of associational life generally and sindicatos in particular. Their occupational organizations had not undergone the turn-of-the-century transformation from mutual societies to resistance leagues that many working-class organizations had; immigrants steeped in the theory and practice of anarchism had come to work in fields and factories, not offices. Through the first two decades of the twentieth century many workers had learned to use the power of concerted action harnessed to a broader political vision. By contrast, collar-and-tie people had emphasized narrower interests through mutual aid and professional associations oriented to patronage and had never formulated a wider conception of politics, along class lines or otherwise. As a result, organized workers faced state-sponsored sindicalismo after 1931 both as a challenge to their independence and as an opportunity. Collar-and-tie people responded to the new labor laws without clear direction.

It might be thought that dire statements about indifference were nothing peculiar to collar-and-tie organizations. Arguably it was the inevitable problem faced by all relatively new groups seeking to attract members and support. Yet complaints of this sort were so common during the 1930s and 1940s that they compel attention to the issue of associative spirit, especially among the vast majority of the collar-and-tie work force that did not belong to a sindicato.[67] For this reason the experience of nonparticipants is as important in gauging the social meaning of collective activity as the experience of participants.

There is no easy way to get at those who did not join sindicatos and the reasons they did not. Not joining may have been the outcome of a conscious decision, as when a person declined the invitation of a friend to take part in an organization. It may simply have been the result of giving priority to other activities, without much thought to collective action. Or it may have been a fear of repression, both by the government and employers. In most cases nonparticipation was probably rooted in all of these. Much of it may have been unconscious; in the context of daily lives many people likely gave little thought to whether or not they should join. In any event, those who remained outside did not leave behind much evidence to help explain their absence. One means of exploring this aspect of associational experience is to focus on the sindicatos' explanations for indifference and attempt to make informed conjectures about those who were not there to speak for themselves.

Preoccupations over status and upward mobility were commonly advanced to explain low participation rates. While Rio's Union of Commercial Employees had existed since shortly after the turn of the century, only in the 1930s did the organization begin to identify its members as workers entitled to the benefits of the new labor laws. In doing so, the union challenged cherished ideals and expectations among Brazil's commercial employees. These aspirations had been most consistently articulated by the Association of Commercial Employees in Rio. The association had come under the domination of employers and accountants during the 1910s and 1920s, but its slogan "employee today, boss tomorrow" still resonated with clerks, bookkeepers, and low-level accountants. So too did its ongoing campaign to raise commercial employees in the public's esteem by insisting on the "nobility and honor of commercial work." The association's president made clear the political implications of this outlook. Rather than rely on the "program of proletarian organizations," wrote Artur Cabrera in 1927, commercial employees should, "through an honest, vigorous, and intelligent collaboration seek gradually to conquer their own position as a boss." In other words, Cabrera counseled commercial employees, however lowly their station, to develop "intellectual and moral self-discipline," to wait their turn, and not involve themselves in political adventures that would only ruin their chances to rise to higher positions.

By 1931 the association was under fire from the union. The assault came against the Association's slogan: in light of economic realities, said the union, "the employee of today will be the employee of tomorrow." In the context of the new labor code union officials sought to persuade commercial clerks that their interests perhaps were not so different from those of other workers. At one level the union's appeal was highly successful. Though it is not known precisely how many ultimately joined the union, the association lost 20,000 of its 43,000 members in 1931, just as the union began to advocate a more assertive stance before employers.[68]

These commercial employees appear not to have abandoned aspirations of upward mobility or to have cashed in their sense of distinction from manual workers. They sought instead to reconcile these ideas with the new imperatives of securing benefits under the 1931 labor code. An article that appeared in the union's magazine in 1931 illustrates the dilemma. In an effort to throw cold water in the faces of his unconscious colleagues, commercial employee Mario José Fernandes argued that the association's hopeful slogan was not accurate. "Don't be fooled!" he admonished colleagues; most employees would remain employees throughout their careers. Yet, because many clerks would indeed become bosses, "more perhaps in commerce than in other areas," he concluded that "all factors indicate that [the employee] at least ought to try to improve his situation."[69]

This article's ambiguity is strong testament to the allure of the association's slogan and to the enduring power of upward mobility and status as
organizing principles of social life. For while attempting to persuade
commercial employees to act more like proletarians in relation to employers, Fernandes felt compelled to reassure members (and potential members) that it was still possible for them to move up. He refused to dash
their dreams lest he drive them away. This suggests that many commercial
employees, wary of a rhetoric identifying them with workers and concerned not to sabotage any chances they might have to "improve their
situation," withheld their participation from the union.

This sentiment appears to have persisted among commercial employees
throughout the 1930s and into the 1940s. In 1937 an activist in São
Paulo's Commercial Employees' Sindicato, repined "worker indifference": "It is astounding that commercial employees who work at petty little jobs (even if in order to get them they had to endure all sorts of sacrifices, studying at night school, etc.) still see sindicalização [unionization]
as *a thing exclusively of interest to [humble and ignorant] workers!*" But
workers, the author wrote angrily, could at least see when unscrupulous
people had taken control of a sindicato and oust them. "What do commercial employees do" faced with a similar situation? They see the problem "as a logical fact about which nothing can be done."[70]

From an activist's point of view the attitude described, which must
have been fairly widespread to call forth such a screed, was simply incom-
prehensible. From another perspective it speaks volumes about the issue of
indifference to the sindicato: among commercial employees the sindicato
and its open exhortation to join other workers appear to have been seen as
inconsistent with their status and a threat to their hope of rising or at least
of remaining a part of the respectable middle class.

This may help explain the resurgence of Rio's Association of Commercial Employees in the 1940s, even though it could not officially represent
its members before government. A decade after losing nearly half its
members, many of whom had gone to the union, the association formulated a position to accommodate the ambiguity of commercial employees'
social place; in 1944 it applauded the government's "formidable accomplishments in labor relations" and at the same time continued to promote
"the well-known lemma, 'today's employee will be tomorrow's boss,'" offering, in a sense, the best of both worlds. Moreover, the association
sought to attract new members by reiterating its policy that "artisans and
workers," the illiterate, and "all those who exercise subaltern functions"
would not be permitted to belong,[71] reinforcing thereby the line between

manual and nonmanual work and between the *culto* and the *inculto* as a basis for organizational identity.

Anxiety of this sort, though rarely so naked, appears to have contributed to low participation among other middle-class employees and professionals, especially since social hierarchy was very much in play throughout the period. The breakaway bank employees' sindicato in São Paulo, Syndiké, with its language of accommodation, hierarchy, and upward mobility indicates that commercial employees were far from alone in their concerns. Spokesmen for emerging professions also expressed reservations about sindicalização. For those seeking to enhance social prestige, the label of worker, even for legal purposes, rubbed against the grain. The author of a 1933 article in the *Revista Paulista de Contabilidade* argued vigorously against a sindicato, even for salaried accountants. Such an organization, insisted Frederico Hermann, Jr., would constitute a step down and implied a "complete negation of our authority as the elite class that we desire to be," for "if accountants accept the conditions imposed on workers' sindicatos, we will be renouncing our highest ideals."[72]

Similarly, the "true" liberal professions—lawyers, doctors, engineers—continued to be "frightened by the word *sindicato*," according to one writer in 1945.[73] Able to see themselves as independent professionals, even if they had the bad luck to earn a salary, many were loath to give up "their dignity, their prestige, their prerogatives" and shrank from being called proletarians. Ashamed of drawing a salary, "which in the modern sense is linked to manual effort," they were, according to one activist, snobs who felt themselves too good to join a sindicato.[74] Liberal professionals did not cringe only from being equated with workers. They worried as well about maintaining a sense of independence before employers and the state, particularly after 1939, when legislation enabled liberal professionals to form state-sponsored sindicatos. Within the ranks of lawyers, doctors, and engineers the tension between the growing numbers of salarymen and those who lived from private practice was palpable. They were separated by income, prestige, and access to the kind of patronage that could guarantee top jobs in the public bureaucracy and business from wealthier clients.

The sindicatos of the liberal professions grew out of this divergence during the 1930s. Because the most prominent members of these professions, those who maintained private practices, were least likely to join, such groups lacked wholehearted support and leadership from those best placed to rally others to collective action. Some stood as obstructionists. Lawyer Noé Azevedo was one. Writing in 1939, he argued that sindicalismo made no sense for lawyers. The sindicato existed to discipline "class struggle," he asserted, to defuse "antagonistic interests" of employers and employees. As the legal profession did not recognize such a distinction within its ranks, there could be no reason to organize in this way. Besides, he said, a sindicato would compromise professional independence, subjecting members to the labor ministry's rigid structure.[75]

Sindicatos of liberal professionals alluded to a host of other reasons to explain lack of interest. Most had to do with the difficult economic conditions of the professions. A common complaint was that intense competition for a limited number of jobs undermined a spirit of solidarity. São Paulo's small lawyers' sindicato rued the "*mors tua, vita mea* attitude" that prevailed among fellow professionals, and the national sindicato of dentists headquartered in Rio worried that practitioners saw in each other "only an enemy to defeat."[76] A related problem was that professionals often worked more than one job or practiced more than one profession. Journalists and accountants, for example, were often so poorly paid that they supplemented their incomes by working at modest commercial jobs or in the public bureaucracies. Not only did this leave them little time to take active part in sindicato life, but by dividing their economic interests between two or more occupational categories, it diluted their loyalties.[77]

Loyalties and interests may also have been divided by the presence of alternatives for professional socializing and identity. Groups such as the Brazilian Education Association, the Brazilian Press Association, the Engineering Club, the Association of Commercial Employees, and the Brazilian Advertising Association, though dominated by elites within each occupational category, gave all members of the profession the opportunity to mingle with more illustrious practitioners or employers. Thus schoolteacher Riva Bauser refused to join a teachers' sindicato because such organizations were for workers, though she enthusiastically became a member of the Brazilian Education Association. There she could mix with intellectuals and educators and immerse herself in national issues by pushing educational reform, rising above her selfish concerns rather then merely pressing for higher salaries and better benefits.[78] Journalist Herculano Siqueira, though a founder of the Sindicato of Professional Journalists of Rio de Janeiro in the mid-1930s, abandoned syndical activity as his career advanced, preferring instead membership in the more respectable and issue-oriented Brazilian Press Association, where he could hobnob with newspaper owners and journalist-intellectuals.[79]

The benefits of belonging to such an association were obvious to many. Commercial employees who felt that sindicato membership was demeaning could join the Association of Commercial Employees and rub shoulders with employers, owners, and accountants, who encouraged them to believe what they were inclined to believe anyway: that it was possible to advance beyond the level of a mere employee or, more realistically, that even as an employee they could be part of higher society, at least vicariously. More instrumentally membership in these associations represented a step toward establishing relationships with employers, well-known professionals, bureaucrats, or even politicians who might be able to offer a pistolão that could make or break a career move at some future time.[80]

Patronage reached far beyond professional organizations. Despite vehement condemnation in the pages of sindicato publications, the idea of career advancement through "political protection and personal sympathy" remained powerful through the 1930s and 1940s, especially in the public sector.[81] A magazine aimed at São Paulo's public grade-school teachers testifies eloquently to the attractions of patronage and to the ways it might undercut solidarity. Writing in 1934, Olavo Leite argued that an "individualist preoccupation" led teachers, men and women alike, to the disturbing position of "combat[ing] political protectionism and at the same time root[ing] around looking for a prestigious name under whose favor he can strengthen his requests for transfer or promotion." As a result, Leite concluded woefully, "We teachers . . . are among the least likely to practice any form of collective unity . . . [because we are] used to receiving official injustices or favors without protests or encomiums."[82] The frustration expressed here was not directed at an abstract market individualism. The problem, rather, was the very concrete individualism of people who knew that their dependence on others could be turned to advantage in a tight job market.

Within public bureaucracies the problem seems to have been particularly acute. According to one commentator in 1937, "identical interests" were not enough to draw federal public servants together. Before 1937 functionaries in various ministries formed their own organizations and sought government recognition independently of functionaries in other ministries.[83] Where Uruguay had a single organization to represent all of the country's salaried bureaucrats, Rio boasted seventy public servants' associations, often working against one another. Fragmentation meant that members of a given sindicato or association could negotiate the circuits of patronage within the ministry more effectively than would have been possible through a larger organization with broader and more politically focused goals. Public functionaries were not passive; they simply were active individually, through work and patronage, rather than collectively.

Nor did patronage cut only one way through associational solidarity. Rumblings of resentment against political protectionism were audible from within collar-and-tie sindicatos during the 1930s. In some cases status, opportunism, and class issues converged. For example, an opposition group within the Commercial Employees' Union charged in 1935 that the organization's important posts always fell to the "well off" with "little interest in the lives of their more exploited colleagues. Or, when they do take an interest, it is not so much to lead the rank and file in a frank struggle against misery; rather they appear as benevolent bourgeois performing an act of charity."[84] More often, the issue appears to have been one of undisguised political entrepreneurialism. In 1935 a member of Rio's medical sindicato lamented the fact that many leaders were concerned only with politics: "They take advantage of the institution exclusively for personal political ends."[85] A member of the national dentists' sindicato in Rio made a nearly identical claim, arguing that a low level of participation allowed organizations to be monopolized by a small number of individuals, "which has unjustly given rise to the legend that [within the sindicatos] political groups dominate that seek only to impose an irreverent bossism."[86] What this writer did not consider was that the legend may have been as much a cause as a consequence of dentists' suspicions. Though the evidence is limited, these examples hint at a more widespread distrust of associational activity among collar-and-tie employees and professionals who simply did not believe that the leadership would act for broader rather than personal ends.

A final indicator of the weak associative spirit among middle-class people was the very low rate of women's participation in sindicatos. Concentrated in certain occupations, especially public administration, teaching, and commerce, women who worked at nonmanual jobs joined sindicatos even less often than did collar-and-tie men and far less often than did working-class women, notwithstanding activists who exhorted their "sisters" to a "duty of solidarity."[87] Certainly women working at nonmanual jobs had limited organizational experience. During the 1920s many female shop clerks and commercial employees had joined and sought to defend their interests through the Brazilian Federation for the Progress of Women.[88] But when sindicatos took shape after 1930, women's specific interests seem to have become lost in the shuffle to assert occupational and class identities, even as the federation's influence declined after suffrage was passed in 1932.

Without the federation to focus women's interests, women who worked at nonmanual jobs had few opportunities to resist the overweening power of men in the professions, even those numerically dominated by women. In some cases male leaders counseled women against aggressive action on their own behalf. In 1933, Everardo Backhauser, president of the Association of Catholic Teachers, agreed that schoolteachers needed to defend their interests collectively. At the same time he insisted that "Catholic teachers judge the value of their work not by the tiny salary with which the state compensates those who serve in the public school system, but by the counsel of the gospel." And though Backhauser pitched his argument in ostensibly neutral (that is, male) gender terms, these words were aimed primarily at women, who vastly outnumbered men as primary-school teachers.[89]

In 1935 the Association of Women Teachers reacted against precisely this situation by condemning "the domination of male leadership in the area of primary-school teaching."[90] The implication was that the men who led the profession's representative organizations had not done enough to address the issue of low salaries and had wholly ignored the fact that men lacked the "maternal instinct" that made women more apt than men for the job of teaching children. Certainly some women joined the association in order to dislodge men from dominant positions within the profession, but since little came of the effort, many must have decided that it simply was not worth the confrontation.

Reasons women stayed aloof from such organizations probably went far beyond male leaders' unresponsiveness to women's concerns. In 1938 the Sindicato of São Paulo Commercial Employees recognized the injustice of the "tremendous disparity between men's and women's salaries and the way employers take advantage of women" and yet still had trouble attracting women to its ranks.[91] An explanation may lie in the fact that few women continued to work with any regularity after they married, and if they did, it was to supplement household income so that children might attend better schools or that the family might afford a servant to perform the most unpleasant domestic chores.[92] If women worked outside the home, they commonly did so at jobs of lesser prestige than their husbands'. A middle-class woman's status was defined less by her own job (if she had one) than by her spouse's and by the overall lifestyle her family led. Though there is little direct evidence for the proposition, it is at least plausible that women in this situation would have shied away from joining a sindicato precisely because it would undercut their own status claims. Moreover, having a wife who stayed home to manage the servant and raise children was a realistic if not always attainable ideal for the families of collar-and-tie men in a way it simply was not for working-class families. Thus most women who entered the collar-and-tie work force when young probably never intended or imagined that their earnings would allow them to live independently.[93] Since their work life as salary earners was tenuous compared to what was referred to as their "more sacred mission" in the home, most probably saw little point in joining organizations to lobby for their interests as employees. Finally Brazilian women had long lived within a culture that discouraged their participation in public and political affairs.[94] Their experience of social reality had until very recently been organized almost exclusively through home life. As women began to emerge into the public sphere, they brought their sensibilities with them. When feminists pushed for the vote, they did so, in part, by claiming that suffrage would elevate their roles as mothers and contribute to social peace.[95]

This lack of experience in the public world of interest-group politics and a greater familiarity with home life may help make sense of Dinah Silveira de Queiroz's advice to her "sisters" from the pages of *O Cruzeiro* in 1945. The "secret to social equilibrium," she opined, was a matter of how the country chose to confront the issue of women's work. It was perfectly fine for women *as individuals* to work outside the home. They were "excellent collaborators" and had an "admirable sense of responsibility." But, she insisted, there should be no women's groups, clubs, or political centers touting a collective agenda on behalf of women. Women might participate in philanthropic organizations, such as the Red Cross or other groups where "domestic aspects predominate," but political clubs, feminist academies, and militant women's organizations simply sapped "precious energies so much more necessary and useful in other sorts of activities. I believe that we [women] can best serve the world as 'individuals.' And the world needs us. We are valuable by ourselves . . . [b]ut we are nothing as a multitude."[96]

Queiroz's views were not universal, because women's roles were in a state of flux. Nevertheless, they do represent the struggle over a long-standing vision that identified women principally with the home and not with politics. Even so, Queiroz's reference to social equilibrium hints she may have had another sort of politics in mind, a politics rooted not in the public sphere of Machiavellian maneuver or ideology but in the intimacies of home life. In the face of a resurgent labor movement, a resurrected communism at the end of the Estado Novo, and an uncertain political situation, her concern for "social equilibrium" suggests the possibility that, in the context of mid-century Rio and São Paulo, class may have weighed more heavily on the minds of middle-class women than feminism.[97]

Though it is hardly a novel claim that many, perhaps most people, in modern societies are disinclined to collective activity, the assertion has rarely been explored for itself. Explanations for tepidness toward sindicalismo by the vast majority of middle-class people can only be tentative. Their voices did not appear in the records of the organizations from which they were absent. Only fragmentary evidence from the organizations themselves exists, with all the evasions, incomprehensions, and misperceptions that attend any effort to understand the motivations of those who were not present to speak on their own behalf. Among the reasons for which so many withheld their participation, fear of repression, status anxiety, the continued force of patronage relationships, an abiding suspicion and distrust of leaders, and the fragile link women had to the world of work stand out.

The indifference sindicatos complained of throughout the 1930s and 1940s, then, was not merely an obstacle in the process of being overcome by a vigorous and vibrant middle-class associational movement. It was, rather, a constituent aspect of the collar-and-tie experience, a crucial element in the emerging political temper of middle-class Brazilians. Contemporary observers expressed concern over a class dispersed. In the early 1940s João Lyra Filho worried that the "competitive spirit" that dominated middle-class life had bred an intractable "individualist sentiment" that undermined cooperation.[98] More pointedly Ruy de Azevedo Sodré argued that overall "the middle class, by its character, has a marked individualist tendency. It is more concerned with its own affairs, individually, than with defending itself through professional organizations or group associations."[99] This is what Dr. Azambuja had feared when he argued to his colleagues at the Medical and Surgical Society that they could not afford to be a "dispersed force" at the mercy of "those who take part in the struggle."

BY 1945 MIDDLE-CLASS Brazilians had gained an uncertain purchase within the corporatist system of labor relations that came to be known as trabalhismo, a mixture of social welfarism, working-class political activity, and economic nationalism. On the one hand, a fair number of collar-and-tie sindicatos represented the interests of occupational groups before the state and expressed an eagerness to collaborate with public authorities. On the other hand, most of these organizations failed to attract large numbers of members. Moreover, after 1939 one of the largest categories of collar-and-tie employees, federal civil servants, was barred altogether from forming sindicatos that could lobby the state. A huge majority of middle-class people remained at the margins of the arena where everyday issues of class relations were being hashed out.

Private associations did seek to regulate and moralize the professions.

Concerned with ethical and professional issues, they generally gave short shrift to the plight of salaried employees. They too insisted that collaboration with government best served the interests of their members and the nation, though they kept a greater distance from the state than groups of salaried employees, among whom numbered many liberal professionals.[100] Proponents of sindicalismo did not oppose such associations. They simply recognized, as the National Engineers' Sindicato remarked of Rio's Engineering Club in 1935, that such groups could not adopt a "program of rigid intransigence" in defense of rights.[101]

The most striking aspect of middle-class associational life up to 1945 can be seen in relation to the history of the labor movement in São Paulo. The labor movement survived the Estado Novo's repression and cooptation by relying on grass-roots resistance and strategic alliances, allowing labor to retain a certain organizational autonomy that carried over to the postwar period.[102] Engagement with the state permitted other components of organized labor to retain influence in politics and government after the war. This was hardly a well-orchestrated effort. Proponents of each strategy rarely saw eye to eye. The crucial point is that the government had to respond to both, knowing that nothing could be taken for granted.

The sindicatos of nonmanual employees and professionals, by contrast, steadfastly expressed their desire to collaborate with the state in maintaining class peace. Faced with few alternatives, these groups acceded, many willingly, to a corporatist model of interest representation linked to a rhetoric of social harmony. Even before the Estado Novo only São Paulo's bank employees demonstrated a willingness to take a more aggressive stance by striking. Most collar-and-tie sindicatos, reflecting widespread concerns for status and fear of working-class upheaval, refused to go so far. Without meaning to, they signaled the state and employers that they could be taken for granted or at least that they could be counted on not to court disorder. By 1946, for instance, commercial employers in São Paulo confidently concluded that their employees, unlike industrial workers, would not strike.[103] Collaboration produced not a close and fruitful relationship with government, but one in which collar-and-tie organizations were very much a second thought to the uncertainties of dealing with what elites saw as a restive working class.

8

Marginalized in the Middle
of Electoral Populism

THROUGHOUT THE ESTADO NOVO industrialists and organized workers took their place at the center of President Getúlio Vargas's political calculations. Vargas reinforced his populist rhetoric by giving workers enforceable rights against their employers through the state's system of labor courts. During the early years of the Estado Novo industrialists continued to oppose Vargas's concessions to workers even as they welcomed the impulse to expand internal markets for manufactured goods.[1] The dynamic tension in which Vargas held these forces began to break down as World War II approached a close. In 1943 Vargas ended Brazil's flirtations with the Axis powers and joined hands with the Allies. Brazil became the only Latin American nation to send troops to the European Theater. Brazil's involvement in a war to protect democracy forced Vargas to loosen his tight grip on internal dissent. War against the Axis gave journalists an opening to champion democracy and to condemn all antidemocratic government, including, by implication, the Estado Novo itself.[2] As an Allied victory neared, Vargas's opponents, not least among them those who had lost power in the Revolution of 1930 and had been stopped from regaining it by the coup of 1937, were emboldened. In 1943 and 1944 several highly publicized manifestos called for the political system to be reopened. By 1944 Vargas had decided he could not stand fast in the face of demands for a return to electoral processes.

This opening did not bring a dramatic shift in middle-class political fortunes. Uneasy political involvement during the 1920s and 1930s carried over to the 1940s, now in the context of national elections. In 1930 Vargas, the Liberal Alliance, and the *Tenentes* had proclaimed that the revolution would "republicanize the republic." Though it was never clear precisely what this meant, most who had supported the dissidents would not have contemplated that twenty years later they would continue to be at the margins of the nation's political life. No longer subordinated to a dominant oligarchy, middle-class Cariocas and Paulistanos by 1950 were pressed between what they saw as an organized and vocal urban working class and well-connected and powerful groups of elites.

The Familiar and the New: The Election of 1945

It is difficult to know how middle-class people perceived and participated in the unraveling of the Estado Novo. Certainly there is no indication that large numbers of middle-class people defended the dictatorship with any vigor. Whatever its earlier accomplishments, Vargas's regime had not warded off the inflationary incubus that continued to haunt tenuous middle-class gains. A 1943 letter from one B. Montenegro to Gustavo Capanema, Vargas's minister of education, was typical of a growing impatience with the government in matters touching middle-class life. "This is not a democracy," said the writer, brandishing the word that was becoming a political mantra. For all the "good will of the great president Getúlio Vargas, even the reasonably well situated [*remediados* (neither rich nor poor)] can no longer educate their children."[3] Before long the pitch of such complaints rose, becoming a constant din, filling column after column in the newspapers and even sparking an effort in São Paulo to organize a "Strike of the Consumer" in 1944.[4]

There was as well a growing sense that Vargas's regime was out of step with the rest of the democratic world. Brazilian troops were fighting and dying in Italy to defend democracy, yet there was no democracy in Brazil. Students and intellectuals took the point on this issue after 1943, calling for Vargas's ouster. Even some of Vargas's staunchest and most public supporters of times past thought the moment for change had come. As early as 1941 the editorial board of *Vida Carioca* had begun to argue that suspension of electoral processes had been a necessary but emphatically "temporary" measure. By 1945 the magazine continued to praise Vargas for his decisive leadership but remarked that as totalitarianism was falling the world over, it was only right that Brazil too should assume the mantle of democracy.[5]

With support among the armed forces slipping, Vargas agreed to elections for late 1945. Two military men emerged as candidates for the presidency. Army General Eurico Dutra ran for the newly minted Social Democratic party (PSD), which, despite its name, owed its existence to Vargas's links to rural political machines controlled by *coronéis*. Air Force

Brigadier Eduardo Gomes ran under the banner of the National Democratic Union (UDN), a loose and unstable amalgam of anti-Vargas forces, ranging from various strands of liberal thought to disgruntled Communists. As in the PSD, behind the UDN's facade of liberalism were the local political machines of coronéis, which had been excluded from political power throughout the 1930s.

Many ordinary citizens remained wary of both parties, fearing oligarchs ousted in 1930 might regain a dominant position. Students, among the more active and notorious opponents of the Estado Novo, held the old guard at arm's length. As a United States embassy cable observed in mid-1944, "The students ... by no means wish for a complete return to the conditions of government as they existed before Vargas."[6] Others expressed greater alarm at the revanchist prospect. A publication of São Paulo commercial employees worried that "the old politicians, the old parties of the Old Republic are back. Hmmm! Old politicians, old parties, Old Republic ... there is something mighty familiar in all this!"[7]

There was also something new: the dramatic increase in the number of eligible voters since the last presidential election in 1930. Not quite 2 million peopled had voted then, less than 6 percent of the total population, not more than 15 percent of adults. In the election of 1945, 6 million people voted, about a third of all adults. By 1950 8 million Brazilians would vote, nearly 40 percent of adults and at least three quarters of all who met the literacy requirement. In the two decades between 1930 and 1950 the number of voting citizens increased fourfold (while population did not even double), and the percentage of the population voting almost tripled.[8] A considerable number of these new participants entered the political arena, not as isolated individuals but as part of a new social force, a politically mobilizable working class.

Having weathered the state's repression and cooptation, organized workers were a force to reckon with by 1945. Vargas saw the change as an opportunity, realizing that he would have to negotiate with workers even as he was trying to bend them to his will if he hoped to prolong his political life beyond the Estado Novo. He knew he must have the urban working-class mass to offset the coronéis, who retained control of a still vast rural electorate. To this end Vargas took a number of dramatic steps to shore up his influence among workers. He struck a bargain with his regime's most famous opponent, Luís Carlos Prestes, the dashing Knight of Hope, who had thrilled urban crowds during the Tenentista uprisings of the 1920s, disappointed many with his betrayal in 1931, helped launch the *Intentona* in 1935, and languished in prison during much of the Estado Novo. In exchange for Prestes's support Vargas released him from prison and took the unprecedented step of legalizing the Communist party. To solidify his own political position, Vargas created the Brazilian Labor party (PTB), which found an enthusiastic following among many workers who saw in it the potential for powerful access to the political arena that had been closed to them for so long. Confident of his footing on the new political terrain, Vargas entered the 1945 election as a third candidate.

It was a short-lived campaign. His courtship of the labor vote gave rise to unresolvable political dilemmas. Throughout the Estado Novo Vargas had curried the favor of industrialists, knowing that without them he could not face down the rural political machines that had been the backbone of oligarchic rule before 1930. Promises of state-led industrial development and assurances of social peace had won him considerable good will. When he began to woo workers with promises of enforcement and expansion of the labor laws, and when thousands of factory hands took to the streets spontaneously to chant, "*Queremos Getúlio*" (we want Getúlio), Vargas's erstwhile allies became concerned. They applauded Vargas the champion of industrial development but were leery of Vargas the populist politician. Aware that if industrialists abandoned him he might not be able to prevent the traditional political elite from returning to power, Vargas withdrew from the race and threw his support to the PSD's Dutra.

By backing Dutra, Vargas sought to balance the various tensions of the post–Estado Novo political reality. Weighing in with the PSD, he was able to accommodate opportunistic rural politicians who could deliver votes in exchange for favors, appease factory owners impressed by the PSD's explicit call for state-led industrial development, and continue to anchor his influence in labor. This arrangement softened the PSD's platform planks on workers' issues. Dutra pledged to enforce the labor laws, including provisions governing minimum wages, workday limitations, vacations, working conditions, medical care, the right to organize and strike, pensions, and the labor courts. These maneuvers represented Vargas's efforts to reorient Brazilian national politics away from the old clientelism and regionalism of oligarchic rule and toward a politics that appealed directly to the mass of urban working people. In other words, class—the relationship between capital and labor—came to rest at the core of political struggle and debate in a political system controlled by electoral contests.

This is what made 1945 a crucial episode in the history of Brazilian politics. It was the first open presidential election since the Revolution of 1930 and the future direction of the political system was at stake. The outcome was unpredictable. In spite of labor's growing strength, the PTB remained poorly organized and the Communist party relatively small, so that the race came down to a match between the PSD and the UDN, closely supervised by the upper echelons of the military hierarchy. The most pronounced differences in the two parties' platforms went to matters of industrialization and labor policy. The PSD explicitly called for industrial development through state intervention in the economy and promised that the labor laws would be scrupulously observed. The UDN's program, by contrast, was not prepared to galvanize industry at the expense of traditional agrarian interests. And beyond a nod to union autonomy and the right to strike, it had little to say on labor issues.[9]

The plight of the splintered middle class was not a major issue for either party as the campaign took off in late 1944. Except for Gomes's blanket pledge to curb inflation and promote "moral and efficient administration" and "rigorous responsibility" in government, neither candidate offered any immediate sop to middle-class voters.[10] Even so, the middle class may have been a factor restraining the candidates from too blatantly appealing for working-class support. Vargas's courting of workers through the PTB and his pact with the Communist party in mid-1945 had doubtless frightened many a solid middle-class citizen. Dutra and Gomes were careful not to follow Vargas's lead. Dutra did not need to. Understanding that workers would not vote for Gomes, he did little more than promise that labor disputes would be resolved peacefully through "impartial organs," allowing the "complete assimilation of classes." Gomes also emphasized "conciliation" and "harmony" between capital and labor, though he seemed less conscious of the electoral strength of workers. He even appeared to contradict his party's commitment to the right to strike by insisting that labor disputes be settled without recourse to "the always pernicious general or partial" work stoppage.[11]

Some insight into the middle class's uneasy political position in 1945 comes from the manifesto of a small leftist party, the Democratic Socialist Union (UDS). While it did not garner great support, the UDS appealed to "the Brazilian people, especially the middle classes and the poor," a faint echo of mid-1930s efforts on the left and right to articulate a middle-class populism. While the Revolution of 1930 had opened up political opportunities for the "middle class," said the manifesto, the "oligarchic framework" had been speedily rebuilt because middle-class people had been so "hostile to an alliance with the urban and rural proletariat." "Their possibilities of affirming autonomy and of forging an alliance with workers," said the manifesto, were finally dashed by the 1937 coup that ushered in the Estado Novo. Since then "the middle classes [had] made only weak efforts to articulate an electoral position."[12]

As an attempt to galvanize the middle class this call to arms left much to be desired. As an assessment of the situation it was coldly honest. The UDS's own analysis suggests that its leaders sensed the difficulty of persuading middle-class people to "affirm an independent politics" and ally themselves with workers. This lack of hope, a kind of admission that the middle class existed only at the margins of "the people," blared out from the banner appeal heading the manifesto: "TO THE BRAZILIAN PEOPLE—TO THE WORKERS OF THE CITIES AND THE COUNTRYSIDE—TO THE YOUNG PEOPLE OF THE FACTORIES AND SCHOOLS." Any potential middle-class reader fearful of being lumped in with mere workers need have read no further.

The uncharismatic Dutra won the day on December 2, 1945: 55 percent to Gomes's 35.[13] He did so with a novel coalition in Brazilian politics: an alliance of local political machines, urban labor support from the PTB, and the favor of urban industrialists linked to the PSD. The UDN's patchwork of oppositionists, from rural elites to Communists upset by the fact that their party had struck a deal with Vargas, simply had not been able to overcome the new political weight of the organized working class. Indeed, the great surprise of the election was not so much Dutra's victory as the performance of the Communist party itself. Its candidate, Yeddo Fiúza, garnered nearly 10 percent of the vote and fourteen Communists went to Congress.

Where did middle-class voters come down? As results from a 1948 poll hint (Table 6), the short answer may be, not overwhelmingly in one camp or another.[14]

Contemporary political commentator Clovis Leite Ribeiro argued in 1948 that this middle-class split was evidence of a political rootlessness rather than of a clear ideological divide. True, a "more refined part of the middle class," by which he seems to have meant a small number of university graduates with links to traditional society, may have tended to vote with the UDN. This, he insisted, had not been the basic problem. Rather, the middle class of salaried employees and professionals had been "left out" of a political equation that had drawn too sharp a distinction between "proletariat and bourgeoisie."[15] Stuck in the middle of class struggle with nowhere to turn, they had voted according to no clear preference or did not vote at all, as Table 6 suggests.

TABLE 6

Poll Regarding Presidential Politics, São Paulo, September 1948

(Percentage of A's, B's, and C's responding)

	A	B	C	Total
Dutra (PSD)	27	36	24	29
Gomes (UDN)	40	25	5	15
Not voting/blank ballot	23	34	47	40
Other*	10	5	25	16

QUESTION: "For whom did you vote in the 1945 presidential election?"
SOURCE: IBOPE 19.
* Votes cast for minor candidates and no answer.

Nor, wrote Ribeiro, did the middle class's political situation improve after Dutra took office. The years between 1945 and 1948 were the "calvary of the middle class, victimized by inflation, by administrative anarchy, and by bad government." He noted, for instance, that in 1946 a São Paulo state decree had allowed a tax break for the purchase of a home up to a maximum of 50,000 cruzeiros. Fine and good, quipped Ribeiro, except not even a "modest middle-class family" could buy a home for anything under 150,000. The middle-class man, he concluded, had few alternatives to "killing himself with work or . . . having recourse to the corruption generated and generalized by inflation" if he hoped to "maintain a certain level of social decency and to educate the children instead of making them take jobs when they turn fourteen."

Having been "entirely abandoned," the middle class, Ribeiro argued, had drifted away from major parties after 1945, at least in Brazil's most populous cities. Not at home in the PSD or the UDN and with little to lose, many middle-class people were willing to experiment politically. This, Ribeiro concluded, was the crucial factor in Adhemar de Barros's successful campaign for São Paulo's governorship in 1947. His Social Progressive party (PSP), newly created for the occasion, attracted a plurality of the state-wide vote and nearly 50 percent in urban areas, a spectacular showing for a party without any history or organization.

Barros's victory was all the more remarkable in that he won without support from mainstream parties—PSD, UDN, PTB—and with Communist backing, the only way he could secure the labor support he needed to overcome Mario Tavares, the candidate backed by the PSD's rural machine. In fact, the political frustration of middle-class Paulistas and Paulistanos was signaled most ostentatiously by their willingness to vote in such large numbers for a man who had struck a bargain with Communists. For

Ribeiro the key to Barros's success was that middle-class voters saw the PSP-Communist alliance as a tactical maneuver rather than an ideological or political commitment. For them Barros was a maverick who could unseat ineffectual mainstream parties but who, unlike Vargas, had no political or ideological affinities for workers. Middle-class voters, averred Ribeiro, saw Barros as being "equidistant from the extremism of Communism or the demagogy of the *queremistas* [working-class supporters of Vargas] and from the conservative parties that had no feeling for their problems—which were fundamental problems of the country." Oriented to the personal ambitions of selfish leaders, these parties had no way to "bring about a politics of unity and national salvation." By casting their ballots for Barros, middle-class voters had said "No!" to the "narrow-minded partisanship" of other parties.[16]

In other words, a middle-class vote for Barros was, in part, a vote against politics as usual. Of course, Ribeiro understood that not all middle-class Paulistas had voted for Barros in 1947. Many who might have probably refused to go along with his play for the Communist vote. And the middle-class gubernatorial vote for Barros did not represent a seismic shift in national political loyalties. Barros's middle-class supporters may have been willing to cast their ballots for a candidate who made a tactical alliance with Communists, but there is no evidence that very many supported the Communist party's program. Moreover, by mid-1948 the PSP had alienated most of its middle-class backers; only about 8 percent of what one poll characterized as middle-class respondents said they would be willing to vote for Barros for president.[17]

The significance of Ribeiro's analysis, then, lies less in the details than in his conclusion that middle-class Paulistanos were splintered among the mainstream parties in the latter half of the 1940s, effectively without a home in national politics. On this view, they voted but lacked access to the levers of power controlled by elites and had nothing like the sense of shared purpose that energized the labor movement.

Politics on a Secondary Plane: The Election of 1950

Ribeiro's analysis helps make sense of a poll conducted in September 1948, purporting to show a high level of frustration with politics in the late 1940s. Six hundred Paulistanos, divided by social and economic category, were asked the question "Are you interested in politics?" Of those queried, 53 percent of upper-class A's, 83 percent of middle-class B's, and 89 percent of lower- or working-class C's said no.[18] The wide gap between

A's, on the one hand, and B's and C's, on the other, is consonant with the fact that the PSD and the UDN were dominated by and acted in the interests of political elites and the powerful economic groups they served.[19] Might there be a basis for distinguishing between the responses of middle-class B's and lower-class C's, despite the similarity suggested by their numbers? Without answers to more a probing inquiry, the only means of approaching this question is to examine the broad context of the responses.

Workers had ample reason to have soured on politics since the election of 1945. The initial excitement of having Vargas negotiate with labor representatives and of electing thirty-six congressmen and one senator in open balloting had faded. In the face of 87 strikes in the first three months of the new administration Dutra seemed to have forgotten that working people had supported him in large numbers. By mid-1946 the new president had begun to denounce communists, who appeared to be gaining ground in workers' unions. Repression of the wider labor movement soon followed. Meetings were broken up; activists, arrested. The Workers' Confederation of Brazil, founded shortly after the 1945 election, was declared illegal. Thereafter nearly 150 unions were "intervened" to "eliminate extremist elements."[20] At times there was violence. In the Massacre of Largo da Carioca in Rio de Janeiro police fired upon a crowd, killing one and wounding several.[21]

In 1947 anticommunist rhetoric reached a fevered pitch and the Brazilian Communist party, the nation's fourth largest political organization, was outlawed. The party's congressional representatives were cashiered and stripped of political rights. In São Paulo governor Adhemar de Barros supported the move, betraying quondam allies. Workers appear to have seen this as evidence that neither Barros, an opportunist pure and simple, nor Dutra, who by 1948 was first and foremost a champion of national industry, could be counted on as a friend of labor.[22]

Thus when Paulistano workers were asked whether they had any interest in politics, their overwhelming no almost surely meant, among other things, that they were fed up with repression and tired of politicians, like Dutra and Barros, who had betrayed their trust. The high percentage of workers who reported not voting or casting blank ballots in 1945 suggests that many may never have put much faith in politics (Table 6).[23] But among those involved in the labor movement, "no" did not necessarily connote a broader sense of resignation to the situation. A distinct combativeness remained. The words of São Paulo mason Antônio Cabrera in 1947 evoke the sentiment: "As workers conscious of our rights and determined to fight for respect of the Constitution, we will not permit our organizations to continue under the threat of brutal interventions."[24] Even after cancellation of the Communist party's political rights, the Communists continued to expand their political base in municipal elections by making agreements with other parties. Perhaps most tellingly, support for Vargas's PTB declined dramatically when it became clear that the party had cooperated with the government's antilabor actions and had known of and failed vigorously to oppose the outlawing of the Communist party. These were the words and actions of people who, while frustrated, constituted a core that continued to believe in the efficacy of collective struggle on behalf of their rights.

By contrast, Ribeiro saw a "dispersed and abandoned" middle class rather than one "animated by a sense of class." Certainly middle-class people had plenty to be upset about. Inflation had not abated in the years since both candidates had promised to rein it in, and government seemed altogether heedless of the ongoing threat to middle-class status. Recent experience counseled little faith in politics, mainstream or otherwise, a legacy painfully confirmed in the political crucible of the 1940s.

Two congresses in the 1940s hint at the middle class's predicament in the unfolding politics of class. In late 1943 representatives of industry and commerce convoked the First Brazilian Economic Congress to discuss economic prospects after the war and the relationship of business to the state. A number of white-collar organizations sent delegates, among them engineers, architects, lawyers, accountants, teachers, shopkeepers, commercial employees, and traveling salesmen. Discussion during three weeks of meetings revolved around issues of industrialization and economic development and, prominently, the problem of labor, though no labor unions participated.[25] After being accused of favoring business groups congress organizer João Daudt ducked for cover and pledged that "the great theme [of] living standards" would be addressed. But when all was said and done, editorialized the opinion magazine *Diretrizes*, the conference had addressed social security, inflation, and welfare policy but had not substantively confronted the broad standard-of-living issue, except as a natural consequence of economic growth. Rather, the conference had focused on how to create incentives for industry. By neglecting this issue, said *Diretrizes*, the congress had all but forgotten about the people.[26] The only solution was for the people, the government, and *técnicos* (technical experts) to act against the overweening power of business in national affairs by working for Brazil's emancipation from economic imperialism and for effective state intervention in the economy.

This reference to the people without so much as a nod to the fact of labor's complete absence from the congress and the implied trust in government and técnicos to counteract business bias bespeaks a viewpoint not widely shared among organized workers in 1943. So while it would be too much to think of *Diretrizes*'s position as representing a middle-class sentiment, the swell of nationalism and the concern expressed over exclusion of the people from a meeting of the "organized classes" likely resonated with many of the collar-and-tie employees and professionals who had had so little to say at the congress. A glimmer of the frustration likely felt among middle-class attendees can be seen in a remark by one of the conference's keynote speakers, spokesman for industry Roberto Simonsen: "The idea to help and protect medium and small industry came from big industry in São Paulo. And who is against it? Lawyers, teachers, groups unrelated to industry."[27]

Three years later nearly 2,000 workers came together at the Congress of Unionized Workers in Rio de Janeiro to undertake frank discussions regarding the future of the labor movement and its relationship to electoral politics. The Communist party had proposed a labor conference for 1946. The labor ministry countered by scheduling a congress of its own. Fearful of being excluded, the Communist party reluctantly agreed to cosponsor the event, which met in Rio for three weeks in September 1946.

Events at the congress exemplify the potential for friction between collar-and-tie groups and organized labor. Two weeks into the proceedings Orval Cunha, president of the Sindicato of Traveling Salesmen, said he had had enough. Aiming to provoke a presidential response, he fired off a telegram to Dutra accusing the Communist party of monopolizing discussion at the congress. This "anarchic current," he said, had dissipated the atmosphere necessary for genuine exchange. From two- to several hundred of the 2,000 delegates in attendance, including a teachers' sindicato from São Paulo, and some workers then stormed out and reconvened in Niterói across Guanabara Bay from Rio. Those who remained, including a small journalists' sindicato, also from of São Paulo, issued a declaration of their own, admitting that many communists were in attendance but noting that a majority of those present were laborites, democrats, liberals, socialists, and even anarcho-syndicalists. In the face of protests from delegates still meeting in Rio, the government sided with the dissidents across the bay and closed the congress down before its official conclusion.[28]

The essence of Cunha's complaint was that the better-organized Communists would always have their way in an open forum. This was a perennial problem for nonradical collar-and-tie groups, which lacked the numbers and focus of many labor organizations. By protesting in a way that led to the congress's being closed, these dissidents gained a momentary ascendancy over the labor movement. It is worth noting that whatever influence they exerted was possible only because Cunha and others had complained about an issue of known concern to the government, Communist infiltration of the labor movement. Here was the dilemma facing a weakly organized middle class: collar-and-tie groups were relatively impotent vis-à-vis organized labor except when making a defensive point the government already agreed with.[29]

By the late 1940s many had begun to wonder whether partisan politics offered any solution to the quandary exemplified in the Brazilian Economic Conference and the Congress of Unionized Workers. Rubens Gil de Alencastro, an *O Cruzeiro* reader, threw up his hands when it came to politics. In a letter to the editor in September 1947 he wrote of his disillusionment, saying that he was "daily more convinced of the bankruptcy of Brazilian political parties." "What should I do, remain neutral or just join any one of them?" he asked with the weary tone of one who was not sure it mattered what he decided.[30] Similarly, in 1948 or 1949 a lawyer from Vitória, Espírito Santo, reprised Alencastro's frustration, though from the perspective of one worried that a politicized working class was eclipsing the middle class: "There is no axis, no unity among the various components of the middle class, from a political viewpoint. There is no party preferred by the middle class," because the political parties sought only to court the "proletariat."[31]

The 1950 presidential campaign appears to have done little to dispel a sense of political abandonment within the middle class. After five years in the wings Getúlio Vargas was back at center stage, recharging the populist language he had debuted between 1938 and 1945. In most of his speeches he addressed himself to "the people" and to "workers of Brazil." As the candidate of the PTB he pledged vigorous enforcement of extant labor laws and new legislation to improve workers' standard of living in accordance with social justice. In a bid for the support of industrialists he promised to "transform [Brazil] into an industrial nation," by overcoming the "myopia of rulers wedded to existing monoculture and to the simple extraction of primary materials." All this could be done, he insisted, "without appeal to class struggle" and in a way that would assure "national unity."[32]

His leading opponent was the losing candidate in 1945, Brigadier Eduardo Gomes of the UDN. Facing Vargas's prolabor, proindustry platform, which promised sustained modernization, jobs, credit, legal protections, and progress with social peace, Gomes and the UDN relied on a vague pledge to protect Christianity against subversion and a sketchy economic program calling for unspecified measures to rein in inflation. Though he entreated the "anonymous army of workers" to vote for him, Gomes was not in tune with the new political style represented by Vargas's campaign. As in 1945 he and the UDN had little to offer workers in exchange for their support. At times he even seemed hostile to their demands, as when he argued for repeal of the minimum-salary law.[33] In the main, however, Gomes and the UDN had one overarching political principle: opposition to Vargas and his populist appeals to workers and employers. São Paulo's major newspaper, *O Estado de São Paulo*, embellished this position, referring to Vargas as the "ex-dictator," denouncing him as the "Argentine candidate" (a swipe at Juan Perón), and repeatedly raising the specter of his links with communism.[34]

Though the UDN expected to the last to win the election, Vargas as the PTB's candidate won with nearly an absolute majority of votes. Gomes ran a weak second, garnering less than a third of the ballots cast. The balance went to the PSD's candidate, who came in a distant third, relying on little more than appeals to Christian morality by its candidate, Cristiano Machado, as a selling point. Once again the UDN had underestimated the power of the labor vote and had slighted Vargas's ability to forge an alliance of disparate interests.[35]

There is no direct evidence of where middle-class voters came down in this election. A 1948 IBOPE poll indicates that middle-class voters in São Paulo remained about as divided as they had been in 1945: 20 percent of B's said they would vote for Vargas, 24 indicated they would vote for Gomes, and most of the rest remained uncommitted.[36] A later poll hints that within a month of the election on October 3, 1950, the tide had turned in Vargas's favor. In early September, just under 50 percent of B's in São Paulo told IBOPE poll takers that they would vote for Vargas, while 37 percent said they would cast their ballots for the UDN's Gomes.[37] Given continuing political uncertainty, it is worth considering the case for each candidate from a middle-class perspective.

A noteworthy aspect of the 1950 presidential race was the UDN's lackluster effort to attract middle-class voters. After its loss in 1945 and its continued decline during Dutra's tenure, the UDN's leadership began to cast about for other sources of electoral support. This prompted UDN president Prado Kelly to claim in 1948 that "the UDN is the party of the middle class and, as such, it is the party of juridical order, democratic stability, and political and individual liberty."[38] Though narrowly conceiving middle-class interests, this recognition of a middle-class constituency carried over to the 1950 election. In an article in *O Estado de São Paulo* in May 1950 Gomes argued that his deflationary policies would rescue the "great mass of consumers" that was being "impoverished day by day." Though he did not refer to the middle class as such, the implication was clear, since "workers are already with [Luís Carlos] Prestes, Getúlio, and Adhemar."[39] Beyond this naked appeal to pocketbooks, Gomes harped on issues of administrative morality and eroding status.[40] Yet for all the rhetoric the UDN remained a party that defended above all the economic interests of landed elites and their hangers-on.[41]

Still middle-class voters could find reasons to side with the UDN enthusiastically or reluctantly, depending on the individual case. Greater attention to middle-class concerns was a welcome novelty. The UDN seemed to recognize that the rising cost of living represented a threat to status. Its emphasis on morality sought to draw those, especially *donas de casa,* who worried that traditional customs were imperiled. Finally, by opposing Vargas, whose politics could be seen to divide the country and whip workers into a frenzy, the UDN offered solace to those who most feared autonomous working-class politics.[42]

In contrast to Gomes, Vargas made no explicit call to the middle class.[43] His chosen audience was almost exclusively workers as the people. Nevertheless, there was enough in his program that many middle-class voters could have preferred him to Gomes. In speeches he spoke passionately of his commitment to creating a modern society by "restoring Brazil on the path to peace and prosperity" and blazing a trail to "national renovation" through an industrialization that would free Brazil from its dependence on foreigners, a theme that resonated to central tenets of Tenentismo, Integralism, and the ANL during the 1920s and 1930s. Moreover, he was known to enjoy support among of coterie of important industrialists pleased with his developmentalist thrust. At the same time he seemed to understand the importance of "supporting and defending the family . . . according to religious tradition and Christian sentiment." He was not blind to the ravages of inflation, even if he pitched the issue in terms of the workers' plight. He insisted over and over that capital and labor could "coexist in harmony" and that *trabalhista* politics was "contrary to class struggle, because in society there are no classes, only men with the same duties and same needs."[44] Who better than a friend of workers to control them? Harking back to rhetoric used to justify the Estado Novo, he blasted "the old parties with new labels" and lamented "public activity that is merely political, empty of economic and social content." Accordingly, he condemned "political professionals" and declared himself a candidate above politics. He linked democracy to well-being, for democracy was not merely a matter of process but also a matter of the "happiness and wealth of each person."[45]

The point of this juxtaposition is to suggest that, at least in São Paulo, there appears to have been no "natural" middle-class choice for president in 1950. Gomes addressed himself to the concerns of status-threatened middle-class people, but his program was weak and backward looking. Vargas did not speak to the middle class as such, though his language and program echoed many of the issues and dilemmas middle-class people had been facing for the past twenty years. For its part the PSD remained a party of rural interests that sought a broader following principally by claiming to be a defender of Christianity, something both Vargas and Gomes were careful to do as well. Hence, the choice among them may not have been so much an option for or against a clear middle-class candidate or agenda. It may instead have been a matter of the weight individual voters gave to a variety of concerns and how they understood their personal problems in the context of the country's situation. Coworkers doubtless differed on these issues. Even family members disagreed.[46]

Without access to the levers of power and in light of complex maneuvers among parties, many may have seen themselves as choosing between evils rather than affirming a political or ideological commitment. Indeed, the fog of dissatisfaction with political process seems not to have lifted for the election. Early in the 1950 campaign, for instance, *O Cruzeiro* (which opposed Vargas) reported receiving over 1,200 letters in one week asking why the political parties had not articulated coherent platforms. If they would but do so, chided the editors, the vote would not be so scattered across numerous parties. "Who is to blame?" asked one letter writer; "mediocre party leaders? The unbridled ambitions of politicians? Has the experiment with national parties failed?"[47] We know nothing of this writer, and middle-class voters had no monopoly on political frustration, but this specific complaint, that the parties had failed to put forth coherent programs, was less likely to have been heard from those who felt represented in national politics, elites through the UDN or the PSD and the substantial numbers of workers who voted for Vargas and the PTB.[48]

The broader significance of the 1950 election is that it marked the consolidation of the experiment in populist politics begun in the mid-1920s. If between 1945 and 1950 the organized working class came under attack by those who feared its political power, Vargas's return to politics and his victory in 1950 assured that in the future organized labor would not be excluded from political participation without a disruption of the democratic process. As a result, politics came to be divided between populists and antipopulists. On the national political stage this translated into a fray between the *Getulistas* and the *Udenistas* over the limits of working-class political participation. As a group middle-class Brazilians stood uneasily amidst the unfolding drama of electoral populism over the following decades.

BY THE EARLY 1950S none of the parties prominent in national electoral contests appear to have held a strong attraction for middle-class Paulistanos and Cariocas. The UDN and the PSD were widely seen as parties of *bacharéis*, mouthpieces for the rural and traditional interests that had resisted change since the 1920s. Vargas's PTB could garner middle-class votes in both cities, but his primary audience remained the industrial working class. Barros's PSP seemed to be nothing more than the personal vehicle of its leader.

Commentators during the 1940s and into the 1950s, would-be spokesmen for the middle class, worried about the consequences of political dispersion. Some simply bemoaned the middle class's individualist sentiment. A few proposed solutions. One author pointed to European middle-class federations as models for the Brazilian middle class to follow.[49] Another called for the creation of a "great party of the middle class" to lead a "broad movement for national unity."[50] In essence these observers wanted a middle class that could serve as a stabilizing and progressive force in Brazilian social and political life. Eyes turned toward Europe and the United States, they thought they knew what such a middle class was supposed to look like. From their perspective the fundamental problem was that the Brazilian middle class simply did not seem to be reading off the right script. By the mid-1950s few remained sanguine of middle-class political prospects.

Some began to worry about the middle class's "alienation from any political or ideological participation in the public life of the country," as a group of ideologues put it in 1948.[51] There was in this a glimmer of recognition that far more was at stake than mere disgruntlement with available political options—or perceived lack of them. Those who concerned themselves with the political prospects of the middle class, from commentators to novelists to ideologues, represented middle-class disdain of politics not merely as a fact but as a deeper attitude about politics itself. On this view, the experience of the 1930s and 1940s amounted to a legacy of failures and frustrations that doused whatever enthusiasm or hope there might have been for political reform after the Revolution of 1930 and corroded a sense of collective faith in the possibilities of politics.

Generalized disaffection for politics was perfectly consistent with individualized, atomistic, interstitial, or opportunistic political involvement. Many paths were open to middle-class men drawn to the game of politics if they were willing to associate themselves with one of the parties.[52] They could run for office or serve as interlocutors between party leaders and the rank and file, pivotal agents in populist efforts to enlist working-class support, especially for the PTB and the PSP.[53] Theirs was a power derived from patrons, a power that nevertheless had real consequences and occasionally allowed a genuine sense of participation in the political system or at least in the machinery of power. For instance, Sr. Abel, a functionary at the National Coffee Institute during the 1930s and 1940s, was also employed by politician Adhemar de Barros, whose bidding he did at election times. By his account he participated in a vote-buying deal in Barros's successful 1947 bid for the governorship of São Paulo. Abel recalled Barros's praising his work before admiring hangers-on. Basking in a reflected glow, he remembered feeling "like a god. Everyone wanted to talk to me, get close to me."[54]

Men like Abel were precisely the sort Clovis Ribeiro condemned in 1948 as "unconscious quislings," who, by giving themselves over to the corruptions of elite-led political parties, had betrayed the cause of the middle class.[55] Through bureaucratic ladder climbing and through the mobilization of connections at just the right moment, some of these rose to positions of power, privilege, and influence in their own right within government.[56] At the other extreme a few within the middle class kept to a radical path. In 1953 French sociologist Jacques Lambert referred to the Communist party as a refuge for discontented elements of the middle class.[57] Students and intellectuals predominated, though modestly successful lawyers such as João Falcão and shopkeepers such as Antônio de Oliveira Marques also worked with the party underground after it was outlawed in 1947.[58]

Middle-class officeholders, political entrepreneurs, and radicals were the exception rather than the rule. For the vast mass of middle-class men and women political participation meant basically one thing, voting—but voting against a backdrop of disenchantment with politics as a whole. Until the late 1920s the Republican parties dominant in each state had known no rivals. Voting, for the relative few who did, had been principally a matter of patronage. By 1945 institutional politics at the national level had been radically transformed to one of parties, programs, and platforms. Patronage persisted, now as an instrument of mass politics oriented to what was perceived as a sharp class divide, the tension between the demands of militant workers and the interests of employers.

Even in the face of the new, older expectations did not entirely vanish.

In 1950 Mario Puell, employee at an import firm in Rio, wrote Osvaldo Aranha, begging help for his future son-in-law. A lawyer by training and already registered with the bar association, the young man wanted to leave his poorly paid job as a bookkeeper at city hall for a position in the city's legal department. Puell noted that in his spare hours this energetic young man would be glad to work in Aranha's firm in order to gain some experience—without pay, of course. By the way, concluded the petitioner, my family and I plan to vote for you in the upcoming presidential election, if you decide to run.[59]

By 1950 Puell's request could be seen as quaint, at least in cities such as Rio de Janeiro and São Paulo. A personal promise by an individual white-collar employee to exchange votes for a job did not carry much weight in a political system concerned with working-class masses. Puell's longing for a politics of personal dependencies, loyalties, and reciprocities may have been touchingly naive, but most in the middle class may not even have been able to console themselves with nostalgia. In the face of what were widely represented as powerful elites and militant workers, failures on both sides of the populist divide could reinforce an abiding sense that politics itself was somehow flawed.

Contemporary observers commonly depicted middle-class politics as little more than the shards of a fragmented political experience in which voters were alienated from partisan contests dominated by elites and workers. "Among us," claimed Ruy de Azevedo Sodré in 1956, "the political parties, which usually have identical programs, have not managed to this point to galvanize public opinion because they have not, unlike what happens in France, Belgium, Holland, sought to address the problems that affect and afflict the middle class." The "working class is united and strengthens itself through its sindicatos" and "employers, with the resources they have, find ways of defending their interests." By contrast, concluded Sodré, "our middle class is completely abandoned to its own fate, forgotten by politicians, at the margin of public life, relegated, alas, to a secondary plane," subject to the "deceitful seductions of left and right" and blinded by the "demagogic mystifications of immediatist and personalist political parties."[60]

Sodré, like Ribeiro a decade earlier, blamed the parties for the middle class's plight of not being able to live up to the supposed accomplishments of the European middle classes. He did not understand that he was uncritically indulging a mythologized narrative of the middle class. Nor did he stop to consider what role willing fragmentation and comforting disillusion might have to do with middle-class political ambivalence.

9

Apolitical Politics

I F   T H E   M I D D L E   C L A S S did not coalesce as a party, vote as a bloc,
establish a clear political direction, or push a unified agenda through its
associations, how can its relationship to the broader political conjuncture
after 1945 be understood? The question too easily tempts the conclusion
that the middle class lacked "political horizons" of its own.[1] This seems
confining. After all, voting patterns, political parties, and well-organized
interest groups are not the whole story of politics. To take class for
granted is to gloss over the deeper questions a society asks itself through
the individuals and groups that make it up. A politics of class is first an
improvised stage play about the means and ends of political activity—the
places different groups occupy in social and political life, the meaning of
politics, the role of class in the social world, and the tension between conflictual and consensual visions of society.

This drama did not play out only, or perhaps even primarily, within
well-established political institutions. For the most part ordinary middle-
class Brazilians (indeed most people of any class) appear simply to have
shifted as best they could, confronting politics largely through the experience of everyday life. Forces of organizational cohesion and dissolution
pulled constantly against one another. In some instances the former prevailed and in others the latter, depending on how the knot of valuations,
preferences, and ideals that bound political sensibilities to the intimacy of
personal and private lives was tied. In this way it is possible to conceptu-
alize a politics of the unorganized and relate it to national politics. The key
to such an analysis is sources representing professional and personal life as
arenas where fundamental issues of social organization were expressed
alongside the ideologies and concrete programs usually associated with a
politics of class.

Técnicos over Politics

In early October 1930 Leonor Solanger, a São Paulo schoolteacher on holiday in Belo Horizonte, began a vacation she would never forget. At 5:30 P.M., October 3, precisely as planned, revolutionaries marched to the home of the commander in charge of Belo's two local infantry regiments and arrested him. Coordinating their actions with compatriots in Rio Grande do Sul and with the support of the governor of Minas Gerais, the revolutionaries published a manifesto calling for the people of Minas to join them in struggle against the oligarchy in São Paulo. Though startled by the suddenness of events, Leonor was not surprised by the insurrectionary movement itself, "with which I was very sympathetic." When the rebels called for volunteers, she was ready to go. She signed up with the local militia and shortly was in the trenches as bullets whistled over her head. "It was a horror," she would later say.

After a short stint with the Belo Horizonte unit she was transferred to the all-woman João Pessoa brigade. In a battle, while dashing to the rear echelons to get more ammunition for the troops, she fell in a hole and broke both legs. She was sent to a hospital to recover and promoted in the field to second lieutenant for her bravery. While she convalesced the revolution triumphed, less than a month after it began. Interviewed at the hospital by a reporter from the popular new magazine *O Cruzeiro*, Leonor expressed no regrets. "I've done my duty," beamed the heroine from her bed. "As soon as I recover I'm going home to teach my students to do their duties as citizens on behalf of the country."[2]

Leonor was only one among thousands of volunteers, many of them young, middle-class people like her, who enlisted with the revolutionary forces during October 1930. For such exceptional people, and for the many others who cheered from behind the lines, the armed struggle of October 1930 was politics and patriotism by other means, a climax to the antioligarchic upheavals of the 1920s. Leonor represents one sense of what politics has meant in the modern age—a means by which ordinary people have at times sought to transcend the personal by concerning themselves with issues affecting the future of the nation. Yet after fighting and being wounded, Leonor thought nothing of direct political power. As far as she was concerned, politics, in the sense of formal, institutional processes by which a society manages itself, was back on the right track. Her duty now was to get on with life. Modestly she wanted nothing more than to return to the classroom and teach her pupils good citizenship.

This positive valuation of a hoped-for formal politics was anything but stable. Leonor and others returned to ordinary life expecting or hoping that their actions and sacrifices had irrevocably changed politics for the better. When a few years on the new regime began to seem not much of an improvement over the old one, some within the middle class revived their struggle through collective, ideological means—Integralism and the ANL. But by 1937 even these experiments had withered in the face of working-class upheaval, police repression, and fear that the Old Regime would be restored. To many, politics itself seemed at fault. Getúlio Vargas grasped this sentiment and made it a centerpiece of his speech justifying the coup of November 1937, which put a stop to politics with an open-ended offer to reform it.[3]

Vargas's inaugural speech was the opening gambit in a bid to manipulate widespread disenchantment with politics as such. Within the Estado Novo regime some saw the issue as a chance to take charge of state functions by seeming to depoliticize them. They recognized the rhetorical and strategic value of linking negative feelings about politics to much-needed measures to modernize Brazil's creaky civil service. And so the new regime played to political frustrations that had smoldered within the emergent middle class. If Leonor had fought on behalf of a better politics, those in charge of federal bureaucracies during the Estado Novo sought to persuade middle-class Brazilians to reject partisan political involvement altogether.

A 1938 article in the civil service's official journal, *Revista do Serviço Público* (the public service review), closely echoed the concerns of many collar-and-tie publications during the 1930s: "Within the ambit of liberal democracy, amidst the jockeying of factional political organizations and the conflict over narrow interests and ambitions that are indifferent to the notion of public good, *the very idea of politics has been devalued* to such an extent that a pejorative sense has come to be associated with the word."[4] Fortunately, concluded the article, the state could offer a substitute for, or at least a counterweight to, a debased politics.

Late the following year the *Revista* went further. It ran an article translated from the German on the best way to organize an insurance system for government employees, a matter of abiding concern among public functionaries the world over. From a Brazilian perspective the most striking aspect of the article is that it explicitly identified public servants as "the nucleus of a new middle class." Austrian Hans Franke argued that middle-class government bureaucrats could bypass politics and obviate class struggle by working to establish a direct link between the state and the people. This was a crucial role, he said, as "the middle classes are showing themselves to be ever more indispensable to the state and to society. They are the permanent bridge between the ruling elite and the directed masses." Freed from a concern for day-to-day survival, middle-class people could be a "civilizing" influence on the "inferior classes."[5] Government functionaries, as a Brazilian commentator put it, would ensure the "political education" of the people so that national unity would not fall victim to competitive politics.[6]

Writers in the *Revista* insisted into the 1940s that this goal could be met if public functionaries would act solely according to their "technical" capacities to advance the "national interest."[7] So long as bureaucrats remained "apolitical," administration would supplant politics "in the old sense of parties."[8] In this way, argued one aspiring civil servant in 1941, government *técnicos* would be able to resolve the fundamental political quandary of the day, antagonism between capital and labor.[9] President Vargas himself weighed in on the matter, assuring public functionaries that administration and technical competence could be a viable alternative to politics. Apoliticism in the nation's service, he declared in a December 1938 speech commemorating Public Servant's Day, would have it own rewards. With "clientelism" and "political ambitions" at an end, public servants could "take part in the life of the State and watch after the public interest with exemplary zeal."[10] In sum, he was inviting middle-class bureaucrats to minimize attachments to conventional politics and instead align themselves with an administrative state.

The idea that public functionaries could find in the state an alternative to conflictual politics did not fall on deaf ears. Government employees had long condemned the corruptions of partisan politics. Through the 1920s and 1930s bureaucrats had crouched in the political trenches. Livelihoods subject to the vagaries of patronage, they denounced the "amorphous" nature of political parties that "meant nothing, represented nothing."[11] As late as 1946 the association of São Paulo's public servants complained bitterly of the "depressing situation" of those who had to beg favors "with hat in hand" because of "a retarded politics."[12] Moreover, the notion that administration and expertise might be an antidote to politics had a long pedigree. In the late nineteenth century positivists had proposed sacking politicians in favor of a technocratic elite.[13] During the 1920s and 1930s *Tenentes*, Santa Rosa, feminists, and Integralists had all called for government by experts in order to bind the nation together and ensure a unity of purpose undermined by political conflict. Even the popular *Vida Carioca* ran an article in 1936 touting the advantages of "administration" over "politics."[14] By the early 1940s the magazine's hostility to the "gangrene of dirty politics" had not diminished.[15]

So when Vargas called upon middle-class bureaucrats to take part in the life of the state, collar-and-tie organizations responded enthusiastically. Engineers and military officers hailed the Estado Novo as a victory for "expertise and experts."[16] Public functionaries, advertising professionals, urban planners, architects, teachers, doctors, social workers, and economists also jumped on the bandwagon.[17] All claimed specialized knowledge through which they would help the state address the problems of a rapidly modernizing society and carry out its tutelary task of ensuring "the political hygiene of the people,"[18] which, "like any technical problem, [is] politically neutral."[19] Nationalist sentiment ran deep among those adopting this stance, not as an abstract idea but as a core element of self-regard and professional opportunity. Accountants offered their expertise and loyalty to the state, asking only that government positions for accountants be limited to licensed practitioners, a reminder that however high sounding the rhetoric, quotidian job concerns were never far out of mind.[20]

More was at stake than just jobs and salaries. An association of public functionaries declared in 1940 that above all its members wanted to be recognized as good citizens performing their duties and "respected for the important function we discharge in the structure of the State and the Nation."[21] *Respect, recognition*—the words of people seeking to transcend politics and ennoble personal life through technical competence. In short the government's discourse of expertise and apoliticism seems to have met with a desire among collar-and-tie groups to cultivate a closer relationship to the state. From the perspective of public functionaries and professionals an idealized bureaucracy came to represent an arena where individual job satisfaction could converge with the public good.

Not everyone could see matters this way. Most commercial clerks, bank tellers, and myriad other private-sector employees probably had little occasion to think of their tasks as serving a greater cause. Many paper-pushing government bureaucrats lost no love on their dull and routinized jobs. Often they had envisioned more glittery and accomplished lives as writers, lawyers, doctors, or politicians. Having settled for bureaucratic work, they could not but pay lip service to the seriousness of their duties. But they easily became, in the words of Cyro dos Anjos's fictional diarist in *Diary of a Civil Servant*, the "militant and nonconforming [who] refus[ed] to put their spirit into the job. . . . They punch the clock with rebelliousness in their souls and scorn in their hands."[22] Others could find ways to punctuate the monotony of bureaucratic life with the quiet thrill of personal power. Almeida Fischer's 1950 short story "Suspicion" concludes with life-long public functionary Seu Floriano feeling "powerful and invincible . . . reconciled with life" because the fortunes of so many others—raises, promotions, overtime—depend on his decision and his signature.[23]

Rebels and petty despots notwithstanding, the ideal of work patriotically performed could be a powerful means of imagining that one's life transcended individual circumstance. In Democrito de Castro e Silva's 1945 novel *Middle Class*, for instance, a young engineering student called Marcelo dreams not of personal gain or politics but of bringing his "professional knowledge" to bear on Brazil's great problems: poverty, lack of infrastructure, education, industrialization. By individual example he hopes to combat the "indifference, criminal apathy, and lack of patriotic conscience of those who put their individual and group interests" before those of the nation. In the end Marcelo wants nothing more than to "fight for an ideal—to see a better life for the Brazilian middle class, still amorphous and fragmented, unlike its foreign counterparts, which live by a different and more human social standard."[24] What is so arresting about Marcelo's story is the combination of nationalism, modernization, containment of class struggle, frustration with politics, and a sense of middle-class identity focused through the idealized middle classes that always lived abroad. Though rarely heard so cleanly as in Silva's fictional representation, these themes resonated in the lives of countless middle-class people, perhaps particularly for those who worked most directly in areas touching on the social question.

Schoolteachers were on the front lines of a massive effort during the 1930s and 1940s to raise Brazil's educational level. Young women, such as Riva Bauser, often attended normal schools in Rio and São Paulo and then lit out for the interior, where they taught the children of rural laborers.[25] Others taught grade school to the children of factory workers, riding the trolley out to where the sparkle of downtown dulled to the sepia hues of gritty industrial districts. Since their students rarely finished primary school, underpaid teachers, mostly women, were responsible above all for trying to ensure basic literacy. With the obvious discomfort of those who must exaggerate, spokesmen often referred to teachers as tutors to the people, educational *técnicos* who would not only teach the nation's masses to read but bring them to civilization.[26] When reflecting more expansively on their role in society, teachers not uncommonly cast themselves in a production far larger than just a literacy campaign. They were the foot soldiers in an epic battle for the hearts and souls of the Brazilian people.

Teachers inclined to pen their sentiments for publication wrote passionately of their mission to instill patriotism, foster "social communion," and make the people a factor for "progress."[27] They were encouraged in this image of themselves by government officials who delivered keynote addresses at normal-school graduation ceremonies. Eminences such as President Getúlio Vargas referred in reverent tones to primary-school teachers as "small, obscure, heroes of daily life," and minister of education Gustavo Capanema called them to the tasks of "teaching what patriotism, family and society mean; tempering the spirit of struggle; inculcating civic courage; and establishing salutary norms of work and discipline."[28]

These norms were at the very heart of the primary-school curriculum. In São Paulo white, native-born women led darker-skinned and immigrant children through readers that examined the history of work in Brazil. Teachers were to emphasize at all turns the importance of work and workers to national progress. So as not to be caught out, they were told how to deflect questions about the brutality of slavery in Brazil by noting that Roman rich men had been unbelievably cruel to their slaves, feeding them to flesh-eating fish or cutting their heads off for sport.[29] Approved history texts depicted Brazil as a nation emerging from backwardness. Didactic primers cued young readers to understand that their place in society was rooted in their being the children of workers. Public schools in São Paulo taught immigrant children that the social division of labor was a natural outcome of economic evolution. By embracing their station, they could become "able workers" with "good hearts and good will" and contribute thereby to Brazil's progress.[30]

The government's interest in transmitting this lesson through the primary-school curriculum was so great that teachers labored under considerable pressure to teach only approved materials and viewpoints. There is no evidence of broad-based dissent from these strictures. Professional publications suggest that most teachers, like Leonor Solanger, saw their broad mission as one of teaching citizenship, which in popular primary schools during the 1930s and into the 1940s meant teaching patriotism and work as well as literacy.

Where grade-school teachers ministered to the popular classes, secondary-school teachers, mostly men in the 1940s, were charged with creating a new Brazilian elite. If Brazil needed the arms of the poor in order to modernize, it needed as well the brains of técnicos. This perception sparked a renewed emphasis on secondary schools during the Estado Novo. Until 1937, said Capanema in a speech to teachers and others at the one hundredth anniversary of the elite Colégio D. Pedro II in Rio, secondary school had been seen as merely preparation for university study, not as an end unto itself. Recent reforms had rectified this situation. Secondary schools, declared the minister of education, were now to be sites for molding the physical, moral, and intellectual personality of adolescents in service to the nation.[31]

Among educators this mission was at times characterized in terms of "preparing the middle classes" for citizenship, leadership, and productive roles in a democratic society.[32] Beyond teaching basic skills—reading, writing, math, science—secondary-school teachers had several tasks. One was to help students choose proper vocations. According to one teacher, the idea was to push pupils to "expand their possibilities for victory in real life" and gain a sense of "general culture," two central aspects of middle-class economic and social life linked to Brazil's modernization.[33] Teachers were also to ensure students' moral preparation and character formation, more necessary than ever for a public service organized around principles of merit. Finally, and especially during the Estado Novo, secondary-school teachers were to make students ready for examinations on a narrative of Brazilian accomplishments. This storyline, taught through history texts and didactic manuals, injected Brazil into the flow of world history and projected a future of "human progress," in which Brazil would participate alongside other "modern" nations. One of the central lessons of this history, according to a 1940 textbook, was that the state had an essential responsibility to regulate relations between capital and labor for the common good and for social peace.[34]

Most teachers had no direct responsibility for professing on such sensitive matters as the social question. Those who did left little evidence of how faithful they were to the dictates of curriculum. The crucial point, however, is that teachers took part in a middle-class profession publicly recognized as having a moral mission to help the nation advance while avoiding social upheaval. Primary-school teachers were to mold workers' children into patriotic laborers who would contentedly take up their role in an industrializing society. Secondary-school teachers were to form the characters and develop the talents of those who would become the next generation of collar-and-tie professionals and public functionaries.

For all the rhetoric, teachers, in general, were poorly paid. Their rewards, according to one lifelong teacher, were intangible, spiritual satisfaction and collaboration with a greater cause.[35] Through teaching, in other words, one might live beyond oneself and engage the great problems of the day without sinking into the morass of competitive, ideological politics. A teacher's journal made the point in 1939: "A nation does not become great only by teaching politics."[36] The highest vocation, insisted this publication, was not to follow the dictates of the state but truly and sincerely to pursue "the ideal of educating the people."[37]

The Estado Novo offered many other opportunities for nonpolitical engagement through public service and technical competence. The labor ministry and its far-flung network of courts and offices brought thousands of middle-class bureaucrats into immediate contact with the social question. Hugo Faria, for example, graduated from secondary school in 1932 and worked at an Italian insurance company in Rio for the next three years.[38] In 1935 he entered a *concurso* for a position as office employee in the ministry of labor. Upon being approved for the post, he became the first public functionary in his modest family, a matter of considerable pride for all concerned. Though privately opposed to the Estado Novo dictatorship when it came, he was dedicated to the system of merit that took shape between 1937 and 1945. Grateful to have "made ourselves through our own merit," he and his colleagues respected Vargas for being "absolutely honest." And so, despite personal misgivings, Faria came to believe that *trabalhismo*, the state-run system governing employer-employee relations, was the best solution for the country's social woes.

While working for the government, Faria took his degree from a Rio law school in 1941. Shortly afterward he applied to be a labor commissioner and was accepted. Posted to the northern reaches of the country, he found himself in the middle of class conflict. He was in Bahia when Communists began to agitate among textile workers. He did not agree with the Communists but did believe they had a right to speak. At the same time he also felt the state had a right to defend itself and its institutions. He was worried, therefore, when the Communist party began to foment strikes in 1947. His task, as he saw it, was to calm workers down, perhaps even save them from themselves. On one occasion he attempted to persuade 6,000 Bahian textile workers not to march on their factories. For three hours he argued and cajoled, telling them that the Communists were pushing them into an action they could not hope to win. He pointed out the twenty most vocal Communist party leaders and asked workers to remember his words when they lost the strike. During the walkout Faria sought to prove that workers' donations to the strike fund were being diverted to the party's coffers. When the strike later collapsed and after hearing suspicions about misdirected funds, the rank and file remembered Faria's speech, tracked down the twenty Communists he had fingered, and beat them to a pulp.

Faria was just one among hundreds of labor commissioners and lawyers who soldiered in the trabalhista labor regime that emerged from the Estado Novo. The system was premised on the idea that tensions between employers and workers could be managed so as to minimize conflict. Within this system public servants such as Faria stood at the line of engagement between antagonists and relied on the power of the state, the keenness of their expertise, and the strength of their convictions to help pacify a troubled and fractious social order.

Apart from commissioners, the system of labor tribunals became a haven for hundreds of law-faculdade graduates. Legislation passed during the Estado Novo allowed individual workers to bring *dissídios individuais* (individual disputes) to the labor courts for adjudication. From the early to the mid-1940s, tens of thousands of workers took advantage of the law, bringing their employers to bar over pay, benefits, and wrongful firings. Complainants appear to have been as likely as, or even more likely than, employers to win such cases.[39] Some labor judges, of course, abused their positions, as workers' protests about one high-handed jurist indicate.[40] But it appears to have been at least as common for these magistrates to see themselves as being "neutral on the side of labor."[41] This suggests that judges had a certain measure of discretion in relation to industrial elites, which often caused employers to demur at the treatment they received.

More expansively, it allowed judges to imagine that by restraining the excesses of employers and reconciling workers to their situation they were contributing decisively to the mission of ensuring progress with social peace. At the same time, their power to mediate conflict was limited. Nowhere was this fact made clearer than when labor tribunals began to hear *dissídios coletivos* (collective disputes). Under the same 1943 law that had empowered labor judges to hear individual disputes, unions were permitted to bring employers before a labor tribunal on collective issues of wages and working conditions. Employers who merely griped at facing individual workers in court initially refused to go along with collective disputes. That part of the law remained in abeyance until 1945. The political moment, however, forced employers to loosen up. The open presidential election of that year, with its populist rhetoric and explicit appeal to organized labor, gave the state leverage against employers. By 1946, the number of dissídios coletivos had risen to 420. Workers appear to have welcomed the change, seeing the labor courts, according to São Paulo's communist newspaper *Hoje*, as "one of the few organisms in which agents of reaction" were not ensconced.[42] But as Vargas's influence faded and as Dutra turned away from labor in the late 1940s, collective adjudications came to be seen as a threat to "the structure of the economy" (as individual disputes were not) and their numbers declined, falling to under 150 in 1950, a lesson both to middle-class bureaucrats as well as to workers of the constraints under which they labored.[43]

Perhaps no occupation drew more middle-class people into intimate contact with issues of class than social work, which emerged as a distinct profession in the late 1930s in Brazil. Labor strikes in the mid-1930s and a growing public concern for the living conditions of workers fanned a reformist impulse dating back to the Catholic social-action movement of the 1920s.[44] Drawing on U.S. and European models Brazilian students of urban social problems began to argue that an ambitious plan of "social assistance" could improve the lives of the poor and help them "adjust to their circumstances."[45] The point, argued one social-work textbook, was to promote social "equilibrium" by conciliating "conflicts of interest" so as to "awaken a sympathy between the boss and the worker."[46] Sympathy, in turn, would restore "human dignity" and instill a "spirit of mutual respect," which would bring about the "genuine emancipation of the worker."[47] The technical competence of middle-class bureaucrats was thought central to realizing these goals. As one proponent put it, social work was to be a means of "restoring social order" through the practical and direct action of "specialists" and "técnicos."[48]

This impetus to confront the dislocations of a modernizing society gathered momentum in social-work schools founded in Rio de Janeiro and São Paulo starting in 1936. By the mid-1940s, universities, religious foundations, business groups, and municipal governments had launched their own schools.[49] Thousands of young people passed through these institutions during the late 1930s and 1940s. A majority were women, in some schools by a two- or three-to-one margin. One school's application forms indicate that students' fathers generally held collar-and-tie jobs, though a few identified their fathers as industrial workers or craftsmen. Application forms indicate that virtually all students claimed some secondary-school education.[50] Photographs of graduation ceremonies and on employment forms suggest that the vast majority of aspiring social assistants or social educators (Brazilian variants on *social worker*) were white or near white.

What reasons did these young women and men offer for wanting to become social assistants? Personal information forms at two different schools offer an impressionistic sense of motivations.[51] Most students cited one or more of patriotism, humanism, religious sentiment, and a desire for social peace alongside more instrumental hopes for career success and the attractions of technical mastery as reasons for attending. After admitting that they had never had meaningful contact with working-class people, many expressed concern for the harsh conditions of workers' lives and especially for their ignorance, their immorality, and their lack of hygiene. As Lêlza Guemata Gomes put it in 1947, she wanted to be "a little more useful to humanity" by addressing the problem of workers' education, which was "the most basic possible. They live in promiscuity, their diets are precarious, and hygiene is unknown among them."[52]

Curricula indicate that students were exposed to a broad conceptual and practical framework for making sense of social problems. Handwritten answers to examination questions at one school show that students were required to discuss the functioning of capitalism and be familiar with the basic tenets of communism, socialism, and liberalism.[53] At a social-work school in Rio a study outline for a written and oral exam in "social politics" covered a number of points, including benefits and limitations of state intervention in social problems, effects of proletarianization, aspects of the social question in Brazil, problems of the middle classes in Brazil, the meaning of strikes, and the function of labor courts.[54]

These issues were not taught in a spirit of open-ended inquiry. Exams, papers, projects, and the grades given them indicate that there were right and wrong answers. Students were required to see communism and liberalism as belonging in the same conceptual box, where liberalism promoted a selfish struggle among individuals and communism constituted a mistaken but understandable group response to the misery left in the wake of unfettered individualism and materialism. The effect was social disorder. The better exams generally resolved this dilemma by referring either to a vague "Christian social doctrine" or to an equally vague notion of a secular middle way between liberalism and communism.[55] Against conflictual models of social relations championed by liberalism and Marxism, they proposed a consensual view of social interaction governed by sympathy among classes, acceptance of established social hierarchies, and an abiding sense of nationalism.

Details of this framework were often ignored outside the classroom in favor of a rough-and-ready moralism. In 1942 Maria Hortência do Nascimento e Silva, graduate of the Social Institute in São Paulo and social assistant for the municipal government in Rio, studied the lives of Rio's *favelados*. Her charge was to diagnose their problems and suggest solutions. She focused on why poor people had such a tough time understanding the need for hard work and a moral family life. Her report, entitled "Impressions of a Social Assistant on Work in the Favela," was a compilation of statistics, interviews, and personal observations which bore the deep imprint of someone from the outside clinically examining the lives of the poor. Silva condemned favela life, noting its "misery, depravity, indolence and sensuality." Drawing on long-standing notions of race, she explained that "our *mestiço* does not like the idea of work. ... He is mediocre and pursues mediocrity." Nor, she said, was he motivated by the idea of upward mobility: "Freed from hunger, he does not aspire to more." "This," she concluded, "was the life of the greater part of our working class." She offered no solution beyond trying to educate workers to better work habits.[56]

Silva's characterization of family life in the favela is equally revealing. Waxing domestic, she noted that "the idea of 'family life' brings to mind a nice little place, a gay window, a comfortable chair, a child playing, a woman cooking, and a man, tired but content, relaxing near the radio." Quite other was what she saw in the favela: "Among the working class, 'family life' means a small and somber room, without air or sunlight, a stiff and angular chair, a leak in the ceiling, a large number of children screaming, a lamentable woman, and an exhausted man who curses his own destiny." This extremity, she argued, undermined morality, as a result of which workers could not lead upright lives. Recognizing that their condition was not altogether of their own making, she proposed that "a comfortable and clean little house is indispensable for the worker to discover and appreciate the happiness of the family unit."[57]

Silva's report was just what it seems: an investigation of the dismal living conditions of Rio's working poor. Their plight was regrettable, perhaps remediable in small ways, especially through education. What stands out, however, is that Silva all but ignored her training. According to the Social Institute's curriculum, she was supposed to analyze poverty in terms of its relationship to the excesses of liberal capitalism. Yet she declined so systemic a critique, favoring instead a straightforward moralism in her work. So while some social assistants entertained grand visions of "public salvation,"[58] most, like Silva, appear to have seen their task as one of helping the less fortunate by communicating to them the instrumental rudiments of a moral life: thrift, hygienic housekeeping, excellent nutrition, responsibility to family, good work habits, patriotism, and conscientious child-rearing practices.

This spirit of aid for workers characterized one of the largest and most sweeping experiments in social assistance up to 1950, the Industrial Social Service (SESI).[59] Founded under state auspices by private-sector São Paulo industrialists in 1946, SESI claimed a patriotic duty to seek "moral and civic perfection and the development of a spirit of solidarity among classes."[60] Its motto was For Social Peace. The moment was critical. Postwar inflation and the loosening of restrictions on political activity sparked a wave of labor strikes in 1944-45, forcing Vargas to legalize the Communist party. SESI was the São Paulo State Industrial Federation's (FIESP) answer to growing fears among larger industrialists that class conflict was breaking out again after the enforced calm of the Estado Novo. At SESI's inauguration FIESP's president Roberto Simonsen mixed the language of technical competence with that of morality: SESI "técnicos," he stressed, were to undertake an "ethico-educational" effort to "enlighten" workers to the "hierarchy of social functions" and the imperative of "moral order," to the greater end of modernizing Brazil.[61] And though Simonsen hoped SESI would work together with political parties, técnicos themselves insisted that SESI was not a government program and vehemently denied any involvement with partisan politics. Utterly "alien to political questions," wrote one enthusiastic social educator, SESI's basic task was to "fight for democracy in its true sense: harmony among classes and Social Peace."[62]

The system worked through a combination of moral suasion and financial incentive. Employers contributed directly to SESI, which then spent money as needed for various projects, among them housing and food programs, legal aid, social centers, housekeeping, and cooking courses. In exchange for these benefits, workers were to reciprocate their boss's good will by "being more interested in work [and] arriving on time."[63] After all, said an informational pamphlet aimed at factory workers, "the bosses are interested in the well-being of workers, because they recognize that workers hold the nation's prosperity in their hands." SESI requested only that workers try always to be "good Brazilians."[64]

To help factory laborers take advantage of these new opportunities, SESI pledged to staff its facilities with the highest-qualified técnicos it could find. Within two years of its founding hundreds of social educators had fanned out into working-class districts, shock troops in a campaign to deploy social welfare against the "perturbations of agitators and professional *meneurs* [ringleaders] who so often drag workers where they do not want to go." The campaign's goal was to be "merely preventive," though workers were exhorted to be more productive in order to lower the cost of living and allow their families to live in comfort. In effect, middle-class social assistants were charged with convincing workers to participate in the patriotic process of modernizing Brazil.[65]

To this end SESI social educators undertook varied tasks. Men such as Hélvio Pinheiro Lima, for instance, often went into factories or union halls. A principal aim was to prompt workers to discuss work habits and galvanize them to become better at their jobs. This was usually done in the context of study groups and courses on human relations, where workers were warned of the dangers of "maladjustment," lack of "emotional equilibrium," and "indiscipline."[66] A further objective was to persuade laborers to avail themselves of benefits through employers, the state, and Catholic Workers' Circles rather than recur to the independent labor movement. And so, SESI social educators met with workers to tell them how to press grievances against employers.

The potential for political involvement in these jobs was obvious. Some social assistants railed against communism or sought to leverage themselves into positions of influence in partisan politics. In at least one instance social educators were known to have helped industrialist Roberto Simonsen mobilize working-class support for his campaign to win a senate seat in 1947.[67] According to a number of social educators from the period, however, most remained faithful to the idea of social service as a nonpolitical vocation that contributed to social peace.[68]

Women were crucial to SESI's mission. Social assistants targeted working-class women in their capacities as *donas de casa*, even though many of them worked at factory jobs as well.[69] For example, Maria de Lourdes Ribeiro Brescia, daughter of a self-employed stonecutter, holder of university degrees in domestic economics and nutrition, took her first job with SESI in 1948.[70] She taught "courses for housewives" at Domestic Apprenticeship Centers located in working-class neighborhoods, such as Moóca in São Paulo. Women who completed these courses received diplomas at lavish dinner ceremonies, perhaps the only time in their lives they were so honored. And their teachers could watch them receive their diplomas and remark: "Look at how these young ladies, with very rare exceptions, are now free of embarrassment and proudly lift their heads. They don't even seem like women workers."[71] Maria Brescia also visited women's homes to demonstrate techniques: in 1948–49, SESI social educators made nearly 70,000 calls at workers' homes. At lunchtime she often went to factories and talked to women workers about "planning rational meals," convincing them to include vegetables in their menus. With experience she began to write instruction manuals for working-class donas de casa clamoring for a more rigorous introduction to the principles of nutrition. Later she was permitted to devise new courses on her own. On the weekends she and SESI colleagues developed a series called "Little Recipes for You." Bearing the ubiquitous SESI slogan For Social Peace, these booklets were mimeographed and distributed for the edification of working-class women. The dominant sentiment among the social educators of the period, recalls Brescia, was one of passion for the job.

Brescia's work was part of a larger effort by SESI to bring domestic ideals to bear on social tensions. The idea, according to a 1947 social-work textbook, was that tidy and "tranquil" working-class homes would ensure social peace and provide factories with "serene and trustworthy" workers.[72] By 1950 the experiences of Brescia and her colleagues came to be enshrined in a monthly newsletter for working-class women. *A Dona de Casa* (The housewife) contained information about new courses, helpful tips on how to economize, and notices of upcoming SESI-sponsored social events. The newsletter affirmed women in their domestic roles, focusing attention on their valuable contribution to society as donas de casa. Because women and men naturally occupied distinct compartments in society, women should not be unhappy with being part of the "so-called weaker sex." In matters of the home they were "minister of finance, of education, of health, executing within the family all of the jobs men do in society."[73] *A Dona de Casa* also assumed that working-class women would respond to a rhapsodic middle-class conception of the social world. They too could be part of "modernism" and learn proper table manners—"tell your little friend [not to] slurp when she eats soup, but in a gentle way so she does not take offense"—if they would but apply themselves to the task.[74]

Gentle though the message sought to be, most SESI social educators, women and men alike, recognized that they were implicated in what was perhaps the most volatile political issue of the day, the problem of class. Simonsen worried constantly that communists were trying to sabotage SESI.[75] Social assistants were under strict instructions not to mention communism in talking to workers, not even to condemn it. Nor were they to discuss class struggle. They were simply to help workers use SESI's resources. A more direct and confrontational approach, it was feared, might turn workers off or even drive them into the communists' arms.

Except for hewing to broad mandates, however, SESI's social educators enjoyed considerable leeway on the job. They went to factories, attended union hall meetings, taught classes, and visited workers' homes—all without over-the-shoulder supervision. If they were trusted, it was because they aspired to responsibility and respectability, had received a secondary-school education, and had been trained in correct social-work technique. At times they might wield considerable power over individual cases. In February 1949 SESI social educator Leila Maria Junqueira de Mendonça investigated Matarazzo Metallurgical, one of São Paulo's oldest and most prominent metallurgical companies. She found, as workers had charged, that Matarazzo's food, medical, and sports facilities were deficient.[76] In a report to superiors, she recommended that Matarazzo be penalized financially for its failure to provide adequate facilities for its workers. Though her recommendation was accepted by an immediate supervisor, it was reversed when Matarazzo appealed to a higher level. Not all such cases were overturned. Mendonça's example bears examination, however, because it illustrates the possibilities and limits of a salaried técnico's power to effect change and act independently.

It was not uncommon for these mid-echelon employees to run into trouble for their zealousness. After attending a union meeting to talk with workers about their situation and their rights, Hélvio Pinheiro Lima found that he had gone too far.[77] When word got back to his virulently anticommunist superior that he had not squelched debate about an issue that ran contrary to SESI policy, he was fired. Supporters within the organization succeeded in reinstating him, but after this incident social educators were barred from union meetings. Mendonça's and Lima's experiences hint at a formative quandary of the middle-class relationship to technical competence and public service. By teaching patriotism, opining on living conditions, reconciling workers and employees, and writing recipes, many middle-class women and men might set their signatures to the social order through their jobs, though this opportunity for meaningful engagement was intertwined with constraints inherent in their dependent position in a hierarchy of authority and status.

Many doubtless became frustrated and ended by working with scant devotion and no thought to greater meaning. Their only consolation for being trapped in bureaucratic structures may have been small insurgencies: Cyro dos Anjos's rebellious civil servants or the occasional teacher, such as Dona Brites, who made a point of talking about workers' rights to her working-class pupils.[78] The extent and effect of such nonconformity is not known, though nothing indicates that it rose above the level of irritant.

Still, technical competence and public service represented an imagined context in which everyday deeds of individuals could seem to give public expression to shared ideals, visions, and sensibilities without recourse to collective politics. Crucially this possibility was mediated through public and private-sector bureaucracies rather than through competitive politics as such. The very idea of specialization bore within it the notion that a servant of bureaucracy, whether public or private, could quite properly ignore all beyond the ken of his or her expertise, most particularly politics. In effect, some of the space middle-class groups lost to working-class populism middle-class individuals regained through the state's and employers' tutelary relationship to the people. In a sense, the job of middle-class técnicos was to lubricate the imperfect gearing between the government's appeal to workers and the tendency among political elites and industrialists to treat labor as a "problem" to be solved.[79]

The frictions were tremendous. The day-to-day actions of teachers, lawyers, bureaucrats, social workers, industrial psychologists, and countless others laboring on behalf of the public interest were subject to the desires and interests of economically and politically powerful forces above them. At the same time, the egalitarian implications of educating workers, of giving them access to a court system where they might prevail against employers, and of moralizing them, grated against the assumption of fundamental social difference between middle-class técnicos and their inferiors. Ground between these two forces, many may have sought a place where they would not so easily be grist in the mill of class struggle.

Avoiding Contacts with Society

In a modest but comfortable house in São Paulo late one afternoon the voices of two brothers die down from a long and disruptive debate about politics. Carlos, diligent bookkeeper at a respected downtown commercial firm and devoted family man, declares that he simply cannot understand his younger brother Alfrêdo's attraction to radical politics. Alfrêdo, rebel with numerous causes, on the run from police, apple of his mother's eye, insists that he, unlike Carlos, lives for an ideal. With nothing more to say to each other, they allow their long-suffering mother the last word. Pausing for a moment from her endless chores, Dona Lola nods gently and plaintively addresses Alfrêdo:

> It's too bad that you like this life that I do not understand. We could be so happy with a calm life. Don't you think you can find happiness in a peaceful home life? Go to work, come home, talk with friends, go to the movies, have everything balanced, with a clear conscience, then get married, have children, just like I did. Everything quiet and good. Why fight so hard, my son?[80]

This exchange never actually happened. Carlos, Alfrêdo, and Dona Lola are characters in Sra. Leandro Dupré's runaway bestseller *There Were Six of Us*. When it first appeared in 1943, a reviewer hailed this story as the "perfect middle-class novel . . . because of the author's faithfulness to middle-class types, to the thinking of the social group to which she belongs."[81]

What is arresting about this scene is the symbolic coupling of home, politics, and middle-class identity. Dona Lola's words, describing a peace and quiet in sharp contrast to the clangor of social life beyond the walls, intimate an attitude toward politics absent from conventional sources. Much more than just a yearning for domestic tranquillity, Dupré's Dona Lola stood for a kind of counterideal to radical politics and to politics more generally. Through her selfless actions, soft words, and spirit of resignation, Dona Lola embodied the proposition that personal life centered on the home could be a refuge from the outside world.

One way of bringing this sentiment to bear on politics more conventionally understood is to examine a series of novels written between the mid-1930s and the early 1950s: João Calazans's *Petit Bourgeois* (1933), Érico Verissimo's *Crossroads* (1935) and *The Rest Is Silence* (1943), Jader de Carvalho's *Middle Class* (1937), Sra. Leandro Dupré's *There Were Six of Us* (1943) and *Dona Lola* (1949), Democrito de Castro e Silva's *Middle Class* (1945), and Hélio Chaves's *A Bourgeois Family* (1952). Organized around middle-class characters, these books glimpse the gossamer threads linking personal life to the valuations, preferences, and ideals underlying political attitudes.[82] They are evidence of political sensibilities among people aware of but not consciously mobilized around their "middle-classness." One among many competing projections of the good society, the coupling of home and politics descries a political dimension intersecting the ideologies and concrete programs usually associated with the politics of class. The advantage (and risk) of these novels as sources is that they were written and read outside any specific institutional setting. The writing and reading of them thus mirrors the political individualism, or at least the political dispersion, of the Brazilian middle class itself during the 1930s and 1940s.[83] To this extent they offer a corrective to institutional sources that quail in the face of intimate lives, for these stories illumine politics from the perspective of everyday experience.[84]

What privileges these novels is that they locate middle-class life at the center of stories about social relations just as the middle class was coming to be part of Brazil's lived social experience. All of these little dramas revolve around the professional and domestic concerns of their characters: anxieties over jobs, money, relationships, and politics. When describing Brazilian society they rely on a tripartite ordering: bourgeoisie, rich, or upper class; proletariat, working class, or lower class; and petite bourgeoisie or middle class. While in this they mirror contemporary political essays about the middle class,[85] their lexicon of class is ambiguous and unstable, varying from one book to the next and sometimes within a given book. They are compelling sources precisely because they stress above all the unsettled, Janus-like experience of social and political middleness.

A recurrent motif in these novels is the middle-class character who comes into contact with political radicalism. The sparks thrown off by the clash of political ideals with the demands of everyday life put in relief some of the deepest concerns and fears of people who neither shared power with the dominant class nor were organized to articulate interests on their own behalf. Put another way, the fictional portrayal of the radical temptation is a rich vein of insight into middle-class political identity, because the choice of whether or not to take up the leftist cause was pregnant with meaning in a political system that was coming to be defined by the struggle between capital and labor.

Two works from the 1930s offer a window onto this issue through the eyes of protagonists who become involved in left-wing politics. João Calazans's *Petit Bourgeois* and Jader de Carvalho's *Middle Class* portray young men at the beginning of middle-class careers and marriages. Before they are able to realize these ideals, however, they are drawn into radical politics. Calazans's Leandro abandons his girlfriend, who wants nothing more than "a modern little house, like the ones in the women's magazines." He takes to speechifying at workers' rallies and strikes in São Paulo, fantasizing about becoming the "Wladimir Illich of the Americas."[86] Carvalho's Manoel moves from a small town to a coastal city in the Northeast. He imagines great success for himself, but after losing his girlfriend—her well-to-do father will not let her marry a "simple lawyer who doesn't even have a place to die in"—and his job, he embarks on an affair with the young woman's reprobate mother and falls in with communists.[87]

As the stories proceed, both men undertake political and emotional journeys that leave them enervated. In becoming radicals, they turn their backs on middle-class comfort, respectability, and success. Hardened by their trials, both come to feel that they have ascended to new planes of human solidarity. Previously uninvolved in politics of any sort, they now embrace it. As Manoel exclaims bathetically, "While doctors, lawyers, and politicians avoid me, I feel my hunger joining the universal hunger of the exploited. I see my dream losing the last tinge of egoism, dissolving and mixing with the dreams of millions of workers."[88] Both Leandro and Manoel complete their symbolic union with the working class when they are arrested and thrown into jail with ordinary workers. Paradoxically it is at just this moment, while in prison for their sympathies, that their cellmates brand them unreliable "petit bourgeois." The shock of rejection disorients them.

After release from prison each confronts his crisis differently, though they come to similar ends. Leandro repents. Distrusted by workers, disillusioned with a corrupt Communist party leadership, he loses his radical resolve when he falls in love with a young woman. "Lost in a world of dreams" about domestic bliss, he renounces politics once and for all upon receiving word of an inheritance. In celebration he treats himself to a shopping spree, symbolically seeking to reintegrate himself into a respectable lifestyle by purchasing a new hat, shirt, and tie in order to look more "elegant." His plans go awry. Old friends shun him. Bootblacks sneer at his dilapidated shoes and fail to compliment his new hat and tie. At the close of the story he is in limbo between an abandoned radicalism and an irretrievable respectability, part of a "vacillating, indecisive half class ... decimated by the two classes that clash in the struggle to conquer power."[89] Manoel follows a different path to the same end. Neither repudiating radicalism nor seeking to renew contacts with working-class militants, he is caught in the middle. Unemployed, homeless, hungry, and bitter, he wanders aimlessly, collapses on the beach and sleeps outside all night, dreaming about his lost past before radicalism.

What is striking about these two books is their ambiguity toward radical politics and middle-class identity. On the one hand, both protagonists yearn for a sense of solidarity with workers, imagining that they can transcend their personal situation and society's divisions through radical politics. On the other hand, radicalism is possible for these middle-class characters only after a prolonged and painful, almost ritual shedding of middle-class identity. On their descent into radical politics, they throw off friends, aspirations, desires, domestic bliss, and morality. Their struggle finally is an isolating, interior one against the habits and expectations of a lifetime, not one of political awakening in the company of like-minded others. For even when the wrenching transformation is complete, these middle-class radicals find no home among workers, who see them as irredeemably petit bourgeois or middle class.[90] Everything they were as middle-class men invested in hierarchy, respectability, and individual possibility clashed with their participation in working-class politics.

Radicalism's heavy symbolic charge is evident in a number of other novels. In Érico Veríssimo's *Crossroads,* João Benevolo, an unemployed commercial employee in Porto Alegre, proves impervious to the cajoling of his radical friend Sebastião. Rather than despise the rich, João admires them. Trapped by "passive envy," he is silent when "faced with the

Chrysler Imperial, which belongs to the man who left him jobless."[91] Dupré's novel of São Paulo *There Were Six of Us* offers a variation on this
sense of acquiescence.[92] Dona Lola, self-sacrificing mother of Carlos and
Alfrêdo, rejects her neighbor Dona Genú's hatred for the rich. "It's not
their fault we are poor. ... God makes these decisions, and we must simply accept them. ... I have resigned myself."[93]

Veríssimo's *The Rest Is Silence*, set in Porto Alegre, suggests a more
vigorous defense of middle-class identity before the radical temptation.
Two young lovers quarrel over politics. Roberto, from a middle-class
family, is a journalist and militant in the labor movement. Nora is the
daughter and secretary of a writer whose novels are aesthetically but not
politically revolutionary. In a conversation about their relationship Roberto criticizes Nora's father for his "indifference to politics" and argues
that his books are flawed because they do not "indicate the road we must
follow in order to reach an ideal world." Nora quavers at his implication
and fears Roberto "would pronounce that taboo, dangerous, incriminating word. ... No, the best thing was to forget everything. She must not let
him utter the forbidden word." He does not.* Yet the distance between
them seems unbridgeable. Nora cannot give up her family to marry Roberto and recognizes that she is "too fond of cheerful, comfortable surroundings" to bear "poverty and privation." Roberto cannot accept
Nora's "petit-bourgeois" values.[94]

Democrito de Castro e Silva's *Middle Class* introduces a final twist on
the theme of radicalism within the middle class.[95] Two friends in São Paulo
disagree over how workers should pursue their interests. Torquato, lowly
shoe salesman become self-made factory owner, wants his friend Aderaldo to take a job at the plant so that he can have a "better chance in life,"
without "violent and speedy ascents that can cause disequilibrium, disorder, failure." Aderaldo wants no part of a slow rise from shop floor to office. Torquato laments Aderaldo's rejection of upward mobility through
hard work and patience. Where Aderaldo wants "to impose himself
through struggle, through force, through strike," the true path is an individualistic one: "Everyone must resign himself to his luck and try to live,"
declares Torquato. By preferring collective confrontation and protest,
Aderaldo was just a "malcontent" who "did not understand" that "work
could belong to him today, and profits could belong to him tomorrow."

These scenes provide a useful contrast to the earlier two novels. In each
instance the dilemma of middle-class radicalism is explored from the per-

---

*The word is never stated. It was probably something like *communism* or *revolution*.

spective of people who meet radical temptation head on with an irreducible antiradical sensibility: Sebastião's blandishments, Dona Genú's hatred, Roberto's militancy, and Aderaldo's desire for dominion are met by João Benevolo's impotent admiration for the rich, Dona Lola's quiet resignation, Nora's defiant refusal to abandon her comforts and family, and Torquato's romanticized dream of upward mobility. While these do not represent middle-class sensibilities in any direct way, they do suggest an interplay between fascination and fear in the face of radicalism, even as they distill the variety of possible middle-class responses to the radical temptation.

But the acceptance of radicalism and its rejection are not treated as equally likely outcomes in these novels. Authors apparently unsympathetic to the radical cause (Dupré and Silva) depict radicalism as something in contradiction to middle-class life. Even those more sympathetic (Calazans, Carvalho, and Veríssimo) see middle-class radicalism as Quixotic at best. Whatever their differences, all see middle-class identity as being affirmed in the heat of personal confrontation with the radical option. In these stories few embrace radicalism, for it exacts a terrible price from those who do: total surrender of the hopes and dreams that ground middle-class lives. Some characters irretrievably sacrifice comfort and status, understanding what they have lost only after it is too late. Others see the light in the process of defending what they have and who they are.

Strikingly this defense mirrors the individualism of the radical option itself. Envy, resignation, contentedness, and upward mobility are the immediate reactions of middle-class characters who confront the specter of class struggle alone. None of them even briefly considers the possibility of a nonradical, collective response. In these stories, as in collar-and-tie publications, mainstream politics is seen as little more than *politicagem*—political chicanery, patronage, corruption, and factionalism incapable of conducing to the public good—a force that serves only to exacerbate class tensions.

A deep suspicion that mainstream politics in practice was not adequate to the challenge of class is perhaps most compellingly revealed by the father and son industrialists in Hélio Chaves's *A Bourgeois Family*.[96] The father claims to have no politics at all. The omniscient narrator insists otherwise: "His real politics is of another sort, a politics of indirect interest, of corruption and venality, of entrapping and demeaning honest men, in order to manipulate them at will in behind-the-curtain intrigues."[97] Like father, like son. When the son takes over the business and becomes embroiled in labor disputes, he puts together a political cabal of congressmen. In one scene he instructs retainers to vote for a law that would harm workers' organizations. A factory worker who has been elected to Congress refuses to do it and walks out. Others are trapped. A journalist who thinks he hears a still, small voice within is warned that he will "suffer consequences": "Consult your conscience and see which is better: what you had, or the social position that you currently enjoy? ... Then try to think about maintaining the luxury your family now enjoys with the pennies you used to earn, now that you are accustomed to a bigger salary." In the end the man bows to his patron's logic and agrees to vote as directed, a vivid demonstration to readers of the dangers of political involvement.[98]

Also a reminder of the peril of trusting elites with the national interest. For after the vote the son secretly sells out to a "foreign trust," which profits at the expense of national industry. In the bargain he keeps a local factory from closing, for which he is lionized as a champion of Brazil's industrialization and a protector of the working man. Workers whose jobs he has saved cheer and proclaim that he should be a senator. In a fairly obvious swipe at Vargas Chaves has him decline the honor, saying, with a great flourish of false modesty and self-abnegation, that he "will always be a worker, a fighter like you in defense of the supreme collective interest."[99]

In these novels formal, institutional politics is a maleficent force rooted in the pervasive moral deficiency of those who control and benefit from it. Other writers expressed similar concerns. During the 1940s would-be spokesmen for the middle class worried that employers and politicians were pushing the working class toward ever more exotic doctrines by ignoring workers' legitimate demands. Their egoism, their use of politics as a vehicle for personal advancement and narrow favor granting thus threatened the social order as a whole. What Brazilian society needed most, concluded one observer of the middle class, was a genuine moral renewal so that Brazil could become a "serene world, preparing the way for a future without ambition, for collective calm, for the well-being of the family, and for the tranquillity of human work."[100] Other contemporary political analysts said much the same thing, indulging the myth that a strong middle class could keep society from flying apart under the pressures of class conflict.[101] As a public functionary notes in Silva's novel *Middle Class*, "It is imperative that we attend to the formation of the middle class ... because on its stability and security depends the equilibrium of the other two, the upper class and the lower class. To the extent the middle is well adjusted and equidistant from the two extremes, everything will be, as through a law of physics, in perfect balance."[102]

For Silva the key to maintaining this balance was cooperation rather than conflict. Workers have every right to defend their interests, insists protagonist Torquato, but they must do so through "cordiality and not struggle, unity and not discord, mutual confidence and not hate." "Moral reform" must therefore teach people to "love each other as brothers," without undermining social hierarchy because the "distinction of classes," says Torquato, "is a providential condition of human activity." If workers behave themselves, they can rise through individual effort into the middle class, even as the middle class moves up to "a more elevated position" in the social order. Social hierarchy and equilibrium are thus preserved by eliminating the working class as such—not through repression, as elites had so long desired, but through spiritual awakening, cooperation, and upward mobility, along the lines of what the Integralists had hoped for. Unrealistic though it may have been, Torquato's solution bespeaks middle-class fears and attitudes regarding class struggle and betrays an abiding faith in the power of morality as a basis for confronting social uncertainty.[103]

Redemptive moralism was at the very core of what by 1950 was represented as a middle-class political outlook. At a Rio conference in 1940 a commentator argued that morality rather than economics should bind the middle class together: "The problem is primarily moral. ... We must resuscitate and maintain family, moral, and spiritual and professional traditions in order to balance the middle groups between the continual ascension of the working class and the compression of the upper strata."[104] The idea that the middle class could be defined by its morality spread beyond the relatively small circle of middle-class spokesmen. In 1948, responding to a nationwide survey on middle-class attitudes, a lawyer stated that "morally, the middle class leads the most stable life. In high circles (with honorable exceptions) there are all of the vices of the bourgeoisie. In the proletarian classes there is a tendency to loosen family ties."[105]

This outlook resonated with Catholic moral doctrine. Silva's *Middle Class*, for example, quoted papal encyclicals when emphasizing the importance of social peace and class harmony. Tito Prates da Fonseca's paper "The Meaning and Value of the Middle Classes" was given at a Catholic social action conference in 1940. Ruy de Azevedo Sodré presented his paper "In Defense of the Middle Classes" at the first São Paulo State Congress of Christian Families. Catholic social doctrine was in the air. After a revival of Catholic thought in the 1920s Catholic intellectuals in the 1930s and 1940s characterized class struggle as a symptom of the loss of unity and blamed unbridled liberalism and capitalism for creating the class divisions that afflicted Brazilian society. They criticized the bourgeoisie for its egoism and its dominance of Christians and proletarians and argued that Brazil could be saved from the conflagration of class only by adhering to Catholic moral doctrine, downplaying individual competition and group conflict.[106]

This was precisely the point of *A Bourgeois Family*, which, though not laden with religious quotations or imagery, warns in the prologue of impending danger to "Christian civilization." Presenting the problem of morality more graphically than any of the other novels canvassed here, the book concerns the lives of two families, one led by a prominent industrialist, the other headed by a moderately successful government bureaucrat. When the story opens the functionary's family—"ashamed of the proletariat," "sacrificing the stomach for appearances," "pretending in order to show off," and constantly "sniffing at the gold of the rich"—leads a life of reasonable comfort in a smallish beach apartment in Rio, with a radio, a telephone, and a single servant.[107] The functionary himself is a simple man, a fatalist without great ambition, who agrees with everything. He is content to read his newspaper, has no political affiliations, and does not even follow soccer. His wife does not work outside the home. His daughter, Nilda, is able to enjoy some of the pleasures of the beach and club set. The industrialist's family is represented as being more or less typical of the new urban upper class. Their politics are corrupt. Money is their poetry. The son, Armando, a wild youth who is presumptive heir to his father's business, is slothful and irresponsible. The story takes off when the two families are brought together by the marriage of their children: Nilda—"a daughter of the upwardly mobile petite bourgeoisie, eyes turned toward splendor"—weds Armando, who marries down because his parents fear he will not find a match among the proper young women of his own class.[108]

The balance of the novel chronicles the progressive debasement of Nilda's family by the egoism and avarice of bourgeois life. The functionary, previously a man of irreproachable moral qualities who dreamt only of a quiet retirement, abandons his orderly habits of old under the spell of Armando's industrialist father. He is drawn into a life of prolonged drinking jags and visits to bordellos, where they ascend to the second floor, "a place where only society types could go. The middle class had to make do for itself downstairs."[109] Armando, as it turns out, has unnatural and violent sexual proclivities of the sort unfamiliar to young women from moral families like Nilda's. His turpitude in the bedroom coincides with a broader social and political immorality that manifests itself when he takes over his father's business. He becomes a rapacious industrial baron, deaf to what the author characterizes as the minatory roar of the working class. In refusing to consider workers' legitimate demands, Armando advances toward the day when the struggle would become "cruel, without quarter, face to face," a battle, says Chaves, the proletariat would surely win. The tragedy is that there can be no other outcome given bourgeois mentality: "The politics of the calculating ones, of the egoists, is necessarily egoist, even when it appears altruistic."[110]

It is in this spirit of politics-as-dead-end that the writer Tônio Santiago in Veríssimo's *The Rest Is Silence* despairs at the chaos of the social world and declares himself an "apolitical type." He claims he can muster no "firm belief in any political doctrine" and insists that he is "utterly incapable of adjusting himself to parties." He does not counsel indifference to the world's "pangs"—quite the contrary— but he simply does not believe politics has anything to offer.[111]

Instead, this mild-mannered writer reposes his hopes for the future in his personal life at home. Refuge from the agitation of the outside world, home is where his life can be a repudiation of the empty and meaningless lives of the rich and near rich and the desperate lives of the poor, who populate the rest of the novel. At home he teaches his children not to worship money. Where dinnertime conversation among the well-to-do lapses into a discussion of how best to sever a man's head from his body, Tônio's family engages in animated and creative talk. Where the monied seek fame or adventure and have not the "least interest in family life," the novelist aspires to a life of familial closeness and private pursuits, "a life of agreeable routine, with friends, music and books, lived in remarkable equilibrium."[112] Tônio's view of the social world is an extension of his domestic utopia. He believes himself obliged to do whatever possible to help preserve social harmony. So he teaches his children not to pursue the "free satisfaction of [their] inclinations" if doing so would "compromise the social equilibrium." He wants everyone to be happy, well fed, well housed, and able to bathe daily. And while the wealthy lust for the bodies of their mistresses and fancy their own coiffures with nary a thought to the common good, Tônio fervently believes in "the future of his land and his people" and is "serenely confident that something beautiful and magnificent would still emerge some day."[113]

Despite Tônio's exalted view of home life, men do not preside over the domestic sphere in these books; women do. In these stories women play a leading role in the struggle to secure social peace, not despite but precisely because of their alienation from the hurly-burly of politics. Mothers, wives, and girlfriends in tightly rendered domestic persona represent inti-

mate counterpoints to both the radical temptation and the corruptions of
elite politics. In *Petit Bourgeois* Leandro's decision to take up radical politics leads him to abandon a girlfriend who just wanted a normal life and
"a modern little house." He comes full circle later, recanting radical politics, when he finds a new girlfriend. Carvalho's *Middle Class* employs the
same motif: Manoel's radical odyssey begins when his suit to marry a local
businessman's daughter is turned down. In Dupré's *There Were Six of Us*
Dona Lola is immovable in her defense of domestic peace and order
against Alfrêdo's political ravings and adventures. Life is not a matter of
politics, mother tells son. People live by practical sense, not by theories.[114]
And in Veríssimo's *The Rest Is Silence* Nora's steadfast devotion to a
tranquil home life finally vanquishes the darker side of Roberto's soul. After parting "forever" earlier in the story, the two are reconciled. Roberto,
an orphan, realizes that at bottom he is not so much a radical as "a man
searching for a family he had never possessed." A yen for fraternity had
taken him among society's downtrodden and endowed him with a political conscience, but he had never been motivated by "hatred, vengeance, or
violence" against the rest of society. His emotion, the author interjects,
was "bright and placid, not bloody or turbulent." He was driven above all
by a "desire for understanding and brotherhood, yearning for peace and
harmony," rather than a fever for revolutionary upheaval.[115] Here domestic quietude stills the hubbub of class conflict one soul at a time.

Middle-class women in these novels also represent a counterpoint to
the depravity and political immorality of the bourgeoisie. Where the rich
are "bandits" who think only of "themselves, themselves, themselves,"
Dona Lola sacrifices herself day in and day out to hold her home together
in the face of social turmoil. Tônio's wife in *The Rest Is Silence* is a bed-
rock of sanity at the end of the novel. Where the rich are wrapped up in
fantasies of carnal lust and self-centered vanity, Livia imagines herself at
home, secretly putting out Easter baskets for her children.[116] In *A Bourgeois Family* Nilda, who as a young woman had been tempted by the racy
lifestyle of her beach and club friends, becomes a paragon of moral virtue
in the same measure as her husband, Armando, becomes a moral monster
in the bedroom, at the factory, and in politics. Ultimately, however, she too
is tainted by her husband's evil: believing she is sterile, Nilda becomes pregnant by artificial insemination, a sin under Catholic doctrine. She keeps the
secret from Armando, hoping to please him. Instead he accuses her of adul-
tery, revealing that he, not she, is sterile.

The significance of these examples is the role they give women in the
everyday political drama of the 1930s and 1940s: these novelists—and on

this the one female author, Sra. Dupré, was perhaps the most dramatically adamant—make middle-class women into conservators of domesticity and by extension of social peace in the face of a flawed political system.[117] Women's historical alienation from the political sphere and their status as paladins of morality become the basis for a critical perspective on institutional politics. The implication in these books is that men like Tônio and Carlos who properly value the life of home and family could participate with their wives and mothers in the mission of securing society's moral center, even while maintaining a sense of male dominance at home. All others simply play into the hands of working-class radicals and bourgeois egoists, whose struggle generates the politics of class. Women could not force men to behave, but by example and self-sacrifice they could bring a domestically rooted morality to bear on the world outside the home. Though as Nilda's disgrace and as the anxiety expressed throughout the stories suggests, it is clear that the influence ran powerfully also in the other direction.

Their ambivalence notwithstanding, these novels represent middle-class political sensibilities as an inversion of politics as usual. Where formal politics is a matter of *a rua*—the vaguely dangerous world of the street, an arena of amoral, male individualism, where markets, interests, patronage, and politics were the order of the day—proper politics was a matter of *a casa*, the female haven of order, morality, and harmony.[118] Home, then, was a defining experience and a powerful metaphor. Through the fugue between inside and outside, order and disorder, public and private, middle-class characters—and with them middle-class readers—could imagine an engagement with broader political questions while avoiding the formal politics from which they felt excluded. And because donas de casa were in charge of the home, subject to a weakened but sturdy dependence on their husbands, their idealized role came to define much of what anchored middle-class political sensibilities even as formal politics remained deeply patriarchal.

These novels are perhaps best understood as faint snatches of the "essentially antagonistic discourse of social class" from an intimate perspective.[119] Other sources hint that this debate was not confined to fictional homes. Housekeeping manuals and domestic magazines of the 1930s and 1940s reflected a distinctive outlook on the nature and purpose of the home in personal life and wider society. As with the novels considered here, they refer to order, morality, harmony, equilibrium, serenity, tranquillity to describe the ideal home. Isabela Serrano's housekeeping manuals, like the novels, insist that donas de casa had a social mission to "try to improve human society" by "combating egoism" and "correcting the asperity of the masculine character."[120] She also declared a point largely implicit in the novels: a properly ordered home allowed a limited sense of control over one's destiny, whatever else was going on outside. Home, as she put it, was a safe harbor, where the family could "determine its own program for life . . . avoiding futile and pernicious contacts with society."[121]

But home as place and metaphor was not to be merely a refuge. Echoing the novels, lawyer Ruy de Azevedo Sodré argued that the middle class must "make of the home its world" and in so doing serve as the buffer between upper-class vice and lower-class misery.[122] In his book *Problems of the Middle Classes,* João Lyra Filho also linked the values of middle-class home life to broader social and political concerns. If only the middle class could develop a "habit of thrift," he declared, and live by "moral discipline," they would feel no need to "dispute what others have" and would contribute thereby to the "tranquillity of a life of peace and comfort, that would permit harmony among men." In the end it was all a matter of organizing the home properly, concluded Lyra, for "the family is the most stable force for consolidating the social order" and for ensuring a world [of] "collective calm."[123] The political, properly understood, was personal; the world, a well-ordered home.

In wider culture too the home became an important symbol during and after the 1930s. In 1933 sociologist Gilberto Freyre published the first volume in his study of the decline of the patriarchal family in Brazil. *Casa Grande & Senzala* (The masters and the slaves) gained a national reputation almost overnight. To chart the waning of stable dependencies mediated by patriarchal families, Freyre began by constructing an idyllic past. His depiction of colonial plantation life in the Northeast sparked a deep nostalgia among the Brazilian reading public, for at times it seemed to say that Brazilians, whatever their race or status, could get along by reaching back for a lost past. The key to Freyre's argument was the *fazenda* itself, a kind of large home where masters and slaves, men and women, black, white, and mulatto, within a largely uncontested hierarchical order mixed freely in all arenas of daily life, from field to table, to bed, relating but little to the world beyond. Its implicit message was, or was taken to be, that Brazil conceived as a large family could avoid the social divisions among classes and races that seemed to be plaguing Europe and even the United States at the time.[124]

The cultural power of home as place and symbol of social and national conciliation did not simply melt into air. Certain professions, such as social work and teaching, which put middle-class women and men on the front lines of class relations, employed a discourse that sought to project a vision of domestic tranquillity onto the wider public sphere. By locating the reasons for social turmoil in immorality and the male character, the novels examined here drew on the taproot of women's status outside politics to reject class and class struggle as a model for social organization. This suggests that an important factor binding middle-class women and men together in the home and the nation in the face of growing gender tensions was a shared anxiety regarding the uncertainties of politics.

Home, with its moral drapery, had come to be seen as less a place apart than a kind of lyrical force in opposition to the dissonances of a modernizing society. Middle-class women did not thereby gain direct political power, but they did come to be recognized symbolically as the guardians of a politically charged moralism. Middle-class men, for all that they retained their authority in the home, now occupied a more politically ambiguous position than ever. Lacking access to the levers of power wielded by elite men and not empowered through collective action, they now came to be symbolically inscribed within a feminized political space organized around morality, home, and family. On this telling domestically rooted moralism—itself a part of the myth of the middle class[125]—took form as masses of individual middle-class men and women groped toward a principle of order which, by seeming to bind all, could offset what they experienced as relative powerlessness in the emerging competitive politics of class.

A REMARKABLE ASPECT of middle-class life as depicted in the novels canvassed here is the absence of broad-based middle-class collective action. This is an eloquent silence that comments on politics largely by refusing to allude to it. A variety of sources testify that middle-class people did not lack an instinct to connect with matters political; as a group they simply appear to have done so by other than collective means. Technical competence came to be represented as one way middle-class men and women might contribute to national progress and social peace. Novels, housekeeping manuals, and political essays limn another—political moralism rooted in an idealized vision of family and home. As forms of imagined engagement with broader social and political issues, technical competence and domestic moralism had key elements in common, a profound suspicion of politics and formal political process and a sense that morality could overcome social conflict. Ideally this was more than just an antipolitical leeriness of all politics. The hope, as adumbrated in diverse sources, was that politics as such might be redeemed and class conflict

quelled by técnicos and by donas de casa (and their right-thinking husbands) who held the moral, public, and national good above narrow political and partisan interests.

So sublime a role for morality came at a price. Condemnation of formal
politics and political process corroded the attachments necessary for
shared concerns to be expressed collectively.* This was what led contemporary observers to despair of the middle class; while powerful antagonists—employers, workers, and political elites—vied for control of the
material world, middle-class people as a group were seen to have no realistic way of competing politically because they had no home in extant political institutions. Yearning above all for social peace, their suspicion of
politics meant they could only torture themselves by desiring a state of affairs they could do little to bring about.

Though we must be cautious, so unstable and seemingly self-defeating
an outlook raises crucial questions about the connections between everyday life and political contexts. Through their work and in their home lives
middle-class men and women could have political opinions, even offer
scathing critiques of politics as a whole, without feeling obliged to join a
political party or movement. No barrier thwarted partisan engagement,
and political entrepreneurship offered a route to those so inclined. The
story of the vast majority, however, appears to have been another. There
is no knowing exactly what went through people's heads, but technical
competence and domestic moralism shared an advantage over engagement with formal politics: Neither of them interfered with or detracted

---

*It is worth noting that issues of middle-class political alienation and avoidance
are not unique to Brazil. In 1958 C. Wright Mills worried about the political indifference of the vast numbers of "inactionary" middle-class Americans and noted that
available theories did not allow for the view that a stratum might appear on the political stage as politically passive (326–28). Herbert Gans has also written on the implications of "political avoidance" and alienation of middle-class Americans from
political institutions, factors he claims lie at the heart of the American political system. See Gans. Historians of the United States have not explored these insights for
what they might reveal of American political culture. French sociologist Pierre Bourdieu has also written on the growing distance between active political agents and the
ordinary individuals who are the consumers of politics. He has suggested that "apoliticism" may, in certain instances, be a protest against the unrepresentativeness of a
political process dominated by professional politicians who seek above all to "dis-
possess the majority of the people" of their political input (171–202). The Brazilian
case thus is less a case apart than a reminder of the deep contradictions and tensions
inherent in all contemporary political systems. Perhaps more sharply it suggests that
avoidance is more apt to describe political noninvolvement than passivity, and it
highlights the danger of assuming political participation to be natural and normal.

from the arduous task of orienting one's individual life toward securing a place in a competitive social order. The notion that professional and domestic life could express what mattered in their relationship to broader society and that politics as such was debauched gave middle-class people a means by which to acquit themselves from further political entanglements. This was, finally, a vision that located the political impulse where most middle-class people's attention appears to have been focused anyway: the imperatives of work and the sweet burdens of family.

10

Reflections

"THE NATURAL ROLE of twentieth-century man," said General Cummings in Norman Mailer's *The Naked and the Dead*, "is anxiety."[1] Of course, anxiety has played differently depending on the stage and been as evocatively expressed through great moments of upheaval and discord in one time and place as through lingering lives of quiet resignation and small rebellions in another. Living between palpable hope for and profound uncertainty about the future, middle-class men and women in Rio de Janeiro and São Paulo sought to reconcile the insistent force of tradition with the compelling impulse of modernity. In the face of emergent market and bureaucratic relations and persistent hierarchy and patronage they made do through the practices of day-to-day lives, seeking to wrest order from the commotion of their lives.

By 1950 these tensions had become part of the ordinary expectations of social life in modern Brazil. A "National Survey on the Situation of the Middle Classes" conducted during 1949–50 exclusively in cities outside the Rio–São Paulo axis revealed attitudes very close to those in Rio and São Paulo.[2] Drawing on hundreds of interviews and thousands of questionnaires, investigators characterized the middle classes of the various states as having fallen into "financial disequilibrium, lack of resources." The study indicates that these middle-class people aspired to a certain social position and comfort in the face of forces that seemed to work against their attainment, aware that they were caught up in the much larger process by which class had become central to Brazilian politics.[3] Whether recently risen to respectability or fallen from more vaunted positions, most appear to have contemplated with dread the possibility that they might skid from respectability into a nether world of unschooled, oftentimes darker-skinned people who worked with their hands. If they overestimated the danger of organized labor between 1920 and 1950 and too readily conflated these relatively privileged, organized workers with those less fortunate and less vocal, simplification of social reality was crucial to the making of middle-class lives.

And so collar-and-tie associations insisted fiercely that their members were a cut above mere manual workers, which meant everyone from an illiterate ditch digger with no access to a *sindicato* to a literate, highly skilled factory worker who belonged to a union. Individuals sought education to set themselves off from those below and reach up toward those above. Through consumption middle-class *donas de casa* made concrete their claim to a more exalted social standing than workers. But because hierarchies were not altogether stable, because competition implied the possibility of downward mobility, because so many remained dependent on patronage, and because incomes seemed so often inadequate to the task of keeping up appearances, these people who aspired to security and stability ended up living lives of disquiet.

This anxious politics of everyday aspiration bore an unresolved relation to the politics of competing ideologies, parties, and programs. Middle-class political experimentation during the 1930s appears to have grown out of a desire to curb the power of elites while maintaining social peace. The answer many came to, albeit from different directions, was to seek a way of bringing "the people" into institutional politics under proper guidance. This was the essence of the middle-class populisms proposed by Virginio Santa Rosa, the Integralists, and the ANL. There was no one reason these imagined alternatives vanished at the end of the 1930s. Their failure seems to have sharpened a sensibility among middle-class people that had been present all along—a vague intuition that the uneasy combination of partisan, ideological, and patronage politics was itself an impediment to national unity and social peace in a period of heightened class tensions.

And yet the politics of everyday life did not galvanize a broad and lasting middle-class political party or movement. Faced on one side with what were commonly represented as unresponsive and elitist political parties and on the other with what they saw as a militant working class, few middle-class voters seemed to have put much stock in formal politics after 1945.* Despite repeated calls that they act collectively, middle-class

---

*It is worth noting here that Brazilian political theorist Oliveira Vianna long ago articulated an alternative to volunteeristic, associationalist—Tocquevilleian—assumptions as the basis for understanding a political culture marked by the "tenuousness and weak-

Cariocas and Paulistanos appeared on the postwar electoral stage as a voting bloc only episodically and then, according to contemporary observers, only to vent their frustration with the political process as a whole. Clovis Leite Ribeiro attributed Adhemar de Barros's election to the governorship of São Paulo in 1947 to middle-class disillusionment with partisan politics as usual. Likewise, Jânio Quadros's 1953 campaign for mayor of São Paulo, symbolized by the broom with which he promised to sweep out the Augean stables of politics, was, said a pundit, little more than a successful play to "a general desire for order and cleanliness and as such was an appeal directed particularly at the puritanism of the middle class."* In other words, middle-class disdain for politics could have direct, if unpredictable, effects, in part because middle-class people were "politically available" to those who could, even if momentarily, speak to middle-class misgivings.[4]

---

ness of our consciousness of the collective good, of our sentiment of social solidarity and the public interest" (F. Vianna, 321–60). If nothing more, Vianna's work cautions against uncritically employing political theories alien to the historical specificities of Brazil in trying to make sense of Brazilian politics. Particularly it challenges the easy identification of volunteerism with individualism, an equation that is often taken as a first principle of liberal political culture.

Along lines similar to Vianna's, readers of Fernando de Azevedo's *A cultura brasileira* could find a historical-cultural explanation for the middle class's weak associative spirit. The middle class, wrote Azevedo in 1944, had never had a chance to "organize itself." While Azevedo seemed to want to fit the Brazilian middle class into the triumphalist narrative of nineteenth-century Europe by arguing that the advent of the Republic in 1889 represented a victory of the middle class against slavery, monarchy, and aristocracy, he betrayed his lack of faith in that storyline as applied to Brazil by concluding that the Brazilian middle class remained without political influence. During the Republic an "urban bourgeoisie" of *bacharéis* had formed the core of a new political class after 1889, but they had not been able to loosen the "landholding aristocracy's" stranglehold on the political system. Brazilian political culture, said Azevedo, thus combined an individualism lacking any notion of "common interest or spirit of cooperation" with the master-slave/patron-client relationship that had been at the center of the social system of slavery. In this situation, he seemed to be saying, there was no clear political part for the middle class. Of course, he was assuming that the middle class's political role had been clearer in other places and at other times, which begs the question regarding the myth of an idealized middle class (95, 117).

*"Porque venceu Jânio Quadros," *Cadernos de nosso tempo* 1 (Mar. 1953): 99–102. The reference to puritanism is a curious one, suggesting how common it was for Brazilian commentators to understand the Brazilian middle class as part of a supposedly universal narrative grounded in the history of the English and American middle classes. Indeed, in Catholic and poly-religious Brazil, puritanism could have no meaning except by reference to a stereotype of the American middle class. For this author, the oddity of something like a unified middle-class political response could only be understood as something alien to normal Brazilian politics.

A further sense in which the middle class mattered politically was far more diffuse—and for that reason far more difficult to discern. Many could imagine setting their signatures to the social order through other than collective political means. Through bureaucracies public and private, middle-class men and women could imagine a tutelary relationship to the people and recapture something of the dream that had energized political experimentation in the 1930s. Nor was the middle class entirely absent from the political discourse generated by the contest between populists and antipopulists: though explicit mention of the middle class was infrequent compared with the storm of words regarding capital and labor, the irenic language of family, social peace, and class harmony appears to have soothed many in the middle class. Novels, political essays, housekeeping manuals, and white-collar publications reveal that this was not merely a disembodied rhetoric confected by politicians for strategic ends; it was an idiom that implicated a basic aspect of the middle-class experience, the quotidian life of home and family. From a middle-class perspective the problem was that the language of moralism so often understudied more conflictual voices. In lieu of political engagement, then, the middle class came to be represented as its own symbol of social peace, a peace premised on its reticence to take part in the politics of class.

This was the rub that gave rise to the political quandaries of the middle class. To working-class militancy and to elite power the moralism of a fissile middle class counterpoised two imperatives: an insistence on the naturalness of hierarchical distinctions vis-à-vis those below and a leveling desire to hold those above to a standard of behavior incompatible with a politics of egoism. Workers might gain more for themselves and elites might retain power, but the middle-class claim to moral superiority made it possible to believe that neither was a legitimate political outcome. Here was an imagined escape route from irrelevance and complicity in a dangerous, corrupt, and unresponsive political system.

Escape led to a further trap, however, for political moralism expressed shared but not collectively articulated concerns. According to the Brazilian Institute of Economics, Sociology, and Politics (IBESP), a São Paulo group that at times purported to speak for the middle class, moralism rooted in an "alienation from any political or ideological participation in the public life of the country" deflected middle-class people from bringing their viewpoint directly to bear on politics. This left them open to manipulation. "By criticizing the rulers for their vices or their evil actions, and by proposing that they be replaced by others, the middle class, *ipso facto*, leaves intact the very conditions that led to material and spiritual discontent in the first place." Only in times of crisis, said IBESP ideologues in 1954, could the middle class have any political influence, and then only through the military "with its traditional links to the middle class, whose discontent it expresses and directs."[5]

Hence the vicissitudes of middle-class politics up to 1950. As individuals, middle-class Cariocas and Paulistanos, and likely others as well, had acquired a stake in a modernizing nation, but having lost their bid to articulate populism on middle-class terms, they distrusted political elites and recoiled from undifferentiated absorption into the people. This was why the middle class as such was largely absent from the explicit political representation of class at the national level, unlike organized workers and employers. Middle-class people benefited enormously from expanding white-collar labor markets, growing educational opportunities, rising incomes, and greater access to consumer goods. Yet none of these seemed to flow from any politics they had undertaken, but from the wellspring of modernization itself. As a result, the pressure their everyday lives exerted on those who wielded power remained invisible. Beneficiaries of modernization, they could feel themselves victims of a process that never seemed to deliver quite what it promised and over which they felt themselves to have little influence.

As long as economic growth continued to fuel industrialization, urbanization, and expansion of public- and private-sector bureaucracies—the founts of middle-class employment, income, status, and hopes—there was little reason to question this state of affairs. Middle-class Brazilians could live by the promise that brighter days were still ahead because, in Stefan Zweig's almost carnivalesque inversion of the usual relationship between Brazil and Europe, they lived in a "country of the future."[6] Meanwhile moralistic disdain for political engagement could seem safely virtuous. If middle-class people could not make the world live up to their moral vision, at least they could imagine standing apart from the unseemly, undignified contest that clove society. Naturally such arrangements could not last. As class antagonisms widened during the 1950s and as it began to dawn that economic growth might not last forever, middle-class people appear either to have chosen sides or to have looked on as politics unraveled.[7]

The story told here is a reminder that beneath the celebratory epic of the middle class have lain more involuted tales. Stuck between combatants in a context of distrust for politics as such, the Brazilian middle class could not "make their will triumph in national politics," as French sociologist Jacques Lambert had brazenly predicted they would. Rather, according to lawyer Ruy de Azevedo Sodré in 1952, they had been "relegated to a secondary plane" in the nation's public life. Unable or unwilling to act as a conflict group, middle-class men and women, on this view, seem to have embodied in their day-to-day lives the notion that their situation, though far from perfect, was preferable to unbridled class warfare. Far from being antimodern, this outlook represented the dynamic conservatism of modernity, an outlook rooted in the reluctant affinities of class and energized by the most powerful political force in rapidly changing societies: the diffuse sense that the good life, or at least a life considerably better than most, is best protected and advanced through individual striving at work and at home. Individuals might take up an ideological or partisan banner, but by 1950 the middle class generally was not aligned with programmatic liberalism or conservatism, corporatism, Christian Democracy, or any of several brands of leftist political thought.

Such fluidity hardly seems surprising. Politics is as meaningfully expressed in the imagined relationship between everyday life and broader social questions as in supposedly well-articulated political programs. Day-to-day lives are never as sharply cut as ideologies or parties would have them be. Uncertainty and unsettledness are not merely passing phenomena. For most people they are central and unavoidable facts of modern lives. Disconcerted by their situation, some may seek certainties through ideological conviction or partisan commitment. Such attachments usually bear the stamp of an anxious ambivalence. Put another way, frustration, apathy, indifference, accommodation, fear, contentedness, resignation, and indecision frame the way huge numbers of people, perhaps most, have related to partisan, ideological conflict in the twentieth century.

Enthusiasm for the idea of a collective middle-class politics in the 1930s and its decline in the 1940s may be interpreted in this light. Populism has generally been understood in terms of passive masses whose nature it is to follow or else as a kind of wrestling match between highly organized, militant workers and highly organized, strident employers, with a contested state bestride the conflict. The problem with these formulations is that they cannot account for the far more fractured experience of populism in practice.[8] They shed no light on how different class and nonclass discourses were articulated with one another.[9] Nor can they say much about how the rhetoric and reality of *the people* were constructed through fragile and temporary accommodations among various segments of the popular classes. The principal reason for this is a failure to consider what role the bulk of the masses, the unorganized or diffusely organized elements of society, played in the politics of populism.

It is here that middle-class political ambivalence impinged directly upon electoral politics. To the extent that the contest between populists and antipopulists defined national politics during the post-1945 period, there was simply no clear consensus within the middle class on the legitimacy of competitive politics as a means of mediating social change. In their individualized suspicion of ideological and partisan struggle and in their fear of class conflict, a great bulk of middle-class men and women appear to have embraced their political confinement even as they were being lured into a snare not entirely of their own making. Their part in the unstable politics of electoral populism was expressed in manifold ways by their uneasiness at having to be a part at all. Eschewing active political engagement, most understood that politics was unavoidable. For many, technical competence and domestic moralism constituted an effort to face this irresolvable quandary.

The disagreement between Lambert and Sodré over middle-class political prospects, therefore, was far more than just an outsider and an insider failing to see eye to eye. Lambert's reliance on a presumed transition from hierarchy to egalitarianism, from patronage to merit, from relationalism to individualism is yoked to another, that from tradition to modernity. But as Sodré perceived, if only dimly, the Brazilian middle class in the 1950s was not in the process of passing from so-called tradition to so-called modernity; it was formed by the tug between the two.

This conclusion carries important implications. Middle-class political unsettledness cannot be laid solely to the fact of its betwixt-and-between social position. Structure cannot be denied, but there are other reasons not to think of the middle class in terms of whether it was democratic or corporatist, liberal or conservative, populist or antipopulist—or even whether it was political in any straightforward way. In Brazil's industrializing, urbanizing, market-oriented social order the conflicting impulses of hierarchy and egalitarianism, patronage and merit, relationalism and individualism, the "shifting involvements" between public and private,[10] the ambivalence toward politics as such, and the great power of everyday life to shape political sensibilities simply do not permit such neat labels, for they imply a mingling of attitudes toward politics that cannot be captured by the doctrines and ideologies that have generally been taken as a basis for understanding political behavior.

What has made the idea of the middle class so attractive in the twentieth century is its assurance of progress with social peace—unambiguous, unpolitical modernization. As a free-floating idea, it was easily appropriated as universalizable norm by intellectuals seeking broad truths and by ordinary people seeking to make sense of lives in turbulent societies. The further in time and place it drifted from its origins, the more obvious the gap between its promise and the experience of those who tried to live by it.

It was in trying that middle-class men and women left their mark on the social order in subtle rather than spectacular ways. Stubborn preoccupation with status led them to accept an unresolved tension between hierarchical imperatives and egalitarian impulses that profoundly influenced social relations among all classes. Hopes of rising and fears of falling played a critical role in defining the unstable relationship between individual pursuits and associative spirit so central to the problems of modern political culture. Their buying power, attention to advertising, and anxious desire for consumer goods gave shape to Brazil's urban culture in terms of modernity as an achievable ideal, exerting thereby an indirect influence on economic policy making. By trying and failing to establish middle-class populisms during the 1930s, they laid the basis for future middle-class critiques from right and left and did much to frame the context within which politics was made and remade after 1945. The interplay between the collaborationism of collar-and-tie *sindicalismo* and the mass uninvolvement of middle-class salary earners in direct political activity allowed government to focus on controlling a more restive industrial labor movement. By eagerly embracing technical competence and domestic moralism, middle-class men and women sought to stand between workers and employers, strengthened connections between state and society, and articulated the nation to itself, even as they called into question the whole enterprise of competitive politics as the basis for a peaceful social order. In doing so, they helped paper over the fact that private and public aspirations did not converge to produce a mannerly, harmonious politics, as it was assumed they should. Finally their lives are testimony to the power of market relations to condition social and political possibilities; whatever else they thought they were doing, middle-class people were constantly engaged by the defining dilemmas of the market.[11]

For all their yearning there was no equipoise in the lives of middle-class men and women after 1950. During the heady days of the campaign during 1951–54 to establish a national oil industry, middle-class people surely thrilled to the idea that Brazil would declare its economic independence from the United States and Europe. Bureaucrats might respond to initiatives of political and economic elites, but they were responsible for carrying out the immense program of public relations necessary to build political support for Vargas's bold stroke. Nor was the matter confined to government offices. In its fervor, the campaign reprised the nationalism of Tenentismo, Integralism, and the ANL. With the zeal of those who swell to the idea of selfless duty in behalf of the nation (and knowing that the issue would sell papers), Rio's popular press turned their pages over to the campaign, encouraging readers to write letters declaring "the oil is ours." Throughout the country, but especially in larger cities, municipal, neighborhood, factory, professional, women's, student, and union commissions sprang up to broadcast the nationalist message.[12] Middle-class people were crucial in this effort, for without having to face the disruptions of class politics they could once again see themselves as helping the state lead the people toward the greater good of the nation.

Yet just as the campaign was rushing toward its successful conclusion (the national oil company, Petrobrás, was established by law in October 1953), many in the middle class surely watched with apprehension São Paulo's massive Strike of 300,000 in March and April 1953. Vargas the nationalist president might be able to rally the people to declare Brazil's independence from economic imperialism but Vargas "the father of the poor" and champion of workers seemed unable to contain an organized working class whose militancy seemed to know few bounds. So when junior army officers published the "Colonel's Memorandum" in February 1954, demanding higher salaries "compatible with their social position" and condemning the "spirit of political partisanship, sower of discord and conflict" and the "subversive violence of communism," many middle-class people were heartened to hear words vibrating to their anxieties. As the Memorandum pointed out, the government's proposal to raise the minimum wage by 100 percent would allow an unskilled worker to earn almost as much as many university graduates.[13] From this perspective, the last straw may have come shortly thereafter. In his May Day speech of 1954, Vargas declared himself the "indefatigable friend and defender of workers" and exhorted them to take politics by storm in the next year's presidential election: "As citizens your views will bear weight at the polls. As a class, you can make your ballots the decisive numerical force. You constitute the majority. Today you are with the government. Tomorrow you will be the government."[14] The menace of class conflict could not have been more explicit.

The political crisis following Vargas's suicide in 1954 appears to have sharpened disdain for politics within the middle class. A power struggle between *getulistas* and *antigetulistas* over the election of 1955 was resolved only when the army stepped in to assure Juscelino Kubitchek's succession to the presidency. The years following were ones of great optimism and accomplishment. Kubitschek lived up to his pledge to accelerate

Brazil's modernization. Industrial growth hummed along at nearly 13 percent a year between 1957 and 1961, middle-class job and educational opportunities expanded, and a full-blown consumer culture came of age.

Yet middle-class anxiety was not at an end. Macedo Dantas's 1959 novel *João classe média* was an emblem of continued uncertainty in day-to-day middle-class life.* The story is diarylike account by a public functionary who realizes he cannot adequately provide for his family on a government paycheck. To make ends meet, he turns to after-hours *bico*. Over time these jobs come to make up a greater part of the family's sustenance than the salary he draws from his respectable day job. Finally he is drawn into a shady deal that leads him down the path of quotidian corruption, just the sort of thing a moralistic middle class spent so much time decrying. As the story ends, he has paid off the refrigerator his wife had desired for so long and bought the family a new television set on installment. His daughters are doing reasonably well in school. His wife's teeth are fine. The family's financial difficulties have been taken care of.[15]

The narrative is driven by what Dantas sees as the animating force behind middle-class lives in the late 1950s, the continuing inability to resolve the predicament of always wanting and expecting more than could be had, in an economy that seemed to grow by leaps and bounds without ensuring broad-based economic security. The novel is a satirical jeremiad that seeks to waken middle-class readers to the paradox of their situation. And so, João does attain middle-class levels of consumption—the refrigerator, a television set—but only by sacrificing occupational respectability and moral purity. To drive the point home, Dantas does not permit his antihero to despair. Instead, João concludes sardonically that middle-class "happiness" is possible . . . with a little imagination.

As with the novels canvassed earlier, Dantas's tale appears not to contemplate the possibility of a collective middle-class response to the crisis. João makes do for himself through work, moral flexibility, and a capacity for willing self-delusion. Perhaps broad middle-class support for moralizing presidential candidate Jânio Quadros in 1960 was a reaction to the quandaries and compromises João Classe Média represented. A schoolteacher who refused to consort with "clientelistic" politicians and proposed a dynamic economic program, Quadros was neither a getulista nor

---

*The protagonist writes in the first chapter that he changed his given name, João da Silva, to João Classe Média, because it seems to express his situation. João Classe Média translates more-or-less to Joe Middle Class, conveying a sense of ordinariness. The translation, however, loses a further play on the Portuguese *João ninguem*, which means something like "Joe nobody."

an antigetulista. This endeared him to the broad mass of those who felt they had never found a place in the struggle between populists and antipopulists. His election to the presidency in 1960 promised to redress the middle class's alienation from politics, a hope dashed by his sudden resignation in 1961.

The ensuing crisis, in which Vice-President João Goulart took office, found no resolution until the military coup of 1964. As the economy slowed after 1962 and as inflation surged, Goulart found himself unable to reconcile the workers and employers who made up a brittle coalition. Many within the middle class became anxious when Goulart, a Vargas protégé, began to side with organized labor after 1963. Anxiety became fear after March 13, 1964, when Goulart unambiguously aligned himself with workers against employers in an outdoor speech broadcast live to television and radio sets in middle-class homes and apartments all over the nation. Less than a week later, on March 19, women's groups with many middle-class members, galvanized by church, business, and military leaders, called as many as half a million men and women into the streets of São Paulo to protest Goulart's turn. They demanded that the military step in to restore order. On March 31, 1964, military leaders agreed, ousting Goulart in a bloodless coup.

The middle class's part in the coup cannot be reduced to a politics of interest or to their supposed slavish dependence on elite sectors. Concrete interests and subordination to elites mattered, but there were other reasons middle-class people widely feared Goulart's maneuvers in 1964 and either backed the coup or looked on in resignation. From the perspective developed in this book, the shock of Goulart's radicalization did not draw its charge solely from rational calculation or committed ideological opposition. Stronger for some than others, it was as well a visceral sense that middle-class identity itself was at stake. Moreover, what appears to have been a widespread initial willingness to abide by the coup, or at least not meaningfully oppose it, may have owed as much to a weary sense that politics had failed once again as to anything like firm principles or clearly defined sectoral interests.

Thus what in the abstract might appear to have been an antidemocratic sensibility may instead have grown out of middle-class political experience over the preceding decades: the abuse of democratic processes during the Old Republic, their suspension after the Revolution of 1930, the failure of efforts to establish a middle-class populism, the not unwelcome dictatorship of the Estado Novo, and the unresponsiveness and chaos of the electoral arena after 1945. If middle-class people reposed little faith in competitive politics as a means of organizing national life, it is not so difficult to understand how large numbers of them might not have been particularly disturbed by its interruption in 1964, particularly in the midst of an economic downturn. After all, the main character in Sra. Leandro Dupré's 1949 novel *Dona Lola* at one point reflects that "Democracy is a great thing": A humble vegetable seller had become rich and now had a lovely house and silk dresses, and her son Julinho had bought a house, drove a car, and ate at the best restaurants.[16] In this light it may make sense to think of the middle class not as inherently authoritarian but as enablingly ambivalent.

Military rule in the 1960s and 1970s appears not to have unriddled the middle-class conundrum. Filmmakers began to take up the problem through movies set during the years leading up to 1964. *São Paulo Sociedade Anônima* (Luís Sérgio Person, 1965), *O Desafio* (Paulo César Saraceni, 1966), and *Terra em Transe* (Glauber Rocha, 1967) all explored recent political events from a middle-class perspective. The films revolved around the diverse ways middle-class men and women relied on ideals, morality, and willing illusion as responses if not precisely answers to the quandaries of Brazil's modernization and the undeniable realities of class struggle.[17] At bottom all seemed to be saying that middle-class people remained unsettled on key questions of Brazilian modernity: how to face a developmentalism that never quite delivered the security and stability it augured, what attitude to adopt with regard to democracy, and how to confront the politics of class.

By all accounts the following decades did not resolve to greater clarity. Military governments that provided collar-and-tie jobs, expanded educational opportunities, kept inflation down, contained organized labor, and ensured a continual flow of consumer goods might enjoy tacit middle-class support. But middle-class people might also call for a return to democracy to protest the arrest and disappearance of sons and daughters who had opposed the regime or simply found themselves in the wrong place at the wrong time. And when the economy faltered, they might seek redress through sindicatos and professional organizations. In the difficult years between 1975 and 1981, when economic growth dropped from 1968–74's double-digit average to under 6 percent and inflation gathered steam, large numbers of doctors, teachers, public functionaries, bank clerks, engineers, journalists, and many others went out on strike dozens of times.

Even so, only a relatively small minority ever participated in such actions. Most, far more concerned with the struggles of day-to-day life, subsumed the political to the private. On this front prospects seemed bleak through the late 1970s and into the 1980s. In 1979 an op-ed piece in *Folha de São Paulo* asked, "What will become of the middle class?" implying that the future was not bright.[18] A series of São Paulo newspaper editorials are a measure of the situation in the early 1980s. Pundits asked whether "the middle classes exist" lamented the middle class's "difficult history" and bemoaned the confusion of a middle class lost in its own "labyrinth."[19] A decade later—Latin America's "lost decade"—the middle class's plight had become a symbol for doubts regarding the future of Brazil's modernization. Glossy magazines put the middle class "on the couch" in order to psychoanalyze a dour if well-attired social group that seemed to have slipped into an almost delusional state as its status eroded. Or, perhaps to rationalize a growing gap between a break-away elite of prosperous professionals and business executives and a downwardly mobile or at best stagnant middle class, the same magazines made "heroes" of unemployed middle-class professionals and employees who prowled the beaches peddling jewelry or sandwiches to those who still had money to buy.[20] Whether on the couch or on the beach, such people, at least as depicted in the popular press, seemed still to have found no place in politics. The patterns and forces that had taken shape by 1950 continued to be renewed nearly half a century later, even as the very concept of a durable middle class was being called into question by contemporary conditions, as it always had been.*

---

*In this regard Roberto Unger's argument for the position that "everything is politics" offers insight. Glossing Unger's discussion of late twentieth-century Brazilian politics, I would argue that the political dilemmas of the mid-century Brazilian middle class grew out of middle-class people's desperation to believe that the politics of social conflict could be avoided, even as they sensed, however dimly, that it could not. If class interests were self-evidently unavoidable to organized employers and workers at mid-century (and the extent to which and ways this was so raise important questions), they appear not to have been so obviously inescapable to the middle class. Indeed, it might be possible to see middle-class Brazilians at mid-century as having been uneasily balanced on the razor's edge between, on the one side, taking up an open-ended politics that would have depended, in Unger's words, on embracing "a range of unmistakably contestable views of social possibility" not reducible to a "routinized conception of reality," a politics in which they would have had no idea how they might fare, and, on the other side, abandoning any notion of class interests of their own whatever, with equally uncertain prospects (71). We may speculate that this balancing act expressed itself politically not by radicalizing the middle class (or most of it, anyway), but by driving middle-class people into the dynamic conservatism of those who know they have a great deal to lose by going either of two directions, despite the discomfort of their position.

IN HIS ESSAY "Development and Other Mirages" Octávio Paz plumbed what he referred to as Mexico's "disturbing sort of modernity."[21] What Paz seems to have sensed, if only vaguely in 1972, is that Latin Americans have always experienced the modern as a kind of invented tradition rooted in the "fantasies and dreams of [a] modernity" originating outside Latin America, fantasies and dreams that have never quite matched up to the lived reality within but have been every bit as real and concrete as other aspects of social life.[22]

Brazilian modernists recognized this dilemma long ago. In his *Anthropophagite Manifesto* of 1922, Oswald de Andrade sought to make a virtue of the fact that Brazilians had little choice but to confront their society through ideas and models that had come to life elsewhere.[23] Playing on Brazil's exotic image in the eyes of Europeans and Americans, he declared unflinchingly that in the modern world Brazilians would have to "cannibalize" and make their own that which was not, with all the attendant contradictions. In social and political life as well as in art he seemed to be calling for a recognition that there could be no sharp line between inside and outside, national and foreign, new and old, traditional and modern.

Andrade was well before his time.[24] For while middle-class Brazilians have had a healthy appetite for devouring the images, products, and aspirations of modernity, they have been largely free of the self-consciousness he seemed to demand. In the end, they could not or would not understand what Mario de Andrade glimpsed in his poems about the frantic, fractionate, "hallucinated" São Paulo of the early 1920s—that modernity, whatever else it might be, whatever promise it might hold, was not balanced and orderly but "Harlequinate!"[25] Against the experience of modernity as perpetual disorder in the here and now, middle-class men and women have consoled themselves by imagining modernity as the unfolding of an achievable order in the here to come. Wanting to believe with Silva's protagonist Torquato that the middle class "will always have to exist" because "it is necessary and can never disappear," they have lived by ceaselessly reviving their faith that finally ideal could win out over history.

In this they have differed little from their counterparts in the United States and Europe. For if "myth is a story everyone already knows," the myth of the middle class has been the longed-for story of the future in modernizing capitalist societies during the twentieth century.[26] Constantly brought up short by their lack of ownership, power, and organization, middle-class Brazilians were never able to surrender themselves completely to the myth.* If a

---

*If this has been less obviously the case in the United States and Europe, it is be-

hazy sense of paradox did not burn off into a clear awareness of their situation, it was because work, home, and morality seemed to provide the means by which to make livable lives amidst the ordeal of change.

---

cause the tenuousness of the middle classes there has been masked by postwar prosperity. This is one crucial way the experience of Latin American countries bears on the historical narratives of the West: Latin American particularities often puncture the pretense of the West's universalities, revealing them to be mythologized versions of European or American experience. This does not imply that the general simply dissolves into unrelated particulars. Rather, it compels us to embrace a wider world of historical particularities and then go about reimagining our more general stories. In this case a rethinking begins with subverting the cherished tropes of the middle-class storyline, so that supposedly clear distinctions between public and private, personal and political, traditional and modern come to be seen as unstable and contingent in the face of changing social and political contexts—as much for Europe and the United States as for Latin America.

Reference Matter

Abbreviations

The following abbreviations are used in the Notes:

AEC	Associação dos Empregados do Comércio
AFPESP	Associação dos Funcionários Públicos do Estado de São Paulo
AGC	Arquivo Gustavo Capanema, Centro de Pesquisa e Documentação, Fundação Getúlio Vargas
AGV	Arquivo Getúlio Vargas, Centro de Pesquisa e Documentação, Fundação Getúlio Vargas
AN	Arquivo Nacional
AOA	Arquivo Osvaldo Aranha, Centro de Pesquisa e Documentação, Fundação Getúlio Vargas
APEB	Arquivo Pedro Ernesto Batista, Centro de Pesquisa e Documentação, Fundação Getúlio Vargas
Boletim da AEC	*Boletim da Associação dos Empregados do Comércio*
Boletim da OAB	*Boletim da Ordem dos Advogados Brasileiros*
CEBRAP	Centro Brasileiro de Pesquisa
CPDOC	Centro de Pesquisa e Documentação, Fundação Getúlio Vargas
DIFEL	Difusão Editorial, S.A.
EDUFF	Editôra Universidade Federal Fluminense
ESSRJ	Arquivo Geral, Universidade Federal Fluminense Escola de Serviço Social do Rio de Janeiro
FGV	Fundação Getúlio Vargas
IBGE	Instituto Brasileiro de Geografia e Estatística
IBOPE	Instituto Brasileiro de Opinião e Estatística

IDORT	Instituto da Organização Racional do Trabalho
MJ	Ministério da Justiça, Arquivo Nacional
Revista do SMB	*Revista do Sindicato Médico Brasileiro*
RSP	*Revista do Serviço Público*
SESI	Serviço Social da Indústria
TSN	Tribunal de Segurança Nacional, Arquivo Nacional
UCLA	University of California, Los Angeles
UEC	União do Empregado no Comércio
UFF	Universidade Federal Fluminense
USP	Universidade de São Paulo

Notes

With regard to publications of occupational groups, it should be noted that volume and issue numbers are often inconsistent or absent because of changes in or oversights by the publications' editorial boards. It is also not uncommon for publications to lack pagination. I have in all instances given the most accurate citation possible.

Chapter 1

1. D. Silva, 55.
2. *Diretrizes*, 6: 148 (May 6, 1943).
3. Dupré, *Dona Lola*, 139–40.
4. See Certeau.
5. Nabuco, 111.
6. Lambert, 80.
7. See Wahrman.
8. Thackeray, 84–85.

9. Wahrman, 415–19. Long before Nabuco the middle class had been offered as the standard against which the progress of nations should be measured. In 1828 William Mackinnon published his book *On the Rise, Progress, and Present State of Public Opinion, in Great Britain, and Other Parts of the World*, wherein he evaluated the success and prospects of the world's nations, including Brazil and Mexico, by the presence or absence of a middle class. Mackinnon, 207–320.

10. Quoted in Wahrman, 416.

11. See, e.g., Rostow.

12. See, e.g., Whittaker; International Institute of Differing Civilizations; Lipset; Porter and Alexander.

13. See, e.g., Alba, 7: "One can no longer harbor the hope [that the middle class can become a social class whose interests coincide with those of society in general]. Day by day, the middle class becomes less and less a factor of social change and more and more a part of the vast parasitology of Latin America." See also, Adams, 47–48; Dealy, 82–83 n. 23. This is the view that has led to what Michael Jiménez calls the "elision" of the middle classes in the history of modern Latin America. See Jiménez, "The Elision."

14. See, e.g., Whittaker.

15. More subtle practitioners of the dependency approach for the modern period did discuss the middle class, though rarely in any full-bodied way. See Cardoso and Faletto; Donghi; Bergquist, *Labor in Latin America.*

16. There have been some notable exceptions. David Parker's *The Idea of the Middle Class* makes a similar point in the Peruvian context. See also Loaeza and Contla for Mexico and Covarrubias for Chile.

17. Weffort, 68.

18. Berman, 16.

19. The broad point regarding the incongruities of living an ideal modernity thought of as being located in Europe and the United States has begun to be explored for the Latin American context. See Schwarz, 19–32; Ortiz; Canclini, 44–54.

20. Obviously I am not talking about a manufacturing middle class, or bourgeoisie, on which there is a substantial literature for Latin America. See, e.g., Cerutti; Collado; Villalobos; Gorender. A small number of Brazilian and American scholars have written in a sustained fashion on a white-collar/professional middle class. They have been pivotal to the framing of this work. See Forjaz; Jaguaribe; Pinheiro; Saes; Skidmore, *Politics.*

21. I have found Giddens, Bourdieu, Hirschman, MacPherson, and Polanyi particularly helpful in understanding the centrality of market relations in social life.

22. This view of class walks a tight and tortuous line between recent criticisms of class. In particular I take very seriously the concern to explore the "limits of social explanation, i.e., in what senses the political cannot be inferred from the social." Jones, 11. I take this to mean that attention to language, while it unbalances strong structural accounts of politics, does not deny class a lived reality or sever any connection between social life and politics.

23. I use *middle class* rather than *middle classes* because I want to emphasize unity within the disunity of this social grouping, lest I end up with nothing more than a congeries of small, unrelated groups. Except when a particular source does so, I do not employ the term *petit bourgeois.* It is much less frequently used than some variant of *middle class* and carries with it a nineteenth-century European sense that seems less appropriate for Brazil. I often employ *collar-and-tie* or *white collar* when discussing situations in which the work lives of nonmanual, salaried employees appears to be central. I use *middle class* rather than *middle sectors* or *middle groups* because the people with whom I am concerned so often used *class* to describe their position in a society whose politics was laced with the language of class. Here I diverge from Johnson, who used *middle sectors* in order "to convey the idea of 'middleness' without paralleling any fixed criteria of 'middleness' employed in areas outside Latin America" (Johnson, ix). While I am deeply sympathetic to Johnson's concern not to impose a European or American category on Latin American reality, my point is that we cannot think about the middle class except by considering its relationship to the idea of the middle class originating outside Latin America. Latin Americans helped impose the category upon themselves.

24. T. Fonseca, 192.

25. Antonio García long ago grasped the importance of this fact in explaining

what he referred to as "the radical alienation of the middle classes from their own image" (123).

26. In this latter regard, I am thinking of those who have followed Michel Foucault.

27. Sofer, 167. The interpretation offered here is directed toward a mid-range conceptualization of the middle class in Brazilian social and political life. The touchstone is always the issue of class from the perspective of the people who lived it. Thus I am not concerned except incidentally with the more broadly interpretive, historical-sociological questions of whether the middle class was or was not an agent of capitalist development and democratic government.

28. Masterman, 301.

29. Johnson, vii.

30. Eliade, 23–28.

Chapter 2

1. R. Graham, *Patronage*, 233–63.

2. F. Fernandes, *A revolução burguesa*, 149–97.

3. Florestan Fernandes refers to Brazilian society in the nineteenth century as one of "castes and estates."

4. Hardman and Leonardi, 35, 91–94.

5. Quoted in Stein, *Vassouras*, 61.

6. See E. Costa, 81–82.

7. Thomas Ewbank, quoted in R. Graham, "The Onset of Modernization," 111.

8. Luccock, 107; F. Vianna, 181; R. Graham, *Britain*, 16.

9. F. Vianna, 180. Graham points out that tradesmen and craftsmen were lumped with manual laborers, even if they owned property. R. Graham, *Patronage*, 33.

10. T. Bastos, 50.

11. Kidder and Fletcher, 335.

12. Freyre, *The Mansions*, 178. Canes were a symbol of respectability through much of the nineteenth century, and municipalities often limited their use to the old, to the infirm, and to "respectable persons" (*pessoas decentes*). That commercial clerks could and did use them in public places indicates that they fell on the respectable side of an important social divide.

13. Freyre, *The Mansions*, 227.   14. R. Graham, *Patronage*, 34 n. 53.

15. Ibid., 32.   16. A. Costa.

17. T. Menezes, 35.

18. Quoted in R. Graham, *Patronage*, 33.

19. Quoted in R. Graham, "The Onset of Modernization," 112.

20. Baer, 21. Sugar as a proportion of exports dropped from 30 percent in 1820 to 12 percent in 1880.

21. See Stein, *Vassouras*, 16; Hermann, 122–24. This pattern did not begin to reverse itself until around 1900, principally in the state of São Paulo, where smallholders occupied land during the western expansion of coffee between 1900 and 1930. See Font, 14–16.

22. Many sold off their slaves to larger *fazendeiros*, alienating their only other source of independent capital to those who were coming to monopolize available sources of capital and credit. "They have been reduced to dependents of big planters," as a contemporary put it in 1855. Quoted in Stein, *Vassouras*, 48. See also Nabuco, 111: "Small land holding does not exist except through indulgence."

23. Burns, 242.

24. Wells, *Exploring*, 11–20, 30.

25. Quoted in Chaloub, 48.

26. E. Costa, 146–47.

27. Merrick and Graham, 66; Census 1890: xii.

28. S. Graham, 19, 187.

29. Luz, 49–66.

30. Merrick and Graham, 75.

31. Pôrto.

32. Hahner, *Poverty*, 82.

33. Census, 1895: xxxviii–xxxix.

34. Associação dos Empregados no Comércio do Rio de Janeiro, 119–22.

35. Hahner, *Poverty*, 83.

36. Nabuco, 111.

37. Ibid., 126–27.

38. Quoted in Stein, *Vassouras*, 125.

39. Naglé, 158.

40. Monteiro, 15.

41. This figure does not take returns into consideration. This is a difficult matter to pin down. Available evidence suggests Brazilian returns were low by international standards, perhaps somewhere in the range of 30 to 40 percent (Holloway, 40–42, 179; Merrick and Graham, 90–96).

42. In 1872 just over 100,000 people worked as commercial employees in Brazil. In 1900 the number surpassed 320,000. Bureaucracy too expanded during these years. Between 1872 and 1900 the number of public employees more than quadrupled, from just under 11,000 to more than 45,000, at a time when total population did not even double (Census 1920 4[5]: viii–ix).

43. Census 1920, 4(5): viii–ix.

44. In 1890 roughly one third of workers in manufacturing industries were black or mulatto, while only 10 percent of commercial employees were (Merrick and Graham, 76). Apparently the number of nonwhites reported in the liberal professions, public employment, and the officer corps was so small that it was not worth the trouble of breaking the statistic down by race.

45. J. Aranha, 19.

46. R. Graham, *Britain*, 277–97.

47. Eakin; R. Graham, *Britain*, 232–51.

48. E. Cunha, 86–87.

49. Ridings, 202–33.

50. R. Graham, *Patronage*, 107–9.

51. Font provocatively contests the hegemony of what he calls Big Coffee from the outset of the Republic. Font, 35–86, 123–48.

52. Love, 11.

53. The best descriptions of urban politics before the Revolution of 1930 are Conniff, *Urban Politics*, and J. M. Carvalho, *Os bestializados*.

54. Topik, "Middle-Class," 95, 96; Hahner, "Jacobinos," 129–33. See also J. M. Carvalho, *Os bestializados*; S. Queiroz.

55. F. Vianna, 216. Villela and Suzigan, chs. 3–4. Most of these establishments were quite small, employing fewer than twenty employees.

56. Merrick and Graham, 92.

57. F. Viana, 216; Census 1920 4(5): 172–73.

58. F. Viana, 216; Census 1920 4(5): 24–25.

59. Lobo, 449.

60. Chaffee; Census 1920 4(5): viii–ix, cxxi.

61. Stein, *The Brazilian Cotton Manufacture*, 20–21.

62. Quoted in Morse, 209.

63. See Greenfield.

64. Quoted in Hahner, *Poverty*, 162.

65. Nor was urbanization confined to Rio and São Paulo. In 1920 there were four times as many cities with 30,000 or more inhabitants in Brazil as in 1872, giving rise to an urban culture in virtually every state of the union. See Alessio; P. Pinheiro, 458–60.

66. Hallewell, 209.

67. Census 1920 2(1): 514–15; 4(5): 170–71.

68. Romero and Guimarães, 77.

69. Census 1920 2(1): cxxvi.

70. The number of construction workers per 1,000 population declined from 120.3 to 72.7. "Other" workers—probably many small producers and artisans—fell from 88.1 per 1,000 to 8.5. Census 1920 2(1): cxxi.

71. Nuto Santana's novel *A fábrica* (1923) speaks of the desperate attempts among working-class youths to get ahead in life.

72. AGC 35.05.16g, III–5.

73. Conniff, *Urban Politics*, 43.

74. Miceli, 26; Herrman, 244. By the 1920s there were reports of marriages between "poor cousins" and the daughters of Italian immigrants. Durham, 43.

75. Monteiro, 17. Though not all were nonmanual employees, roughly 100,000 people were employed by local, state, and federal governments in 1920 (Census 1920 2[5]: xii).

76. Canêdo, *O sindicalismo*, 30.

77. Banking was a relatively new activity and responded to a new set of economic impulses that distanced it from the fazenda. Even so, banks did not start holding concursos until the 1930s, and even then sponsorship remained important, because the number of qualified applicants was high.

78. Monteiro, 62.

79. Camargo, 126.

80. Carelli, 48. Some immigrants appear to have hailed from the middle class in their countries of origin. Lemme 1: 24.

81. Census 1920 2(1): 514–15.   82. P. Lima.

83. Monteiro, 33–34.   84. Census 1920 2(1): 514–15.

85. Elliot, 81–82. For a good discussion of the immigrant work ethic, see Paoli, "Labor," 42–48.

86. E. Cardoso.

87. Monteiro, 22.

88. *Vida Doméstica* 1:4 (Jun. 1920).

89. Romero and Guimarães, 52 (emphasis supplied).

90. Much of the data and a good deal of the analysis in what follows originated in Conniff's "Voluntary Associations."

91. Ibid., 78; idem, *Urban Politics*, 43.

92. G. Amado, *Eleição*, 48.

93. Hardman and Leonardi, 193–98.

94. Fausto, *Trabalho urbano*, 182–85.

95. Hahner, *Poverty*, 285–86.

96. Quoted in French, *The Brazilian Workers' ABC*, 74.

97. See R. Barbosa, *Obras*, 46:1, 5–60, 120.

98. Love, 9.

99. Antônio Leão Velloso, "A greve," *Correio da Manhã*, 14 Feb. 1921, 2, col. 1. I was alerted to this editorial by Bakota, 14.

100. *Correio da Manhã*, 8 Apr. 1921, 2, col. 3. I was alerted to this letter by Bakota, 35. One of the servants was a live-in cook and maid; the other was a laundress who came to the house.

101. A. Guimarães, 71.

102. Sáes, *Classe média e sistema político*, 63; Hallewell, 457.

103. Dean, *The Industrialization*, 83–104; Albert, 262–63.

104. Chafee, 120; Topik, *The Political Economy*, 20–21.

105. Baer, 34, 41; Mello and Tavares, 123–25.

106. *Vida Doméstica* 3:72 (Jan. 1924).

107. "A ambição no empregado no comércio," *Boletim da AEC* 3:25 (Jul. 1927): 59.

108. As advertised in *Vida Doméstica* 3:78 (Jul. 1924).

109. *Vida Doméstica* 3:77 (Jun. 1924). This was part of the magazine's broader campaign to introduce its readers to the notion of the "affordable house" by publishing plans for such a house in each issue. See also *Vida Doméstica* 6:114 (Sept. 1927).

110. Conniff, *Urban Politics*, 30.

111. *U.S. Commerce Reports* 23 (Jan. 16, 1920): 294–95.

112. "Dificuldades do lar carioca—crónica de um pãe de família," *Vida Doméstica* 3:74 (Mar. 1924).

113. Quoted in Besse, "Freedom and Bondage," 18.

114. Quoted in Canêdo, *O sindicalismo*, 49.

115. Nogueira. This document included a 1926 report analyzing a proposed vacation law for the Conselho Nacional de Trabalho.

116. Centro dos Industriais de Fiação e Tecelagem de Algodão, 99–101.

117. Lemme 1: 142–43.

118. See Eakin; Skidmore, "Racial Ideas"; Stepan.

119. Bomilcar, 125–34.

120. Ibid., iv, 140.

121. Ibid., 131.

122. Quoted in Dean, *The Industrialization*, 166.

123. Conniff, *Urban Politics*, 58.

124. See A. Prestes, 397–460.

125. See ibid., appendices 1–6, 397–405.

126. Quoted in J. M. Carvalho, *Os bestializados*, 68–69.

127. In 1906 the winning candidate garnered 97.9 percent of 300,000 votes cast. In 1918 the victor won 99.1 percent of 400,000 votes cast. See Love, 9.

128. Detailed accounts of the revolt are available in J. M. Carvalho, *Os bestializados*; Needell, "The *Revolta*."

129. R. Barbosa, "A crise moral," 140 (first quotation); G. Amado, "As instituições" (second quotation).

130. Brandão, 59.

131. Font has complicated the usual story of industrialists aligning with the PD and planters with the PRP in São Paulo. He argues instead that by 1920 the Paulista economy was not decisively dominated by the large coffee fazenda and that the PD represented a rearguard action by the planter elite to preserve their political position under the guise of liberal reform of the exclusionary PRP (Font, 135).

132. Prado, 21–25; Forjaz, *Tenentismo e Aliança Liberal*, 40–44.

133. Conniff, *Urban Politics*, 74–77.

134. M. Guimarães, 225–26, 264.

135. "Todas as associações de classes são 'casos de polícia,'" in ibid., 62.

136. Weffort, 48.

Chapter 3

1. Col. Leite Ribeiro, "O patrão e o caixeiro noutros tempos e nos de agora," *Boletim da AEC* 4:31 (Jan. 1928): 197–98. I have discovered no biographical information on Ribeiro. From the tone of his speech it is plausible to think that he was an employer. His rank of colonel was probably an honorific indicating links to a landed family. While the association was dominated by employers, a majority of members were employees.

2. See, e.g., Franklin de Oliveira, "Comerciários—a luta pela sobrevivência." *O Cruzeiro* 20 (Jun. 19, 1948): 9. *O Cruzeiro* was Brazil's largest circulation magazine at the time, and its readership was predominantly middle class. See IBOPE 12 and IBOPE 14.

3. After a relatively shallow dip between 1929 and 1932, industrial output expanded by an average 11.3 percent annually between 1933 and 1939, 5.4 percent from 1939 to 1945, and 9.6 percent from 1947 to 1961. Baer, 49, 81. The latter period also saw substantial capital formation.

4. Singer, 63–65.

5. Census statistics are notoriously inconsistent and unreliable, so any estimate of what proportion of Rio's total population got their livings at white-collar jobs must be qualified. A lower-end estimate is to sum all those who had at least some secondary-school or university education. In Rio this comes to over 250,000 people over age ten in 1940, roughly one-sixth of Rio's total population over the age of ten, about 18 percent. Since the number of literate people was substantially greater (nearly 1 million), it is likely that many in white-collar jobs were

autodidacts, especially among older people. A higher estimate can be had by adding white-collar employees across industry, commerce, credit, real estate, services, public employment, and liberal professions. This sum comes to roughly a third of Rio's remunerated work force. Correcting for family size (by one 1946 poll, middle-class Paulistanos had the fewest children of any social class; see IBOPE 11, p. 8), it does not seem unreasonable to think that 25–30 percent of Rio's population may have been tied to these kinds of jobs in 1940. See Census 1940 16: 18–33, 230–31, 246–47, 280–81, 314–15, 324–35, 330–31, 338–39, 346–47, 352–53. The 1940 census does not provide this kind of breakdown for the city of São Paulo, but similar calculations for 1950 show that the range was comparable, though its distribution favored private-sector administrative employees over public functionaries. Census 1950 1: 240–241.

6. Census 1920 2(1): 514–15; Census 1940 16: 20–23, 26–20; Census 1950 24(1): 30–35; Pereira.

7. In 1920 20,000 people were employed in federal, state, and municipal administrations in Rio. By 1950 the number had swelled to over 50,000. Similarly, 7,000 teachers in 1920 became 23,000 in 1950, mostly women. By the 1940s women made up as much as one-quarter of all public servants and by 1950 nearly half of all sales-floor clerks in the retail sector.

8. Paulo de Assis Ribeiro, "A reorganização geral dos serviços da Prefeitura do DF," *RSP* 2:112 (Apr.–May, 1939): 40.

9. As a proportion of the nonagricultural work force the self-employed fell from 17 to 11 percent in Rio between 1940 and 1950 and from 21 to 13 percent in São Paulo. The number of small storekeepers dropped from 7.5 to 5 percent in Rio and from 7 to 5 percent in the state of São Paulo over the same period. Census 1940 16: 22–23; Census 1940 17(1): 20–29; Census 1950 24(1): 30–31; Census 1950 25(1): 32–35. The number of people involved in small shop production in Rio appears to have declined significantly from 1920 to 1940. Conniff, *Urban Politics*, 43.

10. See Pereira, 323.

11. T. Fonseca, 192.

12. Hutchinson, "Hierarquia de prestígio," 33–34.

13. F. Vianna, 180.

14. A. Lima, *O problema do trabalho*, 73.

15. Editorial, *União* 1:1 (Jul. 29, 1931): 1.

16. Dulcídio Costa, "O preposto comercial," *União* 1:4 (Oct. 1931): 9.

17. Editorial, *União* 1:1 (Jul. 29, 1931): 1.

18. J. Fonseca Pinto, "A jornada das 8 horas," *Revista Comercial dos Varejistas* 1:1 (Nov. 1931): 2.

19. *Pesquisa sobre o padrão de vida*, 63, 70, 72.

20. See IBOPE 15, p. 18. This study was based on 770 interviews in the city of São Paulo and 220 in the interior city of Campinas.

21. *Pesquisa sobre o padrão de vida*, 63, 70–72.

22. AN, Belo Horizonte Labor Court, 1ª Junta, no. 640/641, Cx. 001A, Pacote 03/A, 12.12.40.

23. A 1949 study of Rio commercial employees found that fully 50 percent of employees in the sample attended secondary or technical school while working. *Pesquisa sobre o padrão de vida*, 73. By contrast, a 1947 São Paulo survey found that 17 percent were in school while working. IBOPE 18, p. 65. This study was based on 700 interviews in São Paulo and 200 in Campinas.

24. O. Andrade, *Chão*, 18.

25. "En defesa de estabilidade aos dois anos de serviço," *Bancário* 7:38 (Jul. 1943): 6.

26. Imperial. The 1940 census concluded that Rio bank employees as a group had the highest proportion of secondary-school- and university-educated employees (about 40 percent) of all occupations except the liberal professions. Census 1940 16: 20–21. By 1950 the number had jumped to 60 percent. Census 1950 24(1): 24–26.

27. Salma Bamel, "A autocrítica," *Syndiké* 1:6 (Oct. 1935): 2.

28. "Primeiro congresso brasileiro de bancários," *Bancário* 6:33 (Aug. 1940): 3.

29. Quoted in Canêdo, *O sindicalismo*, 43.

30. Luis Amaral, "Um aumento geral de ordenado," *Syndiké* 1:1 (May 1935): 5.

31. Heitor A. Eiras Garais, "O funcionalismo público," *Revista da AFPESP* 2: 14 (Aug.–Sept. 1934): 41–42.

32. "Bota difícil de descalçar . . . " *Vida Carioca* 18:142 (Sept. 1938).

33. Mario Newton, "Quadros de funcionamento e cursos de aperfeiçoamento," *Nossa Classe* 1:1 (Sept. 1936): 5.

34. See, e.g., "Laboratórios que assalariam médicos," *Boletim do SMB* 9: 97/98 (Jan.–Feb. 1937): 1901; *Correio da Manhã*, 21 May 1932, 2, col. 8.

35. A. Faria, 144.

36. "As profissões liberais," *Engenharia* 2:15 (May 1943): 297.

37. J. A. Carvalho, *Cargos*, 112, 139.

38. Rolando Monteiro, "Primeiro congresso médico syndicalista," *Boletim do SMB* 3 (special issue, Jul. 1931): 15.

39. "A irrenunciabilidade de direito dos trabalhadores intellectuaes," *Revista do Trabalho* 10:2 (Feb. 1942): 39.

40. "O Sr. Gilberto Freyre e os engenheiros brasileiros," *Engenharia* 1:8 (Oct. 1942): 2–3.

41. *Revista Paulista de Contabilidade* 12:105 (Mar. 1933): 52–53.

42. Fernando Segismundo, "Os trabalhos manuais no ensino secundário," *Diretrizes*, Sept. 1941, 3, 22.

43. Benedicto Silva, "A profissão de administrador," *RSP* 5:31 (Jul. 1942): 45.

44. Ibid., 5.

45. *Vida Doméstica* 19:238 (Feb. 1938).

46. M. Cunha, 64.

47. Byron T. Freitas, "Importância das funções do supervisor," *RSP* 7:2/1 (Apr. 1944): 51.

48. Benedicto Silva, "A profissão de administrador," *RSP* 5:3/1 (Jul. 1942): 5.

49. "Plano dos conhecimentos necessários à formação de uma assistente social," AGC 37.07.05, I–24.

50. AGC 37.07.05g, I–30, 325.

51. "O comércio progressista dos bairros," *Vida Carioca* 14:104 (Jul. 1934).

52. "Figuras da cidade: o vendeiro," *Revista Comercial dos Varejistas* 1:1 (Nov. 1931): 5.

53. See generally *Revista Comercial dos Varejistas, O Lojista, Vida Carioca.* See also reports on small commerce in *A Manhã* for July 1935. I was unable to locate any publications specific to small producers or artisans. To this extent the analysis is incomplete, because they formed a significant element of Rio's and São Paulo's industrial parks. See F. Vianna, 234–35.

54. "Uma fiscalização vexatória e absurda," *Revista Comercial dos Varejistas* 2:15 (Jan. 1933): 4.

55. "Os grandes exportadores de laranjas do Brasil," *Vida Carioca* 15:108 (Jan. 1935).

56. Veríssimo, *Crossroads*, 204.

57. M. Cunha, 98.

58. "Os engenheiros são generais na batalha da industrialização," *Diretrizes*, no. 173 (Oct. 21, 1943): 11, 14.

59. Bailly, *Manual*, 9; Imperial, 76.

60. Andrade Sobrinho, 49.

61. Victor de Carvalho, reprint of speech, *Revista da AFPESP* 2:10 (Jan. 1934): 3–7.

62. *AEC* 7 (Oct.–Dec. 1951). See also speech by Valentim Bouças, *O Estado de São Paulo*, 24 Jun. 1934, 4, col 1.

63. Arnaldo Nunes, "Contador e literatura," *Revista Paulista de Contabilidade* 2:247 (Jan. 1945): 10–11.

64. Quoted in Canêdo, *O sindicalismo*, 49.

65. See, e.g., "Primeiro congresso brasileiro de bancários," *Bancário* 6:33 (Aug. 1940): 3.

66. Mario Pinto Serva, "A educação de si mesmo," *Syndiké* 3:23 (May 1937): 4.

67. *Syndiké* 3:23 (May 1937): 11. There is no indication of what this class entailed. In general white-collar associations pushed literature, music appreciation, and theater in addition to practical courses to enhance career skills.

68. Pacheco.

69. Quoted in Paoli, "Working-Class São Paulo," 204.

70. A 1933 novel about Brás suggests just how much workers knew of those who lived across the river, and vice versa. Domestic servants surely were intimate with the goings-on in the homes of the wealthy and the middle class. Wealthy young men cruised Brás in search of young working-class women for temporary sexual liaisons. Many of these women, in turn, were often willing to gamble on the possibility that they would be able to marry well and move to the other side. If the novel is any indication, most were disappointed. See Galvão.

71. There were significant exceptions to the rule. Smaller and less prestigious banks are one example, for the rate of tuberculosis among bank employees was extremely high. There was an ongoing debate over whether working conditions

or nutrition of poorly paid bank employees was the cause. "'Classe privile-
giada,'" *Bancário* 4:21 (Nov. 1938): 1. See also Canêdo, *O sindicalismo*, 43.
   72. Lessa, 12; Pacheco, ch. 2; "O aumento do funcionalismo," *Diretrizes*, no.
171 (Oct. 7, 1943): 6.
   73. M. Cunha, 99.
   74. Fernandes and Bastide, 196.
   75. Andrews, 126. Photographs tend to confirm the general absence of dark-
skinned people from collar-and-tie occupations. While the occasional black or
more commonly the darker-skinned mulatto face appears in pictures of association meetings and social events, more telling is the fairly homogeneous lightness
of skin at such gatherings.
   76. E. Costa, 240–41.
   77. Andrews, 134.
   78. Paoli, "Working-Class São Paulo," 208–9.
   79. Bailly, *Manual*, 8.
   80. See, e.g., "Notas para o funcionário," *RSP* 4:3/3 (Sept. 1941): 215; José
Palmeiro, "Faltas ao serviço e horários de trabalho," *RSP* 8:3/3 (Sept. 1945): 60–
64.
   81. Igautimozy Cataldi de Sousa, "Seleção do pessoal para os serviços públicos da união, estados, e municípios," AN, Presidência da República, DASP, Ser.:
Pessoal, Subser.: Seleção, Cx. DASP 1234, pp. 31–32. See also "O trabalho das
mulheres," *Engenharia* 3:29 (Sept. 1944): 5–6; Bailly, *Manual*, 8.
   82. M. Cunha.
   83. *Voz Comerciária* 1:4 (Oct. 1937): 2.
   84. IBOPE 7, p. 7. See also Editorial, "O público e seus servidores," *RSP* 7:2/2
(May 1944): 1.
   85. Veríssimo, *Crossroads*, 43.
   86. See, e.g., Iguatimozy Cataldi de Sousa, "Seleção do pessoal," 1234; Editorial, "A mulher e o serviço público," *RSP* 4:2/2 (Jun. 1941): 3–4.
   87. Salvador Ferrigno, "Regulamentação do trabalho do advogado que com
carater de emprêgo presta serviços de natureza jurídica a entidade de direito pri-
vado," *Boletim da OAB* 7:35 (Jul. 1950): 9.
   88. "O contador moderno," *O Contabilista* 1:1 (Oct. 1937): 19.
   89. "O homen serviçal," *Syndiké* 1:9 (Jan. 1936): 49–51.
   90. "Disciplina, alma das realizações," *Syndiké* 1:4 (Aug. 1935): 1–2.
   91. *Boletim da OAB-SP* 13:48 (Apr.–Jun. 1946): 209; *RSP* 1:1 (Nov. 1937):
4; *Publicidade* no. 39 Jun. 1944, 33.
   92. Backhauser, 37–39.
   93. "O que é e o que representa a actividade de um cadastro," *Bancário* 7:35
(Mar. 1941): 12; A. Nunes, 53.
   94. Luis do Amaral, "Sejamos úteis," *Syndiké* 1:7 (Nov. 1935): 19.
   95. Cap. Aloysio Miranda Mendes, "A disciplina, as virtudes e a profissão
militar,"*A Defesa Nacional* 23:260 (Jan. 1936): 89. See also, "A profissão," *Defesa Nacional* 25:287 (Apr. 1938): 428.

96. Wladimir Pinto, "A felicidade," *Vida Doméstica* 18:233 (Aug. 1937).
97. Freitas, 91.
98. Ferraz, 114–15 (quotation). Pacheco; D. Silva, 111; Anjos, 45, 161–62.
99. Hutchinson, "Hierarquia de prestígio," 32.
100. R. Sodré, 16.
101. The director of Rio's Grajaú Tennis Club barred workers, preferring medical students, lawyers, engineers, military officers, public functionaries, and bank and commercial employees. J. Queiroz; Bauser.
102. Durval Borges, *Estudos*, 64–65.
103. Fischer, 228.
104. While three-quarters of the students who said they came from upper-middle and middle-class families labeled themselves middle class, 87 percent of those who admitted to being from lower-middle-class families did so.

Chapter 4

1. M. Cunha, 38–39.
2. D. J. Stamoto, "Escola de Comércio Alvares Penteado," *Revista Paulista de Contabilidade* 10:79/80 (Jan.–Feb. 1931): 32 (emphasis added).
3. *O Estado de São Paulo*, 21 May 1936, 15, col. 1; 23 May 1936, 16, col. 4; 24 May 1936, 27, col. 2.
4. Ibid., 19 May 1936, 18, col. 6; 24 May 1936, 27, col. 2.
5. Ibid., 31 May 1936, 29, col. 1.
6. See, e.g., ibid., 4 Jun. 1950, 54–56.
7. The classifieds should not be taken as fully representative of the collar-and-tie labor market. According to one observer in 1945, want ads were "somewhat discredited" in Brazil as a means of securing mid- and high-level employees, particularly among Brazilian firms. Foreign firms were more likely to use the classifieds. This suggests that local firms were able to tap into an informal network of job seekers to which foreign firms had only limited access. Freitas, 82.
8. "Estágio e cultura," *Syndiké* 1:2 (Jun. 1935): 22–23.
9. Associação de Professoras, "Exposição do Problema," AGC 36.07.00g, II-17.
10. Fávero, 134.
11. Sebastião Barroso, "A medicina e a profissão médica na atualidade," *Revista do SMB* 1:1 (Nov. 1929): 163 (quotation). See also "Editorial—Até quando?!" *Revista do Syndicato Odontológico Brasileiro* 1:8 (Aug. 1936); Galileu Cintra, "Função social do advogado," *O Advogado* 1:1 (Jan. 1938): 6; "Observações e commentários," *Revista do Clube de Engenharia* 1:7 (Apr. 1935): 342–44; J. J. da Gama e Silva, "Chomâge dos intelectuais," *O Advogado* 2:4/5 (Jan. 1939): 167; Dilermando Xavier Porto to O. Aranha, May 5, 1938, AOA, *Pedidos*, 1938; Hermano de Góes Artigas to O. Aranha, Nov. 21, 1938, AOA, *Pedidos*, 1938.
12. Rolando Monteiro, speech, *Boletim do SMB* 5:54 (Jun. 1933): 541–43.
13. Coelho, 70.
14. *O Cruzeiro* 7 (Oct. 12, 1935): 48–49.

15. Alceu Marinho Rego, "Místicos e mágicos da advocacia," *Diretrizes*, May 1941, 12–13.

16. Ibid.

17. These were often men with degrees from fly-by-night institutions or with forged credentials. Carvalho Neto, 115.

18. Mario de Azambuja, "Sobre a necessidade de um sindicato médico," *Boletim do SMB* 8:87 (Mar. 1936): 1573–79.

19. "A profissão médica no Brasil," *Boletim do SMB* 6:69 (Sept. 1934): 987–88.

20. "O rádio e o futebol: as melhores profissões," *Diretrizes* 2:1 (Apr. 1939): 46–50.

21. *A Manhã*, 13 Aug. 1935, 6, col. 4.

22. Evaldo de Oliveira, "Comentário profissional—boa sorte rapazes," *Revista de Química e Farmácia* 8:9–12 (Oct.–Dec. 1943): 179.

23. Carneiro, 6.

24. Dôria, 232; Aurelio Monteiro, *Correio da Manhã*, 18 Jan. 1940, 3. Herculano Siqueira, whose father had owned a tailor shop, worked as a proofreader and editor at a newspaper while studying medicine in Rio in the early and mid-1930s. Instead of going into medicine when he graduated in 1936, he continued in journalism. In 1946 he switched over to advertising, where he built his career. See Siqueira.

25. *O Cruzeiro* 7 (Oct. 12, 1935): 48–49.

26. A. Siedler to O. Aranha, Oct. 3, 1944, AOA, *Pedidos*, 1944.

27. Wladimir Alves de Souza, "O custo do exito," *A Casa*, nos. 153–54 (Feb.–Mar. 1937): 43. Although little is known about architects, it is worth noting that in the closely related and much larger profession of engineering close to half of the members of the National Sindicato of Engineers appear to have been employed in public service. See "Sócios do Clube de Engenharia," *Revista do Clube de Engenharia*, May–Dec. 1940, Jan.–Oct. 1941, Jan.–Feb. and May–Jun. 1942.

28. IBOPE 10, p. 8.

29. Rolando Monteiro, *Boletim do SMB* 5:54 (Jun. 1933): 542–43.

30. *Publicidade,* no. 38 (May 1944): 43.

31. AN, Presidência de República, DASP, Ser.: Pessoal, Subser.: Orientação e fiscalização, Cx. DASP no. 1234, 1937–50. After 1938 the "accumulation" of public jobs became much more difficult, because a "disaccumulation" law forbade this kind of piggybacking.

32. IBGE, "Ocupação suplementar."

33. Dr. Salvador Ferrigno, "Regulamentação do trabalho do advogado que com carater de emprêgado presta serviços de natureza jurídica a entidade de direito público," *Boletim da OAB* 7:35 (Jul. 1950): 13.

34. They were not successful. Editorial, "A mulher e o serviço público," *RSP* 4:2/2 (Jun. 1941): 3–4.

35. Benedicto Silva, "A profissão de administrador," *RSP* 5:3/1 (Jul. 1942): 5. See also Newton Correia Ramalho, "Organização dos serviços industriais do estado," *RSP* 3:3/1 (Jul. 1940): 7.

36. Freitas, 80.

37. M. Cunha, 63–64.

38. Silveira Costa, "A necessidade do estudo da propaganda no Brasil," *Publicidade*, no. 2 (Jan. 1941): 17. The single quotation marks indicate words that appeared in English in the original, which was otherwise in Portuguese.

39. *O Estado de São Paulo*, 5 May 1920, 8, col. 1.

40. *O Cruzeiro*, issue for the second week of January 1934.

41. *O Cruzeiro* 9 (Jun. 24, 1937): 30. The same ad ran in *Vida Doméstica* 21:9 (Nov. 1940) 49, adding the claim that the tonic would eliminate "cerebral weakness, nervous dyspepsia, neurasthenia, memory loss, loss of appetite and energy."

42. *O Cruzeiro* 9 (Sept. 11, 1937): 28.

43. *O Cruzeiro* 18 (Dec. 15, 1945): 74.

44. Ibid., 100; Dec. 28, 1946.

45. Cited in Canêdo, *O sindicalismo*, 43.

46. Dupré, *Dona Lola*, 140.

47. *Correio da Manhã*, 28 May 1940, 6, col. 2.

48. These numbers must be approached carefully. Beatriz Wahrlich has concluded that between 1937 and 1962 slightly more than 10 percent of those signed up for exams actually were finally approved for employment. Wahrlich, 458.

49. See, e.g., Luiz Pinto, "O DASP—sua atuação na vida do Brasil," *RSP* 7:3/1 (Jul. 1944): 42–48. Richard Graham notes for the nineteenth century that admission to an exam depended on an "intelligent and energetic effort to line up patrons," and even then favoritism and *pistolão* (a letter from a patron in behalf of a client) could overturn results. Graham, *Patronage*, 254.

50. *RSP* 3:4/1 (Oct. 1940): 78.

51. Editorial, "Reflexões sôbre o sistema de mérito," *RSP* 8:3/3 (Sept. 1945): 1.

52. Lemme 1: 170.

53. Hermeto Lima, "Funcionários de hontem e de hoje," *Revista da Semana*, Feb. 26, 1927, 34.

54. "No mundo da lua," *Vida Carioca* 17:129 (Apr. 1937).

55. See, e.g., Editorial "Necessidades do funcionalismo," *Revista da AFPESP* 1:1 (Nov. 1932): 20; "Clama nas cesses," *A Defesa Nacional* 20:227 (Jan. 1933): 1–3; *Boletim do SMB* 5:56 (Aug. 1933): 604; Célio de Barros, "Promoção por merecimento," *Nossa Classe* 1:1 (Sept. 1936): 17.

56. Cleto Seabra Velloso, "Porque não ha concurso na assistência?" *Boletim do SMB* 8:91 (Jul. 1936): 1709–10.

57. Iguatemozy Cataldi de Sousa, "Seleção do pessoal para os serviços públicos da União, estados e municípios," AN, Presidência de República, DASP, Ser.: Pessoal, Subser.: Seleção, Cx. DASP no. 1234, pp. 25–26.

58. See H. Faria, 32; L. Lopes, 424–49.

59. H. Faria, 3–5.

60. See, e.g., "Conversa fria de jornalista," *Voz Comerciária* 4:35 (Nov. 1940): 3. Osvaldo Aranha's *pedido* (a letter from a client to a potential patron requesting help) responses reveal that after 1937 he frequently put people off on the basis that the position being requested was available only through concurso.

See, e.g., letter O. Aranha to Juventino Pinheiro Salgado Lins, Feb. 4, 1941, AOA, *Pedidos*, 1941; Gustavo Capanema to Profa. Amanda Colanier, Dec. 20, 1941, AGC 34.09.25.

61. M. Cunha, 95.

62. Frederico Lane, "O conceito do povo," *Diretrizes*, no. 179 (Jan. 6, 1944): 5.

63. See Wahrlich, 439.

64. See L. Graham, 100, 125–28; Beatriz Wahrlich, "O sistema do mérito," *RSP* 20:3/1 (Aug. 1957): 237–54. Graham argues that the merit approach "achieved its apogee during the Estado Novo, only to be destroyed by the return of party politics in 1946."

65. Canêdo, *O sindicalismo*, 44.

66. Tullio, 8–9.

67. Napoleão Bolivar de Araripe Sucupira, Jan. 8, 1945, AOA, *Pedidos*, 1945. All letters are to Osvaldo Aranha, unless otherwise indicated. See also Olavo Anibal Nascentes to Gustavo Capanema, AGC 34.09.25-A2. I have focused on letters from the Aranha archive because the pedidos of other figures had not yet been made available.

68. João Bittencourt, Mar. 22, 1941, AOA, *Pedidos*, 1941. Aranha denied the request. Similar valiant efforts to establish family connections were common. In a 1933 letter a writer claimed to be the "daughter of the brother of your grandfather and a cousin of your mother." Leopoldina de Freitas, Jun. 12, 1933, AOA, *Pedidos*, 1933. In 1934 a primary-school teacher insisted that his son was Aranha's godchild, though they had not heard from Aranha since the baptism. Claiming there was no future in teaching, the petitioner asked only for "a modest job . . . of any intellectual sort." José Alfredo Silva, Apr. 16, 1934, AOA, *Pedidos*, 1934.

69. It is hard to know whether this represented a change. With the broad influx of people to the cities it is possible that petitioners began to understand that their hometown circle of connections would not take them very far and so they began to write to people they did not know. Only further research can shed further light on such questions.

70. José Moreira de Oliveira, Jun. 3, 1944, AOA, *Pedidos*, 1944.

71. Alvaro Henrique Bouson, Mar. 9, 1938, AOA, *Pedidos*, 1938.

72. Antônio L. da Cunha, Nov. 10, 1938, AOA, *Pedidos*, 1938.

73. Adalberto Tavares do Santos Lima, Jan. 30, 1948, AOA, *Pedidos*, 1948.

74. Dilermando Xavier Porto, May 5, 1938, AOA, *Pedidos*, 1938.

75. AN, Secretaria da Presidência, Pedidos, Ser.: Pessoal, Subser.: Pessoal Civil, Movimentação de Pessoal, 1936, Proc. 5546, Lapa, Rio de Janeiro, Jun. 19, 1936. There is no indication of action.

76. Waldemar Augusto Machado, Jun. 10, 1938, AOA, *Pedidos*, 1938.

77. Clementino de Moura Beleza, Jun. 14, 1944, AOA, *Pedidos*, 1944.

78. José Pinho Corrêa Netto, Aug. 22, 1949, AOA, *Pedidos*, 1949.

79. Veríssimo, *Crossroads*, 226. See also Dupré, *Eramos seis*, 101; D. Silva, 97, 116, 133; Chaves, 67–69.

80. See, e.g., ESSRJ, folders of Lery Tavares da Silva and Flora Amélia de Oliveira.

81. The broad subject of patronage deserves an extended treatment not possible here. There is no historical work for the twentieth century comparable to Richard Graham's *Patronage and Politics* for the nineteenth. For an anthropological perspective, see Leeds.

82. See, e.g., Anna Aparecida de Sá, Jan. 1931, AOA, *Pedidos*, 1931 (on behalf of father); E. Teixeira Guimarães, Oct. 12, 1931, AOA, *Pedidos*, 1931 (father on behalf of daughter's husband); Olympia Carneiro da Cunha, Feb. 30, 1938, AOA, *Pedidos*, 1938 (mother on behalf of son); Julieta Carvalho Cardoso, Jun. 19, 1938, AOA, *Pedidos*, 1938 (wife on behalf of husband); Sra. Diego Soares Munhoz, Apr. 19, 1944, AOA, *Pedidos*, 1944 (wife on behalf of husband); Viuva Desembargador Amando Arambuja. Feb. 23, 1944, AOA, *Pedidos*, 1944 (mother on behalf of son); Lygia Debrize Geduzzi, Dec. 12, 1948, AOA, *Pedidos*, 1948 (wife on behalf of husband).

83. Maria da Gloria, Sept. 22, 1948, AOA, *Pedidos*, 1948.

84. Editorial, "A mulher e o seu público," *RSP* 4:2/4 (Jun. 1941): 3–4.

85. Floriano Cordoville, Aug. 2, 1944, AOA, *Pedidos*, 1944.

86. There were those who complained about the merit system as well. One public servant wrote a memorandum to his superior in 1943, arguing that he had been the victim of "injustices of the system of 'merit.'" He had always been punctual, assiduous, "giving to the state my greatest effort." And yet he had been passed over and could perceive no objective criteria by which this should be so. See Motta.

87. See Tullio.

88. Mário Natal e Silva, Feb. 15, 1944, AOA, *Pedidos*, 1944. Aranha helped him but he failed to get the job. In his second request he moderated his ambition, seeking only to be a staff lawyer at the Banco do Brasil, where some of his friends already worked. Aranha denied the request.

89. D. Silva, 42.

90. *O Estado de São Paulo*, 24 Jun. 1934, 4, col. 1.

91. Genolino Amado, "Os intelectuais e os problemas da cultura no Brasil," *Diretrizes* 2:24 (Apr. 1940): 9–11.

92. Hallewell, 286–87.

93. IBGE, *O ensino—1935*: 406–7, 444–45; *O ensino—1945*: 476–79; Bastide, 10. Three-quarters of these schools were private.

94. Women constituted roughly 45 percent of all those possessing a diploma from some sort of secondary school in Rio in 1940. In the census category embracing the widest number and variety of professional training programs, men tended to concentrate in commercial schools (men, 75 percent; women, 25 percent), and women in social work (men, 28 percent; women, 72 percent) and normal schools (men, 8 percent; women, 92 percent). The vast majority of both men and women with some sort of secondary-school degree had a general curriculum. Census 1940 16(1): 20–31.

95. Pôrto, 28.

96. Ministério de Educação e Saude, 11.

97. IBGE, *O ensino—1935*, 406–7, 444–45; *O ensino—1945*, 476–79. For a

listing of some of the new faculdades approved during the 1930s, see AGC 35.05.16g, III–5. Alongside the legitimate institutions there was a shady industry of degree mills. See Austregildo de Ataíde, "Mercado de diplomas profissionais," *Diário da Noite*, 14 Jan. 1938.

98. Hallewell, 286–87.

99. "Uma revolução universitária," *Diretrizes*, Aug. 1941, 12–13, 18.

100. See, e.g., Andrade Sobrinho, 32.

101. Census 1940 16(3): 21; 17(1): 23; Census 1950 24(1): 24; 25(1): 24.

102. J. J. da Gama e Silva, "Pela dignidade de uma nobre classe," *O Advogado* 1:3 (Sept. 1938): 69.

103. "Notas para o funcionário," *RSP* 3:3/2 (Aug. 1940): 136.

104. See, e.g., Bailly, *Pontos de concurso para escriturário* and *Pontos de concurso para oficial administrativo*.

105. *O Cruzeiro* 18:6 (Dec. 29, 1945): 102.

106. M. Cunha, 105–6.

107. *O Cruzeiro* 22 (May 13, 1950): 101.

108. AGC 38.04.18g, I, I–7.

109. *O Cruzeiro* 20 (Jan. 17, 1948): 57.

110. See IBOPE 21, p. 5. The study was based on interviews with 1,067 consumers and 197 druggists.

111. See, e.g., Victor Vianna, "O esforço das elites e a depressão monetaria," *Syndiké* 1:5 (Sept. 1935): 29; "O contador moderno," *O Contabilista* 1:1 (Oct. 1937): 19.

112. APEB 32/36.00.00/1.

113. See, e.g., Viuva Protogenes Guimarães, Jul. 1938, AOA, *Pedidos*, 1938; José Moreira de Oliveira, Jun. 13, 1944, AOA, *Pedidos*, 1944; Alvaro Maia, Feb. 22, 1945, AOA, *Pedidos*, 1945.

114. Freitas, 91.

115. Andrade Sobrinho, 11.

116. *Revista Comercial dos Varejistas* 1:6 (Apr. 1932), back cover.

117. *Vida Carioca* 14:100 (Feb. 1934). See also *Vida Carioca* 15:112 (Jul. 1935); *Vida Carioca* 15:113 (Aug. 1935); *Nossa Classe* 4 (Jun. 1939): 8; *Publicidade*, Jan. 1942, 14; *O Cruzeiro* 19 (Aug. 9, 1947): 41; *O Cruzeiro* 22 (Jul. 29, 1950): 53.

118. *Revista da Semana*, Dec. 15, 1945, 112. According to the census of 1940, less than 10 percent of Rio's population had insurance of any sort, though a 1947 study claimed that roughly 20 percent of Rio commercial employees had life insurance. This suggests that the rate was substantially higher for those who worked in the collar-and-tie sector. *Pesquisa sobre padrão de vida*; Census 1940 16: 34; IBOPE 16, p. 63.

119. P. Nunes, *35 anos*.

120. "Místicos e mágicos da advocacia," *Diretrizes*, May 1941, 12–13.

121. *O Estado de São Paulo*, 14 May 1936, 15.

122. AN, Presidência da República, DASP, Ser.: Pessoal; Subser.: Seleção, Técnico de Administração, 1940–41.

123. Of the 116,000 people in Rio in 1940 who had completed secondary school or university, 109,000 were white. Fewer than 1,000 blacks had finished secondary school, and about 5,500 mulattoes had. See Census 1940 16: 18–19.

124. See Fernandes and Bastide, 188–204.

125. Census 1950 24(1): 24–25; Pinto, 84–85.

126. Beals; Hutchinson, "Social Mobility Rates"; Hutchinson, *Mobilidade*, 207–29.

127. Hutchinson, *Mobilidade*, 207–29. The study also found a somewhat lower rate of upward mobility for members of native Brazilian, as opposed to immigrant families, which it attributed to a "traditionally rigid system of status."

128. D. Silva, 93.

129. Lyra Filho, 67.

130. D. Silva, 48.

131. Mgr. Blachat, "As educadoras frente à crise atual: alguns problemas da educação contemporânea," *Servir* 3 (Dec. 1950).

132. Dupré, *Eramos seis*, 49.

133. See, e.g., Ivan Bandeira de Gouvêa, Jul. 21, 1938, AOA, *Pedidos*, 1938; Floriano Cordoville, Aug. 2, 1944, AOA, *Pedidos*, 1944.

134. T. Fonseca, 189.

Chapter 5

1. Needell, *A Tropical* Belle Époque, 169–70.

2. See Canêdo, *O sindicalismo*, 34–37.

3. See, e.g., *Syndiké* 1:10 (Feb. 1936): 13; "Custo de vida," *Bancário* 4:16 (Mar. 1938): 1–4; A. Carneiro Leão, "Uma classe ameaçada," *Educação*, no. 9 (Jan. 1941): 13–14; "O custo de vida cresceu muito," *Publicidade*, no. 4 (Mar. 1941); *Voz Comerciária* 8:92 (Feb. 1946): 5.

4. "O aumento do funcionalismo," *Diretrizes* 6:171 (Oct. 7, 1943): 6.

5. "Observações e comentários," *Revista do Clube de Engenharia* 1:7 (Apr. 1935): 342–44.

6. Editorial, "O nivel de vida do trabalhador nacional," *Bancário* 4:17 (Apr. 1938):2.

7. Benedicto Silva, "Contra a carestia—cooperativismo," *RSP* 8:1/2 (Jan. 1945): 28–36.

8. IBOPE 11, p. 48. This study sampled 100 São Paulo housewives from each of A, B, and C groups; 65 married and single A men; 200 married and single B men; and 135 married and single C men.

9. Sindicato dos Bancários, 13.

10. Because of the lack of systematic studies the issue is a tangled one for the middle class. It appears, nevertheless, that collar-and-tie employees generally out-earned manual workers. See Owensby, 193–200. Evidence of working-class incomes is better. See John Wells, "Industrial Accumulation."

11. IBOPE 11, p. 9. See also IBOPE 17, p. 6.

12. "Como vive o povo em São Paulo, a cidade milionária," *Diretrizes* 6:146 (Apr. 15, 1943): 7, 23, 26.

13. A 1940 article in *Vida Doméstica* noted that "if our middle and rich classes, as a rule, eat excessively and inconsiderately, the proletarian classes nourish themselves badly, deficiently because of their financial problems and above all because of their ignorance." "A alimentação brasileira," *Vida Doméstica*, no. 264 (Mar. 1940): 16. See also Paoli, "Working-Class São Paulo"; John Wells, "Industrial Accumulation."

14. Dra. Nathercia Silveira, "Seção feminina—a mulher deve trabalhar," *Bancário* 4:15 (Feb. 1938): 2–4.

15. Census 1940 16: 28; *Pesquisa sobre o padrão de vida*, 70.

16. Franklin de Oliveira, "Comerciários—A luta pela sobrevivência," *O Cruzeiro*, Jun. 19, 1948, 9.

17. *Pesquisa sobre o padrão de vida*, 70–72.

18. IBOPE 17, p. 7. This study was based on interviews with 2,227 B's and 2,736 C's in São Paulo.

19. The greatest number of commercial employees was drawn from among those under 21 who contributed to the family income of their parents. *Pesquisa sobre o padrão de vida*, 97, 118, 120. One study of the living conditions of commercial employees in São Paulo indicated an inverse relationship between total family income and the salaries of commercial employees within the family. Put another way, commercial employees who earned the least were part of families with the greatest total income, suggesting that among the most poorly paid commercial employees were young people, many of them students, who supplemented the income of fathers who worked in more lucrative areas than commerce. IBOPE 15, p. 31.

20. See, e.g., Sebastião Barroso, "A medicina e a profissão médica na actualidade," *Revista do SMB* 5:11 (Nov. 1929): 165; Backhauser, 68.

21. *O Estado de São Paulo*, 5 Sept. 1946, 4.

22. Andrade Sobrinho, 12.

23. "O aumento do funcionalismo," *Diretrizes* 6:171 (Oct. 7, 1943): 6.

24. M. J. Pimentoso Velloso, "Crise econômica do Brasil," *Bancário* 14:3/4 (Mar.–Apr. 1948): 1.

25. "Salário profissional dos jornalistas," *Revista do Trabalho* 12:12 (Dec. 1944): 10; Stanislaw Fischolowitz, "Política em relação aos funcionários públicos," *RSP* 4:4/2 (Nov. 1941): 70.

26. Prof. J. Scantimburgo, *Diário de São Paulo*, 27 Apr. 1946, 4.

27. E. Roosevelt, "Uma mensagem para a classe média," *Diretrizes*, Jul. 1941, 2.

28. "O rádio e o futbol: as melhores profissões," *Diretrizes* 2:1 (Apr. 1939): 46–50.

29. IBOPE 11, p. 48.

30. Salgado, *O espírito* 10: 39.

31. Dupré, *Eramos seis*, 29, 32, 39, 101.

32. Lyra Filho, 88.

33. Andrade Sobrinho.

34. John Wells, II:312.

35. Ibid., 321.

36. Pacheco, ch. 10. Other novels set in middle-class homes are less specific but give more or less the same impression. Dupré, *Eramos seis*; Veríssimo, *Crossroads*; D. Silva. See also J. Cordeiro de Azevedo and Braz Jordão, "Evolução dos interiores," *A Casa* 147 (Aug. 1936): 8–13.

37. IBOPE 4, p. 10; IBOPE 14, p. 36. IBOPE 14 polled 1,000 *O Cruzeiro* readers in Rio and 1,000 in São Paulo, in equal proportions men and women in a 1:3:2 ratio for A, B, and C groups.

38. IBOPE 11, p. 3.

39. Joel Silveira, "O arranha-céu democratizou Copacabana," *Diretrizes*, Apr. 1941, 4.

40. A household advice book in 1945 noted that, while in Europe only the rich could afford servants, this was not so in Brazil. Serrano, *Minha casa*, 143. The "budget for a middle-class family of seven," published by a government agency, included the cost of a servant. See *Syndiké* 1:10 (Feb. 1936): 13. An IBOPE study concluded that A's had, on average, three servants; B's, one; and C's, virtually none. IBOPE 11, p. 8.

41. Cassilda Martins, "A crise do lar," *Schola* 1:5 (Jun. 1930): 147–54.

42. "Creados modernos," *Vida Doméstica*, no. 205 (Apr. 1935).

43. John Wells, II: 309.

44. Pacheco, ch. 3.

45. *Revista do Professor* 1:1 (Mar. 1934); *O Cruzeiro* 18 (Sept. 1945): 51 (Singer advertisement).

46. IBOPE 11, p. 48.

47. Detective novels and stories, many in translation from English, and locally produced police novels, or *policiais*, were very popular. IBOPE 13.

48. In Rio in 1940 less than one-fifth of industrial workers over ten had finished grade school. Few had any secondary schooling, as those in industry listed as having a secondary-school diploma were probably managers and office employees. Census 1940 16: 20.

49. Some sense of the options parents and students faced can be had from *Oportunidades de educação*.

50. Three studies between 1934 and 1940 found that working-class households spent less than 1 percent on education and books. Wells, II: 306.

51. IBOPE 11, p. 14.

52. See, e.g., A. Carneiro Lima, "Uma classe ameaçada," *Educação*, no. 9 (Jan. 1941): 13.

53. *O Cruzeiro* 1 (Nov. 10, 1928): 1.

54. *Vida Doméstica*, no. 166 (Jan. 1932).

55. *O Cruzeiro* 18 (Aug. 24, 1946): 42.

56. *O Estado de São Paulo*, 1 Oct. 1940, 9.

57. See Ramos.

58. See Cortés, 191–94.

59. See Marchand; P. Nunes.

60. "A S.A. Inter-Americana de Propaganda e seus clientes e amigos—a publicidade e o desenvolvimento nacional," *Publicidade*, no. 1 (Sept. 1940): 7.

61. S.A. Inter-Americana de Propaganda, "A publicidade e o desenvolvimento nacional."

62. Eng. Edison Junqueira Passos (graduation address), "Engenheiros-Architectos de 1934," *Revista do Clube de Engenharia* 1:4 (Dec. 1934): 201–2; "Observações e commentários," *Revista do Clube de Engenharia* 1:7 (Apr. 1935): 342–44; "Salário mínimo," *Bancário* 4:19 (Sept. 1938): 4; "A industrialização e o problema do engenheiro," *Diretrizes*, Apr. 22, 1943, 1, 14; "As perspectivas do mercado latino-americano," *Revista Paulista de Contabilidade* 23:237 (Mar. 1944): 6; Alarico Areas, "Os padrões de vida no progresso econômico," *Revista Paulista de Contabilidade* 24:248 (Feb. 1945): 5–7; "Novos contabilistas do Instituto Brasileiro de Contabilidade," *Vida Doméstica*, no. 310 (Jan. 1944): 57; H. Bastos, "Progresso técnico e padrão de vida"; *Resoluções de 1945 do Conselho Nacional de Estudantes*, AGC, 38.04.18g, VIII, VIII–29; "Congresso brasileiro dos problemas médico-sociais de após-guerra," AGC 38.10.09h.

63. "Comentários nacionais—A marcha da industrialização," *Diretrizes*, Apr. 30, 1942, 9.

64. IBOPE 6, p. 7. The study drew on an interview pool consisting of 700 men from various social categories (A, B, C), and of 50 men from each of the following groups: bankers, industrialists, retailers, politicians, intellectuals, land owners, and public functionaries.

65. H. Bastos.

66. *União* 1:6 (Dec. 1931): 9.

67. *Vida Doméstica*, no. 158 (May 1931).

68. Ibid., no. 172 (Jul. 1932).   69. Ibid., no. 208 (Jul. 1935).

70. Ibid., no. 233 (Aug. 1937).   71. Andrade Sobrinho, 12.

72. See Ortiz, 40.   73. Lyra Filho, 70.

74. "Que legislação assiste, no Brasil, a profissão?" interview with Celso Kelly, director of ad agency Agência Continental Ltd., *Diretrizes* 6:170 (Sept. 30, 1943): 9, 18.

75. Serrano, *Minha casa*, 112–13.   76. IBOPE 14, p. 44.

77. Alvim and Peirão, 29.   78. Ibid., 142–43.

79. *Vida Doméstica*, no. 209 (Aug. 1935).

80. *O Cruzeiro* 12 (Oct. 26, 1940): 70.

81. H. Thompson Rich, "Como viver alem dos seus recursos—Vive-se luxuosamente com pequena renda, se se eliminarem coisas não essenciais," *Seleçoes do Reader's Digest*, Jun. 1944, 29.

82. IBOPE 8, pp. 3–12. This study included interviews with 250 A and B housewives.

83. IBOPE 3, table K. This study drew on interviews conducted with 300 A and B women.

84. IBOPE 4, p. 9.

85. IBOPE 1, p. 283. For this study, researchers interviewed 100 A's and 200 B's in Rio and 110 A's and 183 B's in São Paulo.

86. IBOPE 2, p. 301. This study drew on 400 interviews with A and B men and women in Rio and 303 interviews with A and B men and women in São Paulo.

87. IBOPE 15, p. 30.

88. Adão Jr., "Eva sem costela—Progresso," *O Cruzeiro* 18 (Sept. 21, 1946): 80.

89. See cartoon in *O Cruzeiro* 18 (Jul. 6, 1946): 50; 19 (Nov. 9, 1946): 47.

90. "Vida errada," *Vida Doméstica* 5:81 (Dec. 1924).

91. Everardo Backhauser, "O papel do mestre na Escola Normal," *Revista Brasileira de Pedagogia* 1 (May 1934): 196.

92. "Na sociedade," *Vida Carioca* 17:130 (May 1937).

93. Lyra Filho, 195.

94. Cassilda Martins, "A arte de ser dona de casa," *Revista Brasileira de Pedagogia* 1 (Aug. 1934): 119–21. For a discussion of Catholic, as well as positivist, liberal, and socialist views on women, family, and home see Azzi, 85–120.

Many Brazilian women rejected United States feminism as a model. In 1945 Ana Amelia Queiroz Carneiro de Mendonça wrote that she had found American women both unequal and unhappy, because they were trying to deny their "nature by repressing the natural feminine sentiments of tenderness and affection for the family." Ana Amelia Queiroz Carneiro de Mendonça, "A mulher, força política," *O Cruzeiro* 17 (Feb. 3, 1945): 3. See generally Besse, *Restructuring Patriarchy*, ch. 7.

95. "Páginas da vida," *Vida Carioca* 15:108 (Jan. 1935); *Vida Doméstica*, no. 194 (Mar. 1930). See also, "Elogio do lar e da mulher," *Vida Doméstica*, no. 203 (Feb. 1935); Lyra Filho, 190–96.

96. "Penitenciando-nos, mas não retrando-nos," *Vida Carioca* 23:192 (Jun. 1943); "Educação para formar donas de casa—lar feliz é alicerce de todo o edifício social," *Vida Doméstica*, no. 319 (Oct. 1944).

97. *Boletim do Ministério de Trabalho, Indústria e Comércio* 90 (Feb. 1942): 87.

98. Jandyra Gonçalves, "Deve a mulher trabalhar?" *Vida Doméstica*, no. 212 (Nov. 1935).

99. See Veríssimo, *Crossroads*, 335.

100. Serrano, *Minha casa*, 45.

101. Serrano, *Noções*, 148.

102. "Como vive o povo em São Paulo, a cidade milionária," *Diretrizes* 6:149 (May 13, 1943): 9.

103. "O 'eterno feminino' na publicidade," *Vida Doméstica*, no. 234 (Sept. 1937).

104. *Publicidade*, no. 1 (Sept. 1940).

105. *O Cruzeiro* 8 (Nov. 25, 1935): 18.

106. Serrano, *Minha casa*, 141.

107. See *O Cruzeiro* 4 (Jul. 31, 1937): 48; 12 (Jul. 13, 1940): 58; 12 (Aug. 31, 1940): 18; 12 (Sept. 28, 1940): 58; 13 (Nov. 2, 1940): 70; 15 (Jan. 2, 1943): 34; 15 (Feb. 20, 1943): 6; 15 (Jun. 12, 1943): 74; 16 (Aug. 5, 1944): 75; 18 (Dec. 8, 1945): 36; 18 (Sept. 28, 1946): 64.

108. This proportion for C women seems high, given the cost of the magazine, though it is impossible to know, since there are no data on how often a magazine bought by one person passed from hand to hand.

109. *O Cruzeiro* was widely read among all social classes, though numerically B's predominated and seemed to set its tone. IBOPE 14, p. 15.

110. See generally Besse, *Restructuring Patriarchy*, 12–109.

111. The books are Serrano's *Minha casa* and *Noções* and Marialice Prestes's *Problemas do lar*. Among the magazines were *Revista da Semana, Vida Doméstica, O Cruzeiro, Criança—Revista para os Pais,* and *A Casa* in its later incarnation. Note that *O Cruzeiro* published Prestes's book.

112. Serrano, *Minha casa*, 45. She encouraged women to be writers, scientists, musicians, or painters, so long as they did not abandon their central role as mothers and donas de casa. *Minha casa*, 166.

113. Ibid., 18. See also "A casa," *Vida Doméstica*, no. 170 (May 1932); J. Cordeiro de Azevedo and Braz Jordão, "Evolução dos interiores," *A Casa,* no. 147 (Aug. 1936): 10–13.

114. See Carmen Silva, "A felicidade conjugal," *O Ensino* 3:2 (Oct.–Dec. 1938) (the nine "judicious commandments" for ensuring marital bliss); "Os dez mandamentos da mulher superior," *Vida Doméstica*, no. 209 (Aug. 1935).

115. Some felt that the "patriarchal traditions of old" had already passed by 1943. See "O apartamento do homem de trabalho," *A Casa* 22:235 (Dec. 1943): 16–17.

116. Serrano, *Noções*, 25; M. Prestes, 17.

117. Serrano, *Noções*, 162.

118. Ibid., 168.

119. Ibid., 162; Serrano, *Minha casa*, 172.

120. Serrano, *Minha casa*, 61.

121. Ibid., 32.

122. Serrano, *Noções*, 33.

123. "O arranjo da vivenda," *A Casa,* no. 151 (Dec. 1936): 19. See also "Os encantos do lar," *A Casa,* no. 156 (May 1937): 5.

124. Serrano, *Minha casa*, 172.   125. Ibid., 61.

126. Serrano, *Noções*, 173.   127. Ibid., 149.

128. Ibid., 167.

129. See, e.g., "Regras sociaes," *Vida Doméstica*, no. 209 (Aug. 1935).

130. "A casa," *Vida Doméstica*, no. 170 (May 1932).

131. *O Cruzeiro* 22 (Jan. 21, 1950): 70.

132. Dupré, *Eramos seis*, 62.

133. Ibid., 88.

134. *Diretrizes* 1:12 (Mar. 1939): 70.

135. On the elaboration of a cultural sphere of the popular see D. Levine; Rowe and Schelling.

136. D. Silva, 36.

137. Wagley, 123.

138. Lyra Filho, 93.

Chapter 6

1. See A. Prestes, appendix 41, 460–63.

2. Basbaum, 69–71.

3. *O Estado de São Paulo,* 6 Jun. 1920, 3.

4. Forty other military officers, comrades of Prestes during the uprisings of 1922 and 1924, signed a declaration "diverging from the radical and absolute manner" of the May manifesto. See Joffily, 102–3.

5. Távora, 1: 349–66.

6. *Correio da Manhã,* 22 Nov. 1932, 4.

7. See Hardman and Leonardi, 285–89; Conniff, *Urban Politics,* 58; Antunes, 121–25.

8. *Correio da Manhã,* 20 May 1932, 1.

9. Ibid., 19 Jun., 1932, 4.

10. Ibid., 28 Feb. 1932, 4.

11. Carone, "Coleção Azul."

12. Released precisely two years after the revolution's triumph, as Tenentismo was withering, Santa Rosa's 1933 book formed part of a project known as the Blue Collection. The collection consisted of a series of book-length essays on Brazil's condition and prospects. The uneven essays were modeled on European social-political treatises of the time and written from a perspective critical of oligarchic First Republic Brazil. The collection was particularly important because it coincided with the emergence of a middle-class reading public with a voracious appetite for information on social and political affairs. After 1930 the Brazilian publishing industry "understood how the Revolution and the ascent of a new middle class, preoccupied with its own problems and the problems of the country, were changing the perspectives of the country and creating a whole new market for Brazilian authors." L. Lippi, 76, quoting Hallewell, *A indústria brasileira no campo literário* (Bogotá: Jun. 1975, mimeo), 3. See also Hallewell, 336–37.

13. Rosa, *O sentido,* 27–41, 103. As his reference to a German book on the middle class suggests, Santa Rosa understood the Brazilian middle class in explicit comparison to foreign models (34).

14. Ibid., 35, 43, 81.

15. Ibid., 28, 81, 107, 110, 116–26.

16. Ibid., 69, 110. For a less sanguine view of the middle class's political situation see another Blue Collection book, Martins de Almeida, *Brasil errado.*

17. Santa Rosa is less explicit on this point in *O sentido do tenentismo* than in an earlier Blue Collection book, *A desordem* (Disorder), published in 1932. See *A desordem,* 147–55. Disorder was a recurrent theme in the Blue Collection. In addition to Santa Rosa's essays, Afonso Arino de Melo Franco's *Introdução à realidade brasileira* had a chapter entitled "Disorganization and Disorder." Alcindo Sodré's contribution to the collection was called *A gênese da desordem* (The genesis of disorder). In *Brasil errado* Martins de Almeida referred to Brazil's political situation as "organized disorder."

18. The details of this split are discussed in Skidmore, *Politics in Brazil,* and R. Levine.

19. "Manifesto de outubro de 1932," in Salgado, *O integralismo,* 17–28.

20. The following analysis of Integralism is deeply indebted to the insights of Marilena Chauí.

21. Trinidade, 129–41.

22. Ibid., 143.

23. R. Levine, 83, 95.

24. Trinidade, 142–50. Tavares speculates that the Integralists hailed predominantly from the "traditional middle classes (linked in the recent past to the *latifúndio*; their privileges injured by the processes of industrialization and urbanization, independently of their social ascent)" (162).

25. Salgado, *O integralismo,* 61.   26. Pompêo, 53.

27. Trinidade, 146–48.   28. See Williams.

29. A. Lima, *Indicações políticas.* Lima was a spokesman for the Catholic Electoral League, a lay organization that functioned as the political wing of Catholicism.

30. R. Araújo, *Totalitarismo;* Chauí; R. Levine; Tavares; Trinidade.

31. In *What Is Integralism?* Salgado argues that "the study of Brazilian life must be done under the criteria of the Marxist methodology. Affirming this after condemning materialist philosophy in the previous pages may seem strange to the reader. But it is important to understand clearly that while we condemn Marxism as a philosophy, or if we repudiate it as an end or a political process, we Integralists tolerate it as documentation and as a method" (*Obras* 9: 53–54).

32. Venceslau, 67.   33. Salgado, *Obras* 9: 23.

34. Reale 2: 44.   35. Ibid. 3: 216.

36. Salgado, *O integralismo,* 18, 23–24.

37. M. Freitas, 155–56.

38. Salgado, *O integralismo,* 19–20.

39. See Chauí, 112. She talks about Integralism as articulating a worldview at the core of which was the "middle-class-as-people."

40. Quoted in R. Levine, 33.

41. The story of the formation of the ANL and its relationship to radical politics and to Tenentismo is told elsewhere. V. Fonseca; Hernandez; R. Levine.

42. See, e.g., handbills: "Aliança Nacional Libertadora (Rio de Janeiro, maio 1935)," "Ao povo brasileiro," "A 'Aliança Nacional Libertadora,'" "Alliança Nacional Libertadora expõe ao povo os pontos básicos de seu programma," MJ, IJ(1) 132, vol. 1, 2, 4.

43. The first report came from Afonso Henriques, treasurer for Rio's ANL chapter (345). The second came from J. Amado, 257–58.

44. R. Levine, 79.

45. See V. Fonseca, 55–57.

46. A wide variety of labor organizations, including maritime and railroad workers, typesetters, stone workers, public utility workers, and a number of pro-

letarian umbrella organizations, joined student and white-collar groups of commercial employees, bank employees, accountants, and doctors to form the Popular Committee Against Imperialism and Integralism in May 1935. *A Manhã*, 25 May 1935, 7, col. 7.

47. The vast majority of the ANL's membership was white or near white, though the organization did pursue relations with the Frente Negra Brasileira de São Paulo, the small black-consciousness movement. See "Os negros brasileiros confiam na acção da ANL," *A Manhã*, 1 Jun. 1935, 3, col. 3.

48. V. Fonseca, 128–36, 145.

49. Ministério da Fazenda.

50. *A Manhã*, 4 Jul. 1935, 1, col. 1.

51. *A Platea* is an example. See Hernandez, 57.

52. *Juventude*, 15 May 1935, 1, col. 1, attached to *Inquêrito policial do fechamento da ANL em São Paulo, Secção de Segurança Nacional do Ministério da Justiça e Negócios Interiores*, MJ, IJ(1) 1321, vol. 2, #273.

53. "As mulheres em marcha," *A Manhã*, 25 Jun. 1935, 3, col. 1. The number of women activists appears to have been very small, on the order of 5 percent of total membership.

54. See, e.g., *A Manhã*, 4 Jul. 1935, 1, col. 1.

55. See MJ, IJ(1) 1321, vol. 1, "A Alliança Nacional Libertadora: Ao Povo Brasileiro."

56. See *A Manhã*, 4 Jul. 1935, 1, col. 1.

57. See V. Fonseca, 86.

58. "Luís Carlos Prestes a todo o povo do Brasil," *A Manhã*, 5 Jul. 1935, 1–2.

59. See M. Vianna, 132–33.

60. See R. Levine, 102.

61. A 1936 handbill alleged that there were 17,000 political prisoners in Brazil, many tortured or disappeared. See TSN, proc. no. 220, cx. 198, Sept. 1936.

62. *A Manhã*, 30 Jul. 1935, 8, col. 2.

63. See, e.g., AN, *Inquêrito policial*, IJ(1) 1320, vol. 1, nos. 98, 100, 101, 102; IJ(2) 1321, vol. 3, nos. 299, 301, 302, 304; IJ(1), 1321, vol. 4, nos. 439–40, 512; letter from Alcedo B. Cavalcanti to Col. Eduardo Góes, TSN proc. 382, cx. 10.502, Oct. 9, 1937, vol. 1.

64. The best recent narrative of the Intentona is in M. Vianna.

65. "Relatório da Comissão da Eletrificação da E.F. Central do Brazil," *Revista do Clube de Engenharia* 2:14 (Nov. 1935): 682.

66. Lemme 2: 221.

67. Sissón, "Carta aberta ao legislativo," 101–2. For other declarations along the same line, see V. Fonseca, 82–85.

68. Sissón, *Carta aberta à Marinha*, 34.

69. First, they were made after Prestes's July speech and after Sissón's imprisonment in the wake of the Intentona in November 1935. He had every reason to recant his political views in order to secure his own release. Second, Levine has argued that even after the ANL was declared illegal in July, Sissón continued to work in the organization and reshape it along revolutionary lines. R. Levine, 102–3.

70. TSN, proc. no. 382, cx. 41, Oct. 1937.

71. Assorted ANL handbills, MJ, IJ(1) 1321, vols. 1, 2, 4. It is worth noting in this regard that Sissón and Cascardo, two of the ANL's founders, had been Tenentes, many of whom, like Santa Rosa, had favored "technical" over representative government in the early 1930s.

72. Conniff, "Voluntary Associations."

73. Trinidade argues that anticommunism was the single most important reason stated by Integralists for having joined the movement in the first place, followed by sympathy for European fascism, and nationalism (153). This seems to imply more a kind of gut-level hostility than a carefully considered political-philosophical objection.

74. *A Manhã*, 2 Jun. 1935, 6, col. 1. Although the writer was anonymous, I employ the masculine pronoun, since the vast majority of ANL activists were men and since the letter suggests that this person was a bank employee, the vast majority of whom were men.

75. Of course it is possible that *A Manhã* simply fabricated the letter for the obvious propaganda value of such a turncoat.

76. AN, *Inquérito policial*, IJ(1) 1321, vol. 4, no. 409.

77. See Communist party pamphlet attached to the trial record of Taciano José Fernandes before the National Security Tribunal. TSN proc. no. 66, cx. 99, Taciano José Fernandes; "Explicando ao povo—os responsáveis pela crise," *A Manhã*, 11 Aug. 1935, 3, col. 5.

78. Hernandez, 55.

79. "As camadas médias brasileiras em face do momento nacional." This undated document was an analysis of the political moment by Clovis Gusmão. Textual references indicate that it was written after the coup of 1937. It characterizes the ANL as having been organized by the Communist party. The document was picked up by the police in Rio and forwarded to Vargas's office in January 1940.

80. See, e.g., Franco.

81. M. Vianna, 213, 235, 272.

82. *A Manhã*, 7 Sept. 1935, 1–3.

83. Editorial, *Vida Doméstica*, no. 212 (Jan. 1936).

84. "Governo forte" and "Como elles agem—uma cellula communista terrível," *Vida Carioca*, 16:117 (Jan. 1936).

85. "Não somos extremistas!" *A Nota*, 20 Jun. 1936, 8.

86. "A fisionomia do Estado Novo se define," *Diretrizes* 1:1 (Apr. 1938), 3–4.

87. Azevedo Amaral, "A verdadeira natureza do integralismo," *Diretrizes* 1:3 (Jun. 1938): 4.

88. Salgado, *O integralismo*, 21.

89. See generally L. Barreto in Barros, 133, 138, 139, 144, 159–60, 161; Nachman, "Brazilian Positivism."

90. Nachman, "Brazilian Positivism."

91. Barbosa, *Obras*, 33–34, 126–27.

92. Torres, 88. This book was originally published in 1914 and did not receive much attention until republished in 1933 to critical acclaim.

93. Maul, 65. The statement was made by Lima Barreto in a letter to Maul in 1915, after Maul had decided to become involved in Petrópolis politics by running for mayor.

94. A. Prestes, 397–412.

95. *Vida Doméstica*, no. 147 (Nov. 1930); *Vida Carioca* 11:89 (Oct. 1931); Humberto Campos, "Reflexões sobre o momento," *O Cruzeiro* 3 (Nov. 22, 1930).

96. Tigres Bastos, "O mal da política," *Correio da Manhã*, 21 Jan. 1932, 2, col. 2.

97. "Contrarevolução," *Correio da Manhã*, 12 Jul. 1932, 4, col. 5.

98. Santos, 106–7.

99. Salgado, *O integralismo*, 21–22, 27; Reale, *Obras* 3: 168; Salgado, *Obras* 9: 48; *O integralismo*, 18.

100. See, e.g., "A juventude do Brasil," MJ, IJ(1) 1321, vol. 1.

101. See, e.g., Dr. Silvio Boccanera, "A liberadade de sindicato," *Boletim do SMB* 7:80 (Aug. 1935): 1336–48; *Bancário* 3:1 (Jan. 1937): 1; ibid., 3:6 (May 1937): 2; *Anuário do Syndicato Nacional de Engenheiros* (1937), 70.

102. Cap. A. F. Correia Lima, "Hypertrophia federativa," *A Defesa Nacional* 22:255 (Aug. 1935): 913–16.

103. Speech of J. G. Pereira Lima, *Revista do Clube de Engenharia* 2:20 (May 1936): 1080–86.

104. "O momento nacional—É de intensa vibração cívica a hora que passa," *Vida Carioca* 17:128 (Mar. 1937); "O reencontro de 1938—perspectivas de uma luta eleitoral sem precedentes na história do Brasil republicano," 17:128 (May 1937); "A atualidade brasileira," 17:133 (Aug. 1937). The editorial board had hedged its bets, however, praising the army for maintaining a low profile, ready to intervene only if the maintenance of order required they do so.

105. Vargas, *A nova política* 5: 19–32.

106. A. C. Petra de Barros, "O estado forte," *Nossa Classe* 3:4 (Sept. 1938): 4. See also, "Dentro da lei e da ordem," *Bancário* 3:12 (Nov. 1937): 1, 4; "O movimento renovador," *A Panificadora* 8 (Jan. 1938): 3; "Classe desunida," *O Contabilista* 2:4 (Jan. 1938): 8.

The obvious difficulty in gauging these expressions of support is the censorship that took hold during the Estado Novo. The problem is especially acute for the period of most intense censorship, between 1939 and roughly 1943–44. For this reason I have focused on the very earliest praise for the regime, before censorship achieved any bureaucratic or ideological cohesion. *Dicionário histórico-biográfico brasileiro*, 2: 1076; Hons, 68–77. It is worth noting as well that one left-wing journalist recalls DIP censorship as "quite gentle" in terms of prior restraint. Its primary concern was that there be no overt criticism of the government's policies. Peixoto. See also Wainer, 51–52.

107. "Assumpto do dia—a mais sensacional transformação do século sem uma gotta de sangue—Getúlio o estadista genial," *Vida Carioca* 17:136 (Nov. 1937); "A verdadeira democracia," *Vida Carioca* 18:139 (May 1938).

108. Pedro MacCord, "O momento presente e os intellectuaes: o princípio da

igualdade absoluta, um dos grandes absurdos—a evolução da lei e da nova constituição," *Vida Doméstica*, no. 238 (Jan. 1938).

109. Editorial, "É preciso pensar brasileiramente," *Voz Comerciária* 6:47 (Mar. 1942): 3.

110. Dupré, *Eramos seis*, 192.

111. Lemme 2: 217.

112. Murry, 65.

113. A fuller analysis of the discursive construction of populism exceeds the scope of this discussion. See M. Lima.

114. J. Ferreira, 63–90.

115. Thibau, 52.

Chapter 7

1. Mario E. de Azambuja, "Sobre a necessidade de um sindicato médico," *Boletim do SMB* 8 (Mar. 1936): 1573–79.

2. See Erickson; Schmitter; L. Vianna.

3. Though I will not ignore private associations, sindicatos will be at the center of the analysis. In the crucible of the 1930s and 1940s sindicalismo emerged as the conceptual mold according to which the means and ends of associational activity were recast. With the labor laws of 1931 and the Estado Novo the state-sponsored sindicato became the centerpiece of government efforts to subdue an unruly social order.

I deal principally with organizations for which significant runs of publications were available. There were dozens of short-lived organizations that produced no newsletter or journal, and a number of longer-lived organizations so wholly in the shadow of a larger group (such as the lawyers' sindicato in the face of the Order of Brazilian Lawyers) that little or no information is available. This chapter does not pretend to be anything like an institutional history of the organizations discussed. In the main such histories remain to be written.

4. Where 19 mutual aid societies were founded in São Paulo between 1872 and 1900, 26 between 1900 and 1914, and 15 between 1915 and 1929, 42 resistance leagues were established between 1900 and 1914 and 54 between 1915 and 1929.

5. See Ridings.

6. Rio's public functionaries were by far the most extensively organized collar-and-tie sector during the Old Republic, with 80 civil servants' groups claiming 45,000 members in 1921. Conniff, "Voluntary Associations," 67.

7. Schmitter, 148–49.

8. In this context the word *classe* (class) is a synonym of *categoria* (category), here those who earn their livings as bank employees. *Classe* is at times used in the sense of social class, especially after 1930. Context usually indicates which meaning is intended.

9. Quoted in Canêdo, *O sindicalismo*, 53.

10. It is worth noting that bank owners were prepared to fire any who joined, so that fear for one's career doubtless contributed to the reticence to take a more assertive stance. Ibid., 46–47.

11. See A. Oliveira, 30.

12. The law was Decree-Law 19.770 of March 1931. The new law established syndical unity as a governing principle—one organization per occupational group (*categoria*) for a given geographical area—which was a departure from the idea of associational pluralism that had been in place since 1907.

13. Speech by Vargas reprinted in *União* 2:21 (Oct. 1933): 2.

14. E. A. Doment, *União* 1:4 (Oct. 1931):10; Barros, *União* 2:15/16 (Dec. 1932): 15; Getúlio Vargas, *União* 2:21 (Oct. 1933): 2. Available evidence indicates that the union was dominated by better-off members of the profession, who often aligned themselves with employers.

15. See French, *Brazilian Workers' ABC*, 47–55.

16. Canêdo, *O sindicalismo*, 52.

17. Coelho, 17. It is worth noting that Rio's teachers were divided on the sindicato. Some preferred the Institute for Public and Private School Teachers, founded in 1933, which acted more like a mutual aid society than a sindicato. See Editorial, *O Ensino* 1:2 (Jun. 1936).

18. Speech of Dr. Rolando Monteiro, *Boletim do SMB*, special issue (Jul. 1931): 15 (intellectual workers); Reginaldo Fernandes, "A infância do syndicalismo," *Boletim do SMB* 2:16 (Apr. 1930): 66–69 (manual workers); Editorial, "Colabore connosco!" *Boletim do SMB* 4:39 (Mar. 1932): 247–48 (parasitism of bosses). The legislation bringing salaried doctors within the labor code was passed in 1934.

19. Dr. Manoel de Abreu, speech to members of the government, *Boletim do SMB* 4:38 (Feb. 1932): 229–30.

20. "Medicina do estado," *Boletim do SMB*, special issue (Jul. 1931): 24.

21. Canêdo, *O sindicalismo*, 59–61; A. Oliveira, 48–51.

22. Antunes, 122–27.

23. A. Oliveira, 73.

24. While the coalition sought closer contact with the labor movement, it also formulated a new position on the relation sindicatos should bear to politics generally. A document issued in 1934 stated that "the sindicatos have the defense of their *categorias* as their only and exclusive end and are completely distant from any and all movements of a political character." As French points out, the significance of divorcing economic from political issues was that it differed so dramatically from the view characteristic of industrial labor organizations, which had tended to fuse politics and economics. This conceptual separation may have been rooted in the deep suspicion of politics nurtured by middle-class people during this period and in their being more willing than militant workers to trust the state as a social mediator.

25. *O Estado de São Paulo*, 7 Jul. 1934, 4, col. 1.

26. "Duas palavras à classe médica e aos verdadeiros amigos do Sindicato Médico Brasileiro," *Boletim do SMB* 6:69 (Sept. 1934): 997–98.

27. Coelho, 34.

28. "Continuam agitados os médicos de São Paulo," *A Manhã*, 23 Oct. 1935, 7, col. 1.

29. Memorial to Getúlio Vargas from the Brazilian Medical Sindicato, AGC 38.01.08, IV–1. See A. Oliveira, 76; Pacheco; Peixoto.

30. Dr. Silvio Boccanera, "Como definir o sindicalismo," *Boletim do SMB* 6:70 (Oct. 1934): 1029–32.

31. Maria Letícia Ferreira Lima, "A educação e o sindicato," *Revista Brasileira de Pedagogia* 3:24/25 (May–Jun. 1936): 228–442.

32. *A Manhã*, 17 Oct. 1935, 7, col. 4; "Hoje é dia dos comerciários," ibid., 30 Oct. 1935, 1, col. 1.

33. Canêdo, *O sindicalismo*, 113–21.

34. Editorial, "Eleições," *Bancário* 3:1 (Jan. 1937): 4.

35. Salma Bamel, "A autocrítica," *Syndiké* 1:6 (Oct. 1935): 1–4; Vitor Vianna, "O esforço das elites e a depressão monetária," *Syndiké* 1:5 (Sept. 1935): 27–32. This appeal to younger men was clearly aimed at those in the sindicato, whose average age was 25, compared with an average of around 32–33 for Syndiké members. Syndiké members also tended to occupy higher, better-paying positions in the hierarchical structure of bank organizations than sindicato members, as makes sense for employees further along in their careers. In essence Syndiké appears to have been an organization of men in mid-career with solid accomplishments and families to defend. The sindicato was an organization of younger men still finding their way in the white-collar labor market. Canêdo, *O sindicalismo*, 117–20.

36. Editorial, "Os benefícios da syndicalização," *Syndiké* 2:19 (Nov. 1936): 37–38.

37. Luiz André Costa, "Uma entrevista com um bancário," *Syndiké* 1:7 (Nov. 1935): 29–31.

38. Canêdo, *O sindicalismo*, 103.

39. Ibid., 75.

40. These two paragraphs are based on information obtained in interviews with P. Lima, Peixoto, and Siqueira.

41. Omar Campelo, "Sindicalismo," *Boletim do SMB* 7:81 (Sept. 1935): 1356–66.

42. A. C. Petra de Barros, Editorial, *Nossa Classe* 1:1 (Aug. 1936): 3.

43. Vargas, *A nova política*, 6: 133–38.

44. Temistocles Brandão Cavalcanti, "O estatuto dos funcionários e alguns dos seus aspectos," *RSP* 4:112 (Oct.–Nov. 1939): 49.

45. Dec.-lei no. 1.1713, Oct. 28, 1939.

46. Article 136 of the 1937 constitution held that "intellectual, technical, and manual work has the right to protection and special attention from the State. Everyone is guaranteed the right to subsist through honest work, and work, as the individual's means of subsistence, constitutes a good which the State is under obligation to protect."

47. Prof. Millen Improta, speech, *Revista Paulista de Contabilidade* 23:243 (Sept. 1944): 11–16 ("collaboration" and "corporatist"); XYZ, "A procura da felicidade," *Voz Comerciária* 5:39 (Jul. 1941): 1 ("happiness" and "struggle"). See also "Governo e syndicato," *Bancário* 4:16 (Mar. 1938): 1–4; speech of Prof.

José Furtado Simão, *Urbanismo e Viação*, no. 17 (Oct. 1941): 50; "Rumos aos sindicatos," *O Lojista*, no. 114 (Sept. 1943): 1–3.

48. Dr. Silvio Boccanera, "A liberdade de sindicato," *Boletim do SMB* 7:80 (Aug. 1935): 1336–48.

49. Wolfe, chs. 3–4. Bank employees may have been an exception to this generalization.

50. "Sem imprensa livre não haverá povos livres" (interview with Borba), *Diretrizes*, Dec. 30, 1943, 3–4, 20. I also obtained information about this election during my interview with Mario Martins in July 1991. Martins was drafted to run but declined the nomination so that the opposition would not be divided. Martins observed that the election was clean and that Carrazoni, despite his politics, was "an important journalist" and not a *pelego*, or government-controlled syndical leader, as some had claimed. Martins also noted that the sindicato had always depended on close connections in government circles and stated that most of its business with public authorities was transacted through these contacts.

51. "A liberdade de imprensa será assegurada pela victoria das nações democráticas" (interview with Carrazoni), *Diretrizes*, Jan. 6, 1944, 3, 10.

52. Editorial, *Boletim do SMB* 11:129 (Sept. 1939): 2902–6.

53. A. Nunes, 24.

54. See "Associação de professoras, exposição do problema," AGC 36.07.00g, pasta II–17; Editorial, *Bancário* 9:16 (Mar. 1938): 4; *Boletim do Centro dos Professores da 5a CEE* 4 (Jul.–Sept. 1938); *Formação* 1 (Aug. 1938): 9–25; "Bibliotecas, um problema nacional," *Diretrizes*, Jun. 17, 1943, 17–18; Francisco Ichaso, "O anúncio como função social," *Publicidade*, Aug. 1943, 6; "A economia dos servidores públicos," *Diretrizes*, Sept. 2, 1943, 13, 20; "Que e legislação assiste, no Brasil, a profissão de publicidade," *Diretrizes*, Sept. 1943, 9, 18; Prof. Millen Improta, speech, *Revista Paulista de Contabilidade* 23:243 (Sept. 44):11–16.

55. AFPESP, "Vantagens e serviços."

56. See "O que é o que representa a atividade de um cadastro," *Bancário* 7:35 (Mar. 1941): 12; "O lojista e o público," *O Lojista*, no. 10 (Jul. 1934):1.

57. A. Faria, 144–49.

58. For example, Rio's doctors' sindicato suspended publication of its journal to protest government interference in editorial decision. Editorial, *Boletim do SMB* 13:145 (May 1946).

59. "A necessidade do estímulo," *O Bancário* 10:39 (Jan. 1944):1. The São Paulo journalists' sindicato is another, much less important example of this. See Seixas.

60. Quoted in French, *The Brazilian Workers' ABC*, 95.

61. See Canêdo, *Bancários*, 56–60. Despite bank employees' willingness to strike, Canêdo emphasizes the importance of their difference from workers. Canêdo, *O sindicalismo*, 206.

62. "Despertae, empregado do comércio," *União* 1:9 (May, 1932): 18.

63. Theofilo Souzas Carvaho, "De rebus . . ." and "Pela união da classe," *Revista do Professor* 1:4 (Jun.–Jul. 1934): 7, 12.

64. *Boletim do SMB* 7:74 (Feb. 1935): 1154.

65. See, e.g., Editorial, *Revista do Sindicato Odontológico Brasileiro* 1:1 (Jan. 1936): 13 ("skepticism"); Cleto Seabra Veloso, "Um programma de ação," *Boletim do SMB* 9:97/98 (Jan.–Feb. 1937): 1899–1900; A. Lourenço Cabral, "Classe desunida a dos contabilistas," *O Contabilista* 1:3 (Dec. 1937): 8 ("lack of cooperation").

66. Editorial, "Apreciável iniciativa," *O Lojista*, no. 133 (Apr. 1945): 1–3.

67. Taken together, bank employees, liberal professionals, commerce employees, teachers, and bureaucrats reported about a 17 percent rate of sindicato membership in Rio in 1940, compared with 28 percent of those performing manual work in industry or transportation services. Rates differed within categories. Bank employees were said to have a much higher rate of participation (34 percent) than any other white-collar or professional category, though their numbers were small. See IBGE, "Número de pessoas." Because of methodological problems these data are better used as a basis for comparison than as a means of gauging actual participation rates. Because the government had every reason to pad the numbers, actual rates may have been lower than reported.

68. In 1930 the association had reached an all-time high of nearly 43,000 members. In 1931 some 20,000 of these left the organization. See Associação dos Empregados no Comércio, 166, 175. The association spent the next thirteen years trying to rebuild.

69. Mario José Fernandes, "O empregado de hoje será ... o empregado de amanhã," *União* 1:6 (Dec. 1931): 8.

70. M. O. Marco, "A indiferença do trabalhador," *Voz Comerciária* 1:4 (Oct. 1937): 3 (emphasis in the original).

71. Editorial, *Boletim da AEC* 1:2 (Jul. 1944): 22–24; 1:3 (Aug. 1944): 9.

72. Frederico Hermann, Jr., "Sindicalização da classe dos contadores," *Revista Paulista de Contabilidade* 12:112–13 (Oct.–Nov. 1933): 242–43.

73. Fávero, 141.

74. Bandeira, 5–25.

75. Dr. Noé Azevedo, "A ordem dos Advogados e o Sindicato dos Profissionais," *Boletim da OAB* 6:21 (Jul. 1939).

76. Editorial, *O Advogado* 1:1 (Jan. 1938): 1; "Editorial—até quando?!" *Revista do Syndicato Odontológico Brasileiro* 1:8 (Aug. 1936): 1.

77. In this regard it is worth a reminder that many bank employees held secondary-school and university degrees, which means that they may have had a greater interest in maintaining contact with the liberal profession of their training than in joining the sindicato linked with their jobs. See *Bancário*, 6:33 (Aug. 1940): 2.

78. Bauser.

79. Siqueira.

80. The contacts made in such places offered opportunities to join patronage-based groups known as *panelinhas*, through which careers could be advanced. See Leeds.

81. Celio de Barros, "Promoção por merecimento," *Nossa Classe* 1:2 (Sept. 1936): 17.

82. Olavo Leite, "Do ensino e do professorado," *Revista do Professor* 1:3 (May 1934): 6.

83. Editorial, *Nossa Classe* 2:4 (Jan. 1937): 16.

84. "Hoje é dia dos comerciários," *A Manhã*, 30 Oct. 1935, 1, col. 5. This struggle against opportunistic and self-serving leaders had a history. An article in the union's journal in 1931 suggested that some among the rank-and-file members may have resisted incorporation into a larger organization dominated by elites by trying to form organizations of their own. Leaders of the union felt sufficiently threatened that they wrote a memorandum to the labor minister in 1931, arguing that the government had to do something to stop splinter associations from organizing themselves into sindicatos. According to the leaders, these splinters "lacked well-defined ideas, lacked any assets, and what is most remarkable and worthy of note, *lacked the support of the more specialized professionals*," such as themselves (emphasis added). See "A unidade de nossa classe e a syndicalização—combatendo a possibilidade de serem expedidos títulos de syndicatos aos que não podem tel-os," memorial ao ministro de Indústria e Trabalho Lindolfo Collor, *União* 1:3 (Sept. 1931): 8, 12.

85. Dr. Sílvio Boccanera, "A liberdade sindical," *Boletim do SMB* 7:80 (Aug. 1935): 1336–48.

86. Dr. Luiz Cesar Pannain, "A classe odontológica e suas associações no Brasil," *Revista do Syndicato Odontológico Brasileiro* 1:2 (Feb. 1936): 53–54.

87. Where 24 percent of 21,000 women factory workers reported sindicato membership in 1940, only 8 percent of 27,000 in white-collar occupations did so. Calculated from IBGE, "Número das pessoas."

88. Hahner, *Emancipating the Female Sex*, 167–68.

89. Everardo Backhauser, "A syndicalização do professor católico—fins e organização das Associações de Professores Católicos," *Boletim da Associação de Professores Católicos* 11 (Sept.–Oct. 1933): 77–82.

90. Associação de Professoras, "Exposição do problema," AGC 36.07.00g, pasta II–17.

91. "Salários femininos," *Voz Comerciária* 2:6 (May 1938): 6.

92. Jandyra Gonçalves, "Deve a mulher trabalhar," *Vida Doméstica*, no. 212 (Nov. 1935).

93. See Hahner, *Emancipating the Female Sex*, 90.

94. See Azzi.

95. See Hahner, *Emancipating the Female Sex*, 149.

96. Dinah Silveira Queiroz, "Minhas irmãs e o mundo," *O Cruzeiro* 17:13 (Jan. 20, 1945): 3.

97. See Hahner, *Emancipating the Female Sex*, 165–66; Besse, *Restructuring Patriarchy*, 201.

98. Lyra Filho, 67.

99. R. Sodré, 26.

100. Some were more likely to do so than others. The Engineers' Club in Rio, with so many of its members on the public payroll, was particularly keen to persuade the government of its desire to cooperate with big projects. The Brazilian

Education Association sought close links with the government in order to advance educational reform. The Order of Lawyers, by contrast, rarely commented on the matter one way or the other.

101. "Relatório," *Anuário do Sindicato Nacional de Engenheiros* (1934–35).

102. See generally, French, *The Brazilian Workers' ABC*; Wolfe.

103. IBOPE 9, p. 39. This study was based on interviews with 800 people in São Paulo from five social groupings: the middle class, the working class, rural workers, commerce, and industry.

Chapter 8

1. See P. Fonseca, 249–328; Leme, 137–82; Weinstein, *For Social Peace*, 79–113.

2. See, e.g., Wainer, 65.

3. Letter from B. Montenegro to Gustavo Capanema, Aug. 9, 1943, AGC 36.11.20g, folder 5.

4. Cable no. 16761, Harold Tewell to Department of State, Jul. 7, 1944, Commodities Division, National Archive (USA), FW 832.5017/8–2244.

5. "O Estado Novo," *Vida Carioca* 21:175 (Nov. 1941); "Dez de Novembro," ibid., 23:197 (Nov. 1943); "Os funerais do totalitarismo," ibid., 25:209 (Mar. 1945).

6. Memorandum, Jul. 10, 1944, National Archives (USA), FW 832.00/6–2344.

7. Hugo Leplat, "Nós e as eleições," *Voz Comerciária* 7:80 (Feb. 1945): 1.

8. See Love, 9.

9. See Chacon, 411–41.

10. Chacon, 414, 436. I discovered only one passing reference to the middle class in a campaign speech by Gomes, describing them as victims of inflation along with many others, including manual workers. Gomes, 40.

11. French, *The Brazilian Workers' ABC*, 117.

12. Carone, *A Terceira República*, 433–43.

13. Tribunal Superior Eleitoral.

14. IBOPE 18. This study must be taken cautiously. Three years had elapsed since the election, and the only indication of methodology is that the sample was chosen "in proportions adequate to the socio-economic categories."

15. Ribeiro.

16. Ibid., 76.

17. IBOPE 20, p. 3.

18. IBOPE 19, p. 1. This study polled 600 men and women in São Paulo, whether or not eligible to vote.

19. Even so, the high level of disaffection among A's counsels against assuming too easily that elites always and everywhere see politics in a positive light.

20. Skidmore, *Politics*, 67.

21. Carone, *A Quarta República*, 10–19.

22. See French, "Workers."

23. Even if the actual number of blank ballots cast in 1945 was lower, a higher

number reported in 1948 could itself be taken as a sign of frustration with the possibilities of open politics.

24. Quoted in French, *The Brazilian Workers' ABC*, 227.

25. Anais.

26. "As responsabilidades do Congresso de Economia," *Diretrizes*, Dec. 2, 1943, 1–14; "O Congresso de Economia e os problemas brasileiros," ibid., Dec. 19, 1943, 6; "Em torno do Congresso de Economia," ibid., Dec. 23, 1943, 3.

27. Anais 2: 494.

28. See *O Estado de São Paulo*, 21 Sept. 1946, 12, col. 7; 22 Sept. 1946, 1, col. 5; 25 Sept. 1946, 1, col. 5.

29. Of course, the possibility that Cunha and other dissidents were in cahoots with the Labor Ministry to sabotage the event should not be discounted. Given that the protest came within two days of the congress's end, however, this seems less likely to have been the case.

30. *O Cruzeiro* 20 (Sept. 13, 1947): 4.

31. Appendix to Sodré, "Em defesa das classes médias."

32. Vargas, *A campanha*, 19, 29, 41, 68, 70–71, 91, 94, 217–18, 273, 280, 291, 295, 300, 379, 595, 635.

33. See *O Estado de São Paulo*, 1 Oct. 1950, p. 7, col. 6.

34. Quoted in Benevides, 81. Other anti-Vargas publications, such as the weekly *O Cruzeiro*, made similar remarks.

35. After unsuccessfully pursuing an alliance with the PSD, Vargas and the PTB forged an accord with Adhemar de Barros's PSP, creating a kind of populist front. See D'Araujo, 60–68.

36. The surveyers asked São Paulo voters whom they would prefer if an election were held that moment (the election was still two years off). Eight percent of A's, 20 percent of B's, and 48 percent of C's said they would vote for Vargas running under the PTB's banner. Seventeen percent, 24 percent, and 5 percent, respectively, said they would vote for Gomes. Barros was favored by 8 percent of B's and 5 percent of C's. With regard to the candidates, there was a slight gender gap among B's: B (middle-class) women were evenly split (19 and 19) between Vargas and Gomes; B men preferred Gomes to Vargas 28 to 21. IBOPE 20, p. 3.

37. IBOPE 22, p. 1. This study involved interviews with 600 men and women of the three social groupings. It is worth noting that in this poll a larger percentage of A's than in 1948 also indicated they would vote for Vargas, 17 percent versus 8 percent. Days before the election, the percentage of B's saying they would vote for Vargas rose to over 60 percent. IBOPE 23, p. 1. As always, given the size and variability of IBOPE's B category, it would be a mistake to assume from this that middle-class voters were solidly behind Vargas, though it does undermine the idea that the UDN was the party of the middle class. Indeed, among B's polled in São Paulo, 14 percent preferred the PTB, 22 percent the UDN, 11 percent the PSP, and 9 percent the PSD. IBOPE 22, p. 6.

38. Quoted in Benevides, 214.

39. Quoted in ibid., 79.

40. Benevides argues persuasively that the UDN sought to articulate a middle-class appeal after 1950 through these two issues (ibid., 217).

41. This statement holds most firmly for the national UDN. At the local level party politics was less ideological and more likely to be oriented to local patronage.

42. Benevides argues persuasively that while the UDN was the only national political party to address itself explicitly to the middle class, it was not for that reason a party of the middle class. Benevides, 217–18. It played to middle-class anxieties regarding progressive immiseration by inflation and falling salaries and its anger at corruption, but had little to say about economic development, a matter that by the 1950s was of abiding concern to many middle-class people and very much implicated in their everyday lives. See also Soares, 144.

43. I discovered the phrase "middle class" only once in Vargas's published speeches from the 1950 campaign, and that as part of a list of "workers, the middle class, and all Brazilians." Vargas, *A campanha*, 546.

44. Vargas can only have been helped in this regard by the Communist party's opposition to his candidacy. See "Manifesto de agosto de 1950," in Vinhas, 140–58.

45. Unless otherwise indicated, references in this paragraph are to campaign speeches contained in Vargas, *A campanha*, 50, 70, 87, 216, 218, 312, 350, 511–12, 570, 576, 596, 609, 618, 623, 629, 641.

46. Picaluga dedicated her book on the UDN in Rio de Janeiro to "my mother, *getulista*, to my father, *brigaderista*, in whose home political debate was always free."

47. *O Cruzeiro* 22 (Feb. 18, 1950): 19.

48. The social background of these letter writers was not available, though it is worth noting that according to one IBOPE market survey, there may have been 100,000 B *O Cruzeiro* readers in Rio de Janeiro in 1945, 37,000 A's, and 31,000 C's. IBOPE, 5, 10, 11, 22. This study was based on 1,000 interviews, 500 men and 500 women, divided roughly into a 1:3:2 proportion for A:B:C.

49. T. Fonseca, 191–93.

50. Ribeiro, 72.

51. "Situação política brasileira" and "O moralismo e a alienação das classes médias," *Cadernos de nosso tempo* 2 (Jan.–Jun. 1954): 103–20, 150–59. For a description of the Brazilian Institute for Political Studies, which later became the Institute of Advanced Brazilian Studies, see Schwartzman, 3–6; *Dicionário histórico-biográfico*, 1617–19.

52. See, e.g., Picaluga 2: 116–27.

53. French, *The Brazilian Workers' ABC*, 269–73. Much research remains to be done to uncover the extent of such political activity.

54. Bosi, 157.

55. Ribeiro, 72.

56. For example, engineer Mauro Thibau started by overseeing construction projects for the government and later became the Minister of Mines and Energy in the 1960s. Ernane Galvêas, who started as a clerk in the Banco do Brasil, ended up as president of the Central Bank in the late 1960s. See Thibau; Galvêas.

57. Lambert, 153–54.

58. Falcão, 373–77; French, *The Brazilian Workers' ABC*, 233; Chilcote, 121.

59. Mario Puell to Osvaldo Aranha, Apr. 27, 1950, AOA, *Pedidos*, 1950.

60. R. Sodré, 15, 25, 27.

Chapter 9

1. Weffort, 68.

2. Ary Pitombo, "Leonor Solanger—A odysséa de uma professora que combateu nas hostes revolucionárias," *O Cruzeiro* 3 (Nov. 22, 1930): 20.

3. Vargas, *A nova política* 5: 19–32.

4. Azevedo Amaral, "Política e serviço público," *RSP* 2:1 (Apr. 1938): 13–15 (emphasis added). Amaral was one of the more prominent authoritarian writers of the Estado Novo.

5. Hans Franke, "Algumas considerações sôbre o seguro dos funcionários públicos," *RSP* 4:1/2 (Oct.–Nov. 1939): 16–17.

6. Josué Montello, "Dois argumentos democráticos da nova administração brasileira," *RSP* 5:3/1 (Jul. 1942): 65–66.

7. M. Pio Corrêa Jr., "A orientação administrativa do Estado Novo," *RSP* 1:4 (Mar. 1938): 8.

8. Urbano C. Berquó, "Efficiência administrativa e sabotagem burocrática," *RSP* 2:1 (Apr. 1938): 5–6.

9. A. Fernandes. Essays of this sort were required of all who aspired to secure one of the prestigious, merit-based bureaucratic positions of *técnico de administração* within the federal government.

10. Vargas, *A nova política* 6: 133–38.

11. Manoel Rezende, "A representação de classes e o projeto da Constituinte"; Armando Prado, "O Brasil do passado e o Brasil do futuro" (reprint of speech delivered at the Rio de Janeiro Municipal Theater, May 30, 1932), *Revista da AFPESP* 1:1 (Nov. 1932): 7.

12. Associação dos Funcionários Públicos do Estado de São Paulo, "Do funcionário público," 6.

13. Nachman, "Brazilian Positivism," 11; "Positivism, Modernization."

14. "Factor administração, em vez de factor política," *Vida Carioca* 16:120 (May 1936).

15. "O Estado Novo—'Brasil omnia vincit,'" ibid. 22:188 (Nov. 1942).

16. See, e.g., *Revista do Clube de Engenharia* 4:38 (Nov. 1937), 1712; "Interesses profissionais," *Engenharia* 1:1 (Oct. 1942), 70; *Revista do Clube Militar* 15:63 (Jan.–Feb. 1942): 40–43; Prof. Felipe dos Santos Reis, "A engenharia de após guerra," *Revista do Clube de Engenharia* 11:104 (Mar. 1945): 70–74.

17. See, e.g., Armando Godoy, "As consequências sociaes e econômicas dos principios do urbanismo," *Revista do Clube de Engenharia* 2:14 (Nov. 1935): 711–19; "A casa do pobre—construida em duas etapas," *A Casa*, 17:180 (May 1939): 32–33; F. Baptista de Oliveira, "O problema da casa popular," *Urbanismo e Viação*, no. 3 (Apr. 1939): 69–100; "Processo ativo de assistência social," *O Ensino* 6:21 (Apr.–Jun. 1941): 41.

18. Walter Ramos Poyares, "A nova sociedade e a propaganda," *Publicidade*, no. 34 (Dec. 1943): 25.

19. "Urbanismo e democracia," *Engenharia* 34 (Aug. 1945): 488–89.

20. See, e.g., Editorial, "Classe desunida," *O Contabilista* 2 (Jan. 1938): 8; Prof. Millen Improta, speech, *Revista Paulista de Contabilidade* 23:243 (Sept. 1944): 11–16.

21. AFPESP, "Vantagens e serviços."   22. Anjos, 45.

23. Fischer, 229.   24. D. Silva, 107, 115, 116.

25. Bauser.

26. See, e.g., Wilson Moura, "Instrução primária," *O Ensino* 3:12 (Jan.–Mar. 1939).

27. Joaquim Elydio da Silveira, "Educar," *O Ensino* 1:2 (Jun. 1936): 13 ("social communion"); Elza Figueira de Melo, "Educação cívica," *O Ensino* 5:21 (Apr.–Jun. 1941): 10 ("progress").

28. *Anuário do Colégio*, 38; *Revista de Educação Pública* 1:4 (Oct.–Dec. 1940): 471–74.

29. Bittencourt, 150.

30. Ibid., 160.

31. *Anuário do Colégio*, 48–50.

32. *Documentário do Primeiro Congresso*, 33; Onofre Penteado Junior, "A formação do professorado secundário," *Boletim do Sindicato dos Professores de Ensino Secundário e Primário de São Paulo* 4:15 (Aug.–Oct., 1944): 2.

33. Penteado Junior, "A formação do professorado secundário," *Boletim do Sindicato dos Professores de Ensino Secundário e Primário de São Paulo* 4:15 (Aug.–Oct., 1944): 1.

34. Bittencourt, 91.

35. Backhauser, 63.

36. "O ensino," *O Ensino* 4:13 (Apr.–Jun. 1939): 27.

37. Ibid.

38. H. Faria.

39. According to a document detailing statistical data on the national and regional labor courts between 1944 and 1954, of over 131,000 complaints filed by workers between 1941 and 1945, workers won 18 percent, employers won 9 percent, and settlements of some sort were reached in 40 percent. The remaining cases were lumped under the rubric "other decisions." See Secção de Estatística, "Poder Judiciário, Justiça do Trabalho, Produção Verificada nos Diversos Orgãos" (Rio de Janeiro: 1995), cited in French, *Brazilian Workers' ABC*, 311 n. 63.

40. *Voz Comerciária* 1 (Oct. 1937): 2.

41. French, *Brazilian Workers' ABC*, 87.

42. Ibid., 171.

43. In 1943, only 30 collective cases were brought; in 1944 only 1. The political moment loosened restrictions on the law, so that 134 were brought in 1945 and 420 in 1946. Thereafter the number dropped: 295 in 1947; 183 in 1948; 143 in 1949; and 134 in 1950. See French, *Brazilian Workers' ABC*, 161, 333 n. 32.

44. On the origins of professional social work see Arlette Lima, *Serviço social*.

45. Pedro Poppe Gyrão, "A participação do assistente social num programa de higiene geral do trabalho," *RSP* 12:2/3 (Jan. 1950): 10.

46. M. Pinheiro, 9, 92.

47. *Síntese do Primeiro Congresso*, 16.

48. Faro, 92.

49. The Leo XIII Foundation was founded in 1944. The State University of Rio de Janeiro created a department of social assistance also in 1944. São Paulo's main business group created the Industrial Social Service in 1946.

50. *Projeto Memória*, application form files.

51. One form explicitly asked students to explain their decisions. The other provided a space for "Other," where students commonly volunteered reasons. *Projeto Memória*, pastas dos estudantes.

52. ESSERJ, folder of Nêlda Guemata Gomes.

53. ESSERJ, student folders.

54. Curso de Educadores Sociais, "Pontos para os exames."

55. See, e.g., ESSERJ, folders of: José Oliveira de Paula Antunes, Maria Aparecida Guimarães, Eulalia da Conceição Leite, Filamêa Xavier da Matta, Auxiliadora de Oliveira.

56. M. Silva, 82–84.

57. Ibid., 84.

58. Poppe Gyrão, "A participação do assistente social," 11.

59. Another was SENAI, the National Industrial Training Service. SESI and SENAI were at the center of efforts by a vanguard of São Paulo industrialists to bring Taylorism, Fordism, and rational techniques generally to bear on production and labor relations. The indispensable work here is Weinstein's, *For Social Peace*.

60. SESI, *O que é o SESI?*

61. Simonsen, 6–12.

62. Rubens Arantes de Souza, "O educador social e o centro social no. 2—Brás," *O Educador Social* 1:2 (Feb. 1952): 6.

63. SESI, *O que é o SESI*, 23.

64. "O que é o SESI?" *SESI-Jornal* 1:1 (Apr. 1948): 1.

65. Aldo M. Azevedo, "Serviço social e SESI,'" *Serviço Social* 7 (Mar.–Jun. 1948): 53–54.

66. SESI, *Curso.*

67. See Weinstein, "The Industrialists," 402.

68. Brescia; Castellano; H. Lima.

69. See Weinstein, *For Social Peace*, 145–60.

70. Brescia.

71. Quoted in Weinstein, *For Social Peace*, 247.

72. M. Pinheiro, 94.

73. *A Dona de Casa* 2:19 (Aug. 1951): 4.

74. "Etiqueta—o uso dos talhares," *A Dona de Casa* 2:14 (Mar. 1951): 3.

75. Letter from Roberto Simonsen to Euvaldo Lodi, Apr. 27, 1947, Confederação Nacional de Indústria, Rio de Janeiro, uncatalogued documents.

76. Arquivo, SESI, Proc. 289/439/636, Jul. 18, 1950, Metallúrgica Matarazzo.

77. H. Lima.

78. Bosi, 274.

79. This is one of Weinstein's indispensable insights regarding the practice of populism in Brazil. Weinstein, *For Social Peace*, 219–79.

80. Dupré, *Eramos seis*, 240–41.

81. *Diretrizes*, 6:148 (May 6, 1943): 15 When the book's tenth edition appeared in 1957, Monteiro Lobato reiterated the point, insisting that Dona Lola, the book's protagonist, "thinks and talks exactly like all women" of the "middle class" in Brazil.

82. As with all literary sources the issues of production and reception are complicated. In keeping with the social realism of the period (see Putnam), most of these books described the experiences, expectations, and anxieties of people defined by work and home, ordinary people who went to great lengths to lead decent, respectable, and often unremarkable lives. Authors hailed from backgrounds bespeaking familiarity with the lives they depicted. Their fathers tended to be pharmacists, schoolteachers, public functionaries, and commercial clerks. Their mothers commonly graduated from normal schools and worked as teachers. All had at least secondary-school educations. A number had attended university. They earned their livings as teachers, commercial clerks, journalists, lawyers, or public functionaries. All lived in or near a large city.

It is impossible to know precisely who or how many people read these books. Some were bestsellers. Others were not. Context may be the best guide to the general audience to which they were addressed. They were published during a period of dramatic change in literacy and the book market. See Fiorentino, 15, 23, 140; Hallewell, 333–40, 399–413. Perhaps central to this phenomenon was what one student of the matter has referred to as a "rising middle class" of book buyers, the large number of urban-dwelling, salaried employees and professionals that had emerged over the three decades after the turn of the century. See Hallewell, 336. Within this new segment of the book market leisure and a desire to make sense of a postoligarchic, industrializing, urbanizing, class-divided nation led to an "obsessive preoccupation with personal and material matters," causing "the habit of reading to increase dramatically," as an accountant noted in 1936 (Nunes, 24). Or as Hallewell has put it, the "ascent of a new middle class, preoccupied with its own problems and the problems of the country, was changing the perspectives of the country and creating a whole new market for Brazilian authors." Hallewell, cited in L. Oliveira, 70.

83. These novels are particularly valuable historical sources because of the literary context within which they emerged. During the 1930s and 1940s literature became an important instrument for chronicling the profound transformations of Brazilian society. The new social fiction of this period explored the clash between old patriarchal and new industrial orders, sought to understand the rapid urbanization of what had been a rural society, recorded the rise of social groups, and laid bare the political tensions that resulted. For working-class novels in the United States and Britain, see Denning and Fox.

84. Estado Novo censorship raises questions about only two of the books: Dupré's *Eramos seis* (1943) and Versíssimo's *The Rest Is Silence* (1943). There is no indication that either of them was written under pressure from or at the behest of the DIP. Though not unfriendly to the regime, neither explicitly supported it. Indeed, both authors to all intents and purposes ignored the matter. Both books sold very well.

85. See T. Fonseca; Ribeiro; R. Sodré.

86. Calazans's novel was first published in 1933. He was born in Vitória, Espírito Santo, and worked as a mid-level public functionary. He was described by a contemporary as "not accepting his petite-bourgeois condition" and "blowing a lot of cultural smoke," as a result of which he vacillated between communism and "hiding in the shadow of power" (Ponzi, 191). Ponzi notes that Calazans went back and forth on whether to call his novel *Petit Bourgeois* or *Middle Class*. This was his only novel of any note. *Enciclopédia* 1: 364.

87. Carvalho was the son of a schoolteacher in Ceará. In 1928 he founded a newspaper called *A Esquerda* (The left). He took a law degree in 1931 and worked as a journalist thereafter. During the 1930s and 1940s he published a variety of novels and poetry. In 1947 he founded the *Diário do Povo* (The people's daily), which he ran for fifteen years (R. Menezes, 2: 322).

88. Jader de Carvalho, 9.

89. Calazans, 173–76.

90. This gulf between middle-class and working-class radicals was real. Peralva, 233–42; Chilcote, 130.

91. Veríssimo, *Crossroads*, 52. The book was originally published in Portuguese in 1935 as *Caminhos cruzados*. It won a literary prize the same year. It quickly became a bestseller, going into six editions by 1943. It was translated into English in 1943 and Spanish in 1945. See Hallewell, 325–26.

Veríssimo was the son of a successful Rio Grande do Sul pharmacist. His uncle was a rancher and Tenentista, who accompanied Prestes on the march across Brazil in 1924. At a young age Veríssimo began working as a retail clerk in dry goods. After scraping together some cash, he was able to open a pharmacy of his own. He failed for "lack of a capacity for capitalist life." He moved to Porto Alegre, where he ended up working as an editor and translator at a publishing house. He published his first novel in 1933. He wrote many more novels, continued to write as a journalist, and eventually became one of Brazil's better-known authors. See Gonzaga, 223; R. Menezes 5: 1301–2; *Enciclopédia* 2: 1344.

92. Dupré, *Eramos seis*. The book was extremely popular, going through three editions in its first year alone and eight editions in ten years. Sra. Dupré, née Maria José Fleury Monteiro, was born in the state of São Paulo to a schoolteacher and housewife. She married an engineer. She wrote several family novels, achieving her first commercial and literary success with *Eramos seis*, which was made into a movie in Buenos Aires; it was followed by a sequel, *Dona Lola*, in 1949. R. Menezes 2: 452; Z. Cardoso, 99–101.

93. Dupré, *Eramos seis*, 106–7.

94. Veríssimo, *The Rest Is Silence*, 369–70.

95. D. Silva, 48, 120–21. Silva was born in Pernambuco. He worked as a tax agent for the federal government. He wrote a number of novels, essays, and collections of poetry. He was a law student when he published *Classe média*. He took his degree is 1947. During the 1940s he wrote three books of essays as well as *Classe média*. He later wrote but did not publish a sociological monograph entitled "Da importância política, social, e econômica da classe média" ("Of the Political, Social, and Economic Importance of the Middle Class"), suggesting his abiding concern with the subject. R. Menezes 4: 1180; *Enciclopédia* 2: 1243.

96. I have discovered no biographical information on Chaves.

97. Chaves, 61.

98. Ibid.,117–18.

99. Ibid., 120–22.

100. Lyra Filho, 237.

101. See T. Fonseca, 190; IBOPE 6; Lyra Filho, 101; Ribeiro, 71–72.

102. D. Silva, 38–39, 137.

103. Ibid., 60, 72, 75.

104. T. Fonseca, 191.

105. R. Sodré, 37.

106. The most prominent of these was Alecu Amoroso Lima. See his *Problema da burguezia*, *Mitos do nosso tempo*, and *O problema do trabalho*.

107. Chaves, 2.

108. Ibid., 1.

109. Ibid., 48.

110. Ibid., 78.

111. Veríssimo, *The Rest Is Silence*, 69, 79, 193–94, 229, 299, 336, 375, 408, 481, 484.

112. Ibid., 193, 408.

113. Ibid., 69, 484.

114. Dupré, *Dona Lola*, 59–60.

115. Veríssimo, *The Rest Is Silence*, 450–51, 462–65.

116. Ibid., 484.

117. Sra. Dupré does not appear to have been merely idiosyncratic. Her success produced epigones, who, according to one student of the matter, wrote for middle-class readers. Z. Cardoso, 107–8.

118. See S. Graham, 3–9; Matta, *A casa*, 13–70.

119. Jamison, 76.

120. Serrano, *Noções*, 249.

121. Serrano, *Minha casa*, 149.

122. R. Sodré, 20.

123. Lyra Filho, 211, 237.

124. In this regard the best measure of how the book was received are the reviews that appeared in the Brazilian press between *Casa grande*'s publication in 1933 and the mid-1940s. E. Fonseca. See R. Araújo, *Guerra*; Needell, "Identity."

125. See Wahrman, 377–408

Chapter 10

1. Mailer, 177.

2. "Síntese da pesquisa de âmbito nacional sôbre a situação das classes médias," attached to R. Sodré, "Em defesa," 32. The survey involved hundreds of interviews and 2,000 questionnaires. Unfortunately the raw data from the survey are not available. The nature of middle-class life in smaller cities away from the Rio–São Paulo hub remains unexplored.

3. The most specific complaint along these lines was the deficiencies of secon-

dary and university education in the various states. No doubt close investigation of each region would reveal important particularities. In some places, for instance, patronage may have been more important than in Rio and São Paulo. Nevertheless, the broad interplay of market and patronage imperatives appears to have been common to virtually all of urban Brazil by 1950. See, e.g., Dain Borges. Without further research into regional variations, it is difficult to generalize about the details of politics. The 1949–50 survey suggests that the frustration with politics was widespread around the country.

4. "A crise ministerial e a nova política do Sr. Getúlio Vargas," *Cadernos do nosso tempo,* no. 1 (May 1953): 98.

5. "Situação política brasileira" and "O moralismo e a alienação das classes médias," *Cadernos do nosso tempo,* no. 2 (Jan.–Jun. 1954): 103–20, 150–59. See also "Os tanques da democracia," *O Cruzeiro* 22:20 (Jul. 1, 1950): 17; Maria Eugenia Celso, "A última arrancada," *O Cruzeiro* 18:6 (Dec. 1, 1945): 1; "O grande soldado," *Vida Carioca* 25:211 (Jun. 1945); "O bom militarismo," *Vida Carioca* 24:201 (Jul. 1944); Homero de Castro Jobim, "O melhor meio de servir à patria," *Diretrizes* 5:133 (Jun. 14, 1943): 2; "Um grande soldado," *Vida Carioca* 21:169 (May 1941); Col. Souza Decca, "As forças armadas na formação da nacionalidade," *Diretrizes* 2:18 (Aug. 1939): 45–46; "A vocação pacificadora do Exército Nacional," *Vida Doméstica* 12:124 (Apr. 1931).

6. Zweig.

7. This is where my argument converges with an older critique of modernization, which severed the presumed link between modernization and democratic processes. See, e.g., O'Donnell.

8. There are some important exceptions. See Braun; French, *The Brazilian Workers' ABC*; James; Steve Stein; Weinstein, *For Social Peace.*

9. For a theoretical perspective on this issue, see Laclau.

10. See Hirschman, *Shifting Involvements.*

11. These observations beg as many questions as they answer. If work and home were central aspects of middle-class experience, a more fine-grained sense of relationships between men and women in both spheres is indispensable. Perhaps in this way we might find new ways of approaching the unstable boundaries between public and private, personal and political. If middle-class men served as intermediaries of a political system they did not control, only a closer examination of those who played the role of internuncio between the people and the institutions of formal politics and statecraft can reveal the relationship between political engagement and the politics of the apolitical and their connection to the practice of populism. If some joined smaller political parties, we need to know more about how and why they did so. If morality was one of the suns around which middle-class social life revolved, the force of religion in mediating everyday life and politics, perhaps especially in the lives of women, must be more finely calibrated. If egalitarian and hierarchical imperatives both ran through middle-class lives, their effect on quotidian relations with people of other classes remains to be more fully exposed. If patriotism was expressed in the everyday practice of technical competence and domesticity, its link to nationalism more broadly un-

derstood must be clarified. If racial difference set the middle class off from those below, the tortuous paths that led to the myth of racial democracy must be found and cleared. And if São Paulo and Rio de Janeiro are indispensable to understanding an emergent middle class, that understanding can be only partial without a keen eye to other areas of Brazil's geographic and social vastness.

As the breadth of these questions indicates, there can be no one approach to the middle class. Studies like this one which focus on the middle class at a fairly high level of generality must take their place alongside studies of individual occupational groups or associations or government offices or of towns, neighborhoods, or even individual households and families. There can only be a collage, not a portrait.

12. Wirth, 171–73.

13. O. Ferreira, 122–29.

14. *Correio da Manhã*, May 4, 1954, quoted in Skidmore, *Politics*, 134.

15. Dantas, 145.

16. Dupré, *Dona Lola*, 140.

17. Bernardet.

18. Antonio Zago, "O que será da classe média," *Folha de São Paulo*, 10 Jun. 1979.

19. See the following articles from *Jornal da Tarde*: Leôncio Martins Rodrigues, "Existem as classes médias," and José Jobson de Andrade Arruda, "Uma história difícil: a classe média no Brasil," 25 Apr. 1981; José Pastore, "O laberinto da classe média," 26 Sept. 1981.

20. "Crise na cabeça: A classe média no divã," *Manchete*, Feb. 8, 1992, 68–73; Waldemar Zusman, "A dança das classes," *Idéias—Ensaios, Jornal do Brasil*, 8 Mar. 1992, 4–6; Luciano Peluso and Simone Goldberg, "Heróis da sobrevivência," *Isto É*, Jul. 12, 1995, 124–29.

21. Paz, 43, 52.

22. See Berman, 232.

23. O. Andrade, "Anthropophagite Manifesto."

24. The tenor of Andrade's concern for the ambiguities of modernity anticipate critiques that have been raised more recently in a variety of contexts. See Berman; Canclini; Unger. I am grateful to Gildo Brandão and Luís Soares for the conversation that brought Andrade to mind in this context.

25. M. Andrade, 54–57. Andrade noted in his "Extremely Interesting Preface" to this volume of poetry that he could not "represent a modern orientation which as yet he himself does not totally comprehend" (5).

26. Tournier, 184.

References

Libraries, Archives, and Organizations

Arquivo Edgard Leuenroth, Universidade de São Paulo, Campinas, São Paulo
    Arquivo do Instituto Brasileiro de Opinião Pública e Estatística (IBOPE)
Arquivo Geral, Universidade Federal Fluminense, Escola de Serviço Social do
    Estado do Rio de Janeiro (ESSERJ)
Arquivo do Instituto de Direito Social, São Paulo
Arquivo Nacional, Rio de Janeiro (AN)
    Ministério da Justiça e Negócios Interiores (MJ)
    Ministério de Educação e Saúde
    Secretaria da Presidência da República
    Tribunal de Segurança Nacional (TSN)
Arquivo do Serviço Social da Indústria, São Paulo
Associação Brasileira da Imprensa, Rio de Janeiro
Associação dos Empregados no Comércio, Rio de Janeiro
Biblioteca, Fundação Getúlio Vargas, Rio de Janeiro
Biblioteca Municipal, São Paulo
Biblioteca Nacional, Rio de Janeiro
Centro de Pesquisa e Documentação, Fundação Getúlio Vargas, Rio de Janeiro
    (CPDOC)
    Arquivo Osvaldo Aranha (AOA)
    Arquivo Pedro Ernesto Batista (APEB)
    Arquivo Gustavo Capanema (AGC)
    Arquivo Lindolfo Collor (ALC)
    Arquivo Marcondes Filho (AMF)
    Arquivo Getúlio Vargas (AGV)
    Projeto de História Oral
Club de Engenharia, Rio de Janeiro
Club Militar, Rio de Janeiro
Confederação Nacional da Indústria, Rio de Janeiro
Firestone Library, Princeton University, Princeton, New Jersey

Library of Congress, Washington, D.C.
Mudd Library, Yale University, New Haven, Connecticut
Ordem dos Advogados Brasileiros, Rio de Janeiro and São Paulo
Sindicato dos Bancários, Rio de Janeiro
Sindicato dos Comerciários de São Paulo, São Paulo
Sindicato do Empregado no Comércio do Rio de Janeiro, Rio de Janeiro
Sindicato dos Engenheiros, Rio de Janeiro
Sindicato dos Jornalistas Profissionais, Rio de Janeiro and São Paulo
Sindicato Médico Brasileiro, Rio de Janeiro
Sterling Memorial Library, Yale University, New Haven, Connecticut

Sources Cited

Adams, Richard N. *The Second Sowing: Power and Secondary Development in Latin America*. San Francisco: Chandler, 1967.

O Advogado—Mensário dos interesses da classe. São Paulo.

AEC (Órgão da Associação dos Empregados no Comércio do Rio de Janeiro). Rio de Janeiro.

Alba, Victor. *Alliance Without Allies: The Mythology of Progress in Latin America*. New York: Praeger, 1965.

Albert, William. *South America and the First World War: The Impact of the War on Brazil, Argentina, Peru, and Chile*. Cambridge: Cambridge University Press, 1988.

Alessio, Nancy. "Urbanização, industrialização e estrutura ocupacional (1872–1920)." *Dados* 7 (1970): 103–17.

Almeida, Martins de. *Brasil errado*. Rio de Janeiro: Schmidt, 1932.

Alvim, Zuleika, and Solange Peirão. *Mappin: Setenta anos*. São Paulo: Ex Libris, 1985.

Amado, Gilberto. "As instituições políticas e o meio social no Brasil." In *À margem da história da República (idéias, crenças, e affirmações): Inquérito por escritores da geração nascida com a República*. Rio de Janeiro: Anuário do Brasil, 1924, 57–78.

———. *Eleição e representação*. Rio de Janeiro: Pongetti, 1946.

Amado, Jorge. *O cavaleiro da esperança: Vida de Luís Carlos Prestes*. Rio de Janeiro: Record, 1981.

Anais. Primeiro Congresso Brasileiro de Economia. Nov. 25–Dec. 18, 1943. Vol. 1 (1943); vol. 2 (1944). Rio de Janeiro.

Andrade, Mário de. *Hallucinated City—Paulicea Desvairada*. Kingsport, Tenn.: Vanderbilt University Press, 1968.

Andrade, Oswald de. "Anthropophagite Manifesto." In Dawn Ades, ed., *Art in Latin America: The Modern Era, 1820–1980*. New Haven: Yale University Press, 1989, 312–13.

———. *Marco zero, II—Chão*. Rio de Janeiro: José Olympio, 1945.

Andrade Sobrinho, José Moacir de. "Composição do vencimento e níveis da remuneração do funcionário público." *Revista do Serviço Público* 4, no. 1 (Feb. 1941): 5–51.

Andrews, George Reid. *Black and White in São Paulo, Brazil, 1888–1988.* Madison: University of Wisconsin Press, 1991.

Anjos, Cyro dos. *Diary of a Civil Servant.* London: Fairleigh Dickinson University Press, 1988.

Antunes, Ricardo. *Classe operária, sindicatos, e partido no Brasil: Da Revolução de 30 até a Aliança Nacional Libertadora.* São Paulo: Cortez, 1988.

Anuário do Colégio D. Pedro II, 1937–1938. Rio de Janeiro, 1938.

Anuário do Syndicato Central de Engenheiros. Rio de Janeiro, 1932–33, 1933–34, 1934–35, 1938.

Anuário do Syndicato Nacional de Engenheiros. Rio de Janeiro.

Aranha, J. P. da Graça. *Chanaan.* Rio de Janeiro: Briguiet, 1943.

Araújo, Oscar Egídio de. "A alimentação da classe obreira em São Paulo." *Revista do Arquivo Municipal de São Paulo* 69 (Aug. 1940): 91–113.

Araújo, Ricardo Benzaquen de. *Guerra e paz: Casa-Grande & Senzala e a obra do Gilberto Freyre nos anos 30.* Rio de Janeiro: Ed. 34, 1994.

———. *Totalitarismo e revolução: O integralismo de Plínio Salgado.* Rio de Janeiro: Zahar, 1987.

Associação dos Empregados no Comércio do Rio de Janeiro: *Um século, 1880–1980.* Rio de Janeiro, 1980.

Associação dos Funcionários Públicos do Estado de São Paulo. "Do funcionário público." *Primeiro Congresso Nacional dos Servidores Públicos.* Rio de Janeiro, 1946.

———. "Vantagens e serviços que a AFPESP oferece aos seus associados e famílias." São Paulo, 1940.

Azevedo, Fernando de. *A cultura brasileira.* São Paulo: Nacional, 1944.

Azzi, Riolando. "Família e valores no pensamento brasileiro (1870–1950). Um enfoque histórico." In Ivete Ribeiro, ed., *Família e valores: Sociedade brasileira contemporânea.* São Paulo: Loyola, 1987, 85–120.

Backhauser, Everardo. *O professor: Ensinar é um prazer.* Rio de Janeiro: Agir, 1946.

Baer, Werner. *The Brazilian Economy: Growth and Development.* New York: Praeger, 1983.

Bailly, Gustavo Adolpho. *Manual do funcionário público.* Rio de Janeiro: A. Coelho Branco, 1938.

———. *Pontos de concurso para escriturário.* Rio de Janeiro, 1940.

———. *Pontos de concurso para oficial administrativo.* Rio de Janeiro, 1940.

Bakota, Carlos. "Nationalism and the Crisis of the Middle Classes in Brazil, 1914–1922." Ph.D. diss., UCLA, 1973.

Bancário (Órgão do Sindicato Brasileiro de Bancários). Rio de Janeiro.

Bandeira, Armando C. "O médico precisa ser amparado." *Quarto congresso de sindicalismo médico.* Rio de Janeiro, 1944.

Barbosa, Rui. "A crise moral." In *Ruínas de um governo.* Rio de Janeiro: Guanabara, 1931, 133–88.

———. *Obras completas.* Vol. 46, pt. 1. Rio de Janeiro: Ministério de Educação e Saúde, 1942.

Barros, Maciel de, ed. *Obras filosóficas de Luís Pereira Barreto*. Vol. 1. São Paulo: Grijalbo, 1967.

Basbaum, Leôncio. *Uma vida em seis tempos*. São Paulo: Alga Omega, 1976.

Bastide, Roger. *Sociologie du Brésil*. Paris: Université de Paris, 1951.

Bastos, Humberto. "Progresso técnico e padrão de vida." *O Brasil no após-guerra*. São Paulo: IDORT, 1944.

Bastos, Tavares. *Os males do presente e as esperanças do futuro*. São Paulo: Nacional, 1939, originally published in 1861.

Bauser, Profa. Riva. Interview with author, Rio de Janeiro, Feb. 14, 1992.

Beals, Ralph. "Social Stratification in Latin America." *American Journal of Sociology* 58, no. 4 (Jan. 1953): 327–39.

Benevides, Maria Victoria de Mesquita. *A UDN e o udenismo: Ambigüedades do liberalismo brasileiro (1945–1964)*. Rio de Janeiro: Paz e Terra, 1981.

Bergquist, Charles. *Labor in Latin America: Comparative Essays on Chile, Argentina, Venezuela, and Colombia*. Stanford, Calif.: Stanford University Press, 1986.

Berman, Marshall. *All That Is Solid Melts into Air: The Experience of Modernity*. New York: Penguin, 1982.

Bernardet, Jean-Claude. *Brasil em tempo de cinema: Ensaio sôbre o cinema brasileiro de 1958 a 1966*. Rio de Janeiro: Civilização Brasileira, 1967.

Besse, Susan. "Freedom and Bondage: The Impact of Capitalism on Women in São Paulo, Brazil, 1917–1937." Ph.D. diss., Yale University, 1983.

———. *Restructuring Patriarchy: The Modernization of Gender Inequality in Brazil, 1914–1940*. Chapel Hill: University of North Carolina Press, 1996.

Bittencourt, Circe Maria F. *Pátria, civilização e trabalho: O ensino de história nas escolas paulistas (1917–1937)*. São Paulo: Ed. Loyola, 1990.

Blackbourn, David. "Between Resignation and Volatility: The German Petite Bourgeoisie in the Nineteenth Century." In G. Crosswick & H. Haupt, eds., *Shopkeepers and Master Artisans in Nineteenth-Century Europe*. London: Methuen, 1984, 35–61.

Boletim da Associação dos Empregados no Comércio. Rio de Janeiro.

Boletim da Associação de Professores Católicos. Rio de Janeiro.

Boletim do Centro dos Professores da 5a CEE (Rio de Janeiro). Rio de Janeiro.

Boletim do Ministério de Trabalho, Indústria, e Comércio. Rio de Janeiro.

Boletim da Ordem dos Advogados Brasileiros—Seção de São Paulo. São Paulo.

Boletim, Sindicato dos Engenheiros do Rio de Janeiro. Rio de Janeiro.

Boletim do Sindicato Médico Brasileiro. Rio de Janeiro.

Boletim do Sindicato dos Professores de Ensino Secundário e Primário de São Paulo. São Paulo.

Boletim do Sindicato dos Professores de Ensino Secundário, Primário e de Artes do Rio de Janeiro. Rio de Janeiro.

Bomilcar, Alvaro. *A política no Brasil ou o nacionalismo radical*. Rio de Janeiro: Leite, Ribero & Maurillo, 1920.

Borges, Dain. *The Family in Bahia, Brazil, 1870–1945*. Stanford, Calif.: Stanford University Press, 1992.

Borges, Durval Rosa. *Estudos sobre sífilis—com especial referência à classe média paulistana.* Rio de Janeiro, 1941.

Bosi, Ecléa. *Memória e sociedade: Lembranças de velhos.* São Paulo: Universidade de São Paulo, 1987.

Bourdieu, Pierre. *Language & Symbolic Power.* J. Thompson, ed. Cambridge: Cambridge University Press, 1991.

Brandão, Otávio. *Agrarismo e industrismo (ensaio marxista-leninista sobre a revolta de São Paulo e a guerra de classes no Brasil).* Rio de Janeiro: n.p., 1926.

Braun, Herbert. *The Assassination of Gaitán: Public Life and Urban Violence in Colombia.* Madison: University of Wisconsin Press, 1985.

Brescia, Dra. Maria de Lourdes Ribeiro. Interview with author, São Paulo, Aug. 9, 1995.

Burns, E. Bradford. *A History of Brazil.* New York: Columbia University Press, 1980.

Cadernos do Nosso Tempo. Rio de Janeiro.

Calazans, João. *Pequeno burgûes.* Rio de Janeiro: José Olympio, 1952.

"As camadas médias brasileiras em face do momento nacional." AGV 40.01.15, xxxiii–17.

Camargo, José Francisco de. *Crescimento da população no estado de São Paulo e seus aspectos econômicos.* Vol. 3. São Paulo: J. Magalhães, 1952.

Canclini, Néstor García. *Hybrid Cultures: Strategies for Entering and Exiting Modernity.* Minneapolis: University of Minnesota Press, 1995.

Canêdo, Letícia Bicalho. *Bancários: Movimento sindical e participação.* Campinas, São Paulo: Universidade de Campinas, 1988.

———. *O sindicalismo bancário em São Paulo—No período de 1923–1944: Seu significado político.* São Paulo: Símbolo, 1978.

Cardoso, Edmundo. *Uma loja, uma vida.* Rio de Janeiro: n.p., 1974.

Cardoso, Fernando Henrique, and Enzo Faletto. *Dependency and Development in Latin America.* Berkeley: University of California Press, 1979.

Cardoso, Zélia. *O romance paulista no século XX.* São Paulo: Academia Paulista de Letras, 1983.

Carelli, Mario. *Carcamanos e comendadores—Os italianos de São Paulo: Da realidade à ficção (1919–1930).* São Paulo: Ática, 1985.

Carnegie, Dale. *Como fazer amigos e influenciar pessôas.* F. Souza, trans. São Paulo: Nacional, 1939.

Carneiro, Levi. *O livro de um advogado.* Rio de Janeiro: A. Coelho Branco, 1943.

Carone, Edgard. "Coleção azul: Crítica pequeno-burguesa à crise brasileira depois de 1930." *Revista Brasileira de Estudos Políticos* 25–26 (Jul. 1968–Jan. 1969): 249–95.

———. *A Quarta República.* São Paulo: DIFEL, 1979.

———. *A Terceira República (1937–1945).* São Paulo: DIFEL, 1976.

Carvalho, Delgado de. *Organização social e política brasileira.* Rio de Janeiro: Record, 1967.

Carvalho, J. A. de. *Cargos de direção no direito do trabalho.* Rio de Janeiro: Jornal do Comércio, 1949.

Carvalho, Jader de. *Classe média.* Recife: Reunidas, 1937.

Carvalho, José Murilo de. *Os bestializados: O Rio de Janeiro e a república que não foi.* São Paulo: Cia. das Letras, 1989.

Carvalho Neto, Antônio Manuel de. *Advogados—como aprendemos, como sofremos, como vivemos.* São Paulo: Saraiva, 1946.

A Casa—Órgão Oficial da Associação dos Construtores Civis do Rio de Janeiro. Rio de Janeiro.

Castellano, Dr. José Feliciano. Interview with author, São Paulo, Aug. 10, 1995.

Census 1890. Directoria Geral de Estatística. *Recenseamento geral da República dos Estados Unidos do Brasil em 31 de dezembro de 1890: Districto Federal (cidade de Rio de Janeiro).* Rio de Janeiro: Leuzinger, 1895.

Census 1920. Brasil Ministério de Agricultura, Indústria, e Comércio. Directoria Geral de Estatística. *Recenseamento do Brasil realizado em 1 de setembro de 1920.* Vol. 2, parts 1–2; vol. 4, parts 1, 4–5; synopse do recenseamento. Rio de Janeiro, 1922.

Census 1940. IBGE. *Recenseamento geral do Brasil (1 setembro de 1940).* Tomo 3 (1950); tomo 15 (1951); tomo 16 (1951); vol. 17, parts 1–3 (1950). Rio de Janeiro.

Census 1950. Brasil Serviço Nacional de Recenseamento, IBGE. *VI recenseamento do Brasil, 1950.* Vol. 1 (1956); vol. 3, part 2 (1957); vol. 4 (1958); vol. 23, tomo 1 (1955); vol. 24, tomos 1–2 (1955–56); vol. 25 tomos 1–3 (1954–55). Rio de Janeiro.

Centro dos Industriais de Fiação e Tecelagem de Algodão. *Relatório de directoria.* Rio de Janeiro: n.p., 1933.

Certeau, Michel de. *The Practice of Everyday Life.* Berkeley: University of California Press, 1984.

Cerutti, Mario. *Burguesía y capitalismo en Monterrey, 1850–1910.* Mexico: Claves Latinoamericanas, 1989.

Chacon, Vamireh. *História dos partidos brasileiros.* Brasília: Ed. Universidade de Brasília, 1981.

Chaffee, Jr., Wilber. "The Cartorial State: A Study of the Growth of the Brazilian Middle Class." *Revista/Review Interamericana* 1, no. 2 (winter 1972): 116–23.

Chaloub, Sydney. *Trabalho, lar e botequim: O cotidiano dos trabalhadores no Rio de Janeiro da 'Belle Époque.'* São Paulo: Brasiliense, 1986.

Chauí, Marilena. "Apontamentos para uma crítica da Ação Integralista Brasileira." In *Ideologia e mobilização popular.* Rio de Janeiro: Paz e Terra, 1985, 17–117.

Chaves, Hélio. *Uma família burguesa.* Petrópolis, Rio de Janeiro, 1952.

Chilcote, Ronald. *The Brazilian Communist Party: Conflict and Integration, 1922–1972.* Oxford: Oxford University Press, 1974.

Coelho, Ricardo B. M. "O Sindicato dos Professores e os estabelecimentos particulares de ensino no Rio de Janeiro, 1931–1950." Master's thesis, UFF, Niterói, 1988.

Collado, María del Carmen. *La burguesía mexicana: El emporio Braniff y su participación política, 1865–1920.* México: Siglo XXI, 1987.

Conniff, Michael. "The Tenentes in Power: A New Perspective on the Brazilian Revolution of 1930." *Journal of Latin American Studies* 10, no. 1 (May 1978): 61–82.

———. *Urban Politics in Brazil: The Rise of Populism, 1925–1945.* Pittsburgh: University of Pittsburgh Press, 1981.

———. "Voluntary Associations in Rio, 1870–1945: A New Approach to Urban Social Dynamics." *Journal of Interamerican Studies and World Affairs* 17, no. 1 (Feb. 1975): 64–81.

O Contabilista—Revista Mensal Illustrada. Rio de Janeiro.

Contla, Calixto Rangel. *La pequeña burguesía en la sociedad mexicana, 1895 a 1960.* México: Universidad Nacional Autónoma de México, 1972.

Correio da Manhã. Rio de Janeiro.

Cortés, C. *Homens e instituições no Rio de Janeiro.* Rio de Janeiro, 1957.

Costa, Antônio Côrrea de Sousa. *Qual a alimentação de que vive a classe pobre do Rio de Janeiro e a sua influência sôbre a mesma classe.* Rio de Janeiro, 1865.

Costa, Emília Viotti da. *The Brazilian Empire: Myths and Histories.* Chicago: University of Chicago Press, 1985.

Coutinho, A., and J. Souza, eds. *Enciclopédia da literatura brasileira.* 2 vols. Rio de Janeiro: Fundação de Assistência ao Estudante, 1990.

Covarrubias, Jaime García. *El Partido Radical y la clase media en Chile: La relación de intereses entre 1888–1938.* Santiago: Ed. Andrés Bello, 1990.

Criança—Revista para os pais. Rio de Janeiro.

O Cruzeiro. Rio de Janeiro.

Cunha, Euclides da. *Rebellion in the Backlands.* Chicago: University of Chicago Press, 1944.

Cunha, Mario Wagner Vieira da. "A burocratização das empresas industriais." Tenure essay for Professorship in administrative sciences and industrial structure. Faculdade de Ciências Econômicas e Administrativas, Universidade de São Paulo, 1951.

Curso de Educadores Sociais. "Pontos para os exames 'escrito e oral' da cadeira de política social (Nov. 1947)." São Paulo: Arquivo do Instituto de Direito Social, 1947.

Dantas, Macedo. *João classe média.* São Paulo: Nacional, 1959.

D'Araújo, Maria Cecília Soares. *O segundo governo Vargas, 1951–1954: Democracia, partido, e política.* Rio de Janeiro: Zahar, 1982.

Dealy, Glenn Caudill. *The Latin Americans: Spirit & Ethos.* San Francisco: Westview Press, 1992.

Dean, Warren. *The Industrialization of São Paulo, 1880–1945.* Austin: University of Texas Press, 1969.

———. *Rio Claro: A Brazilian Plantation System, 1820–1920.* Stanford, Calif.: Stanford University Press, 1976.

A Defesa Nacional. Rio de Janeiro.

Dicionário histórico-biográfico brasileiro, 1930–1983. I. Beloch and A. de Abreu, eds. Rio de Janeiro: Ed. Forense Universitária, 1984.

Diretrizes. Rio de Janeiro.

Documentário do Primeiro Congresso Nacional dos Diretores de Estabelecimentos de Ensino Secundário e Comercial. Rio de Janeiro, 1944.

A Dona de Casa. SESI. Divisão de Assistência Social. São Paulo.

Donghi, Tulio Halperín. *The Contemporary History of Latin America*. Durham, N.C.: Duke University Press, 1993.

Dôria, Alvaro. "O médico fora da profissão." In *Anais do Congresso Brasileiro dos Problemas Médico-sociais do Após-guerra*, Bahia, Jul. 1945, 232–40.

Dupré, Maria José Fleury Monteiro. *Dona Lola*. 5th ed. São Paulo: Brasiliense, 1958.

———. *Eramos seis*. São Paulo: Cia. Ed. Nacional, 1943.

Durham, Eunice Ribeiro. *Assimilação e mobilidade: A história do imigrante italiano num município paulista*. São Paulo: Instituto de Estudos Brasileiros, 1966.

Eakin, Marshall. "Race and Identity: Sílvio Romero, Science, and Social Thought in Late 19th-Century Brazil." *Luso-Brazilian Review* 22, no. 2 (winter 1985): 151–74.

Educação—Revista da Associação Brasileira de Educação. Rio de Janeiro (successor to *Boletim da AEB* and *Schola*).

Eliade, Mircea. *Myths, Dreams, and Mysteries: The Encounter Between Contemporary Faiths and Archaic Realities*. New York: Harper & Row, 1960.

Elliot, Lilian. *Brazil—Today and Tomorrow*. New York: Macmillan, 1917.

Engenharia (Instituto de Engenharia, São Paulo). São Paulo.

O Ensino—Órgão Oficial do Instituto dos Professores Públicos e Particulares. Rio de Janeiro.

Erickson, Kenneth. *The Brazilian Corporative State and Working-Class Politics*. Berkeley: University of California Press, 1977.

O Estado de São Paulo. São Paulo.

Falcão, João. *O partido comunista que eu conheci (20 anos de clandestinidade)*. Rio de Janeiro: Civilização Brasileira, 1988.

Faría, Alvaro de. "O papel do Sindicato dos Médicos." In *Anais do Congresso Brasileiro dos Problemas Médico-sociais de Após-guerra*. Bahia, Jul. 1945, 144–50.

Faría, Hugo. Interview transcript, CPDOC, Projeto de História Oral, transcript no. E–67.

Faro, Stela de. "Recrutamento e formação de quadros." *Primeira Semana de Ação Social*. Rio de Janeiro, Sept. 16–29, 1936.

Fausto, Boris. *A Revolução de 30: História e historiografia*. São Paulo: Brasiliense, 1970.

———. *Trabalho urbano e conflito social (1890–1920)*. São Paulo: DIFEL, 1976.

Fávero, Flamínio. "A organização da classe médica." In *Anais do Congresso Brasileiro dos Problemas Médico-Sociais de Após-guerra*. Bahia, Jul. 1945, 132–43.

Fernandes, Ary de Castro. "O rendimento no trabalho e o Serviço de Assistência Social." Thesis pursuant to concurso for Técnico de Administração, 1941.

Fernandes, Florestán. *A revolução burguesa no Brasil*. Rio de Janeiro: Zahar, 1976.

Fernandes, Florestán, and Roger Bastide. *Brancos e negros em São Paulo*. São Paulo: Nacional, 1959.

Ferreira, Jorge Luiz. "Trabalhadores de Brasil—A cultura política popular no primeiro governo Vargas (1930–1945)." Master's thesis, UFF, Niterói, 1988.

Ferreira, Oliveiros S. *As forças armadas e o desafio da revolução*. Rio de Janeiro: Ed. GRD, 1964.

Fiorentino, Teresinha A. del. *Prosa e ficção em São Paulo: Produção e consumo*. São Paulo: Hucitec, 1982.

Fischer, Almeida. "Suspeita." In *O homem de duas cabeças: Contos*. Brasília: Ed. Brasília, 1971, 89–94.

Fonseca, Edson Nery da. *'Casa-grande e senzala' e a crítica brasileira de 1933 a 1944*. Recife: Ed. Pernambuco, 1985.

Fonseca, Pedro Cezar Dutra. *Vargas: O Capitalismo em construção*. São Paulo: Brasiliense, 1987.

Fonseca, Tito Prates da. "Sentido e valor das classes medias." *Quarta semana de ação social de São Paulo: Conferências, discursos, conclusões votadas*. Rio de Janeiro: Imprensa Nacional, 1942, 187–93.

Fonseca, Victor Marques da. "A ANL na legalidade." Master's thesis, UFF, Niterói, 1986.

Font, Maurício. *Coffee, Contention, and Change in the Making of Modern Brazil*. London: Blackwell, 1990.

Fountoura, Amaral. *Introdução ao serviço social*. Rio de Janeiro: n.p., 1950.

Forjaz, Maria Célia Spina. *Tenentismo e Aliança Liberal (1927–1930)*. São Paulo: Polis, 1978.

———. *Tenentismo e política: Tenentismo e camadas médias urbanas na crise da Primeira República*. Rio de Janeiro: Paz e Terra, 1977.

Franco, Afonso Arino de Melo. *Introdução à realidade brasileira*. Rio de Janeiro: Schmidt, 1933.

Freitas, Byron T. *Administração de pessoal (serviço público, indústria e comércio)*. Rio de Janeiro: n.p., 1945.

Freitas, Madeiras de. "O movimento do sigma." In *Enciclopedia do integralismo—estudos e depoimentos*. Vol. 2. Rio de Janeiro: Clássica Brasileira, n.d., 151–89.

French, John. *Brazilian Workers' ABC: Class Conflict and Alliances in Modern São Paulo*. Chapel Hill: University of North Carolina Press, 1992.

———. "Workers and the Rise of Adhemarista Populism in São Paulo, Brazil, 1945–47." *Hispanic American Historical Review* 68, no. 1 (1988): 1–42.

Freyre, Gilberto. *The Mansions and the Shanties: The Making of Modern Brazil*. Los Angeles: University of California Press, 1986.

———. "Social Life in Brazil in the Middle of the 19th Century." *Hispanic American Historical Review* 5, no. 4 (Nov. 1922): 593–609.

O Funcionário—Defensor dos Funcionários Públicos e Autárquicos. Rio de Janeiro.

Galvão, Patricia. *Industrial Park: A Proletarian Novel*. Lincoln: University of Nebraska Press, 1995.

Galvêas, Ernane. Interview transcript, CPDOC, Projeto de História Oral, transcript no. E-108.

Gans, Herbert. *Middle-American Individualism: Political Participation and Liberal Democracy*. Oxford: Oxford University Press, 1991.

García, Antonio. "Las clases medias en América Latina: Hacia una teoría de la ambigüedad social." *Cuadernos Americanos* 27, no. 140 (Sept.–Oct. 1968): 122–27.

Giddens, Anthony. *The Class Structure of Advanced Societies*. New York: Barnes & Noble, 1973.

Gomes, Eduardo. *Campanha de libertação*. São Paulo, 1946.

Gonzaga, Sergius. *Manual de literatura brasileira*. Porto Alegre: Ed. Mercado Aberto, 1989.

Gorender, Jacob. *A burguesia brasileira*. São Paulo: Brasiliense, 1981.

Graham, Lawrence. *Civil Service Reform in Brazil: Principle versus Practice*. Austin: University of Texas Press, 1968.

Graham, Richard. *Britain and the Onset of Modernization in Brazil, 1850–1914*. Cambridge: Cambridge University Press, 1968.

———. "The Onset of Modernization in Brazil." In Raymond S. Sayers, ed., *Portugal and Brazil in Transition*. Minneapolis: University of Minnesota Press, 1968, 110–23.

———. *Patronage and Politics in Nineteenth-Century Brazil*. Stanford, Calif.: Stanford University Press, 1990.

Graham, Sandra Lauderdale. *House and Street: The Domestic World of Servants and Masters in Nineteenth-Century Rio de Janeiro*. Austin: University of Texas Press, 1988.

Greenfield, Gerald. "Patterns of Enterprise in São Paulo: A Preliminary Analysis of a Late-Nineteenth Century City." *Social Sciences History* 8, no. 3 (summer 1984): 291–312.

Guimarães, Arthur. *Problemas brasileiros*. Lisbon: A Editora, 1911.

Guimarães, Manuel Luís Lima Salgado, et al., eds. *A Revolução de 30: Textos e documentos*. Vol. 1. Brasília: Universidade de Brasília, 1981.

Hahner, June. *Emancipating the Female Sex: The Struggle for Women's Rights in Brazil, 1850–1940*. Durham, N.C.: Duke University Press, 1990.

———. "Jacobinos versus Galegos: Urban Radicals versus Portuguese Immigrants in Rio de Janeiro in the 1890s." *Journal of Interamerican Studies and World Affairs* 18, no. 2 (May 1976): 125–54.

———. *Poverty and Politics: The Urban Poor in Brazil, 1870–1920*. Albuquerque: University of New Mexico Press, 1986.

———. "Women and Work in Brazil, 1850–1920: A Preliminary Investigation." In D. Alden and W. Dean, eds., *Essays Concerning the Socioeconomic History of Brazil and Portuguese India*. Gainesville: University Presses of Florida, 1977.

Hallewell, Laurence. *O livro no Brasil (sua história)*. São Paulo: Queiroz, 1985.

Hardman, Francisco Foot, and Victor Leonardi. *História de indústria e do trabalho no Brasil (das origens aos anos 20)*. São Paulo: Ática, 1991.

Harrison, Lawrence. *Underdevelopment Is a State of Mind: The Latin American Case*. Lanham, Md.: Madison Books, 1985.

Henriques, Afonso. *Ascensão e queda de Getúlio Vargas*. Rio de Janeiro: Record, 1966.

Hermann, Lucila. *Evolução da estrutura social de Guaratinguetá num período de trezentos anos*. São Paulo: Instituto de Pesquisa Econômica, USP, 1986.

Hernandez, Leila M. G. *A Aliança Nacional Libertadora: Ideologia e ação*. Porto Alegre: Mercado Aberto, 1985.

Hess, David, and Roberto Da Matta, eds. *The Brazilian Puzzle: Culture on the Borderlands of the Western World*. New York: Columbia University Press, 1995.

Hirschman, Albert O. *Rival Views of Market Society and Other Recent Essays*. New York: Viking, 1986.

———. *Shifting Involvements: Private Interest and Public Action*. Princeton: Princeton University Press, 1982.

Holanda, Sérgio Buarque de. *Raízes do Brasil*. Rio de Janeiro: José Olympio, 1969.

Holloway, Thomas. *Immigrants on the Land: Coffee and Society in São Paulo, 1886–1934*. Chapel Hill: University of North Carolina Press, 1980.

Hons, André de Seguin des. *Le Brésil: Presse et histoire, 1930–1985*. Paris: L'Harmattan, 1985.

Humphrey, Hubert H., Sen. "Alliance for Progress—A Firsthand Report from Latin America." *The 1962–63 Sidney Hillman Lecture*. Minneapolis, 1963.

Hunt, Michael H. *Ideology and U.S. Foreign Policy*. New Haven: Yale University Press, 1987.

Hutchinson, Bertram. "Hierarquia de prestígio das ocupações segundo os estudantes universitários." *Educação e ciências sociais* 1, no. 2 (1956): 1–35.

———. *Mobilidade e trabalho*. Rio de Janeiro: Centro de Pesquisas Educacionais, 1960.

———. "Social Mobility Rates in Buenos Aires, Montevideo, and São Paulo: A Preliminary Comparison." *América Latina* 5, no. 4 (Oct.–Dec. 1962): 3–19.

Imperial, Gabriel Corte. *Trabalho por equipe na vida bancária*. Rio de Janeiro: n.p., 1951.

Instituto Brasileiro de Geografia e Estatística (IBGE). *O ensino no Brasil—1935*. Rio de Janeiro, 1936.

———. *O ensino no Brasil—1945*. Rio de Janeiro, 1946.

Instituto Brasileiro de Geografia e Estatística (IBGE). Serviço Nacional de Recenseamento. Gabinete Técnico. "Número de pessoas que declararam pertencer a sindicatos e sua distribuição segundo ramos de atividade, no Districto Federal." Vol. 14, no. 289. *Análises de resultados do censo demográfico de 1940*. Rio de Janeiro, 1946.

———. "Ocupação suplementar." Vol. 7, no. 368. *Análises de resultados do censo demográfico de 1940*. Rio de Janeiro, 1946

Instituto Brasileiro de Opinião Pública e Estatística (IBOPE).

    1. "Pesquisa para Grant Anúncio, S.A. Teste do anúncio 'É proibido a aproximação de extrangeiros' da Firestone." Rio de Janeiro and São Paulo, Oct. 1944.

2. "Estudo de mercado realizado no Rio de Janeiro e São Paulo por incumbência da GM." Rio de Janeiro and São Paulo, Nov. 1944.

3. "Estudo de mercado para Estabelecimentos Canadá." Rio de Janeiro and São Paulo, Dec. 1944.

4. Pesquisa de opinião pública sôbre preferências e conveniências do público da capital de São Paulo a respeito da propriedade e locação de imóveis para moradia, levada a efeito durante o mês de dezembro de 1945." Rio de Janeiro and São Paulo, Jan. 1995.

5. "Pesquisa levada a efeito no Distrito Federal, por solicitação dos Diários Associados, durante o mês de julho de 1945, com o objetivo de estudar a atitude do público em relação a jornais e revistas." Rio de Janeiro, Jul. 1945.

6. "Pesquisa de opinião pública realizada no Distrito Federal, durante o período nov.–dec. 1945, para 'O Observador Econômico,' com o objetivo de estudar a atitude do público em geral e das chamadas classes conservadoras, em face das perspectivas do ano 1946 para o Brasil." Rio de Janeiro, Nov.–Dec. 1945.

7. "Conceito de repartições públicas." Rio de Janeiro, Feb. 1946.

8. "Estudo de mercado para apurar a atitude das donas de casa das classes A e B, revendedores e emprezas importadoras, sôbre um novo tipo de escovão para assoalho, a pedido da Pan-American de Propaganda." São Paulo, Feb. 1946.

9. "Pesquisa de atitudes públicas e políticas realizada nesta capital no mês de março 1946." São Paulo, Mar. 1946.

10. "Pesquisa de opinião pública por incumbência de Panam Propaganda, Ltda., na capital de São Paulo e no Distrito Federal, durante o período de 5 a 12 março de 1946." São Paulo and Rio de Janeiro, Mar. 1946.

11. "Pesquisa sôbre padrão de vida levada a efeito na capital de São Paulo, durante o mês de julho 1946, por solicitação e suporte financeiro da Associação Comercial de São Paulo." São Paulo, Jul. 1946.

12. "Pesquisa sôbre alguns hábitos de leitura e poder aquisitivo dos leitores de jornais, levada a efeito no Distrito Federal, durante os meses de outubro e novembro de 1946." Rio de Janeiro, Oct.–Nov. 1946.

13. "Pesquisa sôbre preferências de revistas juvenís e policiais a pedido do Sucursal do Globo." São Paulo, Oct.–Nov. 1946.

14. "Pesquisa sôbre o poder aquisitivo dos leitores da revista 'O Cruzeiro,' levada a efeito no Distrito Federal a na capital de São Paulo, durante o mês de novembro 1946." Rio de Janeiro and São Paulo, Nov. 1946.

15. "Estudo sôbre as condições de vida do comerciário em São Paulo e Campinas—Estado de São Paulo levado a efeito pelo IBOPE durante o mês de julho de 1947, por incumbência de Serviço Social do Comércio-Regional de São Paulo." São Paulo, Jul. 1947.

16. "Habitos de alimentação, higiene e saúde, vida cultural e social dos comerciários." São Paulo, capital e interior, Jul. 1947.

17. "Pesquisa sôbre o desemprego levada a efeito em São Paulo, no mês de agosto de 1947, por incumbência da Associação Comercial de São Paulo." São Paulo, Aug. 1947.

18. "Survey performed at Rio de Janeiro and São Paulo, during the month of March 1948, by commission of the Reader's Digest." Rio de Janeiro and São Paulo, Mar. 1948.

19. "Pesquisa de opinião pública sôbre materia política realizada nesta capital, no mês de setembro de 1948." São Paulo, Sept. 1948.

20. "Pesquisa de opinião pública realizada nesta capital no mês de outubro de 1948." São Paulo, Oct. 1948.

21. "Investigação de mercado sôbre fortificantes, levada a efeito em São Paulo, Rio de Janeiro, Juiz de Fora, e Três Rios, durante o mês de novembro 1948, por incumbência da McCann-Erikson Corp." São Paulo and Rio de Janeiro, Nov. 1948.

22. "Pesquisa de opinião pública sobre materia política realizada pelo IBOPE no período de 6 a 15 de setembro de 1950, na capital de São Paulo." São Paulo, Sept. 1950.

23. "Pesquizas de opinião pública sôbre matéria política realizadas na capital de São Paulo e cidades de Santos, e Ribeirão Preto, a pedido do Dr. Brasílio Machado Neto, no período de 21 a 22 de Setembro de 1950." São Paulo, Sept. 1950.

International Institute of Differing Civilizations. *Développement d'une classe moyenne dans les pays tropicaux et sub-tropicaux. Development of a Middle Class in the Tropical and Subtropical Countries.* Record of the XXIXth Session held in London from 13th to 16th September, 1955. Brussels, 1956.

James, Daniel. *Resistance and Integration: Peronism and the Argentine Working Class, 1946–1976.* Cambridge: Cambridge University Press, 1988.

Jamison, Frederic. *The Political Unconscious.* Ithaca, N.Y.: Cornell University Press, 1981.

Jiménez, Michael. "'In the Middle of the Mess': Rereading John J. Johnson's *Political Change in Latin America* Thirty Years Later," paper given at the Latin American Studies XV International Congress, Miami, Dec. 1989. Photocopy in possession of author.

———. "The Elision of the Middle Classes and Beyond: History, Politics and Development Studies in Latin America's Short Twentieth Century." In Jeremy Adelman, ed., *Colonial Legacies* (forthcoming, Routledge).

Joffily, José. *Revolta e revolução: Cinquenta anos depois.* Rio de Janeiro: Paz e Terra, 1979.

Johnson, John J. *Political Change in Latin America: Emergence of the Middle Sectors.* Stanford, Calif.: Stanford University Press, 1958.

Jones, Gareth Stedman. *Languages of Class: Studies in English Working-Class History, 1832–1982.* Cambridge: Cambridge University Press, 1983.

Kidder, Daniel P., and J. C. Fletcher. *Brazil and the Brazilians.* Philadelphia: J. B. Lippincott, 1857.

Kocka, Jürgen. "The Middle Classes in Europe." *Journal of Modern History* 67 (Dec. 1995): 786–806.

———. *White-Collar Workers in America, 1890–1940: A Social-Political History in International Perspective*. London: Sage, 1980.

Laclau, Ernesto. "Toward a Theory of Populism." In *Politics and Ideology in Marxist Theory*. London: Verso, 1977, 143–200.

Lambert, Jacques. "Le Brésil: Structure sociale et institutions politiques." *Cahiers de la Fondation Nationale des Sciences Politiques* 44 (Paris, 1953).

Lears, T. J. Jackson. "From Salvation to Self-Realization: Advertising and the Therapeutic Roots of the Consumer Culture, 1880–1930." In Richard W. Fox and T. J. Jackson Lears, eds., *The Culture of Consumption: Critical Essays in American History, 1830–1930*. New York: Pantheon, 1983, 1–19.

Leeds, Anthony. "Brazilian Careers and Social Structure: A Case History and Model." In Dwight Heath, ed., *Contemporary Cultures and Societies of Latin America*. New York: Random House, 1974, 285–307.

Leme, Marisa Saenz. *A ideologia dos industriais brasileiros, 1919–1945*. Rio de Janeiro: Vozes, 1978.

Lemme, Paschoal. *Memórias*. Vols. 1–2. São Paulo: Cortez, 1988.

Lessa, Origines. *O livro do vendedor (noções sobre a arte de vender)*. São Paulo: Propaganda, 1939.

Levine, Daniel, ed. *Constructing Culture and Power in Latin America*. Ann Arbor: University of Michigan Press, 1993.

Levine, Robert. *The Vargas Regime: The Critical Years, 1934–1938*. New York: Columbia University Press, 1970.

Lima, Alceu Amoroso. *Indicações políticas, da revolução à constituição*. Rio de Janeiro: Civilização Brasileira, 1936.

———. *Mitos de nosso tempo*. Rio de Janeiro: José Olympio, 1943.

———. *Problema da burguesia*. Rio de Janeiro: Schmidt, 1932.

———. *O problema do trabalho*. Rio de Janeiro: Agir, 1947.

Lima, Arlette Alves. *Serviço social no Brasil: A ideologia de uma década*. São Paulo: Cortez, 1982.

Lima, Hélvio Pinheiro. Interview with author, São Paulo, Jul. 21, 1995.

Lima, Maria Emília A. T. *A construção discursiva do povo brasileiro: Os discursos de 1 de maio de Getúlio Vargas*. Campinas, São Paulo: Unicamp, 1990.

Lima, Paulo Mota. Interview with author, Rio de Janeiro, Jan. 31 and Feb. 4, 1991.

Lipset, Seymour Martin. "Some Social Requisites of Democratization." *American Political Science Review* 53 (Mar. 1959): 69–105.

Loaeza, Soledad. *Clases medias y política en México: La querella escolar, 1959–1963*. México: El Colégio de México, 1988.

Lobo, Eulália. *História do Rio de Janeiro (Do capital comercial ao capital industrial e financeiro)*. Vol. 2. Rio de Janeiro: IBMEC, 1978.

O Lojista (Órgão Oficial do Sindicato dos Lojistas). Rio de Janeiro.

Lopes, Luís Simões. Interview transcript, CPDOC, Projecto de História Oral, Jul. 13, 1981.

Love, Joseph. "Political Participation in Brazil, 1881–1969." *Luso-Brazilian Review* 7, no. 2 (Dec. 1970): 3–24.

Luccock, John. *Notes on Rio de Janeiro and the Southern Parts of Brazil, Taken During a Ten-Year Residence in That Country from 1808 to 1818.* London: S. Leigh, 1820.

Luz, Nícia Vilela. *A luta pela industrialização do Brasil.* São Paulo: Alfa Omega, 1978.

Lyra Filho, João. *Problemas das classes médias: Economia, amor, desportos.* Rio de Janeiro: Pongetti, 1942.

MacPherson, C. B. *The Political Theory of Possessive Individualism—Hobbes to Locke.* New York: Oxford University Press, 1983.

Mackinnon, William A. *On the Rise, Progress, and Present State of Public Opinion, in Great Britain, and Other Parts of the World.* London, 1929; rep. Shannon, 1971.

Mailer, Norman. *The Naked and the Dead.* New York: Holt, Rinehart & Winston, 1958.

A Manhã. Rio de Janeiro.

Marchand, Roland. *Advertising the American Dream: Making Way for Modernity, 1920–1940.* Berkeley: University of California Press, 1985.

Martins, Mario. Interview with author, Rio de Janeiro, Jul. 21, 1991.

Masterman, C. F. G. *The Condition of England.* London: Methuen, 1909.

Matta, Roberto da. *Carnivals, Rogues, and Heroes: An Interpretation of the Brazilian Dilemma.* Notre Dame, Ind.: University of Notre Dame Press, 1991.

———. *A casa e a rua: Espaço, cidadania, mulher, e morte.* Rio de Janeiro: Guanabara Koogan, 1991.

Maul, Carlos. *Grandezas e misérias da vida jornalística (memórias).* Rio de Janeiro: Livraria S. José, 1968.

Mayer, Arno. "The Lower Middle Class as Historical Problem." *Journal of Modern History* 47 (Sept. 1975): 409–36.

Mello, João Manoel Cardoso de, and Maria Conceição Tavares. "The Capitalist Export Economy in Brazil, 1884–1930." In R. Conde and S. Hunt, eds. *The Latin American Economies: Growth and the Export Sector, 1880–1930.* New York: Homes & Meier, 1985, 82–136.

Menezes, Raimundo. *Dicionário literário brasileiro.* Vols. 1–3. São Paulo: Saraiva, 1969.

Menezes, Tobias Barreto de. *Um discurso em mangas de camisa.* Rio de Janeiro: São José, 1970.

Merrick, Thomas, and Douglas Graham. *Population and Economic Development in Brazil, 1800 to the Present.* Baltimore: Johns Hopkins University Press, 1979.

Miceli, Sérgio. *Intelectuais e classe dirigente no Brasil (1920–1945).* São Paulo: DIFEL, 1979.

Mills, C. Wright. *White Collar: The American Middle Class.* New York: Oxford University Press, 1953.

Ministério de Educação e Saude. Diretoria do Ensino Secundário. *Documentário 4.* Rio de Janeiro, May 1954.

Ministério da Fazenda. Serviço de Estatística Econômica e Financeira. *Índice do custo de vida na cidade do Rio de Janeiro nos anos de 1912 a 1941*. Rio de Janeiro: Imprensa Nacional, 1942.

Monteiro, Tobias. *Funcionários e doutores*. Rio de Janeiro: Francisco Alves, 1919.

"O moralismo e a alienação das classes." *Cadernos de nosso tempo* 2, no. 2 (Jan.–Jun. 1954): 150–59.

Morley, Morris H. *Imperial State and Revolution: The United States and Cuba, 1952–1986*. Cambridge: Cambridge University Press, 1937.

Morris, R. J. *Class, Sect, and Party: The Making of the British Middle Class*. Manchester: Manchester University Press, 1990.

Morse, Richard. *From Community to Metropolis: A Biography of São Paulo, Brazil*. New York: Octagon, 1974.

Motta, Américo Celestino de. *Memorial*. Rio de Janeiro, 1943.

Murry, John Middleton. *Between Two Worlds: An Autobiography*. London: Jonathan Cape, 1935.

Nabuco, Joaquim. *Abolitionism: The Brazilian Antislavery Struggle*. Robert Conrad, trans. Urbana.: University of Illinois Press, 1977.

Nachman, Robert. "Brazilian Positivism as a Source of Middle Sector Ideology." Ph.D. diss., UCLA, 1972.

———. "Positivism, Modernization, and the Middle Class in Brazil." *Hispanic American Historical Review* 57, no. 1 (spring 1977): 1–23.

Naglé, Jorge. *Educação e sociedade na Primeira República*. São Paulo: USP, 1974.

Needell, Jeffrey. "Identity, Race, Gender, and Modernity in the Origins of Gilberto Freyre's *Oeuvre*." *American Historical Review* 100, no. 1 (Feb. 1995): 51–77.

———. "The *Revolta contra vacina* of 1904: The Revolt against 'Modernization' in *Belle-Époque* Rio de Janeiro." *Hispanic American Historical Review* 67, no. 2 (May 1987): 233–69.

———. *A Tropical* Belle Époque: *Elite Culture and Society in Turn-of-the-Century Rio de Janeiro*. Cambridge: Cambridge University Press, 1987.

Nehemkis, Peter. *Latin America: Myth and Reality*. Westport, Conn.: Greenwood Press, 1964.

Nogueira, Otávio Pupo. *A indústria em face das leis do trabalho*. São Paulo: Salesiano, 1935.

Nolan, Mary. *Visions of Modernity: American Business and the Modernization of Germany*. Oxford: Oxford University Press, 1994.

Nossa Classe–Revista de União Geral dos Funcionários Civis do Brasil. Rio de Janeiro.

Nunes, Arnaldo. *Que é a contabilidade*. Rio de Janeiro: Instituto da Ordem dos Contabilistas, 1936.

Nunes, Pedro. *35 anos de propaganda*. Rio de Janeiro: Gernasa, 1970.

O'Donnell, Guillermo. *Modernization and Bureaucratic-Authoritarianism: Studies in South American Politics*. Berkeley: Institute of International Studies, University of California, 1979.

Oliveira, Ana Lúcia Valença de Santa Cruz. *Sindicalismo bancário—origens*. São Paulo: Oboré, 1990.

Oliveira, Lúcia Lippi. "Elite intelectual e debate político nos anos 30." *Dados*, no. 22 (1979): 75–97.

Oportunidades de educação na capital do país: Informações sobre escolas e cursos, para uso de pais, professores, e estudantes. Rio de Janeiro: INEP, 1941.

Ortiz, Renato. *A moderna tradição brasileira*. São Paulo: Brasiliense, 1988.

Owensby, Brian. "'Stuck in the Middle': Middle Class and Class Society in Modern Brazil, 1850–1950." Ph.D. diss., Princeton University, 1994.

Pacheco, Jacy. *Bancário . . . (misérias de uma profissão)*. Rio de Janeiro: Getúlio Costa, 1943.

A Panificadora—Mensal da Associação dos Proprietários de Padarias, Rio de Janeiro.

Paoli, Maria Célia Pinheiro Machado. "Labour, Law, and the State in Brazil, 1930–1945." Ph.D. diss., Birkbeck College, University of London, 1988.

———. "Working-Class São Paulo and Its Representations, 1900–1940." *Latin American Perspectives* 14, no. 2 (spring 1987): 204–25.

Parker, David. *The Idea of the Middle Class: White-Collar Workers and Peruvian Society*. College Station: Pennsylvania State University Press, 1998.

Paz, Octavio. *The Other Mexico: Critique of the Pyramid*. New York: Grove Press, 1972.

Peixoto, Armando. Interview with author, Rio de Janeiro, Feb. 24 and Aug. 6, 1991.

Peralva, Osvaldo. *O retrato*. Rio de Janeiro: Globo, 1962.

Pereira, L.C. Bresser. "The Rise of the Middle Class and Middle Management in Brazil." *Journal of Interamerican Studies* 3 (Jul. 1962): 313–26.

Pesquisa sobre o padrão de vida do comerciário do Distrito Federal. Rio de Janeiro, 1949.

Picaluga, Izabel Fontenelle. *Partidos políticos e classes sociais: A UDN na Guanabara*. Petrópolis, Rio de Janeiro: Vozes, 1980.

Pinheiro, Maria Esolina. *Técnica de serviço social*. São Paulo, 1947.

Pinheiro, Paulo Sérgio. "Classes médias urbanas: Formação, natureza na vida política." *Revista Mexicana de Sociologia* 37, no. 2 (Apr.–Jun. 1975): 445–74.

Pinto, L. A. Costa. *O negro no Rio de Janeiro, revoluções raciais numa sociedade em mudança*. São Paulo: Nacional, 1953.

Polanyi, Karl. *The Great Transformation: The Political and Economic Origins of Our Time*. New York: Beacon, 1957.

Pompêo, A. *Porque é que sou integralista*. São Paulo: n.p., 1935.

Ponzi, Alfio. *De binóculo na varanda: Memórias*. João Pessoa, Paraíba: n.p., 1986.

Porter, Charles, and Robert Alexander. *The Struggle for Democracy in Latin America*. New York: Macmillan, 1961.

Pôrto, Agenor. *Da vida de um médico*. Rio de Janeiro: Pongetti, 1962.

Prado, Maria Lígia Coelho. *A democracia ilustrada (o Partido Democrático de São Paulo, 1926–1934)*. São Paulo: Ática, 1986.

Prestes, Anita. *A coluna Prestes*. São Paulo: Brasiliense, 1990.

Prestes, Marialice. *Problemas do lar*. São Paulo: O Cruzeiro, 1945.

Projeto Memória: *50 anos da Faculdade de Serviço Social, Universidade Estadual do Rio de Janeiro*. Rio de Janeiro: Universidade Estadual do Rio de Janeiro, 1994.

Publicidade. Rio de Janeiro.

Putnam, Samuel. "The Brazilian Social Novel, 1935–1940." *Inter-American Quarterly* 2, no. 2 (Apr. 1940): 5–12.

Queiroz, Dr. Júlio Arantes de Sanderson. Interview with author, Rio de Janeiro, Aug. 5, 1991.

Queiroz, Suely Robles Reis de. *Os radicais da República—Jacobinismo: Ideologia e ação, 1893–1897*. São Paulo: Brasiliense, 1986.

Ramos, Ricardo. *História da propaganda no Brasil*. São Paulo: USP, 1972.

Reale, Miguel. *Obras políticas (1a fase—1931–1937)*. Vols. 2–3. Brasília: Ed. Universidade de Brasília, 1983.

Revista do Arquivo Municipal de São Paulo. São Paulo.

Revista da Associação dos Funcionários Públicos do Estado de São Paulo. São Paulo.

Revista Brasileira de Pedagogia—Órgão Oficial da Confederação Católica Brasileira de Educação. Rio de Janeiro.

Revista do Clube de Engenharia. Rio de Janeiro.

Revista Comercial dos Varejistas. Rio de Janeiro.

Revista Paulista de Contabilidade (Instituto Paulista de Contabilidade). São Paulo.

Revista do Professor—Órgão do Professorado Paulista. São Paulo.

Revista de Química e Farmácia. Rio de Janeiro.

Revista da Semana. Rio de Janeiro.

Revista do Serviço Público. Rio de Janeiro.

Revista do Syndicato Odontológico Brasileiro. Rio de Janeiro.

Revista do Trabalho. Rio de Janeiro.

Ribeiro, Clovis Leite. "A classe média e as eleiçoes de 19 de janeiro." *Digesto Econômico* 3, no. 29 (Apr. 1947): 71–77.

Ridings, Eugene. *Business Interest Groups in Nineteenth-Century Brazil*. Cambridge: Cambridge University Press, 1994.

Romero, Sylvio, and Arthur Guimarães. *Estudos sociaes: O Brasil na primeira década do século XX*. Lisbon: A Editora, 1911.

Rosa, Virginio Santa. *A desordem*. Rio de Janeiro: Schmidt, 1932.

———. *O sentido do tenentismo*. São Paulo: Alfa Omega, 1976.

Rosenberg, Emily S. *Spreading the American Dream: American Economic and Cultural Expansion, 1890–1945*. New York: Hill and Wang, 1982.

Rostow, W. W. *The Stages of Economic Growth: A Non-Communist Manifesto*. New York: Cambridge University Press, 1990.

Rowe, William, and Vivian Schelling. *Memory and Modernity: Popular Culture in Latin America*. New York: Verso, 1991.

Roxborough, Ian. "Modernization Theory Revisited: A Review Article." *Comparative Studies in Society and History* 30, no. 4 (Oct. 1988): 753–61.

Saes, Décio. *Classe média e política na Primeira República brasileira (1889–1930)*. Petrópolis, Rio de Janeiro: Vozes, 1975.

———. *Classe média e sistema político no Brasil*. São Paulo: Queiroz, 1985.

S.A. Inter-Americana de Propaganda. "A publicidade e o desenvolvimento nacional. Manifesto para augmento de capital dirigido aos nossos amigos e accionistas." Rio de Janeiro, 1940.

Salgado, Plínio. *O espírito da burguesia*. São Paulo: Ed. das Américas, 1956.

———. *O integralismo perante a nação*. Rio de Janeiro: Livraria Clássica Brasileira, 1955.

———. *Obras completas*. Vol. 9. São Paulo: Ed. das Américas, 1959.

Santos, José Maria dos. *Notas à história recente*. São Paulo: Brasiliense, 1944.

Schmitter, Philippe. *Interest Conflict and Political Change in Brazil*. Stanford, Calif.: Stanford University Press, 1971.

Schola—Revista da Associação Brasileira de Educação (successor to *Boletim da AEB* and precursor to *Educação*). Rio de Janeiro.

Schwartzman, Simon, ed. *O pensamento nacionalista e o "Cadernos de nosso tempo."* Brasília: Ed. Universidade de Brasília, 1981.

Schwarz, Roberto. *Misplaced Ideas: Essays on Brazilian Culture*. London: Verso, 1992.

Seixas, Marly Rodrigues Martins. "Sindicato dos Jornalistas Profissionais no Estado de São Paulo: 1937–1962." Master's thesis, USP, São Paulo, 1980.

Seleções do Reader's Digest. São Paulo.

Serrano, Isabela de Almeida. *Minha casa*. Petrópolis, Rio de Janeiro: Vozes, 1945.

———. *Noções de economia doméstica (de acôrdo com os novos programas para o curso ginasial do ensino secundário)*. São Paulo: Nacional, 1954.

Serviço Social. Rio de Janeiro.

Serviço Social da Indústria (SESI). Departamento Regional de São Paulo. Divisão de Orientação Social. *Curso de relações humanas para o trabalhador*. São Paulo, 1950.

———. *O que é o SESI?* São Paulo, 1947.

Servir—Boletim da Associação de Educadoras Católicas. Rio de Janeiro.

SESI-Jornal—Órgão dos Funcionários do SESI. São Paulo.

Silva, Democrito de Castro. *Classe média*. Rio de Janeiro: Guaíra, 1945.

Silva, Maria Hortência do Nascimento e. *Impressões de um assistente social sobre o trabalho na favela*. Rio de Janeiro: n.p., 1942.

Simonsen, Roberto. "Discurso pronunciado o 25 de julho de 1946, em São Paulo, na instalação do Primeiro Conselho Consultivo do SESI." Arquivo do SESI.

Sindicato dos Bancários de São Paulo. "As dívidas e a estabilidade—memorial ao Ministro de Trabalho." São Paulo, Dec. 1939.

Singel, Daniel. *The War Within: From Victorian to Modernist Thought in the South, 1919–1945*. Chapel Hill: University of North Carolina Press, 1982.

Singer, Paul I. "Força de trabalho e emprêgo no Brasil, 1920–1969." São Paulo: CEBRAP, 1971.

Sintese do Primeiro Congresso Brasileiro de Serviço Social. São Paulo, Feb. 1947.

Siqueira, Herculano. Interview with author, Rio de Janeiro, May 9, 1991.

Sissón, Roberto. *Carta aberta à Marinha de Guerra.* Rio de Janeiro, 1937.

———. "Carta aberta ao legislativo." *Diário do Poder Legislativo.* Rio de Janeiro, Dec. 24, 1936.

"Situação política brasileira." *Cadernos de nosso tempo* 2, no. 2 (Jan.–Jun. 1954): 103–20.

Skidmore, Thomas. *Politics in Brazil, 1930–1960: An Experiment in Democracy.* Oxford: Oxford University Press, 1986.

———. "Racial Ideas and Social Policy in Brazil, 1870–1940." In Richard Graham, ed., *The Idea of Race in Latin America, 1870–1940.* Austin: University of Texas Press, 1990.

Soares, Gláucio Ary Dillon. *Sociedade e política no Brasil: Desenvolvimento, classe e política durante a Segunda República.* São Paulo: DIFEL, 1973.

Sodré, Alcindo. *A genêse da desordem.* Rio de Janeiro: Schmidt, 1933.

Sodré, Nelson Werneck. "O tenentismo acabou." *Cadernos de Debate* 1 (1976): 51–54.

Sodré, Ruy de Azevedo. "Em defesa das classes médias." *Primeiro Congresso Estadual de Famílias Cristãs*, São Paulo, 1957.

Sofer, Eugene. "Recent Trends in Latin American Labor Historiography." *Latin American Research Review* 15, no. 1 (1980): 167–76.

Stein, Stanley. *The Brazilian Cotton Manufacture: Textile Enterprise in an Underdeveloped Area, 1850–1950.* Cambridge: Harvard University Press, 1957.

———. *Vassouras: A Brazilian Coffee County, 1850–1900—The Roles of Planter and Slave in a Plantation Society.* Princeton: Princeton University Press, 1985.

Stein, Steve. *Populism in Peru: The Emergence of the Masses and the Politics of Social Control.* Madison: University of Wisconsin Press, 1980.

Stepan, Nancy. *The Hour of Eugenics: Race, Gender, and Nation in Latin America.* Ithaca, N.Y.: Cornell University Press, 1991.

Susman, Warren. *Culture as History: The Transformation of American Society in the Twentieth Century.* New York: Pantheon, 1984.

Syndiké—Revista de Bancários (Publicação Oficial do Syndicato de Funcionários Bancários). São Paulo.

Tavares, José Nilo. *Conciliação e radicalização política no Brasil.* Petrópolis, Rio de Janeiro: Vozes, 1982.

Távora, Juarez. *Uma vida e muitas lutas.* Vol. 1. Rio de Janeiro: José Olympio, 1973.

Thackeray, William Makepeace. *The Four Georges.* London: Adam and Charles Black, 1910.

Thibau, Mauro. Interview transcript, CPDOC, Projeto de História Oral, transcript no. E–128.

Topik, Steven. "Middle-Class Brazilian Nationalism, 1889–1930: From Radicalism to Reaction." *Social Science Quarterly* 59, no. 1 (Jun. 1978): 93–104.

———. *The Political Economy of the Brazilian State (1889–1930).* Austin: University of Texas Press, 1987.

Torres, Alberto. *O problema nacional brasileiro.* Vol. 16. São Paulo: Brasiliense, 1978.

Tournier, Michel. *Le vent paraclet.* Paris: Gallimard, 1977.

Tribunal Superior Eleitoral. *Dados estatísticos* 1, no. 11. Rio de Janeiro, 1946.

Trinidade, Hélgio. *Integralismo—O fascismo brasileiro na década de 30.* São Paulo: DIFEL, 1979.

Tullio, Marco. *Do pistolão como instituto jurídico.* 2nd ed. Rio de Janeiro: n.p., 1952.

Unger, Roberto Mangabeira. *Social Theory: Its Situation and Task—A Critical Introduction to Politics, A Work in Constructive Social Theory.* Cambridge: Cambridge University Press, 1987.

União—Órgão da União dos Empregados no Comércio do Rio de Janeiro. Rio de Janeiro.

Unión Panamericana. *Materiales para el estudio de las clases medias en América Latina.* Washington, D.C., 1950.

United States Commerce Reports. Washington, D.C., United States Department of Commerce.

Urbanismo e Viação—Uma revista de enthusiasmo pela engenharia brasileira. Rio de Janeiro.

Vargas, Getúlio. *A campanha presidencial.* Rio de Janeiro: José Olympio, 1951.

———. *A nova política brasileira.* Vols. 5–11. Rio de Janeiro: José Olympio, 1938.

Velho, Gilberto. *Individualismo e cultura: Notas para uma antropologia da sociedade contemporânea.* Rio de Janeiro: Zahar, 1987.

Venceslau, José, Jr.. *O integralismo ao alcance do todos.* Rio de Janeiro, 1935.

Veríssimo, Érico. *Crossroads.* New York: Macmillan, 1943.

———. *The Rest Is Silence.* New York: MacMillan, 1946.

Vianna, Antônio. "Manoel Querino." *Revista do Instituto Geográfico e Histórico da Bahia* 54, no. 2 (1928): 304–16.

Vianna, Francisco José de Oliveira. *História social de econômica capitalista no Brasil.* Vol. 1. Niterói: EDUFF, 1988.

Vianna, Luís Werneck. *Liberalismo e sindicato no Brasil.* Rio de Janeiro: Paz e Terra, 1976.

Vianna, Marly de Almeida Gomes. *Revolucionários de 35: Sonho e realidade.* São Paulo: Cia. das Letras, 1992.

Vida Carioca. Rio de Janeiro.

Vida Doméstica, Rio de Janeiro.

Villalobos, Sergio. *Origen y ascenso de la burguesía chilena.* Santiago: Ed. Universitária, 1987.

Villela, Annibal, and Wilson Suzigan. *Government Policy and the Economic Growth of Brazil, 1889–1945.* Rio de Janeiro: IPES, 1977.

Vinhas, Moisés. *O Partidão: A luta por um partido de massas, 1922–1974.* São Paulo: Hucitec, 1982.

Voz Comerciária. São Paulo.

Wagley, Charles. *An Introduction to Brazil.* New York: Columbia University Press, 1963.

Wahrlich, Beatriz M. de Souza. *Reforma administrativa na era de Vargas*. Rio de Janeiro: Fundação Getúlio Vargas, 1983.

Wahrman, Dror. *Imagining the Middle Class: The Political Representation of Class in Britain, c. 1780–1840*. Cambridge: Cambridge University Press, 1995.

Wainer, Samuel. *Minha razão de viver: Memórias de um repórter*. Rio de Janeiro: Record, 1987.

Weffort, Francisco. *O populismo no Brasil*. Rio de Janeiro: Paz e Terra, 1978.

Weinstein, Barbara. *For Social Peace in Brazil: Industrialists and the Remaking of the Working Class in São Paulo, 1920–1970*. Chapel Hill: University of North Carolina Press, 1996.

———. "Industrialists, the State, and the Issues of Worker Training and Social Services in Brazil, 1930–1950." *Hispanic American Historical Review* 70, no. 3 (1990): 379–404.

Wells, James. *Exploring and Traveling Three Thousand Miles Through Brazil from Rio de Janeiro to Maranhão*. Vol. 1. Philadelphia: J. B. Lippincott, 1886.

Wells, John. "Industrial Accumulation and Living Standards in the Long Run: The São Paulo Industrial Working Class, 1930 to 1975, Part I." *Journal of Development Studies* 19, no. 2 (Jan. 1983): 145–69; Part II, 19, no. 3 (Apr. 1983): 297–320.

Wiarda, Howard. "Did the Alliance 'Lose Its Way,' or Were Its Assumptions All Wrong from the Beginning? and Are Those Assumptions Still with Us?" In L. Ronald Scheman, ed., *The Alliance for Progress*. New York: Praeger, 1988, 95–118.

Whittaker, Arthur. "The Pathology of Democracy in Latin America." *American Political Science Review* 44, no. 1 (Mar. 1950): 101–18.

Williams, Margaret Todaro. "Integralism and the Brazilian Catholic Church." *Hispanic American Historical Review* 54, no. 3 (Aug. 1974): 431–52.

Wirth, John. *The Politics of Brazilian Development, 1930–1954*. Stanford, Calif.: Stanford University Press, 1970.

Wolfe, Joel. *Working Men, Working Women: São Paulo and the Rise of Brazil's Industrial Working Class, 1900–1955*. Durham, N.C.: Duke University Press, 1993.

Zunz, Olivier. "Class." In S. Kutler, ed., *Encyclopedia of the United States in the Twentieth Century*. New York: Scribners, 1996.

Index

In this index an "f" after a number indicates a separate reference on the next page, and an "ff" indicates separate references on the next two pages. A continuous discussion over two or more pages is indicated by a span of page numbers, e.g., "57–59." *Passim* is used for a cluster of references in close but not consecutive sequence.

Library of Congress Cataloging-in-Publication Data

Owensby, Brian Philip
    Intimate ironies : modernity and the making of middle-class
lives in Brazil / Brian P. Owensby.
    p.   cm.
    Includes bibliographical references (p.   ) and index.
    ISBN 0-8047-3360-0 (cloth : alk. paper)
    1. Middle class—Brazil—History.   2. Social change—
Brazil.   I. Title.
HT690.B7095   1999
305.5'5'.0981—dc21   98-46129
                                                                CIP

This book is printed on acid-free, recycled paper.

Original printing 1999
Last figure below indicates year of this printing:
08 07 06 05 04 03 02 01 00 99